This Book may be ... N DAYS

THE BOOK OF
CHRISTIAN
CLASSICS

Anthology
of
CLASSIC CHRISTIAN
LITERATURE

Edited by

MICHAEL WILLIAMS

TUDOR PUBLISHING COMPANY

New York · 1937

New Edition January, 1937

PN6071. R3
W72

MANUFACTURED IN THE UNITED STATES OF AMERICA
AT THE VAN REES PRESS

INTRODUCTION

HIS book appears at a time when not only Western civilization—European and American —but the civilizations, and the cultures less than civilized, of Asia and Africa as well, are in a condition of violent crisis. The whole world is affected by a malaise of the soul, a confusion of the mind, a conflict of social, philosophical, scientific, artistic and literary systems, theories and experiments. As Mr. Christopher Dawson has said: * "In every department of life traditional principles have been shaken and discredited, and we do not yet know what is going to take their place. There are those who hold that Europe has had her day and that our culture has entered the first stage of an inevitable process of decay, while others believe that we are only beginning to realize the possibilities of modern science and that we are about to see the rise of a new social order which will far transcend anything that the world has known. One thing is certain—the old order is dead; and with the old order there has passed away that traditional acceptance of the truth of Christianity and that general recognition of Christian moral principles, which even in the nineteenth century still retained so strong a hold on the minds of men."

That Christianity was the determining element in Western civilization, few would deny, even those who (like Gibbons or Nietzsche or Marx) attribute to its influence a poisonous, and ultimately destructive, character. That it sought not merely the spiritual hegemony of the West, of Europe and America, but that of the whole world, also is indisputable. For its mission is necessarily universal. Local or national or continental or social— or, in fact, any geographical or anthropological—limitations are inconsistent with its system and repugnant to its spirit. It is, of

* *Essays in Order*, New York: The Macmillan Company, 1931. P. V.

course, quite true that the super-national quality of Christianity is not only opposed, and apparently frustrated, by those races and nations as yet unconverted, and by those masses of peoples formerly Christian who have lapsed from, or who now consciously repudiate, Christianity, but also by those nominal Christians, or partial Christians, who throughout nineteen centuries of the Christian effort have in practice placed their racial or national interests and ambitions above the claims of their religion. Nevertheless, such failures or defeats or retardations of the universalism of Christianity at any one time, or in any one place, or in many places simultaneously, are not to be regarded as proofs of Christianity's integral failure, or its final frustration. Invariably, because of the supremacy of the spiritual power of Christianity given to it by God, and maintained intact by His Church—which is more than God's organized instrument: which is His living Body on earth, in which all Christians are incorporated (including multitudes not consciously Christian yet truly so because the innermost will of their souls to possess Truth and Goodness and Love constitute their "baptism of desire"), Christianity rises again after all falls caused by the human weakness of individuals, or groups of individuals, and resumes its interrupted work. History abounds in instances of this power of revival—that might even be called the power of resurrection.* They begin at the very cradle of the Church. In that meeting of the Apostles of Christ which the orthodox historians of the Church recognize as the first Council, of Jerusalem, Christianity broke away decisively from the local and national and racial conditions and restrictions which after the death of Christ threatened to circumscribe and limit the new dispensation. Jewish thought, sentiment, practices, aspirations, all played upon, and deeply influenced, the little group to whom Christ had said: "Going therefore, teach ye all nations: teaching them to observe all things whatsoever I have commanded you; and behold, I am with you all days, even to the consummation of the world."

That the new revelation in its actual operations among men should merely be one more cult among the many schools of religious life within Judaism was the wholly probable thing to

---

* See Book II Chapter VI: The Five Deaths of the Faith, in *The Everlasting Man*, by G. K. Chesterton. New York: Dodd, Mead & Company, 1925.

have happened. Yet the tremendous decisions of the Apostles—heralded by the even more tremendous words: "It has seemed good to the Holy Ghost and to Us"—to break away from Jewish moorings and take to the high seas of the vast oceans of human life, launched the Ship of Peter, the Church of Christ, upon its universal mission. So it was again after the incredible conquest of the Roman Empire when there arose the danger that the Church would be identified with that empire, her fortunes irrevocably linked with those of the mistress of civilization, and, therefore, threatened with the same destruction that overthrew secular Rome before the irresistible flood of the Barbarian cataclysm. Yet again the Church freed herself from the trammels of the local, the contingent, and extended her universalism. Retaining the sifted intellectual wealth of the Roman and Grecian cultures, and adding it to the heritage brought over from Jewry, Christianity absorbed the Barbarians. They too brought riches of human values—their virility, their tribal customs and laws—to be elevated, purged and refined, and assimilated within the Christian ethos. So, too, when the converted Germanic and Frankish and Slavic peoples, beginning their enthusiastic and tumultuous career of self-realization that led them on to the formation of those groupings which eventually brought about the modern nations of Europe, in their turn instinctively sought to make Christianity simply a factor, if a dominating and superior one, of their national or imperial systems, once more the Church was compelled to fight to maintain her spiritual sovereignty, and her separateness from and superiority to all forms of temporal dominance over her universal mission. The struggle centered about the matter of lay investiture—the claim made, and for centuries more or less successfully exerted, by kings and emperors to name and control bishops and even popes. Feudalism indeed enriched the Church, but at the price of enslaving her to the State. No greater peril ever threatened Christianity. Yet she overcame it. Rising from a condition of subserviency to the rulers of this world, and emerging from possibly the lowest ebb of her own moral and spiritual life, a succession of great champions of her universal spiritual supremacy culminated in Hildebrand the Monk (Pope Gregory VII), who won back the complete freedom of canonical elections, from that of the Pope down to those of the lowest ecclesiastical offices. Then when Feudalism slowly faded out into the new system of nations bound together in a vast Christian commonwealth of which the Pope was the acknowledged head, and at last a sort of approximate unity of culture was achieved for Europe—providing if not the precise model, at least the principle of action, from which to proceed to the Christian unification of the whole world—another crisis arose. The growing spirit of nationalism became even stronger. So did the power of royalism. The revival of the study of Greek and Roman classics, heralding the Renaissance, brought back the fascinating spell of the ancient concept of absolutism that was the ruling principle of Roman law: the theory that supreme power not only in secular but in religious fields should be wielded by the head of the State. In this view, religion was subordinated to the temporal and secular interests of the nation, or of the empire among the nations. The emperor or the king could, and would, and in many cases did, determine what religion his people should follow. (And this idea is reborn again today, as witness Russia, or, to a lesser degree, Fascist Italy, or the claims of the Action Française, or of Hitler in Germany.) Crisis after crisis followed upon this most vital one—the Renaissance, the Reformation and Counter-Reformation, the French Revolution, the Industrial Revolution—down to the world crisis of today, in which not only social systems and theories supposedly verified by materialistic science, and apparently quite new in human experience, clash with and threaten the extinction of Christianity, but in addition all the ideas and principles of the past seem to have reappeared and to have reassumed vitality and pugnacity—raging against and clashing among one another, to be sure, but all alike striking out against the the claims and the remaining powers of Christianity.*

It is no part of my intention—nor indeed do I possess the competence—to explain or to attempt the justification of the doctrine of the Catholic Church, whereby it claims its origin to be divine; and says that its authority to teach the true principles of life, applicable to all, without any exception, of the affairs and the acts of mankind is absolute; and its existence and functioning to be

---

* For a brief yet comprehensive sketch of the Church's conflicts of the past, see *The Church at the Turning Points of History*, by Godfrey Kurth, Helena, Montana, Rt. Rev. Victor Day, 1908.

guaranteed until the ending of the world.* I am simply concerned to point out that such indeed are its stupendous claims, maintained inviolate now for nearly twenty centuries—and which today are being advanced, and pressed, and stressed, in a more vigorous, sustained, and manifold fashion than at any time since before the Counter-Reformation. Whether or not the claims of the Church are accepted or rejected, it is clearly evident that these claims are now a resurgent force and furnish the dynamic impulse which upholds and propels the activities of Catholic thinkers in science, philosophy, literature, sociology, art and statesmanship—who in turn influence or directly control tens of millions of the Catholic masses in all countries of the world. Moreover, this Catholic renaissance attracts and holds an increasing alliance among all who value traditional civilization. This fact constitutes a social phenomenon of extraordinary significance.

The revival of orthodox Christianity does not, of course, constitute the total sum of Christian energies which are now at work contending with, or combining with, other social forces in the vast alembic of the world crisis against the forces of the new barbarians, or the danger of mere social chaos; but by reason of the central and fundamental place of the Catholic Church in Christianity, the increasingly positive nature of the modern revival of the universal mission of the Church is of paramount importance.

This revival is seen perhaps most obviously in the sphere of practical politics—in the widest sense of that term—wherein the Christian principles of the rights and the liberty of the individual, of the paramouncy of the family as the only legitimate central unit of society, and of the sanctity of private property— and of the social duty of achieving the widest possible distribution of private property—supply the philosophical bed-rock for all systems of economics and of government which are opposed to the pagan-materialistic conceptions of State absolutism, whether of Communism, or of Fascism, and, which in a lesser degree, yet essentially, also controvert the injustices and mal-adjustments of modern capitalism. Again, this revival of Christian principles is apparent in the world of pure philosophy and science, where the

* For a study of what Catholic literature means by its constant stressing of the principle of the "supremacy of the spiritual," see *The Things That Are Not Caesar's*, by Jacques Maritain. New York: Charles Scribner's Sons, 1930.

predominance of those materialistic axioms that prevailed during the last century is threatened by spiritual conceptions with which Christianity can at least sign a concordat, so to speak, even if she cannot wholly accept their expressions as wholly consistent with her own dogmas.

It is—or so it seems to me—against such a background—amid such a renaissance of the intellectual and social principles of Christianity—that the publication of any book which is expressive of the universal mission of Christianity must be considered as an event of vital interest to all readers who are concerned with the solution of the crisis of our age. Whether or not they subscribe to the claims of Christianity, or are merely willing to consider whether or not these claims possess any contemporary values, or whether they consider Christianity to have been a failure in the past, a handicap to humanity in the present, and think that the prospect of its continuance in the future is a menace rather than a hope—nevertheless, they cannot get away from that interrogation which Christian literature proposes as the criterion of all human thinking on the basic questions of life—"What think ye of Christ?" Everywhere that question is raised and disseminated by Christian theologians, philosophers, artists, scientists, critics, sociologists and statesmen, who, like the Christian humanists of the Renaissance, or the Augustines and the Schoolmen of the past, apply the permanent principles of their Faith to the problems of their age, and sift the cultural developments of thinkers outside the Christian camp with minds open to recognize and adopt all the truths issuing from any school of thought which are consonant with the doctrines of the Church, which today, as in the past, display their boundless capacity of development.

This book, therefore, is not to be considered a rather negligible contribution to Christian literature, at least in its contemporary aspect, consisting as it does merely of extracts from the corpus of the past, and, even so, restricted to examples from only two of the many main departments of that literature—that of mystical experience, and that of devotional meditation, or essays, in poetry and prose. It might be contended that only a strictly contemporary book—either a single work of artistic creation, or of scholarship—or a volume of extracts from a number of such contemporary works—could appropriately be brought within the purview of modern interest as a vital part of that process of intellectual fermentation sketched above. It might indeed be said that merely to appeal to the past, to open once more the treasure house of the traditional, is simply such a performance as may be expected from Christians when facing the actualities of today—a characteristic yet futile habit of theirs of invoking the ghosts of dead glories when called upon to give an account of what they have to say to the present generation.

But it is precisely amid the present generation, so confused and vacillating among opposing principles, that the ideals of a social order centered upon the supremacy of spiritual conceptions, as transmitted through the traditions of Western civilization, are reasserting their power. The youngest and most promising spirits today are placing representative champions in the arenas of literature and of life to reject and fight against the day-before-yesterday conceptions of mechanical materialism and the automatic cultural "progress" of a shallow humanitarianism. They seek amid the chaos of modernity the star that will lead them at once to ecstasy and to order—the ecstasy of the experience of reality in spiritual life, and the order of reason in their intellectual and social interests. For such searchers after an integralism of human life, the star that once shone at Bethlehem has risen again. They have no desire to escape the bewilderment of today by the road of an impossible return to past conditions. What is most characteristic, and encouraging, in their attitude toward life is their sensitiveness to the demands of contemporary problems, and their keen interest in the unfolding aspects of the future. But if Christian tradition is really of the truth—rather, if Truth itself, permanently vital, and unfolding dynamic contemporary aspects of its fructifying power, is indeed the central meaning of Christian culture—then youth will not be denied; it will no longer be chilled and repressed by the narrow and limited materialism of their fathers and grandfathers of the bourgeois nineteenth century. Such a book as this, it is hoped, will at least indicate certain of the sources of inspiration to which they may turn as starting points for new explorations and fresh adventures in life. "I have come," said the ultimate Author of all Christian literature, He Who was the Word, "that ye shall have life and have it more abundantly."

There are several "notes"—innate and congenital characteristics of all Christian literature—which are perhaps most obviously apparent in the mystical and meditative types selected for this book, which it may be useful briefly to indicate. One is its "supernaturalism"; a second is its sense of mystery; a third is its atmosphere of ecstasy; a fourth is its symbolism; a fifth is its sacramentalism; a sixth is its obedience to a higher authority than its own autonomous laws; the seventh, in which these marks, and, indeed, all other attributes, major or minor, and whether peculiar to its own subject matter or common to all schools of literature, are unified, and directly or indirectly controlled, and this particular thing is absolutely unique, for it is the belief in a God-Man Jesus Christ. There are other religions, and other literatures deriving from these religions, which are based upon a belief in a God, or in many gods: transcendent of humanity—divine beings. Only in Christianity does the Ultimate Divinity become incarnate in a Man. Only Christianity tells men that they may actually share the divinity of their maker—not that they are of the essence of the ultimate (which is Pantheism), nor that they are creatures necessarily and absolutely deprived of all participation in ultimate Divinity, but that they may indeed be defied. There is a prayer said in the Mass which is the very corner-stone of the temple of Christian literature. When the priest blesses the water which represents the faithful and mixes it with the wine which he is to change into the Blood of Christ, he says: "*Deus, qui humanae substantiae dignatatem mirabiliter condidisti, et mirabilius reformasti: da nobis per hujus aquæ et vini mysterium, ejus divinitatis esse consortes, qui humanitatis nostrae fieri dignatus est particeps, Jesus Christi, Filius tuus Dominus noster: Qui tecum vivit et regnat in unitate Spiritus Sancti, Deus; per omnia sæcula sæculorum.*" That is to say: "O God, Who in a marvelous manner didst create and ennoble human nature, and still more marvelously hast renewed it; grant that, by the mystical union of this water and wine, we may be made partakers of His divinity Who vouchsafed to become partaker of our humanity, Jesus Christ, Thy Son, our Lord: Who liveth and reigneth with Thee in the unity of the Holy Ghost, one God, world without end."

The sacramentalism which is supremely evident in this prayer accompanies all Christian literature (except, of course, the heretical and "liberal" varieties which are not here being considered, and which, indeed, by their abandonment of belief in the con-current Divinity-Humanity of Christ, and of the sacramentalism flowing from that belief, are not Christian at all). It may—and has—now and then, in this region or that, degenerate into super-stition, and elevate legend into history, myth into doctrine, symbols into the things symbolized; that is its danger. But Christianity, indeed, is itself the Dangerous Life; but it knows the weapons that, properly used, conquer all dangers. Sacramentalism explains super-naturalism, which, as Father D'Arcy says,* "has nothing to do with the superstitious or the magical, and it is not even to be identified with the miraculous." It may be (curtly, and, of course, most inadequately) defined as "a form of life higher (and absolutely other) than that which we possess by being born of human stock." It inter-penetrates through innumerable chan-nels ("Grace") this human life in time and space with subtle radiations, so to speak, and at times with illuminations and reve-lations of divinity. Hence, also, flows the phenomena of ecstasy, recorded in the lives of the saints, and flowering into passages of supreme yet ever-mysterious beauty in poetry and prose. Not only Christian saints and artists, consciously such, but holy souls and artists not visibly of the Church may be vouchsafed these ineffable experiences, and may achieve at least stammering utterances of the innermost mysteries.† Obviously, too, the sense of mystery which I have given as one of the "notes" of Christian literature is that mystery which one of the ancient Catholic authors (Tertullian, I think, but I do not know) referred to when he said: "*Omnia exeunt in mysterium*"—all things end, or, let us say, find their end, in mystery; but it is not the mystery of nescience; or the mystery of oblivion; it is the mystery of God, which is the mystery of Love, of which Christ was the messenger to man, and of which human sanctity is the reflection, and ecstasy in literature is the remote yet splendid echo. Of the remaining "note" of Christian literature, among the seven listed—the note of obedience to a higher law than the human laws of measure and subject and treatment which prevail in all literatures other than the Christian, and have their

* *Catholicism*, by Rev. M. C. D'Arcy, S.J. New York: Doubleday, Doran & Co., Inc. 1929.

† See *Prayer and Poetry*, by Henri Bremond. London: Burns, Oates & Washbourne, Ltd. 1927.

subordinate yet necessary place therein as well—it will suffice to mention once more the major axiom of Christianity: that Christ, being God, became Man and revealed to all mankind the laws of God. Hence, within Christian literature, while there can be the fullest personal originality, the most complete individuality of expression of original thought, and the most thorough realism in the description of human life, there can be none of these rebellions of disordered genius which lead only to the ecstasies of evil, and the vertigoes of vice, and the abyss of madness for individual rebels, and to chaos in society where and when their rebellions are temporarily successful. God is Love, and true ecstasy is a message from His love. God also is Order in the universe, and in this world, and in man's society, and in man's lasting literature. Such, at any rate, so it seems to me, are some of the meanings and intimations borne across the ages by the Christian classics represented in this book.

The design of this book is traced, then, by the intention to provide insight into the traditional Christian concept, method and personal experience of the spiritual life. Doctrinal agreement on the essential principles of the Catholic Faith is more or less assumed—even in the case of those authors who were not members of the Mother Church. The emphasis is placed upon the fairly normal aspects of mystical experience. As for the omitting of theology and philosophy, *qua* theology and philosophy, from a volume representing the classics of Christian literature, the explanation is obvious: those books (many of which are great as literature) must be read in their entirety; extracts cannot represent their qualities; and the masterpieces are far too obstruse, and far too long, to permit publication in such a book as this.

Organized in four sections, this volume, then, delves into the treasury of the past wherein are to be found the more vivid examples of personal records of spiritual experience to which the literary powers of their writers sufficed to give a permanency not only of psychological value but of literary value as well. The first section offers material largely derived from the lives of the saints. Here the emphasis has been I think advisedly placed on the more Augustinian spiritual types—those in whom individual, personal characteristics flavor and color the records of their soul struggles so that great vistas of adventure peculiar to themselves open up through the mysteries and ecstasies of the world of the spirit without ever wholly losing sight of the parallel highways and by-ways of this world and its concerns. Section Two gives excerpts from the counsel afforded by Christian literature to the individual soul of the reader. The selections are from those classical works which lend themselves best to quotation. The third and fourth sections offer extracts from English writers. In these all shades of thought and experience are represented, though the tradition outlined is in a sense Catholic rather than Protestant. Such a man as Bishop Andrewes represents the High Church Anglican group, while William Law is an example of orthodox Evangelical sentiment. Newman, of course, is the Catholic. The exclusion of certain English writers whose claims to be ranked among the classics of Christian literature are unquestionable, is in keeping with the intention to maintain the spirit if not the exact letter of the law of orthodox Christianity as the binding force which gives a unity to this book which a miscellaneous group of extracts from Catholic and Protestant sources alike could not possess. Hence, such heterodox geniuses as, for example, John Bunyan, are excluded. The poetry selections are, of course, only a very few of what could have been offered. Those chosen are in conformity with the prose selections, and to a very considerable extent emphasize experience rather than doctrine. In conclusion—although in justice this remark ought to come first, for the book itself derives from it—I desire to acknowledge the collaboration of George N. Shuster in the primary design as well as the difficult task of selecting the material of the book, while his wide and accurate scholarship is exemplified in the descriptive notes attached to the selections.

MICHAEL WILLIAMS.

CONTENTS

I

SPIRITUAL AUTOBIOGRAPHY

===

1. ST. AUGUSTINE
BOOK NINTH OF THE *CONFESSIONS*

2. TERTULLIAN
TESTIMONY OF THE CHRISTIAN SOUL

3. ST. FRANCIS OF ASSISI
FROM THE *LITTLE FLOWERS OF ST. FRANCIS*

4. BLESSED JULIANA OF NORWICH
FROM *REVELATIONS OF DIVINE LOVE*

5. ST. TERESA OF AVILA
CHAPTERS VIII, IX AND X OF THE *AUTOBIOGRAPHY*

6. BROTHER LAWRENCE
THE PRACTICE OF THE PRESENCE OF GOD

7. ST. THERESE OF LISIEUX
CHAPTER XI OF THE *AUTOBIOGRAPHY*

8. DANTE ALIGHIERI
CANTOS XXXI, XXXII AND XXXIII OF THE *PARADISO*

1. ST. AUGUSTINE:

BOOK NINTH OF THE *CONFESSIONS*

¶THE memoirs which Saint Augustine, Bishop of Hippo in Africa, wrote for the instruction of his friends form what is probably the most illustrious of all spiritual classics. Combining as it does utter sincerity with absolute humility, this book shows more clearly than any other how a man of the world, a philosopher and rhetorician, trained in the manners of the decadent Roman Empire, gradually became one who lived solely to do the will of God.

St. Augustine was born at Tagaste (now Souk-Ahras, in Algeria, Africa) on November 13, 354. The *Confessions* are the only source of information we possess concerning his childhood, his education and his early career. About 383 he left Africa for Rome, going thence to Milan where he met St. Ambrose and was converted to Christianity. Our knowledge of the details concerning this step is very limited; and though the Saint's baptism is by common consent placed in the year 387, all else is pretty much the material of controversy. The reader may well note that prior to becoming a Christian, St. Augustine was strongly influenced by the writings of Mani (the founder of the Manicheans) and of Plotinus (the author of the *Enneads*). The *Confessions* were apparently written about the year 400. Meanwhile their author had become a priest, a bishop and a noted controversialist. He died in 428.

In accordance with the limitations necessary in a volume of this character—limitations explained in the General Introduction—the editors have followed the custom of printing only one of thirteen books. The translation is that of J. G. Pilkington.*

* From *The Confessions of Saint Augustine*. Translated by J. G. Pilkington. New York: Liveright, Inc.

BOOK NINTH

HE SPEAKS OF HIS DESIGN OF FORSAKING THE PROFESSION OF
RHETORIC; OF THE DEATH OF HIS FRIENDS, NEBRIDIUS AND VERE-
CUNDUS, OF HAVING RECEIVED BAPTISM IN THE THIRTY-THIRD
YEAR OF HIS AGE; AND OF THE VIRTUES AND DEATH OF HIS
MOTHER, MONICA

CHAPTER I

*He praises God, the Author of safety, and Jesus Christ, the Redeemer,
acknowledging his own wickedness.*

 LORD, truly I am Thy servant; I am Thy serv-
ant, and the son of Thine handmaid: Thou hast
loosed my bonds. I will offer to Thee the sacrifice
of thanksgiving." Let my heart and my tongue
praise Thee, and let all my bones say, "Lord,
who is like unto Thee?" Let them so say, and
answer Thou me, and "say unto my soul, I am Thy salvation."
Who am I, and what is my nature? How evil have not my deeds
been; or if not my deeds, my words; or if not my words, my will?
But Thou, O Lord, art good and merciful, and Thy right hand
had respect unto the profoundness of my death and removed from
the bottom of my heart that abyss of corruption. And this was the
result, that I willed not to do what I willed, and willed to do what
Thou willest. But where, during all those years, and out of what
deep and secret retreat was my free will summoned forth in a
moment, whereby I gave my neck to Thy "easy yoke," and my
shoulders to Thy "light burden," O Christ Jesus, "my strength
and my Redeemer"? How sweet did it suddenly become to me to
be without the delights of trifles! And what at one time I feared
to lose, it was now a joy to me to put away. For Thou didst cast
them away from me, Thou true and highest sweetness. Thou didst
cast them away, and instead of them didst enter in Thyself,—
sweeter than all pleasure, though not to flesh and blood; brighter
than all light, but more veiled than all mysteries; more exalted
than all honour, but not to the exalted in their own conceits. Now
was my soul free from the gnawing cares of seeking and getting,

and of wallowing and exciting the itch of lust. And I babbled unto Thee my brightness, my riches, and my health, the Lord my God.

CHAPTER II

As his lungs were affected, he meditates withdrawing himself from public favour.

2. And it seemed good to me, as before Thee, not tumultuously to snatch away, but gently to withdraw the service of my tongue from the talker's trade; that the young, who thought not on Thy law, nor on Thy peace, but on mendacious follies and forensic strifes, might no longer purchase at my mouth equipments for their vehemence. And opportunely there wanted but a few days unto the Vacation of the Vintage; and I determined to endure them, in order to leave in the usual way, and, being redeemed by Thee, no more to return for sale. Our intention then was known to Thee; but to men—excepting our own friends—was it not known. For we had determined among ourselves not to let it get abroad to any; although Thou hadst given to us, ascending from the valley of tears, and singing the song of degrees, "sharp arrows," and destroying coals, against the "deceitful tongue," which in giving counsel opposes, and in showing love consumes, as it is wont to do with its food.

3. Thou hadst penetrated our hearts with Thy charity, and we carried Thy words fixed, as it were, in our bowels; and the examples of Thy servant, whom of black Thou hadst made bright, and of dead, alive, crowded in the bosom of our thoughts, burned and consumed our heavy torpor, that we might not topple into the abyss; and they enkindled us exceedingly, that every breath of the deceitful tongue of the gainsayer might inflame us the more, not extinguish us. Nevertheless, because for Thy name's sake which Thou hast sanctified throughout the earth, this, our vow and purpose, might also find commenders, it looked like a vaunting of oneself not to wait for the vacation, now so near, but to leave beforehand a public profession, and one, too, under general observation; so that all who looked on this act of mine, and saw how near was the vintage-time I desired to anticipate, would talk of me a great deal as if I were trying to appear to be a great person.

And what purpose would it serve that people should consider and dispute about my intention, and that our good should be evil spoken of?

4. Furthermore, this very summer, from too great literary labour, my lungs began to be weak, and with difficulty to draw deep breaths; showing by the pains in my chest that they were affected, and refusing too loud or prolonged speaking. This had at first been a trial to me, for it compelled me almost of necessity to lay down that burden of teaching; or, if I could be cured and become strong again, at least to leave it off for a while. But when the full desire of leisure, that I might see that Thou art the Lord, arose, and was confirmed in me, my God, Thou knowest I even began to rejoice that I had this excuse ready,—and that not a feigned one,—which might somewhat temper the offence taken by those who for their sons' good wished me never to have the freedom of sons. Full, therefore, with such joy, I bore it till that period of time had passed,—perhaps it was some twenty days,—yet they were bravely borne; for the cupidity which was wont to sustain part of this weighty business had departed, and I had remained overwhelmed had not its place been supplied by patience. Some of Thy servants, my brethren, may perchance say that I sinned in this, in that having once fully, and from my heart, entered on Thy warfare, I permitted myself to sit a single hour in the seat of falsehood. I will not contend. But hast not Thou, O most merciful Lord, pardoned and remitted this sin also, with my others, so horrible and deadly, in the holy water?

CHAPTER III

He retires to the villa of his friend Verecundus, who was not yet a Christian, and refers to his conversion and death, as well as that of Nebridius.

5. Verecundus was wasted with anxiety at that our happiness, since he, being most firmly held by his bonds, saw that he would lose our fellowship. For he was not yet a Christian, though his wife was one of the faithful; and yet hereby, being more firmly enchained than by anything else, was he held back from that journey which we had commenced. Nor, he declared, did he wish to be a Christian on any other terms than those that were impos-

sible. However, he invited us most courteously to make use of his country house so long as we should stay there. Thou, O Lord, wilt "recompense" him for this "at the resurrection of the just," seeing that Thou hast already given him "the lot of the righteous." For although, when we were absent at Rome, he, being overtaken with bodily sickness, and therein being made a Christian, and one of the faithful, departed this life, yet hadst Thou mercy on him, and not on him only, but on us also; lest, thinking on the exceeding kindness of our friend to us, and unable to count him in Thy flock, we should be tortured with intolerable grief. Thanks be unto Thee, our God, we are Thine. Thy exhortations, consolations, and faithful promises assure us that Thou now repayest Verecundus for that country house at Cassiacum, where from the fever of the world we found rest in Thee, with the perpetual freshness of Thy Paradise, in that Thou hast forgiven him his earthly sins, in that mountain flowing with milk, that fruitful mountain,—Thine own.

6. He then was at that time full of grief; but Nebridius was joyous. Although he also, not being yet a Christian, had fallen into the pit of that most pernicious error of believing Thy Son to be a phantasm, yet, coming out thence, he held the same belief that we did; not as yet initiated in any of the sacraments of Thy Church, but a most earnest inquirer after truth. Whom, not long after our conversion and regeneration by Thy baptism, he being also a faithful member of the Catholic Church, and serving Thee in perfect chastity and continency amongst his own people in Africa, when his whole household had been brought to Christianity through him, didst Thou release from the flesh; and now he lives in Abraham's bosom. Whatever that may be which is signified by that bosom, there lives my Nebridius, my sweet friend, Thy son, O Lord, adopted of a freedman; there he liveth. For what other place could there be for such a soul? There liveth he, concerning which he used to ask me much,—me, an inexperienced, feeble one. Now he puts not his ear unto my mouth, but his spiritual mouth unto Thy fountain, and drinketh as much as he is able, wisdom according to his desire,—happy without end. Nor do I believe that he is so inebriated with it as to forget me, seeing Thou, O Lord, whom he drinketh, art mindful of us. Thus, then, were we comforting the sorrowing Verecundus (our friendship being un-

touched) concerning our conversion, and exhorting him to a faith according to his condition, I mean, his married state. And tarrying for Nebridius to follow us, which, being so near, he was just about to do, when, behold, those days passed over at last; for long and many they seemed, on account of my love of easeful liberty, that I might sing unto Thee from my very marrow. My heart said unto Thee,—I have sought Thy face; "Thy face, Lord, will I seek."

CHAPTER IV

In the country he gives his attention to literature, and explains the fourth Psalm in connection with the happy conversion of Alypius. He is troubled with toothache.

7. And the day arrived on which, in very deed, I was to be released from the Professorship of Rhetoric, from which in intention I had been already released. And done it was; and Thou didst deliver my tongue whence Thou hadst already delivered my heart; and full of joy I blessed Thee for it, and retired with all mine to the villa. What I accomplished there in writing, which was now wholly devoted to Thy service, though still, in this pause as it were, panting from the school of pride, my books testify—those in which I disputed with my friends, and those with myself alone before Thee; and what with the absent Nebridius, my letters testify. And when can I find time to recount all Thy great benefits which Thou bestowest upon us at that time, especially as I am hasting on to still greater mercies? For my memory calls upon me, and pleasant it is to me, O Lord, to confess unto Thee, by what inward goads Thou didst subdue me, and how Thou didst make me low, bringing down the mountains and hills of my imagination, and didst straighten my crookedness, and smooth my rough ways; and by what means Thou also didst subdue that brother of my heart, Alypius, unto the name of Thy only-begotten, our Lord and Saviour Jesus Christ, which he at first refused to have inserted in our writings. For he rather desired that they should savour of the "cedars" of the schools, which the Lord hath now broken down, than of the wholesome herbs of the Church, hostile to serpents.

8. What utterances sent I up unto Thee, my God, when I read the Psalms of David, those faithful songs and sounds of devotion which exclude all swelling of spirit, when new to Thy true love, at rest in the villa with Alypius, a catechumen like myself, my mother cleaving unto us,—in woman's garb truly, but with a man's faith, with the peacefulness of age, full of motherly love and Christian piety! What utterances used I to send up unto Thee in those Psalms, and how was I inflamed towards Thee by them, and burned to rehearse them, if it were possible, throughout the whole world, against the pride of the human race! And yet they are sung throughout the whole world, and none can hide himself from Thy heat. With what vehement and bitter sorrow was I indignant at the Manichæans; whom yet again I pitied, for that they were ignorant of those sacraments, those medicaments, and were mad against the antidote which might have made them sane! I wished that they had been somewhere near me then, and, without my being aware of their presence, could have beheld my face, and heard my words, when I read the fourth Psalm in that time of my leisure,—how that psalm wrought upon me. When I called upon Thee, Thou didst hear me, O God of my righteousness; Thou hast enlarged me when I was in distress; have mercy upon me, and hear my prayer. Oh that they might have heard what I uttered on these words, without my knowing whether they heard or no, lest they should think that I spake it because of them! For, of a truth, neither should I have said the same things, nor in the way I said them, if I had perceived that I was heard and seen by them; and had I spoken them, they would not so have received them as when I spake by and for myself before Thee, out of the private feelings of my soul.

9. I alternately quaked with fear, and warmed with hope, and with rejoicing in Thy mercy, O Father. And all these passed forth, both by mine eyes and voice, when Thy good Spirit, turning unto us, said, O ye sons of men, how long will ye be slow of heart? "How long will ye love vanity, and seek after leasing?" For I had loved vanity, and sought after leasing. And Thou, O Lord, hadst already magnified Thy Holy One, raising Him from the dead, and setting Him at Thy right hand, whence from on high He should send His promise, the Paraclete, "the Spirit of Truth." And He had already sent Him, but I knew it not; He had sent

Him, because He was now magnified, rising again from the dead, and ascending into heaven. For till then "the Holy Ghost was not yet given, because that Jesus was not yet glorified." And the prophet cries out, How long will ye be slow of heart? How long will ye love vanity, and seek after leasing? Know this, that the Lord hath magnified His Holy One. He cries out, "How long?" He cries out, "Know this," and I, so long ignorant, "loved vanity, and sought after leasing." And therefore I heard and trembled, because these words were spoken unto such as I remembered that I myself had been. For in those phantasms which I once held for truths was there "vanity" and "leasing." And I spake many things loudly and earnestly, in the sorrow of my remembrance, which, would that they who yet "love vanity and seek after leasing" had heard! They would perchance have been troubled, and have vomited it forth, and Thou wouldst hear them when they cried unto Thee; for by a true death in the flesh He died for us, who now maketh intercession for us with Thee.

10. I read further, "Be ye angry, and sin not." And how was I moved, O my God, who had now learned to "be angry" with myself for the things past, so that in the future I might not sin! Yea, to be justly angry; for that it was not another nature of the race of darkness which sinned for me, as they affirm it to be who are not angry with themselves, and who treasure up to themselves wrath against the day of wrath, and of the revelation of Thy righteous judgment. Nor were my good things now without, nor were they sought after with eyes of flesh in that sun; for they that would have joy from without easily sink into oblivion, and are wasted upon those things which are seen and temporal, and in their starving thoughts do lick their very shadows. Oh, if only they were wearied out with their fasting, and said, "Who will show us any good?" And we would answer, and they hear, O Lord, The light of Thy countenance is lifted up upon us. For we are not that Light, which lighteth every man, but we are enlightened by Thee, that we, who were sometimes darkness, may be light in Thee. Oh that they could behold the internal Eternal, which having tasted I gnashed my teeth that I could not show It to them, while they brought me their heart in their eyes, roaming abroad from Thee, and said, "Who will show us any good?" But there, where I was angry with myself in my chamber, where I

was inwardly pricked, where I had offered my "sacrifice," slaying my old man, and beginning the resolution of a new life, putting my trust in Thee,—there hadst Thou begun to grow sweet unto me, and to "put gladness in my heart." And I cried out as I read this outwardly, and felt it inwardly. Nor would I be increased with worldly goods, wasting time and being wasted by time; whereas I possessed in Thy eternal simplicity other corn, and wine, and oil.

11. And with a loud cry from my heart, I called out in the following verse, "Oh, in peace!" and "the self-same!" Oh, what said he, "I will lay me down and sleep!" For who shall hinder us, when "shall be brought to pass the saying that is written, Death is swallowed up in victory?" And Thou art in the highest degree "the self-same," who changest not; and in Thee is the rest which forgetteth all labour, for there is no other beside Thee, nor ought we to seek after those many other things which are not what Thou art; but Thou, Lord, only makest me to dwell in hope. These things I read, and was inflamed; but discovered not what to do with those deaf and dead, of whom I had been a pestilent member,—a bitter and a blind declaimer against the writings behonied with the honey of heaven and luminous with Thine own light; and I was consumed on account of the enemies of this Scripture.

12. When shall I call to mind all that took place in those holidays? Yet neither have I forgotten, nor will I be silent about the severity of Thy scourge, and the amazing quickness of Thy mercy. Thou didst at that time torture me with toothache; and when it had become so exceeding great that I was not able to speak, it came into my heart to urge all my friends who were present to pray for me to Thee, the God of all manner of health. And I wrote it down on wax, and gave it to them to read. Presently, as with submissive desire we bowed our knees, that pain departed. But what pain? Or how did it depart? I confess to being much afraid, my Lord my God, seeing that from my earliest years I had not experienced such pain. And Thy purposes were profoundly impressed upon me; and, rejoicing in faith, I praised Thy name. And that faith suffered me not to be at rest in regard to my past sins, which were not yet forgiven me by Thy baptism.

CHAPTER V

At the recommendation of Ambrose, he reads the prophecies of Isaiah, but does not understand them.

13. The vintage vacation being ended, I gave the citizens of Milan notice that they might provide their scholars with another seller of words; because both of my election to serve Thee, and my inability, by reason of the difficulty of breathing and the pain in my chest, to continue the Professorship. And by letters I notified to Thy bishop, the holy man Ambrose, my former errors and present resolutions, with a view to his advising me which of Thy books it was best for me to read, so that I might be readier and fitter for the reception of such great grace. He recommended Isaiah the Prophet; I believe, because he foreshows more clearly than others the gospel, and the calling of the Gentiles. But I, not understanding the first portion of the book, and imagining the whole to be like it, laid it aside, intending to take it up hereafter, when better practised in our Lord's words.

CHAPTER VI

He is baptized at Milan with Alypius and his son Adeodatus. The Book "De Magistro."

14. Thence, when the time had arrived at which I was to give in my name, having left the country, we returned to Milan. Alypius also was pleased to be born again with me in Thee, being now clothed with the humility appropriate to Thy sacraments, and being so brave a tamer of the body, as with unusual fortitude to tread the frozen soil of Italy with his naked feet. We took into our company the boy Adeodatus, born of me carnally, of my sin. Well hadst Thou made him. He was barely fifteen years, yet in wit excelled many grave and learned men. I confess unto Thee Thy gifts, O Lord my God, creator of all, and of exceeding power to reform our deformities; for of me was there naught in that boy but the sin. For that we fostered him in Thy discipline, Thou inspiredst us, none other,—Thy gifts I confess unto Thee. There is a book of ours, which is entitled *The Master*. It is a

dialogue between him and me. Thou knowest that all things there put into the mouth of the person in argument with me were his thoughts in his sixteenth year. Many others more wonderful did I find in him. That talent was a source of awe to me. And who but Thou could be the worker of such marvels? Quickly didst Thou remove his life from the earth; and now I recall him to mind with a sense of security, in that I fear nothing for his childhood or youth, or for his whole self. We took him coeval with us in Thy grace, to be educated in Thy discipline; and we were baptized, and solicitude about our past life left us. Nor was I satiated in those days with the wondrous sweetness of considering the depth of Thy counsels concerning the salvation of the human race. How greatly did I weep in Thy hymns and canticles, deeply moved by the voices of Thy sweet-speaking Church! The voices flowed into mine ears, and the truth was poured forth into my heart, whence the agitation of my piety overflowed, and my tears ran over, and blessed was I therein.

CHAPTER VII

Of the Church hymns instituted at Milan; of the Ambrosian persecution raised by Justina; and of the discovery of the bodies of two martyrs.

15. Not long had the Church of Milan begun to employ this kind of consolation and exhortation, the brethren singing together with great earnestness of voice and heart. For it was about a year, or not much more, since Justina, the mother of the boy-Emperor Valentinian, persecuted Thy servant Ambrose in the interest of her heresy, to which she had been seduced by the Arians. The pious people kept guard in the church, prepared to die with their bishop, Thy servant. There my mother, Thy handmaid, bearing a chief part of those cares and watchings, lived in prayer. We, still unmelted by the heat of Thy Spirit, were yet moved by the astonished and disturbed city. At this time it was instituted that, after the manner of the Eastern Church, hymns and psalms should be sung, lest the people should pine away in the tediousness of sorrow; which custom, retained from then till now, is imitated by many, yea, by almost all of Thy congregations throughout the rest of the world.

16. Then didst Thou by a vision make known to Thy renowned bishop the spot where lay the bodies of Gervasius and Protasius, the martyrs (whom Thou hadst in Thy secret storehouse preserved uncorrupted for so many years), whence Thou mightest at the fitting time produce them to repress the feminine but royal fury. For when they were revealed and dug up and with due honour transferred to the Ambrosian Basilica, not only they who were troubled with unclean spirits (the devils confessing themselves) were healed, but a certain man also, who had been blind many years, a well-known citizen of that city, having asked and been told the reason of the people's tumultuous joy, rushed forth, asking his guide to lead him thither. Arrived there, he begged to be permitted to touch with his handkerchief the bier of Thy Saints, whose death is precious in Thy sight. When he had done this, and put it to his eyes, they were forthwith opened. Thence did the fame spread; thence did Thy praises burn,—shine; thence was the mind of that enemy, though not yet enlarged to the wholeness of believing, restrained from the fury of persecuting. Thanks be to Thee, O my God. Whence and whither hast Thou thus led my remembrance, that I should confess these things also unto Thee,—great, though I, forgetful, had passed them over? And yet then, when the "savour" of Thy "ointments" was so fragrant, did we not "run after Thee." And so I did the more abundantly weep at the singing of Thy hymns, formerly panting for Thee, and at last breathing in Thee, as far as the air can play in this house of grass.

CHAPTER VIII

Of the conversion of Evodius, and the death of his mother when returning with him to Africa; and whose education he tenderly relates.

17. Thou, who makest men to dwell of one mind in a house, didst associate with us Evodius also, a young man of our city, who, when serving as an agent for Public Affairs, was converted unto Thee and baptized prior to us; and relinquishing his secular service, prepared himself for Thine. We were together, and together were we about to dwell with a holy purpose. We sought for some place where we might be most useful in our service to Thee,

and were going back together to Africa. And when we were at the
Tiberine Ostia my mother died. Much I omit, having much to
hasten. Receive my confessions and thanksgivings, O my God,
for innumerable things concerning which I am silent. But I will
not omit aught that my soul has brought forth as to that Thy
handmaid who brought me forth,—in her flesh, that I might be
born to this temporal light, and in her heart, that I might be
born to life eternal. I will speak not of her gifts, but Thine in
her; for she neither made herself nor educated herself. Thou
createdst her, nor did her father nor her mother know what a
being was to proceed from them. And it was the rod of Thy
Christ, the discipline of Thine only Son, that trained her in Thy
fear, in the house of one of Thy faithful ones, who was a sound
member of Thy Church. Yet this good discipline did she not so
much attribute to the diligence of her mother, as that of a certain
decrepit maid-servant, who had carried about her father when an
infant, as little ones are wont to be carried on the backs of elder
girls. For which reason, and on account of her extreme age and
very good character, was she much respected by the heads of that
Christian house. Whence also was committed to her the care of
her master's daughters, which she with diligence performed, and
was earnest in restraining them when necessary, with a holy severity, and instructing them with a sober sagacity. For, excepting
at the hours in which they were very temperately fed at their
parents' table, she used not to permit them, though parched with
thirst, to drink even water; thereby taking precautions against an
evil custom, and adding the wholesome advice, "You drink water
only because you have not control of wine; but when you have
come to be married, and made mistresses of storeroom and cellar,
you will despise water, but the habit of drinking will remain." By
this method of instruction, and power of command, she restrained
the longing of their tender age, and regulated the very thirst of
the girls to such a becoming limit, as that what was not seemly
they did not long for.

18. And yet—as Thine handmaid related to me, her son—
there had stolen upon her a love of wine. For when she, as being
a sober maiden, was as usual bidden by her parents to draw wine
from the cask, the vessel being held under the opening, before she
poured the wine into the bottle, she would wet the tips of her lips

with a little, for more than that her inclination refused. For this she did not from any craving for drink, but out of the overflowing buoyancy of her time of life, which bubbles up with sportiveness, and is, in youthful spirits, wont to be repressed by the gravity of elders. And so unto that little, adding daily little (for "he that contemneth small things shall fall by little and little"), she contracted such a habit as to drink off eagerly her little cup nearly full of wine. Where, then, was the sagacious old woman with her earnest restraint? Could anything prevail against a secret disease if Thy medicine, O Lord, did not watch over us? Father, mother, and nurturers absent, Thou present, who hast created, who callest, who also by those who are set over us workest some good for the salvation of our souls, what didst Thou at that time, O my God? How didst Thou heal her? How didst Thou make her whole? Didst Thou not out of another woman's soul evoke a hard and bitter insult, as a surgeon's knife from Thy secret store, and with one thrust remove all that putrefaction? For the maid-servant who used to accompany her to the cellar, falling out, as it happens, with her little mistress, when she was alone with her, cast in her teeth this vice, with very bitter insult, calling her a "wine-bibber." Stung by this taunt, she perceived her foulness, and immediately condemned and renounced it. Even as friends by their flattery pervert, so do enemies by their taunts often correct us. Yet Thou renderest not unto them what Thou dost by them, but what was proposed by them. For she, being angry, desired to irritate her young mistress, not to cure her; and did it in secret, either because the time and place of the dispute found them thus, or perhaps lest she herself should be exposed to danger for disclosing it so late. But Thou, Lord, Governor of heavenly and earthly things, who convertest to Thy purposes the deepest torrents, and disposest the turbulent current of the ages, healest one soul by the unsoundness of another; lest any man, when he remarks this, should attribute it unto his own power if another, whom he wishes to be reformed, is so through a word of his.

CHAPTER IX

*He describes the praiseworthy habits of his mother; her kindness
towards her husband and her sons.*

19. Being thus modestly and soberly trained, and rather made
subject by Thee to her parents, than by her parents to Thee, when
she had arrived at a marriageable age, she was given to a husband
whom she served as her lord. And she busied herself to gain
him to Thee, preaching Thee unto him by her behaviour; by
which Thou madest her fair, and reverently amiable, and admirable unto her husband. For she so bore the wronging of her
bed as never to have any dissension with her husband on account
of it. For she waited for Thy mercy upon him, that by believing
in Thee he might become chaste. And besides this, as he was
earnest in friendship, so was he violent in anger; but she had
learned that an angry husband should not be resisted, neither in
deed, nor even in word. But so soon as he was grown calm and
tranquil, and she saw a fitting moment, she would give him a
reason for her conduct, should he have been excited without cause.
In short, while many matrons, whose husbands were more gentle,
carried the marks of blows on their dishonoured faces, and would
in private conversation blame the lives of their husbands, she
would blame their tongues, monishing them gravely, as if in jest:
"That from the hour they heard what are called the matrimonial
tablets read to them, they should think of them as instruments
whereby they were made servants; so, being always mindful of
their condition, they ought not to set themselves in opposition to
their lords." And when they, knowing what a furious husband she
endured, marvelled that it had never been reported, nor appeared
by any indication, that Patricius had beaten his wife, or that there
had been any domestic strife between them, even for a day, and
asked her in confidence the reason of this, she taught them her
rule, which I have mentioned above. They who observed it experienced the wisdom of it, and rejoiced; those who observed it
not were kept in subjection, and suffered.

20. Her mother-in-law, also, being at first prejudiced against
her by the whisperings of evil-disposed servants, she so conquered
by submission, persevering in it with patience and meekness, that

she voluntarily disclosed to her son the tongues of the meddling servants, whereby the domestic peace between herself and her daughter-in-law had been agitated, begging him to punish them for it. When, therefore, he had—in conformity with his mother's wish, and with a view to the discipline of his family, and to ensure the future harmony of its members—corrected with stripes those discovered, according to the will of her who had discovered them, she promised a similar reward to any who, to please her, should say anything evil to her of her daughter-in-law. And, none now daring to do so, they lived together with a wonderful sweetness of mutual good-will.

21. This great gift Thou bestowedst also, my God, my mercy, upon that good handmaid of Thine, out of whose womb Thou createdst me, even that, whenever she could, she showed herself such a peacemaker between any differing and discordant spirits, that when she had heard on both sides most bitter things, such as swelling and undigested discord is wont to give vent to, when the crudities of enmities are breathed out in bitter speeches to a present friend against an absent enemy, she would disclose nothing about the one unto the other, save what might avail to their reconcilement. A small good this might seem to me, did I not know to my sorrow countless persons, who, through some horrible and far-spreading infection of sin, not only disclose to enemies mutually enraged the things said in passion against each other, but add some things that were never spoken at all; whereas, to a generous man, it ought to seem a small thing not to incite or increase the enmities of men by ill-speaking, unless he endeavour likewise by kind words to extinguish them. Such a one was she,—Thou, her most intimate Instructor, teaching her in the school of her heart.

22. Finally, her own husband, now towards the end of his earthly existence, did she gain over unto Thee; and she had not to complain of that in him, as one of the faithful, which, before he became so, she had endured. She was also the servant of Thy servants. Whatsoever of them knew her, did in her much magnify, honour, and love Thee; for that through the testimony of the fruits of a holy conversation, they perceived Thee to be present in her heart. For she had "been the wife of one man," had requited her parents, had guided her house piously, was "well-reported of for good works," had "brought up children,"

as often travailing in birth of them as she saw them swerving
from Thee. Lastly, to all of us, O Lord (since of Thy favour
Thou sufferest Thy servants to speak), who, before her sleeping
in Thee, lived associated together, having received the grace of
Thy baptism, did she devote care such as she might if she had been
mother of us all; served us as if she had been child of all.

CHAPTER X

*A conversation he had with his mother concerning the
kingdom of heaven.*

23. As the day now approached on which she was to depart this
life (which day Thou knewst, we did not), it fell out—Thou, as I
believe, by Thy secret ways arranging it—that she and I stood
alone, leaning in a certain window, from which the garden of the
house we occupied at Ostia could be seen; at which place, removed
from the crowd, we were resting ourselves for the voyage, after
the fatigues of a long journey. We then were conversing alone
very pleasantly; and, "forgetting those things which are behind,
and reaching forth unto those things which are before," we were
seeking between ourselves in the presence of the Truth, which
Thou art, of what nature the eternal life of the saints would be,
which eye hath not seen, nor ear heard, neither hath entered into
the heart of man. But yet we opened wide the mouth of our heart,
after those supernal streams of Thy fountain, "the fountain of
life," which is "with Thee;" that being sprinkled with it according
to our capacity, we might in some measure weigh so high a
mystery.

24. And when our conversation had arrived at that point, that
the very highest pleasure of the carnal senses, and that in the very
brightest material light, seemed by reason of the sweetness of
that life, not only not worthy of comparison, but not even of
mention, we, lifting ourselves with a more ardent affection towards
"the Self-same," did gradually pass through all corporeal things,
and even the heaven itself, whence sun, and moon, and stars shine
upon the earth; yea, we soared higher yet by inward musing, and
discoursing, and admiring Thy works; and we came to our own
minds, and went beyond them, that we might advance as high as

that region of unfailing plenty, where Thou feedst Israel for ever with the food of truth, and where life is that Wisdom by whom all these things are made, both which have been, and which are to come; and she is not made, but is as she hath been, and so shall ever be; yea, rather, to "have been," and "to be hereafter," are not in her, but only "to be," seeing she is eternal, for to "have been" and "to be hereafter" are not eternal. And while we were thus speaking, and straining after her, we slightly touched her with the whole effort of our heart; and we sighed, and there left bound "the first-fruits of the Spirit;" and returned to the noise of our own mouth, where the word uttered has both beginning and end. And what is like unto Thy Word, our Lord, who remaineth in Himself without becoming old, and "maketh all things new"?

25. We were saying, then, If to any man the tumult of the flesh were silenced,—silenced the phantasies of earth, waters, and air,—silenced, too, the poles; yea, the very soul be silenced to herself, and go beyond herself by not thinking of herself,— silenced fancies and imaginary revelations, every tongue, and every sign, and whatsoever exists by passing away, since, if any could hearken, all these say, "We created not ourselves, but were created by Him who abideth for ever:" If, having uttered this, they now should be silenced, having only quickened our ears to Him who created them, and He alone speak not by them, but by Himself, that we may hear His word, not by fleshly tongue, nor angelic voice, nor sound of thunder, nor the obscurity of a similitude, but might hear Him—Him whom in these we love—without these, likeas we two now strained ourselves, and with rapid thought touched on that Eternal Wisdom which remaineth over all. If this could be sustained, and other visions of a far different kind be withdrawn, and this one ravish, and absorb, and envelop its beholder amid these inward joys, so that his life might be eternally like that one moment of knowledge which we now sighed after, were not this "Enter thou into the joy of Thy Lord"? And when shall that be? When we shall all rise again; but all shall not be changed.

26. Such things was I saying; and if not after this manner, and in these words, yet, Lord, Thou knowest, that in that day when we were talking thus, this world with all its delights grew

contemptible to us, even while we spake. Then said my mother, "Son, for myself, I have no longer any pleasure in aught in this life. What I want here further, and why I am here, I know not, now that my hopes in this world are satisfied. There was indeed one thing for which I wished to tarry a little in this life, and that was that I might see thee a Catholic Christian before I died. My God has exceeded this abundantly, so that I see thee despising all earthly felicity, made His servant,—what do I here?"

CHAPTER XI

His mother, attacked by fever, dies at Ostia.

27. What reply I made unto her to these things I do not well remember. However, scarcely five days after, or not much more, she was prostrated by fever; and while she was sick, she one day sank into a swoon, and was for a short time unconscious of visible things. We hurried up to her; but she soon regained her senses, and gazing on me and my brother as we stood by her, she said to us inquiringly, "Where was I?" Then looking intently at us stupefied with grief, "Here," saith she, "shall you bury your mother." I was silent, and refrained from weeping; but my brother said something, wishing her, as the happier lot, to die in her own country and not abroad. She, when she heard this, with anxious countenance arrested him with her eye, as savouring of such things, and then gazing at me, "Behold," saith she, "what he saith;" and soon after to us both she saith, "Lay this body anywhere, let not the care for it trouble you at all. This only I ask, that you will remember me at the Lord's altar, wherever you be." And when she had given forth this opinion in such words as she could, she was silent, being in pain with her increasing sickness.

28. But, as I reflected on Thy gifts, O thou invisible God, which Thou instillest into the hearts of Thy faithful ones, whence such marvellous fruits do spring, I did rejoice and give thanks unto Thee, calling to mind what I knew before, how she had ever burned with anxiety respecting her burial-place, which she had provided and prepared for herself by the body of her husband. For as they had lived very peacefully together, her desire had

also been (so little is the human mind capable of grasping things divine) that this should be added to that happiness, and be talked of among men, that after her wandering beyond the sea, it had been granted her that they both, so united on earth, should lie in the same grave. But when this uselessness had, through the bounty of Thy goodness, begun to be no longer in her heart, I knew not, and I was full of joy admiring what she had thus disclosed to me; though indeed in that our conversation in the window also, when she said, "What do I here any longer?" she appeared not to desire to die in her own country. I heard afterwards, too, that at the time we were at Ostia, with a maternal confidence she one day, when I was absent, was speaking with certain of my friends on the contemning of this life, and the blessing of death; and when they—amazed at the courage which Thou hadst given to her, a woman—asked her whether she did not dread leaving her body at such a distance from her own city, she replied, "Nothing is far to God; nor need I fear lest He should be ignorant at the end of the world of the place whence He is to raise me up." On the ninth day, then, of her sickness, the fifty-sixth year of her age, and the thirty-third of mine, was that religious and devout soul set free from the body.

CHAPTER XII

How he mourned his dead mother.

29. I closed her eyes; and there flowed a great sadness into my heart, and it was passing into tears, when mine eyes at the same time, by the violent control of my mind, sucked back the fountain dry, and woe was me in such a struggle! But, as soon as she breathed her last, the boy Adeodatus burst out into wailing, but, being checked by us all, he became quiet. In like manner also my own childish feeling, which was, through the youthful voice of my heart, finding escape in tears, was restrained and silenced. For we did not consider it fitting to celebrate that funeral with tearful plaints and groanings; for on such wise are they who die unhappy, or are altogether dead, wont to be mourned. But she neither died unhappy, nor did she altogether die. For of this were we assured

by the witness of her good conversation, her "faith unfeigned," and other sufficient grounds.

30. What, then, was that which did grievously pain me within, but the newly-made wound, from having that most sweet and dear habit of living together suddenly broken off? I was full of joy indeed in her testimony, when, in that her last illness, flattering my dutifulness, she called me "kind," and recalled, with great affection of love, that she had never heard any harsh or reproachful sound come out of my mouth against her. But yet, O my God, who madest us, how can the honour which I paid to her be compared with her slavery for me? As, then, I was left destitute of so great comfort in her, my soul was stricken, and that life torn apart as it were, which, of hers and mine together, had been made but one.

31. The boy then being restrained from weeping, Evodius took up the Psalter, and began to sing—the whole house responding —the Psalm, "I will sing of mercy and judgment: unto Thee, O Lord." But when they heard what we were doing, many brethren and religious women came together; and whilst they whose office it was were, according to custom, making ready for the funeral, I, in a part of the house where I conveniently could, together with those who thought that I ought not to be left alone, discoursed on what was suited to the occasion; and by this alleviation of truth mitigated the anguish known unto Thee—they being unconscious of it, listened intently, and thought me to be devoid of any sense of sorrow. But in Thine ears, where none of them heard, did I blame the softness of my feelings, and restrained the flow of my grief, which yielded a little unto me; but the paroxysm returned again, though not so as to burst forth into tears, nor to a change of countenance, though I knew what I repressed in my heart. And as I was exceedingly annoyed that these human things had such power over me, which in the due order and destiny of our natural condition must of necessity come to pass, with a new sorrow I sorrowed for my sorrow, and was wasted by a twofold sadness.

32. So when the body was carried forth, we both went and returned without tears. For neither in those prayers which we poured forth unto Thee when the sacrifice of our redemption was offered up unto Thee for her,—the dead body being now placed by the side of the grave, as the custom there is, prior to its being

laid therein,—neither in their prayers did I shed tears; yet was I most grievously sad in secret all the day, and with a troubled mind entreated Thee, as I was able, to heal my sorrow, but Thou didst not; fixing, I believe, in my memory by this one lesson the power of the bonds of all habit, even upon a mind which now feeds not upon a fallacious word. It appeared to me also a good thing to go and bathe, I having heard that the bath [*balneum*] took its name from the Greek βαλανεῖον, because it drives trouble from the mind. Lo, this also I confess unto Thy mercy, "Father of the fatherless," that I bathed, and felt the same as before I had done so. For the bitterness of my grief exuded not from my heart. Then I slept, and on waking found my grief not a little mitigated; and as I lay alone upon my bed, there came into my mind those true verses of Thy Ambrose, for Thou art—

> "Deus creator omnium,
> Polique rector, vestiens
> Diem decoro lumine,
> Noctem sopora gratia;
> Artus solutos ut quies
> Reddat laboris usui,
> Mentesque fessas allevet,
> Luctusque solvat anxios." [1]

33. And then little by little did I bring back my former thoughts of Thine handmaid, her devout conversation towards Thee, her holy tenderness and attentiveness towards us, which was suddenly taken away from me; and it was pleasant to me to weep in Thy sight, for her and for me, concerning her and concerning myself. And I set free the tears which before I repressed, that they

---

[1] Rendered as follows in a translation of the first ten books of the *Confessions*, described on the title-page as "Printed by J. C., for John Crook, and are to be sold at the sign of the 'Ship,' in St. Paul's Churchyard. 1660":—

> "O God, the world's great Architect,
> Who dost heaven's rowling orbs direct;
> Cloathing the day with beauteous light,
> And with sweet slumbers silent night;
> When wearied limbs new vigour gain
> From rest, new labours to sustain;
> When hearts oppressed do meet relief,
> And anxious minds forget their grief."

might flow at their will, spreading them beneath my heart; and it rested in them, for Thy ears were nigh me,—not those of man, who would have put a scornful interpretation on my weeping. But now in writing I confess it unto Thee, O Lord! Read it who will, and interpret how he will; and if he finds me to have sinned in weeping for my mother during so small a part of an hour,—that mother who was for a while dead to mine eyes, who had for many years wept for me, that I might live in Thine eyes,—let him not laugh at me, but rather, if he be a man of a noble charity, let him weep for my sins against Thee, the Father of all the brethren of Thy Christ.

CHAPTER XIII

He entreats God for her sins, and admonishes his readers to remember her piously.

34. But,—my heart being now healed of that wound, in so far as it could be convicted of a carnal affection,—I pour out unto Thee, O our God, on behalf of that Thine handmaid, tears of a far different sort, even that which flows from a spirit broken by the thoughts of the dangers of every soul that dieth in Adam. And although she, having been "made alive" in Christ even before she was freed from the flesh, had so lived as to praise Thy name both by her faith and conversation, yet dare I not say that from the time Thou didst regenerate her by baptism, no word went forth from her mouth against Thy precepts. And it hath been declared by Thy son, the Truth, that "Whosoever shall say to his brother, Thou fool, shall be in danger of hell fire." And woe even unto the praiseworthy life of man, if, putting away mercy, Thou shouldest investigate it. But because Thou dost not narrowly inquire after sins, we hope with confidence to find some place of indulgence with Thee. But whosoever recounts his true merits to Thee, what is it that he recounts to Thee but Thine own gifts? Oh, if men would know themselves to be men; and that "he that glorieth" would "glory in the Lord!"

35. I then, O my Praise and my Life, Thou God of my heart, putting aside for a little her good deeds, for which I joyfully give thanks to Thee, do now beseech Thee for the sins of my mother.

Hearken unto me, through that Medicine of our wounds who hung upon the tree, and who, sitting at Thy right hand, "maketh intercession for us." I know that she acted mercifully, and from the heart forgave her debtors their debts; do Thou also forgive her debts, whatever she contracted during so many years since the water of salvation. Forgive her, O Lord, forgive her, I beseech Thee; "enter not into judgment" with her. Let Thy mercy be exalted above Thy justice, because Thy words are true, and Thou hast promised mercy unto "the merciful"; which Thou gavest them to be who wilt "have mercy" on whom Thou wilt "have mercy," and wilt "have compassion" on whom Thou hast had compassion.

36. And I believe Thou hast already done that which I ask Thee; but "accept the free-will offerings of my mouth, O Lord." For she, when the day of her dissolution was near at hand, took no thought to have her body sumptuously covered, or embalmed with spices; nor did she covet a choice monument, or desire her paternal burial-place. These things she entrusted not to us, but only desired to have her name remembered at Thy altar, which she had served without the omission of a single day; whence she knew that the holy sacrifice was dispensed, by which the handwriting that was against us is blotted out; by which the enemy was triumphed over, who, summing up our offences, and searching for something to bring against us, found nothing in Him in whom we conquer. Who will restore to Him the innocent blood? Who will repay Him the price with which He bought us, so as to take us from Him? Unto the sacrament of which our ransom did Thy handmaid bind her soul by the bond of faith. Let none separate her from Thy protection. Let not the "lion" and the "dragon" introduce himself by force or fraud. For she will not reply that she owes nothing, lest she be convicted and got the better of by the wily deceiver; but she will answer that her "sins are forgiven" by Him to whom no one is able to repay that price which He, owing nothing, laid down for us.

37. May she therefore rest in peace with her husband, before or after whom she married none; whom she obeyed, with patience bringing forth fruit unto Thee, that she might gain him also for Thee. And inspire, O my Lord my God, inspire Thy servants my brethren, Thy sons my masters, who with voice and heart and

writings I serve, that so many of them as shall read these confessions may at Thy altar remember Monica, Thy handmaid, together with Patricius, her sometime husband, by whose flesh Thou introducest me into this life, in what manner I know not. May they with pious affection be mindful of my parents in this transitory light, of my brethren that are under Thee our Father in our Catholic mother, and of my fellow-citizens in the eternal Jerusalem, which the wandering of Thy people sigheth for from their departure until their return. That so my mother's last entreaty to me may, through my confessions more than through my prayers, be more abundantly fulfilled to her through the prayers of many.

2. TERTULLIAN:
TESTIMONY OF THE CHRISTIAN SOUL

¶Early Christianity must have known many eloquent preachers and able writers. Of those whose work has come down to us, Tertullian is the most interesting despite the extremes to which his thought was led. Quintus Septimus Florens Tertullianus was born about 160, at Carthage; the date of his death is unknown. The longest of his earlier writings is the *Apologeticus,* in which he defended the Christians and castigated their pagan opponents. Later on Tertullian became a rigorist, joining the sect of the Montanists who were adjudged heretics by the Church on account of their excessive moral tenets—*e.g.,* their views that second marriage, after the death of a husband or wife, was a sin. He himself seceded from the Church, and eventually founded a sect of his own.

The Testimony here reproduced is a brief and unusually brilliant essay, which has always been read with especial favor both because of its intrinsic worth and because of the insight it affords into the mentality of the early Christians. Numerous translations have been made. The one here reprinted is that of the *Ante-Nicene Christian Library,* edited (1869) by Alexander Roberts and James Donaldson.*

 F, with the object of convicting the rivals and persecutors of Christian truth, from their own authorities, of the crime of at once being untrue to themselves and doing injustice to us, one is bent on gathering testimonies in its favour from the writings of the philosophers, or the poets, or other masters of this world's learning and wisdom, he has need of a most inquisitive spirit, and a still greater memory, to carry

* From *The Writings of Tertullian,* Vol. I. Edited by the Rev. A. Roberts and James Donaldson. Edinburgh: T. and T. Clark, 1869.

out the research. Indeed, some of our people, who still continued their inquisitive labours in ancient literature, and still occupied memory with it, have published works we have in our hands of this very sort; works in which they relate and attest the nature and origin of their traditions, and the grounds on which opinions rest, and from which it may be seen at once that we have embraced nothing new or monstrous—nothing for which we cannot claim the support of ordinary and well-known writings, whether in ejecting error from our creed, or admitting truth into it. But the unbelieving hardness of the human heart leads them to slight even their own teachers, otherwise approved and in high renown, whenever they touch upon arguments which are used in defence of Christianity. Then the poets are fools, when they describe the gods with human passions and stories; then the philosophers are without reason, when they knock at the gates of truth. He will thus far be reckoned a wise and sagacious man who has gone the length of uttering sentiments that are almost Christian; while if, in a mere affectation of judgment and wisdom, he sets himself to reject their ceremonies, or to convicting the world of its sin, he is sure to be branded as a Christian. We will have nothing, then, to do with the literature and the teaching, perverted in its best results, which is believed in its errors rather than its truth. We shall lay no stress on it, if some of their authors have declared that there is one God and one God only. Nay, let it be granted that there is nothing in heathen writers which a Christian approves, that it may be put out of his power to utter a single word of reproach. For all are not familiar with their teachings; and those who are, have no assurance in regard to their truth. Far less do men assent to our writings, to which no one comes for guidance unless he is already a Christian. I call in a new testimony, yea, one which is better known than all literature, more discussed than all doctrine, more public than all publications, greater than the whole man—I mean all which is man's. Stand forth, O soul, whether thou art a divine and eternal substance, as most philosophers believe—if it is so, thou wilt be the less likely to lie,—or whether thou art the very opposite of divine, because indeed a mortal thing, as Epicurus alone thinks—in that case there will be the less temptation for thee to speak falsely in this case: whether thou art received from heaven, or sprung from earth; whether thou art formed of numbers, or of atoms; whether thine existence begins with that of the body, or thou art put into it at a later stage; from whatever source, and in whatever way, thou makest man a rational being, in the highest degree capable of thought and knowledge,—stand forth and give thy witness. But I call thee not as when, fashioned in schools, trained in libraries, fed up in Attic academies and porticoes, thou belchest forth thy wisdom. I address thee, simple and rude, and uncultured and untaught, such as they have thee who have thee only, that very thing pure and entire, of the road, the street, the workshop. I want thine inexperience, since in thy small experience no one feels any confidence. I demand of thee the things thou bringest with thee into man, which thou knowest either from thyself, or from thine author, whoever he may be. Thou art not, as I well know, Christian; for a man becomes a Christian, he is not born one. Yet Christians earnestly press thee for a testimony; they press thee, though an alien, to bear witness against thy friends, that they may be put to shame before thee, for hating and mocking us on account of things which convict thee as an accessory.

2. We give offence by proclaiming that there is one God, to whom the name of God alone belongs, from whom all things come, and who is Lord of the whole universe. Bear thy testimony, if thou knowest this to be the truth; for openly and with a perfect liberty, such as we do not possess, we hear thee both in private and in public exclaim, "Which may God grant," and, "If God so will." By expressions such as these thou declarest that there is one who is distinctively God, and thou confessest that all power belongs to Him to whose will as Sovereign thou dost look. At the same time, too, thou deniest any others to be truly gods, in calling them by their own names of Saturn, Jupiter, Mars, Minerva; for thou affirmest Him to be God alone to whom thou givest no other name than God; and though thou sometimes callest these other gods, thou plainly usest the designation as one which does not really belong to them, but is, so to speak, a borrowed one. Nor is the nature of the God we declare unknown to thee: "God is good, God does good," thou art wont to say; plainly suggesting further, "But man is evil." In asserting an antithetic proposition, thou in a sort of indirect and figurative way reproachest man with his wickedness in departing from a God so good. So, again, as among

us, as belonging to the God of benignity and goodness, "Blessing" is a most sacred thing in our religion and our life, thou too sayest as readily as a Christian needs, "God bless thee"; and when thou turnest the blessing of God into a curse, in like manner thy very words confess with us that His power over us is absolute and entire. There are some who, though they do not deny the existence of God, hold withal that He is neither Searcher, nor Ruler, nor Judge; treating with especial disdain those of us who go over to Christ out of fear of a coming judgment, as they think, honouring God in freeing Him from the cares of keeping watch, and the trouble of taking note,—not even regarding Him as capable of anger. For if God, they say, gets angry, then He is susceptible of corruption and passion; but that of which passion and corruption can be affirmed may also perish, which God cannot do. But these very persons elsewhere, confessing that the soul is divine, and bestowed on us by God, stumble against a testimony of the soul itself, which affords an answer to these views: for if either divine or God-given, it doubtless knows its giver; and if it knows Him, it undoubtedly fears Him too, and especially as having been by Him endowed so amply. Has it no fear of Him whose favour it is so desirous to possess, and whose anger it is so anxious to avoid? Whence, then, the soul's natural fear of God, if God cannot be angry? How is there any dread of Him whom nothing offends? What is feared but anger? Whence comes anger, but from observing what is done? What leads to watchful oversight, but judgment in prospect? Whence is judgment, but from power? To whom does supreme authority and power belong, but to God alone? So thou art always ready, O soul, from thine own knowledge, nobody casting scorn upon thee, and no one preventing, to exclaim, "God sees all," and "I commend thee to God," and "May God repay," and "God shall judge between us." How happens this, since thou art not Christian? How is it that, even with the garland of Ceres on the brow, wrapped in the purple cloak of Saturn, wearing the white robe of the goddess Isis, thou invokest God as judge? Standing under the statue of Æsculapius, adorning the brazen image of Juno, arraying the helmet of Minerva with dusky figures, thou never thinkest of appealing to any of these deities. In thine own forum thou appealest to a God who is elsewhere; thou permittest honour to be rendered in thy temples to a foreign god. Oh, striking testimony to truth, which in the very midst of demons obtains a witness for us Christians!

3. But when we say that there are demons—as though, in the simple fact that we alone expel them from the men's bodies, we did not also prove their existence—some disciple of Chrysippus begins to curl the lip. Yet thy curses sufficiently attest that there are such beings, and that they are objects of thy strong dislike. As what comes to thee as a fit expression of thy strong hatred of him, thou callest the man a devil who annoys thee with his filthiness, or malice, or insolence, or any other vice which we ascribe to evil spirits. In expressing vexation, or contempt, or abhorrence, thou hast Satan constantly upon thy lips; the very same we hold to be the angel of evil, the source of error, the corrupter of the whole world, by whom in the beginning man was entrapped into breaking the commandment of God, and being given over to death on account of his sin, the entire human race, tainted in their descent from him, were made a channel for transmitting his condemnation. Thou seest, then, who your destroyer is; and though he is fully known only to Christians, or to any other sect that confesses the one true God, yet, as thy hatred of him proves, thou hast had some acquaintance with him as well as others.

4. Even now, as the matter refers to thy opinion on a point the more closely belonging to thee, in so far as it bears on thy personal well-being, we maintain that after life has passed away thou still remainest in existence, and lookest forward to a day of judgment, and according to thy deserts art assigned to misery or bliss, in either way of it for ever; that, to be capable of this, thy former substance must needs return to thee, the matter and the memory of the very same human being: for neither good nor evil couldst thou feel if thou wert not endowed again with that sensitive bodily organization, and there would be no grounds for judgment without the presentation of the very person to whom the sufferings of judgment were due. That Christian view, though much nobler than the Pythagorean, as it does not transfer thee into beasts; though more complete than the Platonic, since it endows thee again with a body; though more worthy of honour than the Epicurean, as it preserves thee from annihilation,—yet, because of the name connected with it, it is held to be nothing but vanity and folly, and, as it is called, a mere presumption. But we are not

ashamed of ourselves if our presumption is found to have thy support. Well, in the first place, when thou speakest of one who is dead, thou sayest of him, "Poor man"—poor, surely, not because he has been taken from the good of life, but because he has been given over to punishment and condemnation. But at another time thou speakest of the dead as free from trouble; thou professest to think life a burden, and death a blessing. Thou art wont, too, to speak of the dead as in repose, when, returning to their graves beyond the city gates with food and dainties, thou art wont to present offerings to thyself rather than to them; or when, coming from the graves again, thou art staggering under the effects of wine. But I want thy sober opinion. Thou callest the dead poor when thou speakest thine own thoughts, when thou art at a distance from them. For at their feast, where in a sense they are present and recline along with thee, it would never do to cast reproach upon their lot. Thou canst not but adulate those for whose sake thou art feasting it so sumptuously. Dost thou then speak of him as "poor" who feels not? How happens it that thou cursest, as one capable of suffering from thy curse, the man whose memory comes back on thee with the sting in it of some old injury? It is thine imprecation that the earth may lie heavy on him, and that there may be trouble to his ashes in the realm of the dead. In like manner, in thy kindly feeling to him to whom thou art indebted for favours, thou entreatest repose to his bones and ashes, and thy desire is that among the dead he may have pleasant rest. If thou hast no power of suffering after death, if no feeling remains,—if, in a word, severance from the body is the annihilation of thee, what makes thee lie against thyself, as if thou couldst suffer in another state? Nay, why dost thou fear death at all? There is nothing after death to be feared, if there is nothing to be felt. For though it may be said that death is dreadful not for anything it threatens afterwards, but because it deprives us of the good of life; yet, on the other hand, as it puts an end to life's discomforts, which are far more numerous, death's terrors are mitigated by a gain that more than outweighs the loss. And there is no occasion to be troubled about a loss of good things, which is amply made up for by so great a blessing as relief from every trouble. There is nothing dreadful in that which delivers from all that is to be dreaded. If thou shrinkest from giving up

life because thy experience of it has been sweet, at any rate there
is no need to be in any alarm about death if thou hast no knowledge that it is evil. Thy dread of it is the proof that thou art
aware of its evil. Thou wouldst never think it evil—thou wouldst
have no fear of it at all—if thou wert not sure that after it there
is something to make it evil, and so a thing of terror. Let us leave
unnoticed at this time that natural way of fearing death. It is a
poor thing for any one to fear what is inevitable. I take up the
other side, and argue on the ground of a joyful hope beyond our
term of earthly life; for desire of posthumous fame is with almost
every class an inborn thing. I have not time to speak of the Curtii,
and the Reguli, or the brave men of Greece, who afford us
innumerable instances of death despised for after-death renown.
Who at this day is without the desire that he may be often remembered when he is dead? Who does not give all endeavour to
preserve his name by works of literature, or by the simple glory
of his virtues, or by the splendour even of his tomb? How is it
the nature of the soul to have these posthumous ambitions, and
to prepare with such amazing effort things it can only use after
its decease? It would care nothing about the future, if the future
were quite unknown to it. But perhaps thou thinkest thyself surer
of continuing still to feel after thy exit from the body than of any
future resurrection, which is a doctrine laid at our door as one
of our presumptuous suppositions. But it is also the doctrine of
the soul; for if any one inquires about a person lately dead as
though he were alive, it occurs at once to say, "He has gone."
He is expected to return, then.

5. These testimonies of the soul are simple as true, commonplace as simple, universal as commonplace, natural as universal,
divine as natural. I don't think they can appear frivolous or feeble
to any one, if he reflect on the majesty of nature, from which the
soul derives its authority. If you acknowledge the authority of the
mistress, you will own it also in the disciple. Well, nature is the
mistress here, and her disciple is the soul. But everything the one
has taught or the other learned, has come from God—the Teacher
of the teacher. And what the soul may know from the teachings
of its chief instructor, thou canst judge from that which is within
thee. Think of that which enables thee to think; reflect on that
which in forebodings is the prophet, the augur in omens, the

foreseer of coming events. Is it a wonderful thing, if, being the gift of God to man, it knows how to divine? Is it anything very strange, if it knows the God by whom it was bestowed? Even fallen as it is, the victim of the great adversary's machinations, it does not forget its Creator, His goodness and law, and the final end both of itself and of its foe. Is it singular then, if, divine in its origin, its revelations agree with the knowledge God has given to His own people? But he who does not regard those outbursts of the soul as the teaching of a congenital nature and the secret deposit of an inborn knowledge, will say that the habit and, so to say, the vice of speaking in this way has been acquired and confirmed from the opinions of published books widely spread among men. Unquestionably the soul existed before letters, and speech before books, and ideas before the writing of them, and man himself before the poet and philosopher. Is it then to be believed, that before literature and its publication no utterances of the sort we have pointed out came from the lips of men? Did anybody speak of God and His goodness, nobody of death, nobody of the dead? Speech went a-begging, I suppose; nay, it could not exist at all (the subjects being still a-wanting, without which it cannot even exist at this day, when it is so much more copious and rich, and wise), if the things which are now so easily suggested, that cling to us so constantly, that are so very near to us, that are somehow born on our very lips, had no existence in ancient times, before letters had any existence in the world—before there was a Mercury, I think, at all. And whence was it, I pray, that letters themselves came to know, and to disseminate for the use of speech, what no mind had ever conceived, or tongue put forth, or ear taken in? But, clearly, since the Scriptures of God, whether belonging to Christian or Jews—into whose olive tree we have been grafted—are much more ancient than any secular literature, or, let us only say, are of a somewhat earlier date, as we have shown in its proper place when proving their trustworthiness; if the soul have taken these utterances from writings at all, we must believe it has taken them from ours, and not from yours, its instruction coming more naturally from the earlier than the later works, which latter indeed waited for their own instruction from the former; and though we grant that light has come from you, still it has flowed from the first fountainhead originally; and we claim as entirely ours, all you may have taken from us and handed down. Since it is thus, it matters little whether the soul's knowledge was put into it by God or by His book. Why, then, O man, wilt thou maintain a view so groundless, as that those testimonies of the soul have gone forth from the mere human speculations of your literature, and got hardening of common use?

6. Believe, then, your own books, and as to our Scriptures so much the more believe writings which are divine, but in the witness of the soul itself give like confidence to nature. Choose the one of these you observe to be the most faithful friend of truth. If your own writings are distrusted, neither God nor nature lie. And if you would have faith in God and nature, have faith in the soul; thus you will believe yourself. Certainly you value the soul as giving you your true greatness,—that to which you belong, which is all things to you, without which you can neither live nor die, on whose account you even put God away from you. Since, then, you fear to become a Christian, call the soul before you, and put her to the question. Why does she worship another? why name the name of God? Why does she speak of demons, when she means to denote spirits to be held accursed? Why does she make her protestations towards the heavens, and pronounce her ordinary execrations earthwards? Why does she render service in one place, in another invoke the Avenger? Why does she pass judgments on the dead? What Christian phrases are those she has got, though Christians she neither desires to see nor hear? Why has she either bestowed them on us, or received them from us? Why has she either taught us them, or learned them as our scholar? Regard with suspicion this accordance in words, while there is such difference in practice. It is utter folly—denying a universal nature—to ascribe this exclusively to our language and the Greek, which are regarded among us as so near akin. The soul is not a boon from heaven to Latins and Greeks alone. Man is the one name belonging to every nation upon earth: there is one soul and many tongues, one spirit and various sounds; every country has its own speech, but the subjects of speech are common to all. God is everywhere, and the goodness of God is everywhere; demons are everywhere, and the cursing of them is everywhere; the invocation of divine judgment is everywhere, death is everywhere, and the sense of death is everywhere, and all the

world over is the witness of the soul. There is not a soul of man that does not, from the light that is in itself, proclaim the very things we are not permitted to speak above our breath. Most justly, then, every soul is a culprit as well as a witness: in the measure that it testifies for truth, the guilt of error lies on it; and on the day of judgment it will stand before the courts of God, without a word to say. Thou proclaimedst God, O soul, but thou didst not seek to know Him; evil spirits were detested by thee, and yet they were the objects of thy adoration; the punishments of hell were foreseen by thee, but no care was taken to avoid them; thou hadst a savour of Christianity, and withal wert the persecutor of Christians.

3. ST. FRANCIS OF ASSISI:

FROM THE *LITTLE FLOWERS OF ST. FRANCIS*

¶SAINT FRANCIS of Assisi (born 1182, or possibly the year previous; died October 3, 1226) was the founder of the Order of Friars Minor. He was the son of Peter Bernadone, a wealthy cloth merchant; and after receiving an education which included some instruction in Latin and French, he was apprenticed to his father. Love of sport and song characterized him as a young man. When he was about twenty he fought in a war with Perugia, was taken prisoner and returned home to fall a victim to a serious illness. Thereupon he began to concern himself with religion, though at first no marked change in his conduct was noticeable. It was a vision, beheld in the Church of St. Damian, in Assisi, which made him resolve to leave the world and serve God. Stripping himself naked in front of the Archbishop's palace, Francis began to beg his living and to work at repairing churches. Before long a number of disciples had joined him, and Pope Innocent III endorsed their work. From this time forward the life of Francis became one of fruitful and self-sacrificing devotion to the "Lady Poverty."

Among the several treatises which constitute the available fund of information concerning St. Francis, the *Little Flowers* (or *Fioretti* in the Italian) have a place apart. They contain more legendary material than do the official biographies, but possess a charm and simple contemporaneousness which other records lack. Accordingly, they have gradually supplanted all other books about the early Franciscan community. They repose upon a Latin work, probably written by Ugulino of Monte Giorgio during the fourteenth century. The modern form is that given by an Italian translator during the same century. There are many English versions. The one here in part reprinted is that published by W. Heywood in 1906.*

* From The *Little Flowers of St. Francis of Assisi*. Translated by W. Heywood. London: Methuen and Company, 1906.

OF THE MOST HOLY STIGMATA OF
ST. FRANCIS
AND OF THEIR CONSIDERATIONS

IN THIS PART WE SHALL BEHOLD WITH DEVOUT CONSIDERATION
THE GLORIOUS, SACRED AND HOLY STIGMATA OF OUR BLESSED
FATHER, MESSER SAINT FRANCIS, THE WHICH HE RECEIVED OF
CHRIST UPON THE HOLY MOUNTAIN OF ALVERNIA

*Because the said stigmata were five, even as the wounds of our Lord
Jesus Christ were five, therefore this treatise will have five considerations.*

*The first consideration will be touching the manner in which St. Francis
came to the holy mountain of Alvernia.*

*The second consideration will be touching the life which he lived, and
the conversation which he held with his companions on the said holy
mountain.*

*The third consideration will be touching the seraphic vision and the
imprinting of the most sacred stigmata.*

*The fourth consideration will be how St. Francis descended from the
mountain of Alvernia, after he had received the sacred stigmata, and
returned to Santa Maria degli Angeli.*

*The fifth consideration will be touching Divine visions and revela-
tions made after the death of St. Francis to holy friars and to other
devout persons concerning the said sacred and glorious stigmata.*

OF THE FIRST CONSIDERATION OF THE MOST HOLY STIGMATA

S to the first consideration, it must be known that,
in 1224, St. Francis, being then forty-three years
old, was inspired of God to depart from the Val
di Spoleto and to go into Romagna, with Friar
Leo his companion; and as he went, he passed at
the foot of the Castello di Montefeltro; in the
which town there was then being held a great banquet and festival for the knighting of one of those Counts of Montefeltro;
and St. Francis, hearing of this festival, and that many gentlefolk
were gathered there from divers lands, said unto Friar Leo: "Let
us go up thither unto this feast, since by God's help we shall

gather some good spiritual fruit." Now among the other gentlemen, who had come thither from that district to that ceremonial,
was a great and rich gentleman of Tuscany, by name Messer
Orlando of Chiusi in Casentino, the which, by reason of the marvellous things which he had heard touching the sanctity and
miracles of St. Francis, bore him great devotion and had very
great desire to see him and to hear him preach. St. Francis then,
having arrived at this town, entered in and gat him to the piazza,
where were assembled all the multitude of those gentlemen; and,
in fervour of spirit, he climbed upon a little wall and began to
preach, taking as the text of his sermon these words in the vulgar
tongue:—

> So great the bliss I hope to see,
> That every pain delighteth me.

And from this text, by the inspiration of the Holy Ghost, he
preached so devoutly and so profoundly, proving the truth thereof
by divers sufferings and torments of holy apostles and of holy
martyrs, by the severe penances of holy confessors, and by the
many tribulations and temptations of holy virgins and of other
saints, that every man stood with eyes and mind fixed upon him,
and hearkened unto him as if it were an angel of God that spoke;
among whom, the said Messer Orlando, being touched in the
heart by God, through the marvellous preaching of St. Francis,
was minded to consult and speak with him after the sermon concerning the affairs of his soul. Wherefore, when the preaching
was done, he drew St. Francis aside and said unto him: "O father,
I would take counsel with thee touching the salvation of my soul."
St. Francis made answer: "Well content am I; but go thou this
morning and do honour to thy friends who have invited thee to
this festival, and dine with them; [and, after thou hast dined,
we will talk together as long as thou shalt please." Messer Orlando, therefore, went to dinner;] and, after dinner, he returned
to St. Francis and laid before him fully all the affairs of his soul
and took counsel with him concerning the same. And finally this
Messer Orlando said to St. Francis: "I have in Tuscany a mountain most apt for devotion, the which is called the mountain of
Alvernia, exceeding solitary, and passing well fitted for such as
would do penance in a place remote from men, and desire a life

of solitude. If it pleases thee, gladly would I give it to thee and to thy companions for the salvation of my soul." St. Francis, hearing so liberal an offer of a thing which he much desired, was exceeding joyful thereat; and praising and thanking first God, and then Messer Orlando, he spake unto him thus: "Messer Orlando, when you shall have returned to your home, I will send unto you some of my companions, and you shall show them that mountain; and, if it shall seem to them fitted for prayer and for the doing of penance, even from this moment do I accept your charitable offer." And, when he had thus spoken, St. Francis departed; and after he had finished his journey he returned to Santa Maria degli Angeli; and Messer Orlando likewise, when the festivities for the making of that knight were ended, returned to his castle, which was called Chiusi, and which was distant a mile from Alvernia. St. Francis, then, having returned to Santa Maria degli Angeli, sent two of his companions to the said Messer Orlando, who, when they were come unto him, welcomed them with very great joy and charity: and, desiring to show them the mountain of Alvernia, he sent with them fully fifty armed men, to the end that they might defend them from the wild beasts; and thus accompanied those friars went up into the mountain and explored it diligently; and at last they came unto a part of the mountain exceeding well fitted for devotion and for contemplation; in the which part there was some level ground; and that place they chose for their habitation and for that of St. Francis; and with the aid of those armed men which were in their company they made a little cell with the boughs of trees, and on this wise, in the name of God, they accepted and took possession of the mountain of Alvernia and of the Place of the friars in that mountain, and departed and returned to St. Francis. And, when they had come unto him, they told him how and in what manner they had taken the said Place upon the mountain of Alvernia, well fitted for prayer and contemplation. Now, when St. Francis heard this news, he rejoiced greatly, and, giving praise and thanks to God, spake unto those friars with happy face, and said: "My sons, we are drawing nigh to our forty days' fast of St. Michael the Archangel; and I firmly believe that it is the will of God that we keep this fast in the mountain of Alvernia, the which by Divine dispensation hath been made ready for us, to the end that we may, through penance, merit from Christ the consolation of consecrating that blessed mountain to the honour and glory of God and of His glorious mother, the Virgin Mary, and of the holy angels." And then, having said these words, St. Francis took with him Friar Masseo da Marignano of Assisi, the which was a man of great wisdom and eloquence, and Friar Angelo Tancredi da Rieti, who was a man of very noble birth, and who in the world had been a knight, and Friar Leo, who was a man of very great simplicity and purity; for the which cause St. Francis loved him much. And with these three friars St. Francis betook himself to prayer, and commended himself and his companions aforesaid to the prayers of the friars which remained behind, and set out with those three in the name of Jesus Christ the Crucified, to go to the mountain of Alvernia; and, as he went, St. Francis called unto him one of those three companions, to wit Friar Masseo, and spake unto him thus: "Thou, Friar Masseo, shalt be our Guardian and Superior on this journey; to wit while we shall be going and abiding together, and we will observe our custom: that either we will say the office, or we will speak of God, or we will keep silence; and we will take no thought beforehand, neither of eating, nor of drinking, nor of sleeping; but when the time to rest for the night shall be come, we will beg a little bread, and will lodge and repose ourselves in that place which God shall make ready for us." Then those three companions bowed their heads, and, signing themselves with the sign of the cross, went forward; and the first evening they came to a Place of friars, and there they lodged. The second evening, by reason of the bad weather and because they were weary, they were not able to reach any Place of friars, or any walled town, nor any hamlet; and when night and the bad weather overtook them, they sought shelter in an abandoned and disused church, and there they laid them down to rest, and, while his companions slept, St. Francis gave himself to prayer; and lo! in the first watch of the night, there came a great multitude of most ferocious demons with very great noise and tumult, and began vehemently to give him battle and annoy; for one plucked him on this side and another on that; one pulled him down and another up; one menaced him with one thing and another accused him of another; and thus in divers manners did they seek to disturb him in his prayer; but they were not able, because God was with him. Wherefore, when St. Francis had borne these assaults of the demons for some time, he began to cry with a loud voice: "O damned spirits, ye can do nothing save that which the hand of God permitteth you; and therefore, in the name of God Omnipotent I tell you that ye may do unto my body whatsoever is permitted you by God, and I will bear it willingly; for I have no greater enemy than this body of mine. Wherefore, if ye take vengeance for me upon mine enemy, ye do me very great service." Thereupon the demons, with very great impetus and fury, laid hold of him and began to hale him about the church and to do him much greater injury and annoy than at first. And then St. Francis commenced to cry aloud and said: "My Lord Jesus Christ, I thank Thee for the great honour and charity which Thou showest me; for it is a token of much love when the Lord thoroughly punisheth His servant for all his faults in this world, to the end that he may not be punished in the next. And I am ready to endure joyfully every pain and every adversity which Thou, my God, mayst vouchsafe to send me for my sins." Then the demons, being put to confusion and conquered by his constancy and patience, left him, and St. Francis, in fervour of spirit, went forth from the church into a wood which was thereby, and there he gave himself to prayer; and, with supplications and tears and beatings of his breast, sought to find Jesus Christ, the Spouse and delight of his soul. And when, at last, he found Him in the secret places of his soul, he now spake reverently unto Him as his Lord; now answered Him as his Judge; now besought Him as his Father; and now talked with Him as to a Friend. On that night and in that wood, his companions, after they were awakened and had come thither to hear and to consider that which he was doing, saw and heard him, with tears and cries, devoutly beseeching the Divine mercy for sinners. Then too he was heard and seen to bewail the Passion of Christ with a loud voice as if he saw the same with his bodily eyes. On that same night they beheld him praying, with his arms held in the form of a cross, uplifted for a great space and raised from the ground, surrounded by a resplendent cloud. And on this wise, in these holy exercises, he passed the whole of that night without sleeping; and thereafter, in the morning, because they knew that, by reason of the fatigues of the night which he had passed without sleep, St. Francis was very weak in body and could ill have travelled on foot, his companions went to a poor labourer of that district, and besought him for the love of God to lend his little ass to St. Francis, their father, who could not go on foot. Now, when this man heard them make mention of Friar Francis, he asked them: "Are ye some of the friars of that friar of Assisi whereof so much good is spoken?" The friars answered: "Yes"; and that it was in truth for him that they asked the beast of burden. Then that good man made ready the little ass, with great devotion and diligence, and led it to St. Francis with great reverence and made him mount thereon; and they continued their journey; and he with them, behind his little ass. And, when they had gone some distance, that villain said to St. Francis: "Tell me, art thou Friar Francis of Assisi?" And St. Francis answered him, "Yea." "Strive thou, then (said the villain), to be as good as all folk hold thee to be, for there are many which have great faith in thee; and therefore I admonish thee, that thou fall not short of that which men hope to find thee." Hearing these words, St. Francis did not disdain to be admonished by a villain, and said not within himself: "What beast is this that admonisheth me?" even as many many proud fellows who wear the friar's habit would say to-day; but forthwith he cast himself to earth from off the ass, and kneeled him down before that villain and kissed his feet, and thanked him humbly, because he had deigned to admonish him so charitably. Then the villain, together with the companions of St. Francis, raised him up from off the ground with great devotion, and set him upon the ass again, and continued their journey. And when they had gone perhaps half way up the mountain; because the heat was very great and the ascent difficult, this villain became exceeding thirsty, so that he began to cry aloud behind St. Francis, saying: "Alas! I am dying of thirst; if I have not something to drink I shall presently swoon away." For the which cause St. Francis dismounted from his ass and betook himself to prayer; and he remained upon his knees with his hands raised to heaven until he knew by revelation that God had heard him. And then St. Francis said to the villain: "Run, go quickly to yonder rock, and there thou shalt find living water, which Jesus Christ, in this hour, hath of His mercy made to issue forth from that rock." So he went to the place which St. Francis had shown him, and found there a fair spring which had come forth from the hard rock at the prayer of St. Francis, and he drank copiously thereof, and was comforted. And it was clearly seen that that fountain was miraculously produced by God through the prayers of St. Francis, because neither before nor after was there ever found, in that place, a spring of water, nor any living water near that place for a great distance round about. When he had thus done, St. Francis, with his companions and with the villain, gave thanks to God for the miracle vouchsafed, and thereafter they continued their journey. And when they drew nigh to the foot of the peak of Alvernia itself, it pleased St. Francis to rest himself a little beneath an oak which was in that place and which is there yet; and, as he sat beneath it, St. Francis began to consider the situation of the place and of the country thereabout; and, while he was thus considering, lo! a great multitude of birds came thither from divers parts, the which, with singing and beating of wings, all showed very great joy and gladness; and they surrounded St. Francis on such wise that some alighted upon his head, and some upon his shoulders, and some upon his arms, some in his bosom, and some about his feet. Now when his companions and the villain saw this they marvelled greatly; whereupon St. Francis, all joyful in spirit, spake unto them thus: "I believe, most dear brethren, that it is the will of our Lord Jesus Christ that we dwell in this solitary mountain, because our sisters and brothers the birds show such joy of our coming." And when he had said these words, they rose up and continued their journey; and finally came unto the place which his companions had chosen at the first. And this sufficeth for the first consideration, to wit how St. Francis came to the holy mountain of Alvernia.

OF THE SECOND CONSIDERATION OF THE MOST HOLY STIGMATA

THE second consideration is touching the conversation of St. Francis with his companions upon the said mountain of Alvernia. And as to this it is to be known; that, when Messer Orlando had heard that St. Francis with three companions had gone up into the mountain of Alvernia to dwell there, he had very great joy thereof; and, on the following day, he set out with many of his retainers and came to visit St. Francis, bearing bread and wine and other victuals for him and for his companions; and, coming, to the place where they were, he found them in prayer; and drawing nigh unto them he saluted them. Then St. Francis rose up and with very great charity and joy welcomed Messer Orlando and his company; and, when he had thus done, he entered into conversation with him; and, after they had talked together and St. Francis had thanked him for the holy mountain which he had given him and for his coming thither, he besought him that he would cause a poor little cell to be made at the foot of a very beautiful beech-tree, which was distant a stone's throw from the Place of the friars, because that spot seemed to him most apt and dedicate to prayer. And straightway Messer Orlando caused it to be built; and, when it was finished, because the evening drew nigh and it was time for them to depart, St. Francis, before they went, preached unto them a little: and, after that he had preached and given them his blessing, Messer Orlando, since he could no longer stay, called St. Francis and his companions aside and said unto them: "My most dear friars, I would not that, in this savage mountain, ye suffered any bodily want, whereby ye might be let and hindered from spiritual things; and therefore I desire (and this I tell you once for all) that ye fail not to send to my house for all that ye need; and, if ye do not do so, I shall take it very ill of you." And, having thus spoken, he departed with his company and returned to his castle. Then St. Francis made his companions sit down and instructed them concerning the manner of life which they, and whosoever desireth to live religiously in hermitages, must lead. And, among other things, he especially laid upon them the observance of holy poverty, saying: "Regard not overmuch the charitable offer of Messer Orlando, that in naught may ye offend our lady and mistress, holy Poverty. Be ye sure that the more we shun Poverty the more the world will shun us; but, if we shall closely embrace holy Poverty, the world will follow after us and will abundantly supply all our needs. God hath called us to this holy religion for the salvation of the world, and hath made this covenant between us and the world; that we should give unto the world a good ensample and the world should provide for us in our necessities. Let us continue, therefore, in holy poverty, because that is the way of perfection and the pledge and earnest of eternal riches." And, after many beautiful and devout words and admonishments touching this matter, he concluded, saying: "This is the manner of life which I lay upon myself and upon you; for I perceive that I draw nigh unto my death, and I am minded to be solitary, and to turn all my thoughts to God and to bewail my sins before Him; and Friar Leo, when it shall seem good to him, shall bring me a little bread and a little water; and on nowise do ye permit any layman to come unto me; but do ye answer them for me." And when he had said these words he gave them his blessing, and gat him to the cell beneath the beech-tree; and his companions abode in the Place, firmly resolved to observe the commandments of St. Francis. A few days thereafter, as St. Francis was standing beside the said cell, considering the conformation of the mountain, and marvelling at the huge chasms and clefts in those tremendous rocks, he betook himself to prayer; and then was it revealed to him of God that those wondrous fissures had been made miraculously in the hour of Christ's Passion, when, even as saith the evangelist, "the rocks were rent." And this, as God willed it, was singularly manifested in that mountain of Alvernia because it was foreordained that, in that place, St. Francis must renew the Passion of our Lord Jesus Christ, in his soul through love and pity, and in his body through the imprinting of the most holy stigmata. Now, when he had received this revelation, St. Francis straightway shut himself up in his cell, and, closing his mind to all earthly things, disposed himself to await the mystery of this revelation. And from thenceforward, because he continued alway in prayer, St. Francis began, more often than heretofore, to taste the sweetness of Divine contemplation; whereby he was ofttimes so rapt in God that he was seen by his companions uplifted from the ground and rapt from out himself. In these raptures of contemplation, not only were things present and future revealed unto him by God, but also the secret thoughts and desires of the friars, even as Friar Leo, his companion, on that day, proved in his own person. For the said Friar Leo being vexed of the devil with a very grievous temptation, not carnal but spiritual, there came upon him a great desire to have some holy thing written by the hand of St. Francis; for he thought that, if he had it, that temptation would leave him, either altogether or in part; nevertheless, albeit he had this desire, for shame and reverence he lacked the courage to speak thereof to St. Francis; but that which Friar Leo told him not, was revealed to him by the Holy Ghost. Wherefore St. Francis called him unto him and made him bring inkhorn and pen and paper, and with his own hand wrote a laud of Christ, according to the desire of the friar, and at the end thereof made the sign of the *Tau*, and gave it unto him, saying: "Take this paper, dearest friar, and keep it diligently until thy death. God bless thee and preserve thee from every temptation. Be not dismayed that thou hast temptations, for then do I hold thee more my friend and a truer servant of God; and I love thee the more the more thou hast fought against thy temptations. Verily I say unto thee that no man may call himself a perfect friend of God until he hath passed through many temptations and tribulations." And when Friar Leo had received this writing with very great devotion and faith, anon every temptation left him; and, returning to the Place, he related to his companions, with great joy, what grace God had done him as he received that writing from St. Francis; and he put it in a safe place and preserved it diligently; and therewith, in after-time, the friars wrought many miracles. And from that hour the said Friar Leo commenced to scrutinise and to consider the life of St. Francis, with great purity and goodwill; and, by reason of his purity, he merited to behold how many a time and oft St. Francis was rapt in God and uplifted from the ground, sometimes for the space of three cubits, sometimes of four, and sometimes even to the height of the beech-tree; and sometimes he beheld him raised so high in the air, and surrounded by such radiance, that scarcely could he see him. And what did this simple friar do when St. Francis was so little raised above the ground that he could reach him? He went softly and embraced his feet and kissed them with tears, saying: "My God, have mercy upon me a sinner; and, for the merits of this holy man, grant me to find Thy grace." And, one time among the rest, while he stood thus beneath the feet of St. Francis, when he was so far uplifted from the ground, that he could not touch him, he beheld a scroll inscribed with letters of gold descend from heaven and rest above the head of St. Francis, upon the which scroll these words were written: "QVI È LA GRAZIA DI DIO—*Here is the grace of God;*" and, after that he had read it, he saw it return again to heaven. By reason of this grace of God which was in him, not only was

St. Francis rapt in God through ecstatic contemplation, but also he was sometimes comforted by angelic visitations. Thus, one day, while St. Francis was thinking of his death and of the state of his Religion after his life should be ended, and was saying: "Lord God, what after my death shall become of Thy mendicant family, the which through Thy goodness Thou hast entrusted to me a sinner? Who shall console them? Who shall correct them? Who shall pray to Thee for them?" While he spake these and such-like words, there appeared unto him the angel sent by God, which comforted him, saying: "I tell thee in God's name that the profession of thy Order shall not fail until the Day of Judgment; and there shall be no sinner so great that, if he shall love thy Order from his heart, he shall not find mercy with God; and no one who persecuteth thy Order maliciously shall live long. Moreover no one, in thy Order, who is very wicked and who doth not amend his life will be able to remain long in the Order. Therefore grieve not thyself if thou see in thy Religion certain friars who are not good, and who observe not the Rule as they ought to do; neither think thou that for this thy Religion languisheth; for there will always be very many therein who will perfectly follow the life of the gospel of Christ and the purity of the Rule; and such as these, as soon as ever their earthly life is done, will go to the life eternal, without passing through purgatory at all; some will follow it, but not perfectly; and these, before they go to paradise, will be in purgatory: but the time of their purgation will be remitted unto thee by God. But for those who observe not the Rule at all, care thou not, saith God, because He careth not for them." And when the angel had spoken these words he departed, leaving St. Francis consoled and comforted. Thereafter, when the feast of the Assumption of Our Lady drew nigh, St. Francis sought to find a fitting spot, more secret and remote, wherein in greater solitude he might keep the forty days' fast of St. Michael the Archangel, the which commenceth on the said feast of the Assumption. Wherefore he called Friar Leo and spake unto him thus: "Go and stand at the doorway of the oratory of the Place of the friars; and, when I shall call thee, do thou return to me." Friar Leo went and stood in the said doorway; and St. Francis gat him thence a space and called loudly. Friar Leo, hearing him call, returned unto him;

and St. Francis said: "Son, search we out another more secret spot whence thou shalt not be able thus to hear me when I shall call thee;" and, as they searched, they saw, on the southern side of the mountain, a lonely place exceeding well fitted for his purpose; but it was impossible to reach it, because there was in front of it a rocky chasm, horrible and fearful, and very great. Wherefore, with much labour they laid a tree across the same, after the fashion of a bridge, and passed over to the other side. Then St. Francis sent for the other friars and told them how he purposed to keep the forty days' fast of St. Michael in that solitary place; and therefore he besought them that they would make him a little cell there, so that for no crying of his might he be heard of them; and, when the little cell of St. Francis was finished, he said unto them: "Go ye to your own Place and leave me here alone; for, with the help of God, I mean to keep this fast in this place without any trouble or disturbance of mind; and therefore let none of you come nigh me, nor suffer any layman to come unto me. But thou, Friar Leo, alone shalt come unto me, once a day, with a little bread and water, and at night once again, at the hour of matins; and then shalt thou come unto me in silence; and, when thou art at the head of the bridge, thou shalt say unto me: *Domine, labia mea aperies;* and, if I answer thee, pass over and come to the cell and we will say matins together; but if I answer thee not, get thee gone immediately." And this St. Francis said because he was sometimes so rapt in God that he heard not nor perceived anything with the bodily senses; and, when he had thus spoken, St. Francis gave them his blessing; and they returned to the Place. Now, the feast of the Assumption being come, St. Francis began the holy fast with very great abstinence and severity, mortifying his body and comforting his spirit with fervent prayers, vigils and flagellations; and in these prayers, ever growing from virtue to virtue, he prepared his mind to receive the Divine mysteries and the Divine splendours, and his body to endure the cruel assaults of the fiends, with whom oftentimes he fought bodily. And among the other times was one when, on a day, as St. Francis came forth from his cell in fervour of spirit, and went to a place hard by, to pray in the cavity of a hollow rock, wherefrom down to the ground there is a very great height, and a horrible and fearful precipice; suddenly the devil came in terrible shape, with tempest and with very great uproar, and smote him to cast him down from thence. Wherefore, St. Francis, not having any place to flee unto, and being unable to endure the passing cruel aspect of the demon, forthwith turned himself round, with his hands and face and with all his body against the rock, commending himself to God, and groping with his hands if, perchance, he might find something to lay hold of. But, as it pleased God, who never allows His servants to be tempted beyond that which they can bear, on a sudden the rock whereto he clung miraculously hollowed itself to the form of his body and so received him into itself; and even as if he had put his hands and face into liquid wax, so was the shape of the face and hands of St. Francis imprinted upon the said rock; and, on this wise, being helped of God, he escaped from the devil. But that which the devil could not then do to St. Francis, namely to cast him down from thence, he did a good while thereafter, when St. Francis was dead, to a dear and devout friar of his, the which, in that same place, was adjusting certain pieces of wood to the end that it might be possible to go thither without peril, for devotion toward St. Francis and toward the miracle which was wrought there; and one day the devil pushed him, when he had a great log on his head which he wished to set there, and caused him to fall down thence with that log on his head; but God, who had saved and preserved St. Francis from falling, through his merits saved and preserved that devout friar of his from the peril of the fall; for, as the friar fell, he commended himself with very great devotion and with a loud voice to St. Francis, who straightway appeared to him and took him and set him on the rocks below, without permitting him to suffer any shock or hurt. Then, the friars, having heard his cry as he fell, and believing that he was dead and dashed to pieces, by reason of the great height wherefrom he had fallen upon the sharp rocks, with great sorrow and weeping took the bier and went from the other side of the mountain to search for the fragments of his body and to bury them. Now, when they had already come down from the mountain, the friar who had fallen met them, with the log wherewith he had fallen upon his head; and he was singing the *Te Deum laudamus,* in a loud voice. And, because the friars marvelled greatly, he related unto them in order all the manner of his falling, and how St. Francis had rescued him from every peril. Then all the friars accompanied him to the place, singing most devoutly the aforesaid psalm, *Te Deum laudamus,* and praising and thanking God together with St. Francis for the miracle which he had wrought in his friar. St. Francis, then, continuing (as hath been said) the aforesaid fast, albeit he sustained many assaults of the devil, nevertheless received many consolations from God, not only through angelic visitations but also through the birds of the air; for, during all the time of that fast, a hawk, which was building its nest hard by his cell, awakened him every night a little before matins, with its cry, and by beating itself against his cell, and departed not until he rose up to say matins; and, when St. Francis was more weary than usual, or weak or sick, this hawk, after the manner of a discreet and compassionate person, uttered its cry later than it was wont to do. And so St. Francis took great joy of this clock, because the great diligence of the hawk drove away from him all sloth, and urged him to prayer: and besides this, sometimes, in the daytime, it would familiarly sit with him. Finally, touching this second consideration, St. Francis, being much weakened in body, both by reason of his great abstinence, and of the assaults of the devil, and desiring to comfort his body with the spiritual food of the soul, began to meditate on the immeasurable glory and joy of the blessed in the life eternal, and therewith he began to pray God that He would grant him to taste a little of that joy. And, as he continued in this thought, anon there appeared unto him an angel, with very great splendour, bearing a viol in his left hand and in his right a bow; and, while yet St. Francis was all amazed at the sight of him, the angel drew his bow once across the viol; and straightway St. Francis heard so sweet a melody that it filled all his soul with rapture and rendered it insensible to every bodily feeling; insomuch that, according to that which he afterward told his companions, he doubted whether, if the angel had drawn the bow back again across the viol, his soul must not have departed out of his body by reason of the intolerable sweetness. And this sufficeth for the second consideration.

OF THE THIRD CONSIDERATION OF THE MOST HOLY STIGMATA

COMING to the third consideration, to wit the seraphic vision and the imprinting of the most holy stigmata, it is to be considered that when the festival of the most Holy Cross of the month of September was drawing nigh, Friar Leo went one night, at the accustomed hour, to say matins with St. Francis, and calling, as he was wont, from the head of the bridge: *Domine, labia mea aperies,* and St. Francis making no answer, Friar Leo turned not back again as St. Francis had commanded him; but, with good and holy purpose, he crossed over the bridge and softly entered the cell; and, finding him not, he thought that he was somewhere in the wood in prayer; wherefore he came forth and, by the light of the moon, went searching softly through the wood; and finally he heard the voice of St. Francis; and, drawing nigh, he saw him on his knees in prayer, with face and hands raised to heaven; and in fervour of spirit he was speaking thus: "Who art Thou, my most sweet God? What am I, most vile worm and Thine unprofitable servant?" And these same words alone did he repeat, and said no other thing. For the which cause, Friar Leo, marvelling thereat, raised his eyes and gazed toward heaven; and, as he looked, he beheld, coming down from heaven, a torch of fire, most beautiful and bright, which descended and lighted upon the head of St. Francis; and from out the said flame he heard a voice come which spake with St. Francis; but Friar Leo understood not the words. Hearing this, and deeming himself unworthy to abide so near to that holy place, where was that marvellous apparition, and fearing also to offend St. Francis, or to disturb him in his contemplation, if he should be perceived by him, he softly drew back, and, standing afar off, waited to see the end; and, gazing fixedly, he saw St. Francis stretch out his hands three times to the flame; and finally, after a long time, he saw the flame return to heaven. Wherefore he gat him thence, deeming himself unseen and glad of the vision, and was returning to his cell. And, as he went confidently, St. Francis perceived him by the rustling which his feet made upon the leaves, and commanded him to wait for him and not to move. Then Friar Leo, obedient, stood still and waited for him, with such fear that, as he afterwards told his companions, he would rather, at that moment, that the earth had swallowed him up than wait for St. Francis, who he thought was angered with him; because with very great diligence he took heed not to offend his fatherhood, lest, through fault of his, St. Francis should deprive him of his company. Then, when he had come up to him, St. Francis asked him: "Who art thou?" and Friar Leo, all trembling, replied: "My father, I am Friar Leo;" and St. Francis said unto him: "Wherefore didst thou come hither, friar little sheep? Did I not tell thee not to come and watch me? For holy obedience, tell me whether thou sawest or heardest aught." Friar Leo replied: "Father, I heard thee speak and say many times: 'Who art Thou, my most sweet God? What am I, most vile worm and Thine unprofitable servant?'" And then Friar Leo, kneeling down before St. Francis, confessed himself guilty of disobedience, in that he had done contrary to his commandment, and besought his pardon with many tears. And thereafter he prayed him devoutly that he would explain those words which he had heard, and would tell him those which he had not understood. Then, seeing that to the humble Friar Leo God had revealed or granted to hear and to see certain things, by reason of his simplicity and purity, St. Francis condescended to reveal and to explain unto him that which he asked; and he spake as follows: "Know, friar little sheep of Jesus Christ, that when I was saying those words which thou heardest, then were shown unto me two lights for my soul; the one of knowledge and understanding of my own self, the other of knowledge and understanding of the Creator. When I said: 'Who art thou, O my most sweet God?' then I was in a light of contemplation wherein I saw the abyss of the infinite goodness and wisdom and power of God; and when I said: 'What am I?' I was in a light of contemplation in the which I beheld the depth of my baseness and misery; and therefore I said: 'Who art Thou, Lord of infinite goodness and wisdom, that deignest to visit me, that am a vile worm and abominable?' And in that flame which thou sawest was God; who in that form spake with me, even as of old He spake unto Moses. And, among other things which He said unto me, He asked me to give Him three gifts; and I made answer: 'Lord, I am all Thine; Thou knowest well that I have nothing beside the habit and the cord and the breeches, and even these three things are Thine; what then can I offer or give unto Thy majesty?' Then God said unto me: 'Search in thy bosom, and give Me that which thou findest therein.' I searched and found a ball of gold; and I offered it to God; and thus did I three times, even as God three times commanded me; and thereafter I kneeled me down three times and blessed and thanked God who had given me wherewith to offer Him. And straightway, it was given me to understand that these three offerings signified holy obedience, highest poverty and most resplendent chastity; the which God, through His grace, hath permitted me to observe so perfectly that my conscience accuseth me of nothing. And as thou sawest me put my hands in my bosom and offer to God those three virtues symbolised by those three balls of gold, which God had placed in my bosom; so hath God given me such virtue in my soul that, for all the benefits and all the graces which He hath granted me of His most holy goodness, I ever praise and magnify Him with heart and mouth. These are the words which thou heardest when I thrice lifted up my hands, as thou sawest. But look to it, friar little sheep, that thou watch me no more; but return to thy cell with the blessing of God, and do thou have diligent care of me; because, a few days from now, God will do such great and marvellous things upon this mountain that all the world shall wonder thereat; for He will do certain new things, the which He hath never done unto any creature in this world." And, when he had spoken these words, he caused the book of the Gospels to be brought unto him; for God had put it in his mind that, by the opening of the book of the Gospels three times, that which it was the will of God to do unto him should be revealed. And, when the book was brought unto him, St. Francis betook himself to prayer; and, when he had finished his prayer, he caused the book to be opened three times by the hand of Friar Leo, in the name of the Most Holy Trinity; and, as it pleased the Divine Providence, in those three times ever there appeared before him the Passion of Christ. By the which thing it was given him to understand that, even as he had followed Christ in the actions of his life, so he must follow Him, and be conformed to Him in afflictions and sorrows and in his passion, before he departed from this life. And from that moment St.

Francis began to taste and to feel more abundantly the sweetness of Divine contemplation and of the Divine visitations. Among the which he had one which was an immediate preparative for the imprinting of the most holy stigmata; and it was upon this wise: On the day before the festival of the most Holy Cross of the month of September, while St. Francis was secretly praying in his cell, the angel of God appeared unto him, and said unto him in God's name: "I exhort thee and admonish thee that thou prepare and dispose thyself, humbly and with all patience, to receive that which God willeth to give thee, and to work in thee." St. Francis made answer: "I am ready to bear patiently everything that my Lord willeth to do unto me;" and, when he had said this, the angel departed. The next day came, to wit the day of the most Holy Cross, and St. Francis, betimes in the morning, or ever it was day, betook himself to prayer before the entrance of his cell, and turning his face towards the East, prayed after this manner: "O my Lord Jesus Christ, two graces do I beseech Thee to grant me before I die: the first, that, during my lifetime, I may feel in my soul and in my body, so far as may be possible, that pain which Thou, sweet Lord, didst suffer in the hour of Thy most bitter passion; the second is that I may feel in my heart, so far as may be possible, that exceeding love, whereby Thou, Son of God, wast enkindled to willingly bear such passion for us sinners." And, when he had continued long time in this prayer, he knew that God would hear him, and that, as far as was possible for a mere creature, so far would it be granted to him to feel the aforesaid things. Having this promise, St. Francis began to contemplate with very great devotion the Passion of Christ and His infinite charity; and so much did the fervour of devotion increase in him that he altogether transformed himself into Jesus through love and pity. And, being thus self-inflamed in this contemplation, on that same morning, he saw, coming from heaven, a Seraph, with six wings resplendent and ablaze; the which Seraph, flying swiftly, drew near unto St. Francis, so that he was able to discern Him clearly, and he perceived that He bore the likeness to a crucified Man; and His wings were so disposed that two wings extended above His head, two were spread out to fly, and the other two covered all His body. Seeing this, St. Francis was sore afraid, and, at the same

time, was filled with joy and grief and wonder. He had passing
great joy of the gracious aspect of Christ, who appeared to him
so familiarly and regarded him so kindly; but, on the other
hand, seeing Him crucified upon the cross, he felt immeasurable
grief for pity's sake. Next, he marvelled much at so strange and
stupendous a vision, knowing well that the infirmity of suffering
agreeth not with the immortality of the seraphic spirit. And, while
he thus marvelled, it was revealed unto him by Him who appeared to him: that that vision had been shown unto him in that
form, by the Divine providence, to the end that he might understand that, not by corporal suffering but by enkindling of the
mind, he must be altogether transformed into the express image
of Christ crucified, in that marvellous vision. Then all the mountain of Alvernia seemed to burn with brightest flame, which
shone forth and lighted up all the mountains and the valleys
round about, even as if the sun had risen upon the earth; wherefore the shepherds, who kept watch in those regions, beholding
the mountain all on fire and so great a light round about it, were
very much afraid, according as they afterward related to the
friars, declaring that that flame continued upon the mountain of
Alvernia for the space of an hour or more. In like manner, by
reason of the brightness of this light, which shone through the
windows into the hostelries of the countryside, certain muleteers,
who were journeying into Romagna, rose up, believing that the
sun had risen, and saddled and loaded their beasts; and, as they
went upon their way, they beheld the said light die out, and the
material sun arise. In the said seraphic vision, Christ, who appeared to St. Francis, spake unto him certain high and secret
things, the which St. Francis was never willing to reveal to any
one during his life; but, after his death, he revealed it, even as
is set forth below; and the words were these: "Knowest thou,"
said Christ, "that which I have done unto thee? I have given
thee the stigmata, which are the tokens of My Passion, so that
thou mayest be My standard-bearer. And even as I, on the day
of My death, descended into Limbo, and, in virtue of these My
stigmata, drew out thence all the souls which I found there;
so to thee do I grant that, every year on the day of thy death,
thou shalt go to purgatory, and in virtue of thy stigmata, shalt
draw out thence all the souls of thy three Orders, to wit minors,

sisters and continents, and also those others who have borne great
devotion unto thee, and shalt lead them unto the glory of paradise, to the end that thou mayest be conformed to Me in death
as thou art in life." Now when, after long and secret converse,
this marvellous vision vanished away, it left an exceeding ardour
and flame of Divine love in the heart of St. Francis, and in his
flesh a marvellous image and imprint of the Passion of Christ.
For anon, in the hands and in the feet of St. Francis the marks
of nails began to appear after the same fashion as he had just
seen in the body of Jesus Christ crucified, the which had appeared
unto him in the form of a seraph; and even so were his hands
and his feet pierced through the midst with nails, the heads
whereof were in the palms of the hands and in the soles of the
feet, outside the flesh; and the points came out through the back
of the hands and of the feet, where they showed bent back and
clinched on such wise that, under the clinching and the bend,
which all stood out above the flesh, it would have been easy to
put a finger of the hand, as in a ring; and the heads of the nails
were round and black. In like manner, in his right side appeared
the likeness of a lance wound, open, red and bloody; the which
oftentimes thereafter spouted blood from the holy breast of St.
Francis, and covered his habit and breeches with blood. Wherefore his companions, before they knew thereof from him, perceiving nevertheless that he uncovered neither his hands nor his
feet, and that he could not put the soles of his feet to the ground;
and therewithal finding his habit and breeches all bloody, when
they washed them, knew certainly that he bore, imprinted on
his hands and feet and likewise on his side, the express image
and likeness of our Lord Jesus Christ crucified. And although
he very earnestly endeavoured to conceal and to hide those most
holy and glorious stigmata which were so clearly imprinted on
his flesh, he perceived that he could but ill conceal them from
his familiar companions; and therefore he stood in very great
doubt, fearing to make public the secrets of God, and knowing
not whether he ought to reveal the seraphic vision and the imprinting of the most holy stigmata. At the last, being goaded
thereunto by his conscience, he called to him certain of his most
intimate friends among the friars, and, setting before them his
doubt in general terms, yet without explaining the actual fact,

he asked their advice; and among the said friars was one of great sanctity, who was called Friar Illuminatus. Now this man, being of a truth illuminate by God, and understanding that St. Francis must have seen marvellous things, answered him after this manner: "Friar Francis, know thou that, not for thy sake only but also for the sake of others, God manifesteth unto thee at divers times His mysteries; and therefore thou hast good reason to fear that, if thou keepest secret that which God hath shown thee for the benefit of others, thou wilt be worthy of blame." Then St. Francis, being moved by these words, with great dread related unto them all the manner and form of the aforesaid vision; adding that Christ, who had appeared unto him, had spoken certain things unto him which he would never repeat as long as he lived. And, albeit those most holy wounds, inasmuch as they were imprinted by Christ, gave very great joy to his heart; nevertheless to his flesh and to his corporal senses they gave intolerable pain. Wherefore, being compelled thereunto by necessity, he chose Friar Leo, as more simple and more pure than the others, and to him he revealed everything; permitting him to see and to touch those sacred wounds and to bind them with certain handkerchiefs, for the allaying of the pain, and to catch the blood which issued and flowed from the said wounds; the which bandages, in time of sickness, he permitted him to change frequently, and even daily, except from Thursday evening to Saturday morning, during which time our Saviour Jesus Christ was taken for our sakes and crucified, slain and buried; and therefore, during that time, St. Francis would not suffer that the pain of the Passion of Christ, which he bore in his body, should be assuaged in anywise by any human remedy or medicine whatsoever. It befel, sometimes, that, as Friar Leo was changing the bandage of the wound in his side, St. Francis, for the pain which he felt when that blood-soaked bandage was plucked away, laid his hand upon the breast of Friar Leo; whereby, from the touch of those sacred hands, Friar Leo felt such sweetness of devotion in his heart, that he well-nigh fell swooning to the ground. And finally, as touching this third consideration, St. Francis having finished the fast of St. Michael the Archangel, prepared himself, by Divine revelation, to return to Santa Maria degli Angeli. Wherefore he called unto him Friar Masseo and Friar Agnolo, and, after

many words and holy admonishments, he commended unto them
that holy mountain with all possible earnestness, telling them that
it behoved him, together with Friar Leo, to return to Santa Maria
degli Angeli. And when he had said this, he took leave of them
and blessed them in the name of Jesus crucified; and, yielding
to their entreaties, he gave them his most holy hands, adorned
with those glorious and sacred stigmata, to see, to touch and to
kiss; and so leaving them consoled, he departed from them and
descended the holy mountain.

OF THE FOURTH CONSIDERATION OF THE MOST HOLY STIGMATA

As touching the fourth consideration, it must be known that, after
the true love of Christ had perfectly transformed St. Francis
into God and into the true image of Christ crucified; having
finished the fast of forty days in honour of St. Michael the
Archangel upon the holy mountain of Alvernia; after the festival of St. Michael, the angelical man, St. Francis, descended from
the mountain with Friar Leo and with a devout villain, upon
whose ass he sat, because by reason of the nails in his feet he
could not well go afoot. Now, when St. Francis had come down
from the mountain, the fame of his sanctity was already noised
abroad throughout the land; for it had been reported by the
shepherds how they had seen the mountain of Alvernia all ablaze,
and that this was the token of some great miracle which God
had wrought upon St. Francis; wherefore, when the people of
the district heard that he was passing, they all flocked to see him,
both men and women, small and great, and all of them with much
devotion and desire sought to touch him and to kiss his hands;
and not being able to resist the devotion of the people, albeit he
had bandaged the palms of his hands, nevertheless, the better
to hide the most holy stigmata, he bandaged them yet more and
covered them with his sleeves, and only gave them his fingers
to kiss. But albeit he endeavoured to conceal and to hide the
mystery of the most holy stigmata, to avoid every occasion of
worldly glory, it pleased God for His own glory to show forth
many miracles by virtue of the said most holy stigmata, and singularly in that journey from Vernia to Santa Maria degli Angeli,

and very many thereafter in divers parts of the world, both during his life and after his glorious death; to the end that their occult and marvellous virtue, and the extreme charity and mercy of Christ, towards him to whom He had so marvellously given them, might be manifested to the world by clear and evident miracles; whereof we will set forth some in this place. Thus, when St. Francis was drawing nigh unto a village which was upon the borders of the county of Arezzo, a woman came before him, weeping sore and holding her child in her arms; the which child was eight years old and had been dropsical for four years; and his belly was so terribly swollen that, when he stood upright, he could not see his feet; and this woman laid that son of hers before him, and besought him to pray God for him; and St. Francis first betook himself to prayer and then, when he had prayed, laid his holy hands upon the belly of the child; and anon, all the swelling disappeared, and he was made perfectly whole, and he gave him back to his mother, who received him with very great joy, and led him home, thanking God and St. Francis; and she willingly showed her son that was healed to all those of the district who came to her house to see him. On the same day St. Francis passed through Borgo San Sepolcro, and or ever he drew nigh unto the walls, the inhabitants of the town and of the villages came forth to meet him, and many of them went before him with boughs of olive in their hands, crying aloud: "Behold the saint! behold the saint!" And, for devotion and the desire which the folk had to touch him, they thronged and pressed upon him; but ever he went on his way with his mind uplifted and rapt in God through contemplation, and, albeit he was touched and held and plucked at by the people, he, even as one insensible, knew nothing at all of that which was done or said around him; neither did he perceive that he was passing through that town or through that district. For, when he had passed through Borgo and the crowd had returned to their homes, that contemplator of celestial things, having arrived at a house for lepers, a full mile beyond Borgo, returned to himself, and, as one who had come from another world, inquired of his companion: "When shall we be near Borgo?" Of a truth his soul, being fixed and rapt in contemplation of heavenly things, had been unconscious of anything earthly, whether of change of place, or of time, or of the people who thronged about him; and this befel many other times, as his companions proved by evident experience. That evening St. Francis reached the Place of the friars of Monte Casale, in the which place a friar was so cruelly sick and so horribly tormented by sickness that his disease seemed rather some affliction and torment of the devil than a natural infirmity; for sometimes he cast himself upon the ground trembling violently and foaming at the mouth; anon all the sinews of his body were contracted, then stretched, then bent, then twisted, and anon his heels were drawn up to the nape of his neck, and he flung himself into the air, and straightway fell flat on his back. Now, while St. Francis sat at table, he heard from the friars of this friar, so miserably sick and without remedy; and he had compassion on him, and took a piece of bread which he was eating, and, with his holy hands imprinted with the stigmata, made over it the sign of the most holy Cross, and sent it to the sick friar; who, as soon as he had eaten it, was made perfectly whole, and never felt that sickness any more. When the following morning was come, St. Francis sent two of those friars who were in that Place to dwell at Alvernia; and he sent back with them the villain, who had come with him behind the ass, which he had lent him, desiring that he should return with them to his home. The friars went with the said villain, and, as they entered the county of Arezzo, certain men of the district saw them afar off, and had great joy thereof, thinking that it was St. Francis, who had passed that way two days before; for one of their women, which had been three days in travail and could not bring to the birth was dying; and they thought to have her back sound and well, if St. Francis laid his holy hands upon her. But, when the said friars drew near, they perceived that St. Francis was not with them; and they were very sad. Nevertheless, albeit the saint was not there in the flesh, his virtue lacked not, because they lacked not faith. O marvellous thing! the woman was dying and was already in her death agony, when they asked the friars if they had anything which the most holy hands of St. Francis had touched. The friars thought and searched diligently, but could find nothing which St. Francis had touched with his hands save only the halter of the ass upon which he had come. With great reverence and devotion those men took that halter and laid it upon the belly of the pregnant woman, calling devoutly on the name of St. Francis and faithfully commending themselves to him. And what more? No sooner had the aforesaid halter been laid upon the woman than, anon, she was freed from all peril, and gave birth joyfully, with ease and safety. Now St. Francis, after he had been some days in the said place, departed and went to Città di Castello; and behold, many of the citizens brought to him a woman, who had been possessed of a devil for a long time, and humbly besought him for her deliverance; because, with her dolorous howlings and cruel shrieks and dog-like barkings, she disturbed all the neighbourhood. Then St. Francis, having first prayed and made over her the sign of the most holy Cross, commanded the demon to depart from her; and he straightway departed, leaving her sane in body and in mind. And, when this miracle was noised abroad among the people, another woman with great faith brought to him her sick child, who was afflicted with a cruel sore, and besought him devoutly that he would be pleased to make the sign of the Cross upon him with his hands. Then St. Francis gave ear unto her prayer, and took the child and loosed the bandage from off his sore and blessed him, making the sign of the most holy Cross over the sore three times, and thereafter with his own hands he replaced the bandage, and gave him back to his mother; and, because it was evening, she forthwith laid him on the bed to sleep. Thereafter, in the morning, she went to take her child from the bed, and found the bandage unloosed, and looked and saw that he was as perfectly whole as if he had never had any sickness at all; save only that, in the place where the sore had been, the flesh had grown over after the manner of a red rose; and that rather in testimony of the miracle than as a scar left by the sore; because the said rose, remaining during the whole of his lifetime, often moved him to devotion toward St. Francis who had healed him. In that city, then, St. Francis sojourned for a month, at the prayer of the devout citizens, in the which time he wrought many other miracles; and thereafter he departed thence, to go unto Santa Maria degli Angeli with Friar Leo, and with a good man, who lent him his little ass, whereupon St. Francis rode. Now, it came to pass that, by reason of the bad roads and the great cold, they journeyed all day without being able to reach any place where they might lodge; for the which cause, being constrained by the darkness and by the bad weather, they took shelter beneath the brow of a hollow rock, to avoid the snow and the night which was coming on. And, being in this evil case and also badly clad, the good man, to whom the ass belonged, could not sleep by reason of the cold; wherefore he began to murmur gently within himself and to weep; and almost did he blame St. Francis, who had brought him into such a place. Then St. Francis, perceiving this, had compassion upon him, and, in fervour of spirit, stretched out his hand toward him and touched him. O marvellous thing! as soon as he had touched him with that hand of his, enkindled and pierced by the fire of the Seraph, all the cold left him; and so much heat entered into him, both within and without, that he seemed to be hard by the mouth of a burning furnace; whence being presently comforted in soul and body he fell asleep; and, according to that which he said, he slept more sweetly that night, among rocks and snow until morning, than he had ever slept in his own bed. Thereafter, on the next day, they continued their journey and came to Santa Maria degli Angeli; and, when they were nigh thereunto, Friar Leo lifted up his eyes and looked toward the said Place of Santa Maria degli Angeli, and saw an exceedingly beautiful Cross, whereon was the figure of the Crucified, going before St. Francis, even as St. Francis was going before Him; and on such wise did the said Cross go before the face of St. Francis that when he stopped it stopped too, and when he went on it went on; and that Cross was of such brightness that, not only did it shine in the face of St. Francis, but all the road about him also was lighted up; and it lasted until St. Francis entered into the Place of Santa Maria degli Angeli. St. Francis, then, having arrived with Friar Leo, they were welcomed by the friars with very great joy and charity. And from thenceforward, until his death, St. Francis dwelt for the greater part of his time in that Place of Santa Maria degli Angeli. And the fame of his sanctity and of his miracles spread continually more and more through the Order and through the world, although, by reason of his profound humility, he concealed as much as he might the gifts and graces of God, and ever called himself the greatest of sinners. Wherefore, on a time, Friar Leo, marvelling within himself and thinking foolishly, said in his heart: "Lo, this man calleth himself a very great sinner in public, and becometh great in the Order, and is so much honoured of God, yet, in secret, he never confesseth any carnal sin. Can it be that he is a virgin?" And therewith he began to desire very earnestly to know the truth; and, fearing to ask St. Francis touching this matter, he betook himself to God; and urgently beseeching Him that He would certify him of that which he desired to know, through the much praying and merit of St. Francis, he was answered and certified, through this vision, that St. Francis was verily a virgin in body. For he saw, in a vision, St. Francis standing in a high and excellent place, whereunto none might go up nor attain to bear him company; and it was told him in spirit that this so high and excellent place signified that perfection of virginal chastity in St. Francis which was reasonable and fitting in the flesh that was to be adorned with the most holy Stigmata of Christ. St. Francis, seeing that, by reason of the Stigmata of Christ, his bodily strength grew gradually less and that he was not able any more to take charge of the government of the Order, hastened forward the General Chapter of the Order; and, when it was assembled, he humbly excused himself to the friars for the weakness which prevented him from attending any more to the care of the Order, as touching the duties of General; albeit he renounced not that office of General because he was not able to do so, inasmuch as he had been made General by the Pope; and therefore he could neither resign his office nor appoint a successor without the express leave of the Pope. Nevertheless he appointed as his Vicar Friar Peter Cattani, and commended the Order unto him and unto the Ministers of the Provinces with all possible affection. And, when he had thus done, St. Francis, being comforted in spirit, lifted up his eyes and hands to heaven and spake thus: "To Thee, my Lord God, to Thee I commend this Thy family, which unto this hour Thou hast committed unto me; and now, by reason of my infirmities, which Thou my most sweet Lord knowest, I am no longer able to take charge thereof. Also do I commend it to the Ministers of the Provinces; and if, through their negligence or through their bad example or through their too harsh correction, any friar shall perish, may they be held to give account thereof to Thee on the Day of Judgment." And in these words, as it pleased God, all the friars of the Chapter understood that he spake of the most holy Stigmata, to wit in that which he said excusing himself by reason of his infirmity: and for devotion none of them was able to refrain from weeping. And from thenceforward he left all the care and government of the Order in the hands of his Vicar and of the Ministers of the Provinces; and he was wont to say: "Now that, by reason of my infirmities, I have given up the charge of the Order, I have no other duty than to pray God for our Religion and to set a good ensample to the friars. And of a truth, I know well that, if my infirmity should leave me, the greatest help which I could render to the Religion would be to pray continually to God for it, that He would defend and govern and preserve it." Now, as hath been said above, albeit St. Francis, as much as in him lay, strove to hide the most holy Stigmata, and, from the time when he received them, always went with his hands bandaged and with stockings on his feet, yet, for all that he could do, he could not prevent many of the friars from seeing and touching them in divers manners, and particularly the wound in his side, the which he endeavoured with special diligence to hide. Thus, a friar, who waited on him, induced him, by a pious fraud, to take off his habit, that the dust might be shaken out of it; and, since he removed it in his presence, that friar saw clearly the wound in his side; and, swiftly putting his hand upon his breast, he touched it with three fingers and thus learned its extent and size; and in like manner his Vicar saw it at that time. But more clearly was Friar Ruffino certified thereof; the which was a man of very great contemplation, of whom St. Francis sometimes said that in all the world there was no more holy man than he; and by reason of his holiness he loved him as a familiar friend, and was wont to grant him all that he desired. In three ways did this Friar Ruffino certify himself and others of the said most holy Stigmata. The first was this: that, it being his duty to wash the breeches of St. Francis, which he wore so large that, by pulling them well up, he covered therewith the wound in his right side, the said Friar Ruffino examined them and considered them diligently, and found that they were always bloody on the right side; whereby he perceived of a surety that that was blood which came from the said wound; but for this St. Francis rebuked him when he saw that he spread out the clothes which he took off in order to look for the said token. The second way was this: that once, while the said Friar Ruffino was scratching St. Francis' back, he deliberately let his hand slip and put his fingers into the wound in his side; whereat, for the pain that he felt, St. Francis cried aloud: "God forgive thee, O Friar Ruffino, that thou hast done this." The third way was that he once begged St. Francis very urgently, as an exceeding great favour, to give him his habit and to take his in exchange, for love of charity. Whereupon the charitable father, albeit unwillingly, yielded to his prayer, and drew off his habit and gave it to him and took his; and then, in that taking off and putting on, Friar Ruffino clearly saw the said wound. Friar Leo likewise, and many other friars, saw the said most holy Stigmata of St. Francis while yet he lived; the which friars, although by reason of their sanctity they were worthy of credence and men whose simple word might be believed, nevertheless, to remove doubt from every heart, sware upon the Holy Book that they had clearly seen them. Moreover, certain cardinals, who were intimate friends of St. Francis, saw them; and, in reverence for the aforesaid most holy Stigmata, they composed and made beautiful and devout hymns and psalms and prose treatises. The highest pontiff, Pope Alexander, while preaching to the people in the presence of all the cardinals (among whom was the holy Friar Buonaventura, who was a cardinal) said and affirmed that he had seen with his own eyes the most holy Stigmata of St. Francis, when he was yet alive. And Madonna Jacopa di Settensoli of Rome, who was the greatest lady of her time in Rome and was most devoted to St. Francis, saw them before he died, and, after his death, saw and kissed them many times with great reverence; for she came from Rome to Assisi, by Divine revelation, to the death-bed of St. Francis; and her coming was after this manner: For some days before his death, St. Francis lay sick at Assisi in the palace of the Bishop, with some of his companions; and, notwithstanding his sickness, he often sang certain lauds of Christ. One day, one of his companions said unto him: "Father, thou knowest that these citizens have great faith in thee, and hold thee for a saintly man, and therefore they may think that, if thou art that which they believe thee to be, thou shouldest, in this thine infirmity, think upon thy death, and rather weep than sing, in that thou art so exceedingly sick; and know that thy singing and ours, which thou makest us to sing, is heard of many, both within and without the palace; for this palace is guarded on thy account by many armed men, who perchance may take bad ensample therefrom. Wherefore I believe (said this friar) that thou wouldest do well to depart hence, and that we should all of us return to Santa Maria degli Angeli; for this is no place for us, among seculars." St. Francis answered him: "Dearest friar, thou knowest that two years ago, when we abode at Foligno, God revealed unto thee the term of my life; and in like manner also He revealed unto me that, a few days hence, the said term shall end, in this sickness; and in that revelation God made me certain of the remission of all my sins, and of the bliss of paradise. Until I had that revelation I bewailed death and my sins; but, since I have had that revelation, I am so full of gladness that I can weep no more; and therefore do I sing, yea, and will sing unto God, who hath given me the blessing of His grace and hath made me sure of the blessings of the glory of paradise. As touching our departure hence, I consent thereunto and it pleaseth me; but do ye find means to carry me, because, by reason of mine infirmity, I cannot walk." Then the friars took him up in their arms and so carried him; and many of the citizens accompanied them. And, coming to a hospice, which was by the way, St. Francis said unto those who carried him: "Set me down on the ground, and turn me toward the city." And, when he was set with his face toward Assisi, he blessed the city with many blessings, saying: "Blessed be thou of God, O holy city, for through thee many souls shall be saved, and in thee shall dwell many servants of God, and from thee many shall be chosen unto the Kingdom of the Life Eternal." And, when he had said these words, he caused them to carry him on to Santa Maria degli Angeli. And, when they arrived at Santa Maria degli Angeli, they bore him to the infirmary and there laid him down to rest. Then St. Francis called unto him one of the companions and spake unto him thus: "Dearest friar, God hath revealed unto me that, of this sickness, on such a day, I shall depart from this life; and thou knowest that the wellbeloved Madonna Jacopa di Settensoli, who is devoted to our Order, if she knew of my death and had not been present thereat, would be sore grieved; and therefore do thou send her word that, if she would see me alive, she come hither at once." The friar made answer: "Father, thou sayest rightly; for in truth, by reason of the great love which she beareth thee, it would be most unseemly if she were not present at thy death." "Go, then," said St. Francis, "and bring me inkhorn and paper and pen, and write as I bid thee." And, when he had brought them, St. Francis dictated the letter on this wise: *"To Madonna Jacopa, the servant of God, Friar Francis, the mendicant of Christ, greeting and the fellowship of the Holy Ghost in our Lord Jesus Christ. Know, well beloved, that Christ the blessed hath, of His grace, revealed unto me that the end of my life is at hand. Therefore, if thou wouldst find me alive, when thou hast seen this letter, arise and come to Santa Maria degli Angeli; for, if thou art not come by such a day, thou wilt not find me alive; and bring with thee hair-cloth to wrap my body in, and the wax which is needed for my burial. Also I beseech thee to bring me some of that food which thou wast wont to give me to eat, when I was sick in Rome."* And, while this letter was being written, it was revealed of God to St. Francis that Madonna Jacopa was coming to him and was already nigh unto the place, and brought with her all those things which he was sending to ask for by the letter. Wherefore, when he had had this revelation, St. Francis told the friar who was writing the letter, not to write further, because there was no need thereof, but to lay aside the letter; whereat the friars marvelled greatly, because he finished not the letter and would not have it sent. And, while they continued thus, lo, after a little while, there was a great knocking at the door of the Place, and St. Francis sent the doorkeeper to open it; and, when he had opened the door, behold, there was Madonna Jacopa, the noblest lady of Rome, with two of her sons, Senators of Rome, and with a great company of men on horseback; and they entered in; and Madonna Jacopa gat her straight to the infirmary, and came unto St. Francis. Of whose coming St. Francis had great joy and consolation, and she likewise, seeing him alive and speaking with him. Then she told him how God had revealed unto her in Rome, while she was praying, the short span of his life, and how he would send for her, and ask for those things, all of which she said that she had brought; and she caused them to be brought to St. Francis and gave him to eat thereof; and, when he had eaten and was much comforted, this Madonna Jacopa kneeled down at the feet of St. Francis, and took those most holy feet, marked and adorned with the wounds of Christ, and kissed and bathed them with her tears, with such limitless devotion that to the friars which were standing by it seemed that they verily beheld the Magdalene at the feet of Jesus Christ; and on nowise might they draw her away from them. And finally, after a long time, they raised her up and drew her aside, and asked her how she had come so duly and so well provided with all those things which were necessary for St. Francis while yet he was alive, and for his burial. Madonna Jacopa replied that, while she was praying one night in Rome, she heard a voice from heaven, which said: "If thou wouldest find St. Francis alive, get thee to Assisi without delay, and take with thee those things which thou art wont to give him when he is sick, and those things which will be necessary for his burial; and I (said she) have done so." So the said Madonna Jacopa abode there until St. Francis passed from this life and was buried; and at his burial she did him very great honour, she and all her company; and she bore all the cost of whatsoever was needed. And thereafter, this noble lady returned to Rome; and there, within a little while, she died a holy death; and for devotion to St. Francis she commanded that her body should be borne to Santa Maria degli Angeli and buried there; and so was it done.

HOW MESSER JEROME TOUCHED AND SAW THE MOST HOLY
STIGMATA OF ST. FRANCIS, WHEREIN AT FIRST
HE DID NOT BELIEVE

At the death of St. Francis, not only did the said Madonna Jacopa and her sons together with all her company see and kiss his glorious and holy Stigmata, but also many citizens of Assisi; among whom was a knight of wide renown and a great man, who was named Messer Jerome, the which doubted much thereof and was incredulous concerning them, even as was St. Thomas concerning those of Christ; and to certify himself and others, in the presence of all the friars and the lay folk, he boldly moved the nails in the hands and feet, and touched the wound in the side before them all. Whereby he was thereafter a constant witness of that verity, swearing upon the Book that so it was, and so he had seen and touched. St. Clare, likewise, beheld and kissed the glorious and sacred Stigmata of St. Francis, together with her nuns, which were present at his burying.

OF THE DAY AND OF THE YEAR OF THE DEATH OF ST. FRANCIS

THE glorious confessor of Christ, Messer St. Francis, passed from this life in the year of our Lord M.CC.XXVI., on the fourth day of October, on Saturday, and was buried on Sunday. That year was the twentieth year of his conversion, to wit when he began to do penance, and was the second year after the imprinting of the most holy Stigmata; and it was in the forty-fifth year from his birth.

OF THE CANONISATION OF ST. FRANCIS

THEREAFTER was St. Francis canonised in M.CC.XXVIII., by Pope Gregory IX., who came in person to Assisi to canonise him. And this sufficeth touching the fourth consideration.

OF THE FIFTH AND LAST CONSIDERATION OF THE MOST HOLY STIGMATA

THE fifth and last consideration is touching certain visions and revelations and miracles which God wrought and showed forth after the death of St. Francis, in confirmation of his most holy Stigmata, and for a declaration of the day and the hour whereon Christ gave them unto him. And as touching this matter, it is to be considered that, in the year of our Lord M.CC.LXXXII., on the . . . day of the month of October, Friar Philip, Minister of Tuscany, at the commandment of Friar John Buonagrazia, Minister-General, in the name of holy obedience, asked Friar Matthew of Castiglione Aretino, a man of great devotion and sanctity, to tell that which he knew concerning the day and the hour whereon the most holy Stigmata were imprinted by Christ on the body of St. Francis; because he heard that he had had a revelation touching the same. Whereupon Friar Matthew, constrained by holy obedience, answered him after this manner: "While I was in the community of Alvernia, last year in the month of May, I one day betook myself to prayer in my cell, which is on the spot where it is believed that that seraphic vision took place. And in my prayer I besought God most devoutly that He would vouchsafe to reveal unto some person the day and the hour and the place wherein the most holy Stigmata were imprinted upon the body of St. Francis; and, when I had continued in prayer and in this petition beyond the first watch, St. Francis appeared to me with very great radiance, and said unto me: 'Son, for what dost thou pray to God?' And I said unto him: 'Father, I pray for such and such a thing.' And he said unto me: 'I am thy Father Francis. Dost thou know me well?' 'Father,' I said, 'yes.' Then he showed me the most holy Stigmata in his hands and feet and side, and said: 'The time hath come when God wills that that, which aforetime the friars have not been curious to know, shall be made manifest for His glory. Know thou then that He which appeared unto me was not an angel, but was Jesus Christ, in the form of a Seraph, who, with his own hands, imprinted on my body these wounds, even as He received them in His body on the cross. And it was after this manner: On the day before the Exaltation of the Holy Cross, an angel came unto me, and in God's name, bade me make me ready unto patience and to receive that which God might will to send me. And I made answer that I was ready to receive and to endure everything which might be God's good pleasure. Thereafter, on the following morning, to wit the morning of [the festival of the] Holy Cross, the which that year fell upon a Friday; at daybreak I came forth from my cell, in very great fervour of spirit, and went to pray in this place where thou now art and where I ofttimes prayed, and, as I prayed, lo, through the air, there came down from heaven, with great swiftness, a young man crucified, in the form of a Seraph with six wings; at which marvellous sight I humbly kneeled me down and began to contemplate devoutly the boundless love of Jesus Christ crucified, and the boundless pain of His passion; and the sight of Him engendered in me such pity that I verily seemed to feel His passion in my own body; and, at His presence, all this mountain shone as doth the sun; and, so descending, He came nigh unto me. And, standing before me, He said certain secret words unto me, the which I have not yet revealed unto any man; but the time draweth nigh when they shall be revealed. Then, after a while, Christ departed, and returned into heaven, and I found myself thus marked with these wounds. Go then,' said St. Francis, 'and tell these things to thy minister nothing doubting; for this is the operation not of man but of God.' And, when he had said these words, St. Francis blessed me and went back to heaven with a great multitude of youths, exceeding bright." All these things the said Friar Matthew said that he had seen and heard, not sleeping but awake. And he sware that he had of a truth told these things to the said minister in his cell at Florence, when he inquired of him concerning the same for obedience' sake.

HOW A HOLY FRIAR, READING THE LEGEND OF ST. FRANCIS IN THE CHAPTER OF THE MOST HOLY STIGMATA, PRAYED SO MUCH TO GOD CONCERNING THE SECRET WORDS, WHICH THE SERAPH SPAKE TO ST. FRANCIS, WHEN HE APPEARED UNTO HIM, THAT ST. FRANCIS REVEALED THEM UNTO THE SAID FRIAR

UPON another time, a devout and holy friar, while reading the legend of St. Francis in the chapter of the most holy Stigmata, began with great travail of spirit to consider what those so secret words could have been, which St. Francis said that he would not reveal to any one while he lived; the which the Seraph had spoken to him when he appeared unto him. And this friar said within himself: "St. Francis willed not to speak these words to any one during his lifetime; but now, after his bodily death, perchance he would tell them, if he were prayed devoutly so to do." And from thenceforward, the devout friar began to pray God and St. Francis that they would vouchsafe to reveal those words; and this friar continuing eight years in this prayer, in the eighth year he merited to be heard on this wise: One day, after eating, thanks having been given in the church, he was in prayer in a certain part of the church, and was praying to God and St. Francis touching this matter, more devoutly than he was wont, and with many tears; when he was called by another friar, who commanded him in the name of the Guardian to bear him company to the town for the good of the Place. For the which cause, he, doubting not that obedience is more meritorious than prayer, as soon as he had heard the commandment of his superior, humbly left off praying and went with that friar that called him. And, as God willed it, he, by this act of ready obedience, merited that which he had not merited by his long praying. Whence, as soon as they had gone forth from the gate of the Place, they met two strange friars, who appeared to have come from a far country; and one of them seemed a young man and the other old and lean; and, by reason of the bad weather, they were all muddy and wet. Wherefore that obedient friar had great compassion for them, and said unto the companion, with whom he was going: "O dearest brother mine, if the business whereon we are going may wait a little, inasmuch as these strange friars have great need to be charitably received, I beseech thee to permit me first to go and wash their feet, and especially those of this aged friar, who hath the greater need thereof; and you will be able to wash those of this younger one; and thereafter we will go about the business of the convent." Then this friar consenting unto the charitable desire of his companion, they went back and received those strange friars very charitably, and took them into the kitchen to the fire to warm and dry themselves; at the which fire eight other friars of the Place were warming themselves. And, after they had been a little while at the fire, they took them aside to wash their feet, even as they had agreed together. And while that obedient and devout friar was washing the feet of the older friar, and removing the mud therefrom, for they were very muddy, he looked and saw that his feet were marked with the most holy Stigmata; and anon, for joy and wonder he embraced them closely, and began to cry aloud: "Either thou art Christ, or thou art St. Francis." At that cry and at those words, the friars, which were at the fire, arose and came thither with great fear and reverence to see those glorious Stigmata. And then, at their prayer, this ancient friar permitted them clearly to see and touch and kiss them. And, while they marvelled yet more for joy, he said unto them: "Doubt not and fear not, dearest friars and sons; I am your father Friar Francis, who, according to the will of God, founded three Orders. And seeing that, for eight years, I have been entreated by this friar, who is washing my feet, and to-day more fervently than ever before, that I would reveal unto him those secret words which the Seraph spake unto me when He gave me the Stigmata, the which words I resolved never to reveal in my lifetime, to-day, by the commandment of God, by reason of his perseverance and the ready obedience with which he left the sweetness of contemplation, I am sent by God to reveal unto him, before you all, that which he asks." And then, turning unto that friar, St. Francis spake thus: "Know, dearest friar, that, when I was upon the mountain of Alvernia, wholly absorbed in the remembrance of the passion of Christ in that seraphic apparition, I was by Christ thus marked on my body with the Stigmata, and then Christ said unto me: 'Knowest thou what I have done unto thee? I have given thee the tokens of My passion, so that thou mayest be My standard-bearer. And even as I, on the day of My death, descended into Limbo, and, in virtue of these My Stigmata, drew out thence all the souls which I found there, and took them to Paradise; so to thee do I grant even from this hour, to the end that thou mayest be conformed to Me in death as thou hast been in life, that, after thou shalt have passed from this life, every year on the day of thy death, thou shalt go to Purgatory, and, in virtue of thy Stigmata which I have given thee, shalt draw out thence all the souls of thy three Orders, to wit minors, sisters and continents, and, beyond this, those others whom thou shalt find there, who have borne devotion unto thee, and shalt lead them into Paradise.' And these words I never spake while I lived in the world." And, when he had said these words, St. Francis and his companion suddenly vanished away. Many friars afterwards heard this from those eight friars, who were present at this vision and at these words of St. Francis.

HOW ST. FRANCIS, AFTER HIS DEATH, APPEARED TO FRIAR JOHN
OF ALVERNIA, WHILE HE WAS PRAYING

ONCE, upon the mountain of Alvernia, St. Francis appeared to Friar John of Alvernia, a man of great sanctity, while he was praying, and abode and talked with him for a very long time; and, at the last, desiring to depart, he spake thus: "Ask of me what thou wilt." Said Friar John: "Father, I pray thee to tell me that which I have long desired to know, to wit what you were doing, and where you were, when the Seraph appeared unto you." St. Francis made answer: "I was praying in that place where is now the chapel of Count Simon da Battifolle, and I was entreating two graces of my Lord Jesus Christ. The first was that He would grant me to feel, in this life, in my soul and in my body, as far as might be possible, all that pain which He had Himself felt at the time of His most bitter passion. The second grace which I asked of Him was in like manner that I might feel in my heart that intense love wherewith He was enkindled to bear so great passion for us sinners. And then God put it in my heart that He would grant me to feel both the one and the other, as much as was possible for a mere creature; the which thing was abundantly fulfilled in me at the imprinting of the Stigmata." Then Friar John asked him whether those secret words which the Seraph had spoken unto him had been even such as were rehearsed by that holy friar aforesaid, who declared that he had heard them from St. Francis in the presence of eight friars. St. Francis replied that the truth was even as that friar had said. Thereupon, Friar John, encouraged by the liberality of the granter, took heart to ask yet more, and said thus: "O father, I beseech thee most earnestly that thou wilt suffer me to behold and to kiss thy most holy and glorious Stigmata; not because I doubt thereof at all, but only for my consolation; for for this have I always yearned." And, St. Francis freely showing them and offering them unto him, Friar John clearly saw and touched and kissed them. And, at the last, he asked of him: "Father, how great consolation had your soul, be-holding Christ the Blessed coming unto you to give you the marks of His most holy Passion? Now wouid to God that I might feel a little of that sweetness!" Then St. Francis made answer: "Seest thou these nails?" Said Friar John. "Father, yes." "Touch yet again," said St. Francis, "this nail which is in my hand." Then Friar John, with great reverence and fear, touched that nail, and immediately, as he touched it, so great a perfume issued there-from, as it were a thin spiral of smoke after the fashion of in-cense, and, entering through the nose of Friar John, filled his soul and body with so much sweetness, that forthwith he was rapt in God in ecstasy, and became insensible; and he remained thus rapt from that hour, which was the hour of Terce, even until Vespers. And of this vision and familiar conversation with St. Francis Friar John never spake unto any man, save only to his confessor, until he came unto his death; but, being nigh unto his death, he revealed it to many friars.

4. BLESSED JULIANA OF NORWICH:
FROM *REVELATIONS OF DIVINE LOVE*

¶TOWARD the close of the fourteenth century, there appeared a book
evidently written by a Benedictine nun living as a recluse in Norwich. Nothing definite is known concerning her identity or further
activities. The *Revelations of Divine Love* are, however, the most
perfect fruit of later mediæval English mysticism. They outline
meditations following an experience during which she became acutely
aware of Christ's love for the soul. Gradually this became the key
to an understanding of the whole of life. Mother Juliana seems to
have been fairly well acquainted with the mystical writers of her day,
but in all probability she was not an educated woman. Accordingly,
the exactness and poetic beauty of her expression, no less than the
keenness of her psychological insight are all the more remarkable.

It has been conjectured that Mother Juliana was born in 1342,
and that she died about 1420. Efforts to secure further information
have failed. In 1902 there appeared an edition of the *Revelations*
with an excellent preface by George Tyrell, S.J. To this the reader
desirous of an interpretation of Mother Juliana's doctrine is referred.
There are in all sixteen revelations, of which that reprinted here is
the fifteenth.*

* From *Blessed Juliana of Norwich: Revelations of Divine Love*. Edited by
George Tyrell, S.J. London, 1902.

THE FIFTEENTH REVELATION

FORE this time I had great longing and desire of Gods gift to be delivered of this world, and of this life; for oft-times I beheld the woe that is here, and the weal and the blessed being that is there. And if there had no pain been in this life, but the absence of our Lord, methought sometime that it was more than I might bear. And this made me to mourn and busily to long. And also of my own wretchedness, slouth and weariness, that me liked not to live and to travel as me fell to do. And to all this our courteous Lord answered for comfort and patience, and said these words: *'Suddenly thou shalt be taken from all thy pain, from all thy sickness, from all thy disease, and from all thy woe. And thou shalt come up above, and thou shalt have me to thy meed, and thou shalt be fulfilled of joy and bliss; and thou shalt never more have no manner of pain, no manner of sickness, no manner misliking, no wanting of will, but ever joy and bliss without end. What should it then grieve thee to suffer a while, sithen it is my will and my worship?'* And in this word (*suddenly thou shalt be taken*) I saw that God rewarded man of the patience that he hath in abiding of Gods will, and of his time; and that man lengeth his patience over the time of his living; for unknowing the time of his passing. This is a great profit; for if a man knew his time, he should not have patience over that time. And also God will that while the soul is in the body, it seem to it self that it is ever at the point to be taken, for all this life and this longing that we have here is but a point. And when we be taken suddenly out of pain into bliss, then pain shall be nought. And in this time I saw a body lying on the earth: which body shewed heavy and fearful, and without shape and form, as it were a swilge [1] stinking myre. And suddenly out of this body sprung a full fair creature, a little child full shapen and formed, swift and lively, and whiter than the lilly, which sharply glided up into heaven. The swilge of the body betokeneth great wretchedness of our deadly flesh: and the littleness of the child betokeneth the cleanness and the pureness of our soul. And I thought

[1] Hideous.

with this body bliveth no fairness of this child, ne of this child
dwelleth no foulness of this body. It is full bliss-ful (for) man to
be taken from pain, more than pain to be taken from man; for if
pain be taken from us, it may come again. Therefore this is a
sovereign comfort, and a bless-ful beholding in a longing soul,
that we shall be taken from pain; for in this behest I saw a merciful compassion that our Lord hath in us for our woe, and a courteous behighting of clear deliverance: for he will that we be
comforted in the over-passing joy. And that he shewed in these
words; *And thou shalt come up above; and thou shalt have me
to thy meed, and thou shalt be fulfilled of joy and bliss.* It is
Gods will that we set the point of our thought in this blissful
beholding as oft-time as we may, and as long time keep us therein
with his grace; for this is a blissful contemplation to the soul that
is led of God, and full much to his worship for the time that it
lasteth. And when we fall again to our self by heaviness and
ghostly blindness, and feeling of pains ghostly and bodily by our
fragility, it is Gods will that we know, that he hath not forget us.
And so meaneth he in these words, and saith for comfort; *And
thou shalt never more have pain in no manner; nor no manner of
sickness, no manner of mis-liking, no want of will, but ever joy
and bliss without end: what should it then agrieved thee to suffer
a while, sithen it is my will and my worship?* It is Gods will that
we take his behests and his comfortings as largely and as mightily
as we may take them. And also he will that we take our abidings
and our dis-eases as lightly as we may take them, and set them at
naught: for the lightlier that we take them, and the less price that
we set at them for love, less pain shall we have in the feeling of
them, and the more thank and meed shall we have for them.

AND thus I understood that what man or woman wilfully choseth
God in this life for love, he may be sure that he is loved without
end, with endless love that worketh in him that grace; for he will
we keep this trustily, that we be as sicker in hope of the bliss of
heaven whiles we are here, as we shall be in surety when we are
there. And ever the more liking and joy that we take in this sickerness, with reverence and meekness, the better liketh him. For as
it was shewed, this reverence that I mean, is a holy, courteous

dread of our Lord, to which meekness is knit; and that is, that a creature see the Lord marvellous great, and her self marvellous litle: for these vertues are had endlesly to the loved of God. And it may now be seen and felt in measure by the gracious presence of our Lord, when it is: which presence in all thing is most desired; for it worketh that marvellous sickerness in true faith, and siker hope by greatness of charity in dread that is sweet and delectable. It is Gods will that I see myself as much bound to him in love, as if he had done for me all that he hath done. And thus should every soul think in regard of his love; that is to say, the charity of God maketh in us such a unity, that when it is truly seen no man can part himself from other. And thus ought each soul to think that God hath done for him all that he hath done. And this sheweth he to make us to love him, and liken him, and nothing dread but him; for it is his will we know that all the might of our enemies is locked in our friends hands. And therefore the soul that knoweth this sickerly, he shall not dread but him that she loveth. All other dreads she set them among passions, and bodily sickness, and imaginations. And therefore though we been in so much pain, woe and disease that us thinketh, we can think right naught but that we are in, or that we feel; as soon as we may we pass it lightly over, and set we it at naught. And why? for God will be known; for if we know him, and love him, and reverently dread him, we shall have patience, and be in great rest. And it should been great liking to us all that he doth. And this shewed our Lord in these words: *'What should it then agrieve thee to suffer a while, seeing it is my will and my worship?'* Now have I told you of xv. Shewings, as God witsafe to minister them to my mind, renewed by lightnings and touchings, I hope, of the same Spirit that sheweth them all. Of which xv. shewings the *first* began early in the morning, about the hour of four; and it lasted shewing by process full fair and soberly, each following other till it was noon of the day, or past.

5. ST. TERESA OF AVILA:
CHAPTERS VIII, IX AND X OF THE
AUTOBIOGRAPHY

¶Saint Teresa (1515-1582) was born in Avila, Spain, and entered the convent of the Carmelites during her eighteenth year. Conscious of having been called to a life of great spiritual fervor, she devoted herself heart and soul to the service of God according to the rule of her Order. This itself she then undertook to reform, blending the loftiest idealism with sound practical sense. Her writings are fairly extensive and have always been regarded, along with those of St. John of the Cross, as the most important source books concerning Spanish Carmelite mysticism. Some critics have endeavored to find a pathological strain in her life and work. These attempts, one may safely assert, are now thoroughly discredited.

The autobiography from which portions are here reprinted was written at a time when, in considerable distress of spirit, she sought out a Jesuit confessor in order to learn whether her experiences came from God. Concerning the actual date of composition there are differences of opinion. The book is notable for its human interest, its great beauty and its value as spiritual testimony. Three chapters have been selected—VIII, IX, X,—which describe the Saint's attainment to sanctity. The version used is that of David Lewis (published in 1870), and revised (1910) by the V. Rev. Benedict Williamson.*

---

* From *The Autobiography of St. Teresa*. Edited by Benedict Williamson. London: Burns, Oates and Washbourne, 1910.

CHAPTER VIII

THE SAINT CEASES NOT TO PRAY. PRAYER THE WAY TO RECOVER
WHAT IS LOST. ALL EXHORTED TO PRAY. THE GREAT ADVANTAGE
OF PRAYER, EVEN TO THOSE WHO MAY HAVE CEASED FROM IT

Of the great advantages she derived from not entirely abandoning prayer
so as not to lose her soul; and what an excellent remedy this is, in order to
win back what one has lost. She exhorts everybody to practise prayer, and
shows what a gain it is, even if one should have given it up for a time, to
make use of so great a good.

 T IS not without reason that I have dwelt so long
on this portion of my life. I see clearly that it will
give no one pleasure to see anything so base; and
certainly I wish those who may read this to have
me in abhorrence, as a soul so obstinate and so
ungrateful to Him Who did so much for me. I
could wish, too, I had permission to say how often at this time I
failed in my duty to God, because I was not leaning on the strong
pillar of prayer. I passed nearly twenty years on this stormy sea,
falling and rising, but rising to no good purpose, seeing that I
went and fell again. My life was one of perfection; but it was so
mean that I scarcely made any account whatever of venial sins,
and though of mortal sins I was afraid, I was not so afraid of them
as I ought to have been, because I did not avoid the perilous occasions of them. I may say that it was the most painful life that can
be imagined, because I had no sweetness in God and no pleasure
in the world.

2. When I was in the midst of the pleasures of the world, the
remembrance of what I owed to God made me sad, and when I
was praying to God my worldly affections disturbed me. This is
so painful a struggle that I know not how I could have borne it
for a month, let alone for so many years. Nevertheless, I can trace
distinctly the great mercy of our Lord to me, while thus im-
mersed in the world, in that I had still the courage to pray. I say
courage, because I know of nothing in the whole world which
requires greater courage than plotting treason against the King,
knowing that He knows it, and yet never withdrawing from His

presence; for, granting that we are always in the presence of God, yet it seems to me that those who pray are in His presence in a very different sense; for they, as it were, see that He is looking upon them, while others may be for days together without even once recollecting that God sees them.

3. It is true, indeed, that during these years there were many months, and, I believe, occasionally a whole year, in which I so kept guard over myself that I did not offend our Lord, gave myself much to prayer, and took some pains, and that successfully, not to offend Him. I speak of this now because all I am saying is strictly true; but I remember very little of those good days, and so they must have been few, while my evil days were many. Still, the days that passed over without my spending a great part of them in prayer were few, unless I was very ill, or very much occupied.

4. When I was ill, I was well with God. I contrived that those about me should be so, too, and I made supplications to our Lord for this grace, and spoke frequently of Him. Thus, with the exception of that year of which I have been speaking, during eight and twenty years of prayer, I spent more than eighteen in that strife and contention which arose out of my attempts to reconcile God and the world. As to the other years, of which I have now to speak, in them the grounds of the warfare, though it was not slight, were changed; but inasmuch as I was—at least, I think so—serving God, and aware of the vanity of the world, all has been pleasant, as I shall show hereafter.[1]

5. The reason, then, of my telling this at so great a length is that, as I have just said, the mercy of God and my ingratitude, on the one hand, may become known; and, on the other, that men may understand how great is the good which God works in a soul when He gives it a disposition to pray in earnest, though it may not be so well prepared as it ought to be. If that soul perseveres in spite of sins, temptations, and relapses, brought about in a thousand ways by Satan, our Lord will bring it at last—I am certain of it—to the harbour of salvation, as He has brought me myself; for so it seems to me now. May His Majesty grant I may never go back and be lost! He who gives himself to prayer is in possession of a great blessing, of which many saintly and

[1] Ch. ix. 10.

good men have written—I am speaking of mental prayer—glory be to God for it! and, if they had not done so, I am not proud enough, though I have but little humility, to presume to discuss it.

6. I may speak of that which I know by experience; and so, I say, let him never cease from prayer who has once begun it, be his life ever so wicked; for prayer is the way to amend it, and without prayer such amendment will be much more difficult. Let him not be tempted by Satan, as I was, to give it up, on the pretence of humility; let him rather believe that His words are true Who says that, if we truly repent, and resolve never to offend Him, He will take us into His favour again, give us the graces He gave us before, and occasionally even greater, if our repentance deserve it. And as to him who has not begun to pray, I implore him by the love of our Lord not to deprive himself of so great a good.

7. Herein there is nothing to be afraid of, but everything to hope for. Granting that such a one does not advance, nor make an effort to become perfect, so as to merit the joys and consolations which the perfect receive from God, yet he will by little and little attain to a knowledge of the road which leads to heaven. And, if he perseveres, I hope in the mercy of God for him, seeing that no one ever took Him for his friend that was not amply rewarded; for mental prayer is nothing else, in my opinion, but being on terms of friendship with God, frequently conversing in secret with Him Who, we know, loves us. Now, true love and lasting friendship require certain dispositions; those of our Lord, we know, are absolutely perfect; ours, vicious, sensual, and thankless; and you cannot, therefore, bring yourselves to love Him, as He loves you, because you have not the disposition to do so; and if you do not love Him, yet, seeing how much it concerns you to have His friendship, and how great is His love for you, rise above that pain you feel at being much with Him Who is so different from you.

8. O infinite Goodness of my God! I seem to see Thee and myself in this relation to one another. O Joy of the angels! when I consider it, I wish I could wholly die of love! How true it is that Thou endurest those who will not endure Thee! Oh, how good a friend art Thou, O my Lord! how Thou comfortest and endurest, and also waitest for them to make themselves like unto

Thee, and yet, in the meanwhile, art Thyself so patient of the state they are in! Thou takest into account the occasions during which they seek Thee, and for a moment of penitence forgettest their offences against Thyself.

9. I have seen this distinctly in my own case, and I cannot tell why the whole world does not labour to draw near to Thee in this particular friendship. The wicked, who do not resemble Thee, ought to do so, in order that Thou mayest make them good, and for that purpose should permit Thee to remain with them at least for two hours daily, even though they may not remain with Thee but, as I used to do, with a thousand distractions, and with worldly thoughts. In return for this violence which they offer to themselves for the purpose of remaining in a company so good as Thine—for at first they can do no more, and even afterwards at times—Thou, O Lord, defendest them against the assaults of evil spirits, whose power Thou restrainest, and even lessenest daily, giving to them the victory over these enemies. So it is, O Life of all lives, Thou slayest none that put their trust in Thee, and seek Thy friendship; yea, rather, Thou sustainest their bodily life in greater vigour, and makest their soul to live.

10. I do not understand what there can be to make them afraid who are afraid to begin mental prayer, nor do I know what it is they dread. The devil does well to bring this fear upon us, that he may really hurt us; if, by putting me in fear, he can make me cease from thinking of my offences against God, of the great debt I owe Him, of the existence of heaven and hell, and of the great sorrows and trials He underwent for me. That was all my prayer, and had been, when I was in this dangerous state, and it was on those subjects I dwelt whenever I could; and very often, for some years, I was more occupied with the wish to see the end of the time I had appointed for myself to spend in prayer, and in watching the hour-glass, than with other thoughts that were good. If a sharp penance had been laid upon me, I know of none that I would not very often have willingly undertaken, rather than prepare myself for prayer by self-recollection. And certainly the violence with which Satan assailed me was so irresistible, or my evil habits were so strong, that I did not betake myself to prayer; and the sadness I felt on entering the oratory was so great, that it required all the courage I had to force myself in. They say of

me that my courage is not slight, and it is known that God has given me a courage beyond that of a woman; but I have made a bad use of it. In the end our Lord came to my help; and then, when I had done this violence to myself, I found greater peace and joy than I sometimes had when I had a desire to pray.

11. If, then, our Lord bore so long with me, who was so wicked—and it is plain that it was by prayer all my evil was corrected—why should any one, how wicked soever he may be, have any fear? Let him be ever so wicked, he will not remain in his wickedness so many years as I did, after receiving so many graces from our Lord. Is there any one who can despair, when He bore so long with me, only because I desired and contrived to find some place and some opportunities for Him to be alone with me—and that very often against my will? for I did violence to myself, or rather our Lord Himself did violence to me.

12. If, then, to those who do not serve God, but rather offend Him, prayer be all this, and so necessary, and if no one can really find out any harm it can do him, and if the omission of it be not a still greater harm, why, then, should they abstain from it who serve and desire to serve God? Certainly I cannot comprehend it, unless it be that men have a mind to go through the troubles of this life in greater misery, and to shut the door in the face of God, so that He shall give them no comfort in it. I am most truly sorry for them, because they serve God at their own cost; for of those who pray, God Himself defrays the charges, seeing that for a little trouble He gives sweetness, in order that, by the help it supplies, they may bear their trials.

13. But because I have much to say hereafter of this sweetness, which our Lord gives to those who persevere in prayer, I do not speak of it here; only this will I say: prayer is the door to those great graces which our Lord bestowed upon me. If this door be shut, I do not see how He can bestow them; for even if He entered into a soul to take His delight therein, and to make that soul also delight in Him, there is no way by which He can do so; for His will is, that such a soul should be lonely and pure, with a great desire to receive His graces. If we put many hindrances in the way, and take no pains whatever to remove them, how can He come to us, and how can we have any desire that He should show us His great mercies?

14. I will speak now—for it is very important to understand it—of the assaults which Satan directs against a soul for the purpose of taking it, and of the contrivances and compassion wherewith our Lord labours to convert it to Himself, in order that men may behold His mercy, and the great good it was for me that I did not give up prayer and spiritual reading, and that they may be on their guard against the dangers against which I was not on my guard myself. And, above all, I implore them for the love of our Lord, and for the great love with which He goeth about seeking our conversion to Himself, to beware of the occasions of sin; for once placed therein, we have no ground to rest on—so many enemies then assail us, and our own weakness is such, that we cannot defend ourselves.

15. Oh, that I knew how to describe the captivity of my soul in those days. I understood perfectly that I was in captivity, but I could not understand the nature of it; neither could I entirely believe that those things which my confessors did not make so much of were so wrong as I in my soul felt them to be. One of them—I had gone to him with a scruple—told me that, even if I were raised to high contemplation, those occasions and conversations were not unfitting for me. This was towards the end, when, by the grace of God, I was withdrawing more and more from those great dangers, but not wholly from the occasions of them.

16. When they saw my good desires, and how I occupied myself in prayer, I seemed to them to have done much; but my soul knew that this was not doing what I was bound to do for Him to Whom I owed so much. I am sorry for my poor soul even now, because of its great sufferings, and the little help it had from any one except God, and for the wide door that man opened for it, that it might go forth to its pastimes and pleasures, when they said that these things were lawful.

17. Then there was the torture of sermons, and that not a slight one; for I was very fond of them. If I heard any one preach well and with unction, I felt, without my seeking it, a particular affection for him, neither do I know whence it came. Thus, no sermon ever seemed to me so bad, but that I listened to it with pleasure; though, according to others who heard it, the preaching was not good. If it was a good sermon, it was to me a most special refreshment. To speak of God, or to hear Him spoken

of, never wearied me. I am speaking of the time after I gave myself to prayer. At one time I had great comfort in sermons, at another they distressed me, because they made me feel that I was very far from being what I ought to have been.

18. I used to pray to our Lord for help; but, as it now seems to me, I must have committed the fault of not putting my whole trust in His Majesty, and of not thoroughly distrusting myself. I sought for help, took great pains; but it must be that I did not understand how all is of little profit if we do not root out all confidence in ourselves, and place it wholly in God. I wished to live, but I saw clearly that I was not living, but rather wrestling with the shadow of death; there was no one to give me life, and I was not able to take it. He Who could have given it me had good reasons for not coming to my aid, seeing that He had brought me back to Himself so many times, and I as often had left Him.

CHAPTER IX

THE MEANS WHEREBY OUR LORD QUICKENED HER SOUL, GAVE HER LIGHT IN HER DARKNESS, AND MADE HER STRONG IN GOODNESS

By what means God began to rouse her soul and give light in the midst of darkness, and to strengthen her virtues so that she should not offend Him.

1. My soul was now grown weary; and the miserable habits it had contracted would not suffer it to rest, though it was desirous of doing so. It came to pass one day, when I went into the oratory, that I saw a statue which they had put by there, and which had been procured for a certain feast observed in the house. It was a representation of Christ most grievously wounded; and so devotional, that the very sight of it, when I saw it, moved me—so well did it show forth that which He suffered for us. So keenly did I feel the evil return I had made for those wounds, that I thought my heart was breaking. I threw myself on the ground beside it, my tears flowing plenteously, and implored Him to strengthen me once for all, so that I might never offend Him any more.

2. I had a very great devotion to the glorious Magdalene, and very frequently used to think of her conversion—especially when

I went to Communion. As I knew for certain that our Lord was then within me, I used to place myself at His feet, thinking that my tears would not be despised. I did not know what I was saying; only He did great things for me, in that He was pleased I should shed those tears, seeing that I so soon forgot that impression. I used to recommend myself to that glorious Saint, that she might obtain my pardon.

3. But this last time, before that picture of which I am speaking, I seem to have made greater progress; for I was now very distrustful to myself, placing all my confidence in God. It seems to me that I said to Him then that I would not rise up till He granted my petition. I do certainly believe that this was of great service to me, because I have grown better ever since.[1]

4. This was my method of prayer: as I could not make reflections with my understanding, I contrived to picture Christ as within me; and I used to find myself the better for thinking of those mysteries of His life during which He was most lonely. It seemed to me that the being alone and afflicted, like a person in trouble, must needs permit me to come near unto Him.

5. I did many simple things of this kind; and in particular I used to find myself most at home in the prayer in the Garden, whither I went in His company. I thought of the bloody sweat, and of the affliction He endured there; I wished, if it had been possible, to wipe away that painful sweat from His face; but I remember that I never dared to form such a resolution—my sins stood before me so grievously. I used to remain with Him there as long as my thoughts allowed me, and I had many thoughts to torment me. For many years, nearly every night before I fell asleep, when I recommended myself to God, that I might sleep in peace, I used always to think a little of this mystery of the prayer in the Garden—yea, even before I was a nun, because I had been told that many indulgences were to be gained thereby. For my part, I believe that my soul gained very much in this way, because I began to practise prayer without knowing what it was; and, now that it had become my constant habit, I was saved from omitting it, as I was from omitting to bless myself with the sign of the cross before I slept.

[1] About the year 1555.

6. And now to go back to what I was saying of the torture which my thoughts inflicted upon me. This method of praying, in which the understanding makes no reflections, hath this property: the soul must gain much, or lose. I mean, that those who advance without meditation make great progress, because it is done by love. But to attain to this involves great labour, except to those persons whom it is our Lord's good pleasure to lead quickly to the prayer of quiet. I know of some. For those who walk in this way, a book is profitable, that by the help thereof they may the more quickly recollect themselves. It was a help to me also to look on fields, water, and flowers. In them I saw traces of the Creator —I mean, that the sight of these things was as a book unto me; it roused me, made me recollected, and reminded me of my ingratitude and of my sins. My understanding was so dull that I could never represent in the imagination either heavenly or high things in any form whatever, until our Lord placed them before me in another way.

7. I was so little able to put things before me by the help of my understanding, that, unless I saw a thing with my eyes, my imagination was of no use whatever. I could not do as others do, who can put matters before themselves so as to become thereby recollected. I was able to think of Christ only as man. But so it was; and I never could form any image of Him to myself, though I read much of His beauty, and looked at pictures of Him. I was like one who is blind, or in the dark, who, though speaking to a person present, and feeling his presence, because he knows for certain that he is present—I mean, that he understands him to be present, and believes it—yet does not see him. It was thus with me when I used to think of our Lord. This is why I was so fond of images. Wretched are they who, through their own fault, have lost this blessing; it is clear enough that they do not love our Lord—for if they loved Him, they would rejoice at the sight of His picture, just as men find pleasure when they see the portrait of one they love.

8. At this time, the *Confessions* of St. Augustine were given me. Our Lord seems to have so ordained it, for I did not seek them myself, neither had I ever seen them before. I had a very great devotion to St. Augustine, because the monastery in which

I lived when I was yet in the world was of his Order;[1] and also because he had been a sinner—for I used to find great comfort in those Saints whom, after they had sinned, our Lord converted to Himself. I thought they would help me, and that, as our Lord had forgiven them, so also He would forgive me. One thing, however, there was that troubled me—I have spoken of it before [2] —our Lord had called them but once, and they never relapsed; while my relapses were now so many. This it was that vexed me. But calling to mind the love that He bore me, I took courage again. Of His mercy I never doubted once, but I did very often of myself.

9. O my God, I am amazed at the hardness of my heart amidst so many succours from Thee. I am filled with dread when I see how little I could do with myself, and how I was clogged, so that I could not resolve to give myself entirely to God. When I began to read the *Confessions*, I thought I saw myself there described, and began to recommend myself greatly to this glorious Saint. When I came to his conversion, and read how he heard that voice in the garden,[3] it seemed to me nothing less than that our Lord had uttered it for me: I felt so in my heart. I remained for some time lost in tears, in great inward affliction and distress. O my God, what a soul has to suffer because it has lost the liberty it had of being mistress over itself! And what torments it has to endure! I wonder now how I could live in torments so great: God be praised Who gave me life, so that I might escape from so fatal a death! I believe that my soul obtained great strength from His Divine Majesty, and that He must have heard my cry, and had compassion upon so many tears.

[1] Ch. ii. 8.

[2] In the Prologue.

[3] St. Augustine, being in great trouble, heard a voice from the house next door, as of boys and girls singing: "Take and read, take and read." Believing these words to be a supernatural answer to his questionings, he took a volume of the Epistles, and, opening it at random, his eyes fell on the words: "Let us walk honestly as in the day: not in rioting and drunkenness, not in chambering and impurities, not in contention and envy: But put ye on the Lord Jesus Christ, and make not provision for the flesh in its concupiscences" (Rom. xiii. 13, 14). This proved the turning-point in his life. *Confess.* bk. viii. chap. xii, § 29.

10. A desire to spend more time with Him began to grow within me, and also to withdraw from the occasions of sin: for as soon as I had done so, I turned lovingly to His Majesty at once. I understood clearly, as I thought, that I loved Him; but I did not understand, as I ought to have understood it, wherein the true love of God consists. I do not think I had yet perfectly disposed myself to seek His service when His Majesty turned towards me with His consolations. What others strive after with great labour, our Lord seems to have looked out for a way to make me willing to accept—that is, in these later years to give me joy and comfort. But as for asking our Lord to give me either these things or sweetness in devotion, I never dared to do it; the only thing I prayed Him to give me was the grace never to offend Him; together with the forgiveness of my great sins. When I saw that my sins were so great, I never ventured deliberately to ask for consolation or for sweetness. He had compassion enough upon me, I think—and, in truth, He dealt with me according to His great mercy—when He allowed me to stand before Him, and when He drew me into His presence; for I saw that, if He had not drawn me, I should not have come at all.

11. Once only in my life do I remember asking for consolation, being at the time in great aridities. When I considered what I had done, I was so confounded, that the very distress I suffered from seeing how little humility I had, brought me that which I had been so bold as to ask for. I knew well that it was lawful to pray for it; but it seemed to me that it is lawful only for those who are in good dispositions, who have sought with all their might to attain to true devotion—that is, not to offend God, and to be disposed and resolved for all goodness. I looked upon those tears of mine as womanish and weak, seeing that I did not obtain my desires by them; nevertheless, I believe that they did me some service; for, specially after those two occasions of great compunction and sorrow of heart, accompanied by tears, of which I am speaking, I began in an especial way to give myself more to prayer, and to occupy myself less with those things which did me harm—though I did not give them up altogether. But God Himself, as I have just said, came to my aid, and helped me to turn away from them. As His Majesty was only waiting for some preparation on my part, the spiritual graces grew in me as I shall

now explain. It is not the custom of the Lord to give these graces to any but to those who keep their consciences in greater pureness.

CHAPTER X

THE GRACES SHE RECEIVED IN PRAYER. WHAT WE CAN DO OUR-
SELVES. THE GREAT IMPORTANCE OF UNDERSTANDING WHAT OUR
LORD IS DOING FOR US. SHE DESIRES HER CONFESSORS TO KEEP HER
WRITINGS SECRET, BECAUSE OF THE SPECIAL GRACES OF OUR LORD
TO HER, WHICH THEY HAD COMMANDED HER TO DESCRIBE

*She begins to explain the graces God gave her in prayer, and how much
we can do for ourselves, and of the importance of understanding God's
mercies towards us. She requests those to whom this is to be sent to keep
the remainder (of this book) secret, since they have commanded her to go
into so many details about the graces God has shown her.*

1. I USED to have at times, as I have said, though it used to pass quickly away—certain commencements of that which I am going now to describe. When I formed those pictures within myself of throwing myself at the feet of Christ, as I said before,[1] and sometimes even when I was reading, a feeling of the presence of God would come over me unexpectedly, so that I could in no wise doubt either that He was within me, or that I was wholly absorbed in Him. It was not by way of vision; I believe it was what is called mystical theology. The soul is suspended in such a way that it seems to be utterly beside itself. The will loves; the memory, so it seems to me, is as it were lost; and the under-standing, so I think, makes no reflections—yet is not lost: as I have just said, it is not at work, but it stands as if amazed at the greatness of the things that it understands; for God wills it to understand that it understands nothing whatever of that which His Majesty places before it.

2. Before this, I had a certain tenderness of soul which was very abiding, partially attainable, I believe, in some measure, by our own efforts: a consolation which is not wholly in the senses, nor yet altogether in the spirit, but is all of it the gift of God. However, I think we can contribute much towards the attaining

[1] Ch. ix. 4.

of it by considering our vileness and our ingratitude towards God—the great things He has done for us—His Passion, with its grievous pains—and His life, so full of sorrows; also, by rejoicing in the contemplation of His works, of His greatness, and of the love that He bears us. Many other considerations there are which he who really desires to make progress will often stumble on, though he may not be very much on the watch for them. If with this there be a little love, the soul is comforted, the heart is softened, and tears flow. Sometimes it seems that we do violence to ourselves and weep; at other times, our Lord seems to do so, so that we have no power to resist Him. His Majesty seems to reward this slight carefulness of ours with so grand a gift as is this consolation which he ministers to the soul of seeing itself weeping for so great a Lord. I am not surprised; for the soul has reason enough, and more than enough, for its joy. Here it comforts itself—here it rejoices.

3. The comparison which now presents itself seems to me to be good. These joys in prayer are like what those of heaven must be. As the vision of the saints, which is measured by their merits here, reaches no further than our Lord wills, and as the blessed see how little merit they had, every one of them is satisfied with the place assigned him: there being the very greatest difference between one joy and another in heaven, and much greater than between one spiritual joy and another on earth—which is, however, very great. And in truth, in the beginning, a soul in which God works this grace thinks that now it has scarcely anything more to desire, and counts itself abundantly rewarded for all the service it has rendered Him. And there is reason for this: for one of those tears—which, as I have just said, are almost in our own power, though without God nothing can be done—cannot, in my opinion, be purchased with all the labours of the world, because of the great gain it brings us. And what greater gain can we have than some testimony of our having pleased God? Let him, then, who shall have attained to this, give praise unto God—acknowledge himself to be one of His greatest debtors; because it seems to be His will to take him into His house, having chosen him for His kingdom, if he does not turn back.

4. Let him not regard certain kinds of humility which exist, and of which I mean to speak. Some think it humility not to be-

lieve that God is bestowing His gifts upon them. Let us clearly understand this, and that it is perfectly clear God bestows His gifts without any merit whatever on our part; and let us be grateful to His Majesty for them; for if we do not recognize the gifts received at His hands, we shall never be moved to love Him. It is a most certain truth, that the richer we see ourselves to be, confessing at the same time our poverty, the greater will be our progress, and the more real our humility.

5. An opposite course tends to take away all courage; for we shall begin to think ourselves incapable of great blessings, if we begin to frighten ourselves with the dread of vain-glory when our Lord begins to show His mercy upon us. Let us believe that He Who gives these gifts will also, when the devil begins to tempt us herein, give us the grace to detect him, and the strength to resist him—that is, He will do so if we walk in simplicity before God, aiming at pleasing Him only, and not men. It is a most evident truth, that our love for a person is greater, the more distinctly we remember the good he has done us.

6. If, then, it is lawful, and so meritorious, always to remember that we have our being from God, that He has created us out of nothing, that He preserves us, and also to remember all the benefits of His death and Passion, which He suffered long before He made us, for every one of us now alive—why should it not be lawful for me to discern, confess, and consider often that I was once accustomed to speak of vanities, and that now our Lord has given me the grace to speak only of Himself?

7. Here, then, is a precious pearl, which, when we remember that it is given us, and that we have it in possession, powerfully invites us to love. All this is the fruit of prayer founded on humility. What, then, will it be when we shall find ourselves in possession of other pearls of greater price, such as contempt of the world and of self, which some servants of God have already received? It is clear that such souls must consider themselves greater debtors—under greater obligations to serve Him: we must acknowledge that we have nothing of ourselves, and confess the munificence of our Lord, Who, on a soul so wretched and poor, and so utterly undeserving, as mine is,—for whom the first of these pearls was enough, and more than enough,—would bestow greater riches than I could desire.

8. We must renew our strength to serve Him, and strive not to be ungrateful, because it is on this condition that our Lord dispenses His treasures; for if we do not make a good use of them, and of the high estate to which He raises us, He will return and take them from us, and we shall be poorer than ever. His Majesty will give the pearls to him who shall bring them forth and employ them usefully for himself and others. For how shall he be useful, and how shall he spend liberally, who does not know that he is rich? It is not possible, I think, our nature being what it is, that he can have the courage necessary for great things who does not know that God is on his side; for so miserable are we, so inclined to the things of this world, that he can hardly have any real abhorrence of, with great detachment from, all earthly things, who does not see that he holds some pledges for those things that are above. It is by these gifts that our Lord gives us that strength which we through our sins have lost.

9. A man will hardly wish to be held in contempt and abhorrence, nor will he seek after the other great virtues to which the perfect attain, if he has not some pledges of the love which God bears him, together with a living faith. Our nature is so dead, that we go after that which we see immediately before us; and it is these graces, therefore, that quicken and strengthen our faith. It may well be that I, who am so wicked, measure others by myself, and that others require nothing more than the verities of the faith, in order to render their works most perfect; while I, wretched that I am! have need of everything.

10. Others will explain this. I speak from my own experience, as I have been commanded; and if what I say be not correct, let him [1] to whom I send it destroy it; for he knows better than I do what is wrong in it. I entreat him, for the love of our Lord, to publish abroad what I have thus far said of my wretched life, and of my sins. I give him leave to do so; and to all my confessors also—of whom he is one—to whom this is to be sent, if it be their pleasure, even during my life, so that I may no longer deceive people who think there must be some good in me. Certainly, I

[1] F. Pedro Ibañez, of the Order of St. Dominic, of the monastery of San Esteban at Salamanca, but for some years reader of divinity at Santo Tomás at Avila.

speak in all sincerity, so far as I understand myself. Such publication will give me great comfort.

11. But as to that which I am now going to say, I give no such leave; nor, if it be shown to any one, do I consent to its being said who the person is whose experience it describes, nor who wrote it. This is why I mention neither my own name, nor that of any other person whatever. I have written it in the best way I could, in order not to be known; and this I beg of them for the love of God. Persons so learned and grave as they are have authority enough to approve of whatever right things I may say, should our Lord give me the grace to do so; and if I should say anything of the kind, it will be His, and not mine—because I am neither learned nor of good life, and I have no person of learning or any other to teach me; for they only who ordered me to write know that I am writing, and at this moment they are not here. I have, as it were, to steal the time, and that with difficulty, because my writing hinders me from spinning. I am living in a house that is poor, and have many things to do. If, indeed, our Lord had given me greater abilities and a better memory, I might then profit by what I have seen and read; but my abilities are very slight. If, then, I should say anything that is right, our Lord will have it said for some good purpose; that which may be wrong will be mine, and your reverence will strike it out.

12. In neither case will it be of any use to publish my name: during my life, it is clear that no good I may have done ought to be told; after death, there is no reason against it, except that it will lose all authority and credit, because related of a person so vile and so wicked as I am. And because I think your reverence and the others who may see this writing will do this, that I ask of you, for the love of our Lord, I write with freedom. If it were not so, I should have great scruples except in declaring my sins: and in that matter I should have none at all. For the rest, it is enough that I am a woman to make my sails droop; how much more, then, when I am a woman, and a wicked one?

13. So, then, everything here beyond the simple story of my life your reverence must take upon yourself—since you have so pressed me to give some account of the graces which our Lord bestowed upon me in prayer—if it be consistent with the truths of our holy Catholic faith; if it be not, your reverence must burn it

at once—for I give my consent. I will recount my experience, in order that, if it be consistent with those truths, your reverence may make some use of it; if not, you will deliver my soul from delusion, so that Satan may gain nothing there where I seemed to be gaining myself. Our Lord knows well that I, as I shall show hereafter, have always laboured to find out those who could give me light.

14. How clear soever I may wish to make my account of that which relates to prayer, it will be obscure enough for those who are without experience. I shall speak of certain hindrances, which, as I understand it, keep men from advancing on this road—and of other things which are dangerous, as our Lord has taught me by experience. I have also discussed the matter with men of great learning, with persons who for many years had lived spiritual lives, who admit that in the twenty-seven years only during which I have given myself to prayer—though I walked so ill, and stumbled so often on the road—His Majesty granted me that experience which others attain to in seven-and-thirty, or seven-and-forty years; and they, too, being persons who ever advanced in the way of penance and of virtue.

15. Blessed be God for all, and may His infinite Majesty make use of me! Our Lord knoweth well that I have no other end in this than that He may be praised and magnified a little, when men shall see that on a dunghill so foul and rank He has made a garden of flowers so sweet. May it please His Majesty that I may not by my own fault root them out, and become again what I was before. And I entreat your reverence, for the love of our Lord, to beg this of Him for me, seeing that you have a clearer knowledge of what I am than you have allowed me to give of myself here.

6. BROTHER LAWRENCE:

THE PRACTICE OF THE PRESENCE OF GOD

¶Brother Lawrence was the name in religion of Nicholas Herman of Lorraine, who served as a soldier, was later employed as a footman, and then entered the order of the Barefooted Carmelites in Paris. He was over eighty when he died, in 1691. Brother Lawrence enjoyed a reputation for sanctity, so that at various times prelates and others sought his company. Thus there came to be the "Conversations on the Practice of the Presence of God," by M. Beaufort, Vicar of Cardinal de Noailles. The book was first published in 1692, and has since been widely reprinted. It is a minor spiritual classic, but one which continues to please and help many in almost all the countries of the world.*

FROM THE PREFACE TO THE ORIGINAL EDITION
1692

¶Although death has carried off last year many of the Order of Carmelites Déchaussés, brethren who have left in dying rare legacies of lives of virtue, Providence, it would seem, has desired that the eyes of men should be cast chiefly on Brother Lawrence, and has made his death the occasion of showing forth the merit of this holy man, who all his life had studied to avoid the gaze of men, and whose saintliness is only fully seen now that he is dead.

Several persons having seen a copy of one of his letters, have desired to see more; and to meet this wish, care has been taken to collect as many as possible of those which Brother Lawrence wrote with his own hand.

* From *The Practice of the Presence of God*. By Brother Lawrence. London: Methuen and Co. N.D.

These letters are so edifying, so rich in unction, and have been found so full of delight by those who have had the joy of reading them, that the first readers have desired not to be alone in profiting by them. It is at their wish that the letters have been printed, for they judge that these writings will prove very useful to souls who are pressing forward to perfection by the Practice of the Presence of God.

All Christians will find herein much that is edifying. Those in the thick of the great world will learn from these letters how greatly they deceive themselves, seeking for peace and joy in the false glitter of the things that are seen, yet temporal: those who are seeking the Highest Good will gain from this book strength to persevere in the practice of virtue. All, whatever their life-work, will find profit, for they will see herein a brother, busied as they are in outward affairs, who in the midst of the most exacting occupations, has learnt so well to accord action with contemplation, that for the space of more than forty years he hardly ever turned from the Presence of God.

CONVERSATIONS

FIRST CONVERSATION

August 3rd, 1666

THE first time I saw *Brother Lawrence* was upon the third of August 1666. He told me that God had done him a singular favour, in his conversion at the age of eighteen.

That in the winter, seeing a tree stripped of its leaves and considering that within a little time the leaves would be renewed, and after that the flowers and fruit appear, he received a high view of the Providence and Power of God, which has never since been effaced from his soul. That this view had set him perfectly loose from the world, and kindled in him such a love for God, that he could not tell whether it had increased in above forty years that he had lived since.

That he had been footman to M. Fieubert, the treasurer, and that he was a great awkward fellow, who broke everything.

That he had desired to be received into a monastery, thinking that he would there be made to smart for his awkwardness, and the faults he should commit: but that GOD had disappointed him, he having met with nothing but satisfaction in that state.

That we should establish ourselves in a sense of GOD's Presence, by continually conversing with Him. That it was a shameful thing to quit His conversation to think of trifles and fooleries.

That we should feed and nourish our souls with high notions of GOD; which would yield us great joy in being devoted to Him.

That we ought to *quicken, i.e. to enliven our faith*. That it was lamentable that we had so little; and that instead of taking *faith* for the rule of their conduct, men amused themselves with trivial devotions, which changed daily. That the way of faith was the spirit of the Church, and that it was sufficient to bring us to a high degree of perfection.

That we ought to give ourselves up entirely to GOD, with regard both to things temporal and spiritual, and seek our satisfaction only in the fulfilling of His will, whether He lead us by suffering or by consolation; for all would be equal to a soul truly resigned. That there was need of fidelity in those times of dryness, or insensibility and irksomeness in prayer, by which GOD tries our love to Him: that *then* was the time for us to make good and effectual acts of resignation, whereof one alone would oftentimes very much promote our spiritual advancement.

That as for the miseries and sins he heard of daily in the world, he was so far from wondering at them, that, on the contrary, he was surprised that there were not more, considering the malice sinners were capable of: that for his part, he prayed for them; but knowing that GOD could remedy the mischiefs they did, when He pleased, he gave himself no farther trouble.

That to arrive at such resignation as GOD requires, we should watch attentively over all the passions, which mingle as well in spiritual things as those of a grosser nature; that GOD would give light concerning those passions to those who truly desire to serve Him. That if this was my design, viz., sincerely to serve GOD, I might come to him (B. Lawrence) as often as I pleased, without any fear of being troublesome; but, if not, that I ought no more to visit him.

SECOND CONVERSATION

September 28th, 1666

THAT he had always been governed by love without selfish views; and that having resolved to make the love of GOD the *end* of all his actions, he had found good reason to be well satisfied with his method. That he was pleased, when he could take up a straw from the ground for the love of GOD, seeking Him only, and nothing else, not even His gifts.

That he had been long troubled in mind from a sure belief that he was lost; that all the men in the world could not have persuaded him to the contrary; but that he had thus reasoned with himself about it: *I did not engage in a religious life but for the love of* GOD, *and I have endeavoured to act only for Him: whatever becomes of me, whether I be lost or saved, I will always continue to act purely for the love of* GOD. *I shall have this good at least, that till death I shall have done all that is in me to love him.* That this trouble of mind had lasted four years, during which time he had suffered much.

That since that time he had passed his life in perfect liberty and continual joy. That he placed his sins betwixt him and GOD, as it were to tell Him that he did not deserve His favours; but that GOD still continued to bestow them in abundance.

That in order to form a habit of conversing with GOD continually, and referring all we do to Him, we must at first apply to Him with some diligence: but that after a little care we should find His love inwardly excite us to it without any difficulty.

That he expected, after the pleasant days GOD had given him, he should have his turn of pain and suffering; but that he was not uneasy about it, knowing very well, that as he could do nothing of himself, GOD would not fail to give him the strength to bear them.

That when an occasion of practising some virtue offered, he addressed himself to GOD, saying, LORD, *I cannot do this unless Thou enablest me:* and that then he received strength more than sufficient.

That when he had failed in his duty, he simply confessed his fault, saying to GOD, *I shall never do otherwise, if Thou leavest me to myself; 'tis Thou must hinder my falling, and mend what is amiss.* That after this, he gave himself no farther uneasiness about it.

That we ought to act with GOD in the greatest simplicity, speaking to Him frankly and plainly, and imploring His assistance in our affairs, just as they happen. That GOD never failed to grant it, as he had often experienced.

That he had been lately sent into Burgundy to buy the provision of wine for the Society, which was a very unwelcome task to him, because he had no turn for business, and because he was lame, and could not go about the boat, but by rolling himself over the casks. That, however, he gave himself no uneasiness about it, nor about the purchase of the wine. That he said to GOD, *It was His business he was about;* and that he afterwards found it very well performed. That he had been sent into Auvergne the year before upon the same account; that he could not tell how the matter passed, but that it proved very well.

So likewise in his business in the kitchen (to which he had naturally a great aversion), having accustomed himself to do everything there for the love of GOD, and with prayer, upon all occasions, for His grace to do his work well, he had found everything easy during the fifteen years that he had been employed there.

That he was very well pleased with the post he was now in; but that he was as ready to quit that as the former, since he was always finding pleasure in every condition by doing little things for the love of GOD.

That with him the *set* times of prayer were not different from other times. That he retired to pray according to the directions of his Superior: but that he did not want such retirement, nor ask for it, because his greatest business did not divert him from GOD.

That as he knew his obligation to love GOD in all things, and as he endeavoured so to do, he had no need of a "director" to advise him; but that he needed much a "confessor" to absolve him. That he was very sensible of his faults, but not discouraged by them: that he confessed them to GOD, and did not plead against Him to excuse them. When he had so done, he peaceably resumed his usual practice of love and adoration.

That in his trouble of mind, he had consulted nobody: but knowing only by the light of faith that GOD was present, he contented himself with directing all his actions to Him, *i.e.* doing them with a desire to please Him, let what would come of it.

That useless thoughts spoil all: that the mischief began there: but that we ought to be diligent to reject them as soon as we perceived their impertinence to the matter in hand, or to our salvation, and return to our communion with GOD.

That at the beginning he had often passed his time appointed for prayer, in rejecting wandering thoughts and falling back into them. That he could never regulate his devotion by certain methods, as some do. That, nevertheless, at first he had *meditated* for some time, but afterwards that went off, in a manner he could give no account of.

That all bodily mortifications and other exercises are useless, but as they serve to arrive at the union with GOD by love: that he had well considered this, and found it the shortest way, to go straight to Him by a continual practice of love, and doing all things for His sake.

That we ought to make a great difference between the acts of the *understanding* and those of the *will*; that the first were comparatively of little value, and the others all. That our only business was to love and delight ourselves in GOD.

That all possible kinds of mortification, if they were void of the love of GOD, could not efface a single sin. That we ought, without anxiety, to expect the pardon of our sins from the blood of JESUS CHRIST, labouring simply to love Him with all our hearts. That GOD seemed to have granted the greatest favours to the greatest sinners, as more signal monuments of His mercy.

That the greatest pains or pleasures of this world were not to be compared with what he had experienced of both kinds in a spiritual state: so that he was careful for nothing, and feared nothing, desiring but one thing only of GOD, viz., that the might not offend Him.

That he had no qualms; for said he, when I *fail* in my duty, I readily acknowledge it, saying, *I am used to do so: I shall never do otherwise, if I am left to myself.* If I fail not, then I give GOD thanks, acknowledging that it comes from Him.

THIRD CONVERSATION

November 22nd, 1666

He told me that the *foundation of the spiritual life* in *him* had been a high notion and esteem of God in faith; which when he had once well conceived, he had no other care, but faithfully to reject at once every other thought, *that he might perform all his actions for the love of God.* That when sometimes he had not thought of God for a good while, he did not disquiet himself for it; but after having acknowledged his wretchedness to God, he returned to Him with so much the greater trust in Him, by how much he found himself more wretched to have forgotten Him.

That the trust we put in God honours Him much, and draws down great graces.

That it was impossible, not only that God should deceive, but also that He should long let a soul suffer which is perfectly surrendered to Him, and resolved to endure everything for His sake.

That he had so often experienced the ready succour of Divine Grace upon all occasions, that from the same experience, when he had business to do, he did not think of it beforehand; but when it was time to do it, he found in God, as in a clear mirror, all that was fit for him to do. That of late he had acted thus, without anticipating care; but before the experience above mentioned, he had been full of care and anxiety in his affairs.

That he had no recollection of what things he had done, once they were past, and hardly realised them when he was about them: that on leaving table, he knew not what he had been eating; but that with one single end in view, he did all for the love of God, rendering Him thanks for that He had directed these acts, and an infinity of others throughout his life: he did all very simply, in a manner which kept him ever steadfastly in the loving Presence of God.

When outward business diverted him a little from the thought of God, a fresh remembrance coming from God invested his soul, and so inflamed and transported him, that it was difficult for him to restrain himself.

That he was more united to God in his ordinary occupations,

than when he left them for devotion in retirement, from which he knew himself to issue with much dryness of spirit.

That he expected hereafter some great pain of body or mind; that the worst that could happen to him would be to lose that sense of GOD, which he had enjoyed so long; but that the goodness of GOD assured him that he would not forsake him utterly, and that he would give to him strength to bear whatever evil He permitted to befall him: and that he therefore feared nothing, and had no occasion to take counsel with anybody about his soul. That when he had attempted to do it, he had always come away more perplexed; and that as he was conscious of his readiness to lay down his life for the love of GOD, he had no apprehension of danger. That perfect abandonment to GOD was the sure way to heaven, a way on which we had always sufficient light for our conduct.

That in the beginning of the spiritual life, we ought to be faithful in doing our duty and denying ourselves; but after that, unspeakable pleasures followed. That in difficulties we need only have recourse to JESUS CHRIST, and beg His grace, with which everything became easy.

That many do not advance in the Christian progress because they stick in penances and particular exercises, while they neglect the love of GOD which is the *end;* that this appeared plainly by their works, and was the reason why we see so little solid virtue.

That there was need neither of art nor science for going to GOD, but only a heart resolutely determined to apply itself to nothing but Him, or for *His* sake, and to love Him only.

FOURTH CONVERSATION

November 25th, 1667

HE discoursed with me very fervently and with great openness of heart, concerning his manner of *going to* GOD, whereof some part is related already.

He told me, that all consists *in one hearty renunciation* of everything which we are sensible does not lead us to God, in order that we may accustom ourselves to a continual conversation with

Him, without mystery and in simplicity. That we need only to recognise GOD intimately present with us, and to address ourselves to Him every moment, that we may beg His assistance for getting to know His will in things doubtful, and for rightly performing those which we plainly see He requires of us; offering them to Him before we do them, and giving to Him thanks when we have done.

That in this conversation with GOD, we are also employed in praising, adoring, and loving Him unceasingly, for His infinite goodness and perfection.

That without being discouraged on account of our sins, we should pray for His grace with a perfect confidence, relying upon the infinite merits of OUR LORD. That GOD never failed offering to us His grace at every action: that he distinctly perceived it, and never failed of it, unless when his thoughts had wandered from a sense of GOD's Presence, or he had forgotten to ask His assistance.

That GOD always gave us light in our doubts, when we had no other design but to please Him, and to act for His love.

That our sanctification did not depend upon changing our works, but in doing that for GOD's sake, which commonly we do for our own. That it was lamentable to see how many people mistook the means for the end, addicting themselves to certain works, which they performed very imperfectly, by reason of their human or selfish regards.

That the most excellent method which he had found of going to GOD, was that of *doing our common business* without any view of pleasing men,[1] and (as far as we are capable) *purely for the love of* GOD.

That it was a great delusion to think that the times of prayer ought to differ from other times: that we were as strictly obliged to adhere to GOD by action in the time of action as by prayer in its season.

That his view of prayer was nothing else but a sense of the Presence of GOD, his soul being at that time insensible to everything but Divine Love. That when the appointed times of prayer were passed, he found no difference, because he still continued

[1] Gal. i. 10; Eph. vi. 5, 6.

with GOD, praising and blessing Him with all his might, so that he passed his life in continual joy; yet hoped that GOD would give him somewhat to suffer, when he should have grown stronger.

That we ought, once for all, heartily to put our whole trust in GOD, and make a full surrender of ourselves to Him, secure that He would not deceive us.

That we ought not to be weary of doing little things for the love of GOD, for He regards not the greatness of the work, but the love with which it is performed. That we should not wonder if, in the beginning, we often failed in our endeavours; but that, at last, we should gain a habit, which would naturally produce its acts in us, without our care, and to our exceeding great delight.

That the whole substance of religion was faith, hope, and love; by the practice of which we become united to the will of GOD: that all beside is indifferent, and to be used only as a means, that we may arrive at our end, and be swallowed up therein, by faith and love.

That all things are possible to him who *believes*, that they are less difficult to him who *hopes*, that they are easier to him who *loves*, and still more easy to him who perseveres in the practice of these three virtues.

That the end we ought to propose to ourselves, is to become, in this life, the most perfect worshippers of GOD we can possibly be, as we hope to be through all eternity.

That when we enter upon the spiritual life, we should consider and examine to the bottom, what we are. And then we should find ourselves worthy of all contempt, and such as do not deserve the names of Christians, subject to all kinds of misery, and numberless accidents which trouble us, and cause perpetual vicissitudes in our health, in our humours, in our internal and external dispositions: in fine, persons whom GOD would humble by many pains and labours, as well within as without. After this, we should not wonder that troubles, temptations, oppositions, and contradictions happen to us from men. We ought, on the contrary, to submit ourselves to them, and bear them as long as GOD pleases, as things highly beneficial to us.

That the higher perfection a soul aspires after, the more dependent it is upon Divine Grace.

[1] Being questioned by one of his own Society (to whom he was obliged to open himself) by what means he had attained to such an habitual sense of GOD, he told him that, since his first coming to the monastery, he had considered GOD as the *end* of all his thoughts and desires, as the mark to which they should tend, and in which they should terminate.

That in the beginning of his novitiate, he spent the hours appointed for private prayer in thinking of GOD, so as to convince his mind of, and to impress deeply upon his heart, the Divine existence, rather by devout sentiments, than by studied reasonings, and elaborate meditations. That by this short and sure method, he exercised himself in the knowledge and love of GOD, resolving to use his utmost endeavour to live in a continual sense of His Presence, and, if possible, never to forget Him more.

That when he had thus in prayer filled his mind full with great sentiments of that INFINITE BEING, he went to his work appointed in the kitchen (for he was cook to the Society); there, having first considered severally the things his office required, and when and how each thing was to be done, he spent all the intervals of his time, as well before as after his work, in prayer.

That when he began his business, he said to GOD, with a filial trust in Him: "O MY GOD, since Thou art with me, and I must now, in obedience to Thy commands, apply my mind to these outward things, I beseech Thee to grant me grace to continue in Thy Presence; and to this end, do Thou prosper me with Thy assistance, receive all my works, and possess all my affections."

As he proceeded in his work, he continued his familiar conversation with his Maker, imploring His grace, and offering to Him all his actions.

When he had finished, he examined himself how he had discharged his duty: if he found *well*, he returned thanks to GOD: if otherwise, he asked pardon; and without being discouraged, he set his mind right again and continued his exercise of the *Presence of* GOD, as if he had never deviated from it. "Thus," said he, "by rising after my falls, and by frequently renewed acts of faith and love, I am come to a state, wherein it would be as difficult for me not to think of GOD, as it was at first to accustom myself to it."

[1] The particulars which follow are collected from other accounts of Brother Lawrence.

As Brother Lawrence had found such comfort and blessing in walking in the Presence of God, it was natural for him to recommend it earnestly to others; but his example was a stronger inducement than any arguments he could propose. His very countenance was edifying; such a sweet and calm devotion appearing in it, as could not but affect all beholders. And it was observed, that in the greatest hurry of business in the kitchen, he still preserved his recollection and his heavenly-mindedness. He was never hasty nor loitering, but did each thing in its season, with an even, uninterrupted composure and tranquillity of spirit. "The time of business," said he, "does not with me differ from the time of prayer, and in the noise and clatter of my kitchen, while several persons are at the same time calling for different things, I possess God in as great tranquillity, as if I were upon my knees at the Blessed Sacrament."

LETTERS

FIRST LETTER [1]

To the Reverend Mother

Y Reverend Mother,—Since you desire so earnestly that I should communicate to you the method by which I arrived at that *habitual sense of God's Presence*, which Our Lord, of His mercy, has been pleased to vouchsafe to me, I must tell you, that it is with great difficulty that I am prevailed on by your importunities, and now I do it only upon the terms, that you show my letter to nobody. If I knew that you would let it be seen, all the desire that I have for your perfection would not be able to determine me to it.

The account I can give you is this. Having found in many books different methods prescribed of going to God, and divers practices of the spiritual life, I thought that this would serve rather to puzzle me, than to facilitate what I sought after, which

---

[1] This letter has no date, but is supposed to have been written the first of this collection.

was nothing else, but how to become wholly GOD's. This made me resolve to give the *all* for the *all:* so after having given myself wholly to GOD, to make all the satisfaction I could for my sins, *I renounced, for the love of Him, everything that was not His; and I began to live, as if there was none but He and I in the world.* Sometimes I considered myself before Him, as a poor criminal at the feet of his judge; at other times, I beheld Him in my heart, as my FATHER, as my GOD; I worshipped Him the oftenest that I could, keeping my mind in His Holy Presence, and recalling it as often as I found it wandering from Him. I found no small trouble in this exercise, and yet I continued it, notwithstanding all the difficulties that I encountered, without troubling or disquieting myself when my mind had wandered involuntarily. I made this my business, as much all the day long as at the appointed times of prayer; for at all times, every hour, every minute, even in the height of my business, I drove away from my mind everything that was capable of interrupting my thought of GOD.

Such has been my common practice ever since I entered into religion; and though I have done it very imperfectly, yet I have found great advantages by it. These, I well know, are to be imputed solely to the mercy and goodness of GOD, because we can do nothing without Him; and *I* still less than any. But when we are faithful to keep ourselves in His Holy Presence, and set Him always before us; this not only hinders our offending Him, and doing anything that may displease Him, at least wilfully, but it also begets in us a holy freedom, and, if I may so speak, a familiarity with GOD, wherewith we ask, and that successfully, the graces we stand in need of. In fine, by often repeating these acts, they become *habitual,* and the *Presence of* GOD is rendered as it were *natural* to us. Give Him thanks, if you please, with me for His great goodness towards me, which I can never sufficiently marvel at, for the many favours He has done to so miserable a sinner as I am. May all things praise him. Amen.—I am, in OUR LORD, Yours, etc.

SECOND LETTER

To the Reverend Mother

My Reverend Mother,—I have taken this opportunity to communicate to you the thoughts of one of our Society, concerning the wonderful effect and continual succour which he receives from *the Presence of* God. Let you and me both profit by them.

You must know that during the forty years and more that he has spent in religion, his continual care has been to be *always with* God; and to do nothing, say nothing, and think nothing which may displease Him; and this without any other view than purely for the love of Him, and because He deserves infinitely more.

He is now so accustomed to that *Divine Presence*, that he receives from it continual succour upon all occasions. For above thirty years, his soul has been filled with joys so continual and sometimes so transcendent, that he is forced to use means to moderate them and to prevent their appearing outwardly.

If sometimes he is a little too much absent from that *Divine Presence*, which happens often when he is most engaged in his outward business, God presently makes Himself felt in his soul to recall him. He answers with exact fidelity to these inward drawings, either by an elevation of his heart towards God, or by a meek and loving regard to Him, or by such words as love forms upon these occasions, as for instance, My God, *behold me, wholly Thine*: Lord, *make me according to Thy heart*. And then it seems to him (as in effect he feels it) that this God of love, satisfied with such few words, reposes again and rests in the depth and centre of his soul. The experience of these things gives him such an assurance that God is always deep within his soul, that no doubt of it can arise, whatever may betide.

Judge from this what contentment and satisfaction he enjoys, feeling continually within him so great a treasure: no longer is he in anxious search after it, but he has it open before him, free to take of it what he pleases.

He complains much of our blindness and exclaims often that we are to be pitied, who content ourselves with so little. God's *treasure*, he says, *is like an infinite ocean, yet a little wave of feeling, passing with the moment, contents us. Blind as we are, we hinder* GOD, *and stop the current of His graces. But when He finds a soul permeated with a living faith, He pours into it His graces and His favours plenteously; into the soul they flow like a torrent, which, after being forcibly stopped against its ordinary course, when it has found a passage, spreads with impetuosity its pent-up flood.*

Yes, often we stop this torrent, by the little value we set upon it. But let us stop it no longer: let us enter into ourselves and break down the barrier which holds it back. Let us make the most of the day of grace, let us redeem the time that is lost, perhaps we have but little left to us: death follows close, let us be well prepared; for we die but once, and a miscarriage *then* is irretrievable.

I say again, let us enter into ourselves. Time presses: there is no room for delay, our souls are at stake. You, I believe, have taken such effectual measures, that you will not be surprised. I commend you for it, it is the one thing needful: we must, nevertheless, always labour at it; for, in the spiritual life, not to advance is to go back. But those whose spirits are stirred by the breath of the HOLY SPIRIT go forward, even in sleep. If the bark of our soul is still tossed with the winds and the storms, let us awake the Lord, Who reposes in it, and quickly He will calm the sea.

I have taken the liberty to impart to you these good thoughts, that you may compare them with your own. They will serve to rekindle and inflame them, if by misfortune (which GOD forbid, for it would be indeed a great evil) they should, though never so little, be somewhat cooled. Let us then *both* recall our *early* fervour. Let us profit by the example and thoughts of this brother, who is little known of the world, but known of GOD, and in untold measure caressed by Him. I will pray for you, do you pray very instantly for him, who is, in OUR LORD,—Yours, etc.

June 1st, 1682.

THIRD LETTER

TO THE REVEREND MOTHER

MY REVEREND AND GREATLY HONOURED MOTHER,—I have received to-day two books and a letter from Sister ——, who is preparing to make her "profession," and upon that account desires the prayers of your holy Community, and yours in particular. I perceive that she reckons much upon them; pray do not disappoint her. Beg of God that she may make her sacrifice in the view of His love alone, and with firm resolution to be wholly devoted to Him. I will send you one of those books which treat of *the Presence of* God, a subject which in my opinion contains the whole spiritual life. It seems to me, that whosoever duly practises it, will soon become spiritual.

I know that for the right practice of it, the heart must be empty of all else; because God wills to possess the heart *alone:* and as He cannot possess it alone unless it be empty of all besides, so He cannot work in it what He would, unless it be left vacant to Him.

There is not in the world a kind of life more sweet and more delightful, than that of a continual walk with God; those only can comprehend it, who practise and experience it. Yet I do not advise you to do it from that motive, it is not pleasure that we ought to seek in this exercise; but let us do it from the motive of love, and because God would have us so walk.

Were I a preacher, I should preach above all other things, the practice of *the Presence of* God: were I a "director," I should advise all the world to it; so necessary do I think it, and so easy.

Ah! knew we but the need we have of the grace and the succour of God, we should never lose sight of Him, no, not for one moment. Believe me; this very instant, make a holy and firm resolution, never again wilfully to stray from Him, and to live the rest of your days *in His Holy Presence*, for love of Him surrendering, if He think fit, all other pleasures.

Set heartily about this work, and if you perform it as you ought, be assured that you will soon find the effects of it. I will assist you with my prayers, poor as they are. I commend myself earnestly to yours, and to those of your holy Community, being theirs, and more particularly,—Yours, etc.

1685.

FOURTH LETTER

To the Same

My Reverend and Greatly Honoured Mother,—I have received from Mdlle. le —— the chaplets which you gave her for me. I wonder that you have not given me your thoughts on the little book I sent you, and which you must have received. Pray, set heartily about the practice of it in your old age; it is better late than never.

I cannot imagine how religious persons can live satisfied without the practice of *the Presence of* God. For my part, as I can, I keep myself retired with Him in the very centre of my soul; and, when I am so with Him, I fear no evil; but the least turning away from Him is to me insupportable.

This exercise does not much fatigue the body; yet it is proper to deprive it sometimes, nay often, of many little pleasures, which are innocent and lawful. For God will not suffer a soul, which would fain be wholly devoted to Him, to take other pleasures than with Him: that is more than reasonable.

I do not say that for this cause we must place any violent constraint upon ourselves. No, we must serve God in a holy freedom, we must do our business faithfully, without trouble or disquiet; recalling our minds to God meekly, and with tranquillity, as often as we find them wandering from Him.

It is, however, needful to put our whole trust in God, laying aside all other cares, and even some particular forms of devotion, very good in themselves, but yet such as one often engages in unreasonably: because, in fact, those devotions are only means to attain to the end, so when by this practice of *the Presence of* God we are *with Him* Who is *our End*, it is then useless to return to the means. Then it is that abiding in His Holy Presence, we may continue our commerce of love, now by an act of adoration, of praise, or of desire; now by an act of sacrifice or of thanksgiving, and in all the manners which our mind can devise.

Be not discouraged by the repugnance which you may find to it from nature; you must do yourself violence. Often, at the outset, one thinks it is lost time; but you must go on, and resolve to persevere in it till death, despite all difficulties. I commend myself

to the prayers of your holy Community, and to yours in particular.
—I am, in Our Lord, yours, etc.
November 3rd, 1685.

FIFTH LETTER

To Madame ——

Madame,—I pity you much. It will be of the greatest moment,
if you can leave the care of your affairs to M. and Mme. ——
and spend the remainder of your life only in worshipping God.
He lays no great burden upon us,—a little remembrance of Him
from time to time, a little adoration; sometimes to pray for His
grace, sometimes to offer Him your sorrows, sometimes to return
Him thanks for the benefits He hath bestowed upon you and is
still bestowing in the midst of your troubles. He asks you to
console yourself with Him the oftenest you can. Lift up your
heart to Him even at your meals, or when you are in company,—
the least little remembrance will always be acceptable to Him.
You need not cry very loud: He is nearer to us than we think.

To be with God, there is no need to be continually in church.
Of our heart we may make an Oratory, wherein to retire from
time to time and with Him hold meek, humble, loving converse.
Everyone can converse closely with God, some more, others less:
He knows what we can do. Let us begin then; perhaps He is just
waiting for one generous resolution on our part; let us be brave.
So little time remains to us to live; you are near sixty-four, and
I am almost eighty. Let us live and die with God: sufferings will
be ever sweet and pleasant to us, while we abide with Him; and
without Him, the greatest pleasures will be but cruel anguish.
May He be blessed for all. Amen.

Accustom yourself, then, by degrees, to worship Him with
your whole strength, to beg His grace, to offer Him your heart,
from time to time throughout the day's business, even every moment, if you can. Do not scrupulously confine yourself to fixed
rules or particular forms of devotion; but act with faith in God,
with love, and with humility. You can assure M. and Mme.
and Mdlle. —— of my poor prayers, and that I am their servant, and in particular, in Our Lord,—Your Brother, etc.

SIXTH LETTER

To the Reverend Father

My Reverend Father,—Not finding my manner of life in books, although I have no difficulty about it, yet, for greater security, I shall be glad to know your thoughts concerning it.

In a conversation some days since with a person of piety, he told me that the spiritual life was a life of grace, which begins with servile fear, which is increased by hope of eternal life, and which is consummated by pure love. That each of these states had its different stages, by which one arrives at last at that blessed consummation.

I have not followed all these methods. On the contrary, from I know not what instincts, I found that they discouraged me. This was the reason why, at my entrance into religion, I took a resolution to give myself up to God, as the best satisfaction I could make for my sins, and for the love of Him to renounce all besides.

For the first years I commonly employed myself during the time set apart for devotion with the thoughts of death, judgment, hell, heaven, and my sins. Thus I continued some years, applying my mind carefully the rest of the day, and even in the midst of my business, *to the Presence of* God, Whom I considered always as *with* me, often as *in* me.

At length I came insensibly to do the same thing during my set time of prayer, which caused in me great delight and consolation. This practice produced in me so high an esteem for God, that *faith* alone was capable to satisfy me in that point.[1]

Such was my beginning; and yet I must tell you, that for the first ten years I suffered much: the apprehension that I was not devoted to God, as I wished to be, my past sins always present to my mind, and the great unmerited favours which God bestowed on me, were the matter and source of my sufferings. During all

---

[1] I suppose he means, that all distinct notions he could form of God were unsatisfactory, because he perceived them to be unworthy of God; and therefore his mind was not to be satisfied but by the views of *faith*, which apprehends God as infinite and incomprehensible, as He is in Himself, and not as He can be conceived by human ideas.

this time I fell often, yet as often rose again. It seemed to me that all creation, reason, and GOD Himself were against me; and *faith* alone for me. I was troubled sometimes with thoughts, that to believe I had received such favours, was an effect of my presumption, which pretended to be *at once* where others arrive only with difficulty; at other times that it was a wilful delusion and that there was no salvation for me.

When I thought of nothing but to end my days in these times of trouble and disquiet (which did not at all diminish the trust I had in GOD, and which served only to increase my faith), I found myself changed all at once; and my soul, which till that time was in trouble, felt a profound inward peace, as if it had found its centre and place of rest.

Ever since that time, I have been and am now walking before GOD in simple faith, with humility, and with love; and I apply myself diligently to do nothing, say nothing, and think nothing which may displease Him. I hope that when I have done what I can, He will do with me what He pleases.

As for what passes in me at present, I cannot express it. I have no pain nor any doubt as to my state, because I have no will but that of GOD, which I endeavour to carry out in all things, and to which I am so submissive that I would not take up a straw from the ground against His order, or from any other motive but purely that of love to Him.

I have quitted all forms of devotion and set prayers, save those to which my state obliges me. And I make it my only business to persevere in His Holy Presence, wherein I keep myself by a simple attention and an absorbing passionate regard to GOD, which I may call an *actual Presence of* GOD; or to speak better, a silent and secret, constant intercourse of the soul with GOD, which often causes in me joys and raptures inwardly, and sometimes also outwardly, so great, that I am forced to use means to moderate them, and prevent their appearance to others.

In short, I am assured beyond all doubt, that my soul has been with GOD these past thirty years and more. I pass over many things that I may not be tedious to you; yet I think it proper to inform you after what manner I consider myself before GOD, Whom I behold as my *King*.

I consider myself as the most wretched of men, full of sores and corruptions, and as one who has committed all sorts of crimes against his King; moved with deep sorrow, I confess to Him all my wickedness, I ask His forgiveness, I abandon myself in His hands, that He may do with me what He pleases. This King, full of mercy and goodness, very far from chastising me, embraces me with love, makes me to eat at His table, serves me with His own hands, gives me the key to His treasures; He converses and delights Himself with me unceasingly, in a thousand and a thousand ways, and treats me in all respects as His favourite. It is thus that I consider myself from time to time in His Holy Presence.

My most usual method is this simple attention and this absorbing, passionate regard to GOD, to Whom I find myself often attached with greater sweetness and delight, than that of an infant at his mother's breast: so that, if I dare use the expression, I should choose to call this state the bosom of GOD, by reason of the inexpressible sweetness which I taste and experience there. If sometimes my thoughts wander from it by necessity or by infirmity, I am soon recalled by inward emotions, so charming and delightful that I am confused to mention them.

I beg you to reflect rather upon my great wretchedness, of which you are fully informed, than upon the great favours which GOD does me, all unworthy and ungrateful as I am.

As for my set hours of prayer, they are only a continuation of the same exercise. Sometimes I consider myself as a stone in the hands of a carver, whereof he wills to make a statue: presenting myself thus before GOD, I beseech Him to render me entirely like Himself, and to fashion in my soul His Perfect Image.

At other times so soon as I apply myself to prayer, I feel my whole spirit and my whole soul lift itself up without any trouble or effort of mine; and it remains as it were in elevation, fixed firm in GOD as in its centre and its resting-place.

I know that some charge this state with inactivity, delusion, and self-love. I avow that it is a holy inactivity, and would be a happy self-love, were the soul in that state capable of such; because, in fact, while the soul is in this repose, it cannot be troubled by such acts, as it was formerly accustomed to, and which were then its support, but which would now rather injure than assist it.

Yet I cannot bear that this should be called delusion; because the soul which thus enjoys God, desires herein nothing but Him. If this be delusion in me, it is for God to remedy it. May He do with me what He pleases: I desire only Him, and would fain be wholly devoted to Him. You will, however, oblige me in sending me your opinion, to which I always pay great deference, for I have a very special esteem for your Reverence, and am, in Our Lord, my Reverend Father,— Yours, etc.

SEVENTH LETTER
To the Reverend Mother

My Reverend and Greatly Honoured Mother,—My prayers, of little worth though they be, will not fail you; I have promised it, and I will keep my word. How happy we might be, if only we could find the Treasure, of which the Gospel tells us,— all else would seem to us nothing. How infinite it is! The more one toils and searches in it, the greater are the riches that one finds. Let us toil therefore unceasingly in this search, and let us not grow weary and leave off, till we have found. [Then follow some private matters, after which the writer goes on to say],

I know not what I shall become: it seems to me that peace of soul and repose of spirit descend on me, even in sleep. To be without the sense of this peace, would be affliction indeed; but with this calm in my soul even for purgatory I would console myself.

I know not what God purposes with me, or keeps me for; I am in a calm so great that I fear nought. What can I fear, when I am with Him? And with Him, in His Presence, I hold myself the most I can. May all things praise Him. Amen.—Yours, etc.

EIGHTH LETTER
To Madame ——

Madame,—We have a God Who is infinitely gracious, and knows all our wants. I always thought that He would reduce you to extremity. He will come in His own time, and when you

least expect it. Hope in Him more than ever: thank Him with
me for the favours He does you, particularly for the fortitude
and patience which He gives you in your afflictions; it is a plain
mark of the care He has for you; comfort yourself therefore
with Him, and give thanks for all.

I admire also the fortitude and bravery of M. de ——. God
has given him a good disposition, and a good will; but there is in
him still a little of the world and a great deal of youth. I hope
that the affliction, which God has sent him, will prove to him a
wholesome medicine, and make him take stock of himself. It is
an occasion very proper to engage him to put all his confidence in
Him, Who accompanies him everywhere: let him think of Him
the oftenest he can, especially in the greatest dangers.

A little lifting up of the heart suffices; a little remembrance of
God, one act of inward worship, though upon a march and sword
in hand, are prayers which, however short, are nevertheless very
acceptable to God; and far from lessening a soldier's courage,
they best serve to fortify it.

Let him think then of God the most he can. Let him accustom
himself by degrees to this small but holy exercise; nobody per-
ceives it, and nothing is easier than to repeat often in the day these
little acts of inward worship. Recommend to him, if you please,
that he think of God the most he can, in the manner here directed:
it is very fit and most necessary for a soldier, who is daily exposed
to dangers of life and often of his salvation. I hope that God
will assist him and all the family, to whom I present my service,
being theirs and in particular,—Yours, etc.
October 12th, 1688.

NINTH LETTER

To the Reverend Mother

My Reverend and Greatly Honoured Mother,—You tell
me nothing new: you are not the only one that is troubled with
wandering thoughts. Our mind is extremely roving, but as the
will is mistress of all our faculties, she must recall it, and carry
it to God, as its last End.

When the mind, for lack of discipline when first we engaged

in devotion, has contracted bad habits of wandering and dissipation, such habits are difficult to overcome, and commonly draw us, even against our will, to things of earth.

I believe that one remedy for this is to confess our faults, and to humble ourselves before GOD. I do not advise you to use multiplicity of words in prayer; discursive forms are often the occasion of wandering. Hold yourself in prayer before GOD, like a poor, dumb, paralytic beggar at a rich man's gate. Let it be *your business* to keep your mind in *the Presence of the* LORD: if it sometimes wanders and withdraws itself from Him, do not much disquiet yourself for that; trouble and disquiet serve rather to distract than to recall the mind; the will must bring it back in tranquillity: if you persevere with your whole strength, GOD will have pity on you.

One way to recall easily the mind in time of prayer, and to preserve it more in rest, is not to let it wander too far at other times. You should keep it strictly in *the Presence of* GOD, and being accustomed to think of Him often from time to time, you will find it easy to keep your mind calm in the time of prayer, or at least to recall it from its wanderings.

I have told you already at large in my other letters of the benefits we may draw from this practice of *the Presence of* GOD. Let us set about it seriously, and pray for one another. I commend myself to the prayers of Sister ——, and of the Reverend Mother ——, and am,—Yours in OUR LORD, etc.

TENTH LETTER

TO THE SAME

The inclosed is an answer to that which I have received from our good Sister ——; pray deliver it to her. She seems to me full of good will, but she wants to go faster than grace. One does not become holy all at once. I commend her to you: we ought to help one another by our advice, and still more by our good examples. You will oblige me by letting me hear of her from time to time, and whether she be very fervent and very obedient.

Let us think often that our only business in this life is to please

GOD; that all besides is perhaps but folly and vanity. You and I have lived more than forty years in religion. Have we employed those years in loving and serving GOD, Who by His mercy has called us to this state and for that very end? I am filled with shame and confusion when I reflect, on one hand, upon the great favours which GOD has bestowed and is still unceasingly bestowing upon me; and, on the other, upon the ill use I have made of them, and my small advancement in the way of perfection.

Since, by His mercy, He gives us still a little time, let us begin in earnest, let us redeem the time that is lost, let us return with a whole-hearted trust to this FATHER *of Mercies*, Who is always ready to receive us into His loving arms. Let us renounce, and renounce generously, with single heart, for the love of Him, all that is not His; He deserves infinitely more. Let us think of Him unceasingly; in Him let us put all our confidence. I doubt not but that we shall soon experience the effects of it in receiving the abundance of His grace, with which we can do all things, and without which we can do nought but sin.

We cannot escape the dangers which abound in life, without the actual and *continual* help of GOD; let us then pray to Him for it continually. How can we pray to Him, without being with Him? How can we be with Him, but in thinking of Him often? And how can we have Him often in our thoughts, unless by a holy habit of thought which we should form? You will tell me that I am always saying the same thing: it is true, for this is the best and easiest method that I know; and as I use no other, I advise the whole world to it. We must *know* before we can *love*. In order to *know* GOD, we must often think of Him; and when we come to *love* Him, we shall *also think* of Him often, *for our heart will be with our treasure!* Ponder over this often, ponder it well.—Yours, etc.

March 28*th,* 1689.

ELEVENTH LETTER

To MADAME ――

MADAME,—I have had a good deal of difficulty to bring myself to write to M. de ――; and I do it now purely because you and

Mme. de —— desire me. Pray write the directions and send it to him. I am very well pleased with the trust you have in GOD: it is my wish that He may increase it in you more and more. We cannot have too much confidence in so good and faithful a Friend, Who will never fail us in this world or the next.

If M. de —— knows how to profit by the loss he has sustained, and puts all his confidence in GOD, He will soon give him another friend more powerful and more inclined to serve him. He disposes of hearts as He pleases. Perhaps M. de —— was too much attached to him he has lost. We ought to love our friends, but without encroaching upon the love of GOD, which must be the chief.

Remember, I pray you, what I have often recommended to you, which is, often to think on GOD, by day, by night, in your business, and even in your diversions. He is always near you and with you: leave Him not alone. You would think it rude to leave a friend alone, who had come to visit you: why then must GOD be neglected? Do not then forget Him, think often of Him, adore Him unceasingly, live and die with Him: this is the glorious employment of a Christian, in a word, this is our profession; if we do not know it, we must learn it. I will endeavour to help you with my prayers, and am, in OUR LORD,—Yours, etc.

October 29*th*, 1689.

TWELFTH LETTER

TO THE REVEREND MOTHER

MY REVEREND AND GREATLY HONOURED MOTHER,—I do not pray that you may be delivered from your troubles, but I pray GOD earnestly that He would give you strength and patience to bear them as long as He pleases. Comfort yourself with Him, Who holds you fastened to the cross; He will loose you when He thinks fit. Happy those who suffer with Him; accustom yourself to suffer in that manner, and seek from Him the strength to endure as much and as long as He shall judge to be needful for you. They who love the world do not comprehend these truths, nor do I wonder at it; for they suffer as lovers of the

world, and not as lovers of Christ. They consider sickness as a
pain of nature and not as a favour from God; and seeing it only
in that light, they find nothing in it but grief and distress. But
they who trust in sickness as coming from the hand of God, as
the effect of His mercy, and the means which He employs for
their salvation, commonly find in it great sweetness and sensible
consolation.

I wish you could convince yourself that God is often nearer
to us and more effectually present with us, in sickness than in
health. Rely upon no other Physician, for according to my apprehension, He reserves your cure to Himself. Place all your trust
in Him and you will soon find the effects, which we often retard
by putting greater confidence in physic than in God.

Whatever remedies you make use of, they will prove beneficial
only so far as He permits. When pains come from God, He alone
can cure them. Often He sends diseases of the body to cure
those of the soul. Comfort yourself with the sovereign Physician
both of soul and body.

I foresee that you will tell me that I am very much at my
ease, that I eat and drink at the table of the Lord. You are right:
but think you that it would be a small pain to the greatest criminal in the world to eat at his king's table and to be served by his
king's hands, without however being assured of pardon? I believe
that he would feel exceeding great uneasiness, and such as nothing could moderate, save only his trust in the goodness of his
sovereign. So I can assure you that whatever pleasures I taste at
the table of my King, my sins ever present before my eyes, as well
as the uncertainty of my pardon, torment me: though in truth,
that torment itself is pleasing.

Be satisfied with the state wherein God has placed you: however happy you may think me, I envy you. Pains and sufferings
would be a paradise to me, while I should suffer with my God;
and the greatest pleasures would be to me a hell, if I could relish
them without Him: all my joy would be to suffer something
for His sake.

In a little time I shall be going to God, I mean going to render
my account to Him.

In this life, what comforts me is, that I see God by faith, and
indeed in such a manner as might make me say at times, *No longer*

I believe—I see. I feel what faith teaches us, and in that assurance, and that practice of faith I will live and die with Him.

Continue then always with GOD; it is the only support and comfort for your affliction. I shall beseech Him to company with you. I present my service to the Reverend Mother Superior, and commend myself to your prayers, and am, in OUR LORD,—Yours, etc.
November 17th, 1690.

THIRTEENTH LETTER

TO THE REVEREND MOTHER

MY GOOD MOTHER,—If we were well accustomed to the exercise of *the Presence of* GOD, all bodily diseases would be much alleviated thereby. GOD often permits that we should suffer a little to purify our souls, and to compel us to continue *with Him.* I cannot understand how a soul, which is with GOD and which desires Him alone, can feel pain: I have had enough experience to banish all doubt that it can.

Take courage, offer to Him unceasingly your sorrows, pray to Him for strength to endure. Above all, acquire a habit of holding constant converse with GOD, and forget Him the least you can. Adore Him in your infirmities, offer yourself to Him from time to time; and in the very height of your sufferings beseech Him humbly and lovingly—as a child his good father—to grant you the aid of His grace and to make you conformable to His holy will. I will help you with my poor halting prayers.

God has many ways of drawing us to Himself. He hides Himself sometimes from us; but *faith* alone, which will not fail us in time of need, ought to be our support and the foundation of our confidence, which must be all in GOD.

I do not know how GOD will dispose of me. I am always more happy. The whole world suffers, yet I, who deserve the severest discipline, experience joys so constant and so great, that I can scarce contain them.

I would willingly ask of GOD a share of your sufferings, but that I know my weakness which is so great, that if He left me one moment by myself, I should be the most wretched man alive.

And yet I know not how He can leave me alone, because faith gives me as strong a conviction as sense can do, and I know that He never forsakes us, till we have first forsaken Him. Let us fear to leave Him. Let us ever abide with Him: let us live and die with Him. Make you this petition for me, as I for you.— Yours, etc.

November 28*th,* 1690.

FOURTEENTH LETTER

To the Same

MY GOOD MOTHER,—I am in pain to see you suffer so long: what gives me some ease, and sweetens the sorrow which I have for your griefs, is that I am convinced that they are tokens of the love GOD has for you. Look at them in this light, and you will bear them more easily. As your case is, it is my opinion that you should leave off human remedies, and resign yourself entirely to the Providence of GOD: perhaps He stays only for that resignation and a perfect trust in Him to cure you. Since, despite all your cares, physic has not had the effect it should, but on the contrary the malady increases, it will not be tempting GOD to abandon yourself into His hands, and look for all to Him.

I told you in my last that sometimes He permits the body to suffer, to cure the sickness of our souls. Have courage, then: make of necessity a virtue; ask of God, not deliverance from the body's pains, but strength bravely to endure, for the love of Him, all that He shall desire, and as long as He shall please.

Such prayers, indeed, are a little hard to nature, but most acceptable to GOD, and sweet to those who love Him. Love sweetens pain: and when one loves GOD, one suffers for Him with joy and courage. Do you so, I beseech you: comfort yourself with Him, Who is the only Physician of all our ills. He is the FATHER of the afflicted, ever ready to succour us. He loves us infinitely more than we can imagine: love Him therefore, and seek no other relief than in Him: I hope you will soon receive it. Adieu. I will help you with my prayers, poor as they are, and I will ever be in OUR LORD,—Yours, etc.

FIFTEENTH LETTER
To the Same

My Very Dear Mother,—I render thanks to Our Lord for having relieved you a little according to your desire. I have been often near expiring, though I was never so much satisfied as then. Accordingly, I did not pray for any relief, but I prayed for strength to suffer bravely, meekly, lovingly. Ah! how sweet it is to suffer with God! However great may be the sufferings, receive them with love. 'Tis Paradise to suffer, and to be with Him; so that, if even now in this life we would enjoy the peace of Paradise, we must accustom ourselves to hold familiar, humble, loving converse with Him: we must prevent our spirit from ever wandering from Him: we must make our heart a spiritual temple, wherein to adore Him unceasingly: we must watch continually over ourselves, that we may not do, nor say, nor think anything that may displease Him. When our minds are thus filled with God, suffering will become full of sweetness, of unction, and of quiet joy.

I know that to arrive at this state, the beginning is very difficult, for we must act purely in faith. But hard though it is, we know also that we can do all things with the grace of God, which He never refuses to them who ask Him for it earnestly. Knock, be instant in knocking, and I answer for it, He will open to you in His due time, and grant you in a moment what He has withheld during the many years. Adieu. Pray to Him for me, as I pray to Him for you. I hope to see Him very soon.—I am entirely yours, in Our Lord.

January 22nd, 1691.

SIXTEENTH LETTER
To the Same

My Good Mother,—God knoweth best what is needful for us, and all that He does is for our good. If we knew how much He loves us, we should be always ready to receive equally, and with indifference, from His hand, the sweet and the bitter; all would please that came from Him. The sorest afflictions never appear intolerable, but when we see them in a wrong light: when we see them in the hand of GOD, Who dispenses them; when we know that it is our loving FATHER, Who abases and distresses us, our sufferings lose all their bitterness, and our mourning becomes all joy.

Let all our business be to *know* GOD: the more one *knows* Him, the more one *desires to know* Him. And as *knowledge* is commonly the measure of *love*, the deeper and more extensive *our knowledge* shall be, the greater will be *our love*: and if our love of GOD be great, we shall love him equally in grief and in joy.

Let us not amuse ourselves, to seek or to love GOD for any sensible favours (how elevated soever) which He has done or may do to us. Such favours, though never so great, cannot bring us so near to GOD, as faith does in one simple act. Let us seek Him often by faith; He is within us,—seek Him not elsewhere. Are we not rude and deserving of blame, if we leave Him alone, to busy ourselves about trifles, which do not please Him,—which perhaps offend Him? He bears with them now, but it is to be feared these trifles will one day cost us dear.

Let us begin to be devoted to Him in good earnest. Let us cast everything besides out of our hearts; He would possess them alone. Beg this favour of Him. If we do what we can on our part, we shall soon see that change wrought in us which we aspire after. I cannot thank Him sufficiently for the relief He has vouchsafed you. I hope from His mercy the favour of seeing Him within a few days.[1] Let us pray for one another.—I am, in OUR LORD, yours, etc.

February 6th, 1691.

[1] He took to his bed two days after, and died within the week.

7. ST. THERESE OF LISIEUX:
CHAPTER XI OF THE *AUTOBIOGRAPHY*

¶THE "Little Flower," as Saint Therese of Lisieux is so popularly known, was a French Carmelite nun who was born in 1873 and died in 1897. She entered the convent at the age of fifteen, having received a special indult, and was there known as Sœur Therese de l'Enfant Jesus (Sister Teresa of the Child Jesus). Her canonization took place in 1925. Shortly before her death she had written that she was "a spring flower which the Master culls for his pleasure." This name has since clung to her; and she is doubtless the best known of modern saints.

Written at the behest of the Carmelite Prioress at Lisieux, the *Autobiography* is not in the strict sense a classic. It is a modern book, and its author was hardly more than a child. The wisdom and genius of St. Teresa of Avila are alike missing, and there is a quality which occasionally can be distinguished from sentimentality only with difficulty. Nevertheless the book has the marvelous freshness and vitality of youth. It is, indeed, a "canticle of love." The present quotation is virtually the whole of Chapter Eleven, and the editor has followed the edition published by the Rev. T. N. Taylor.*

* From *The Little Flower*. Edited by the Rev. T. N. Taylor. New York: Benziger Bros. N.D.

CHAPTER XI
A CANTICLE OF LOVE

T IS not only when He is about to send me some
trial that Our Lord gives me warning and
awakens my desire for it. For years I had cher-
ished a longing which seemed impossible of
realisation—to have a brother a Priest. I often
used to think that if my little brothers had not
gone to Heaven, I should have had the happiness of seeing them
at the Altar. I greatly regretted being deprived of this joy. Yet
God went beyond my dream; I only asked for one brother who
would remember me each day at the Holy Altar, and He has
united me in the bonds of spiritual friendship with two of His
apostles. I should like to tell you, dear Mother, how Our Divine
Master fulfilled my desire.

In 1898 our Holy Mother, St. Teresa, sent my first brother
as a gift for my feast. It was washing day, and I was busy at my
work, when Mother Agnes of Jesus, then Prioress, called me aside
and read me a letter from a young Seminarist, in which he said
he had been inspired by St. Teresa to ask for a sister who would
devote herself specially to his salvation, and to the salvation of
his future flock. He promised always to remember this spiritual
sister when saying Mass, and the choice fell upon me. Dear
Mother, I cannot tell you how happy this made me. Such unlooked-for fulfilment of my desire awoke in my heart the joy
of a child; it carried me back to those early days, when pleasures
were so keen, that my heart seemed too small to contain them.
Years had passed since I had tasted a like happiness, so fresh, so
unfamiliar, as if forgotten chords had been stirred within me.

Fully aware of my obligations, I set to work, and strove to re-
double my fervour. Now and again I wrote to my new brother.
Undoubtedly, it is by prayer and sacrifice that we can help our
missionaries, but sometimes, when it pleases Our Lord to unite
two souls for His Glory, He permits them to communicate their
thoughts, and thus inspire each other to love God more. Of course
an express command from those in authority is needed for this,
otherwise, it seems to me, that such a correspondence would do

more harm than good, if not to the missionary, at least to the Carmelite, whose manner of life tends to continual introversion. This exchange of letters, though rare, would occupy her mind uselessly; instead of uniting her to God, she would perhaps fancy she was doing wonders, when in reality, under cover of zeal, she was doing nothing but producing needless distraction.——And here am I, launched, not upon a distraction, but upon a dissertation equally superfluous. I shall never be able to correct myself of these lengthy digressions, which must be so wearisome to you, dear Mother. Forgive me, should I offend again.

Last year, at the end of May, it was your turn to give me my second brother, and when I represented that, having given all my merits to one future apostle, I feared they could not be given to another, you told me that obedience would double their value. In the depths of my heart I thought the same thing, and, since the zeal of a Carmelite ought to embrace the whole world, I hope, with God's help, to be of use to even more than two missionaries. I pray for all, not forgetting our Priests at home, whose ministry is quite as difficult as that of the missionary preaching to the heathen. . . . In a word, I wish to be a true daughter of the Church, like our holy Mother St. Teresa, and pray for all the intentions of Christ's Vicar. That is the one great aim of my life. But just as I should have had a special interest in my little brothers had they lived, and that, without neglecting the general interests of the Church, so now, I unite myself in a special way to the new brothers whom Jesus has given me. All that I possess is theirs also. God is too good to give by halves; He is so rich that He gives me all I ask for, even though I do not lose myself in lengthy enumerations. As I have two brothers and my little sisters, the novices, the days would be too short were I to ask in detail for the needs of each soul, and I fear I might forget something important. Simple souls cannot understand complicated methods, and, as I am one of their number, Our Lord has inspired me with a very simple way of fulfilling my obligations. One day, after Holy Communion, He made me understand these words of the Canticles: *"Draw me: we will run after Thee to the odour of Thy ointments."* O my Jesus, there is no need to say: "In drawing me, draw also the souls that I love": these words, *"Draw me,"* suffice. When a soul has let herself be taken captive by the inebriating odour of Thy perfumes, she cannot run alone; as a natural consequence of her attraction towards Thee, the souls of all those she loves are drawn in her train.

Just as a torrent carries into the depths of the sea all that it meets on its way, so, my Jesus, does the soul who plunges into the shoreless ocean of Thy Love bring with it all its treasures. My treasures are the souls it has pleased Thee to unite with mine; Thou hast confided them to me, and therefore I do not fear to use Thy own words, uttered by Thee on the last night that saw Thee still a traveller on this earth. Jesus, my Beloved! I know not when my exile will have an end. Many a night I may yet sing Thy Mercies here below, but for me also will come the last night, and then I shall be able to say:

"I have glorified Thee upon earth: I have finished the work which Thou gavest me to do. I have manifested Thy name to the men whom Thou hast given me out of the world. Thine they were, and to me Thou gavest them; and they have kept Thy word. Now they have known that all things which Thou hast given me are from Thee: because the words which Thou gavest me I have given to them; and they have received them, and have known for certain that I came forth from Thee, and they have believed that Thou didst send me. I pray for them: I pray not for the world, but for them whom Thou hast given me, because they are Thine. And all mine are Thine, and Thine are mine; and I am glorified in them. And now I am no more in the world, and these are in the world, and I come to Thee. Holy Father, keep them in Thy name, whom Thou hast given me, that they may be one, as we also are one. And now I come to Thee, and these things I speak in the world, that they may have my joy filled in themselves. I do not ask that Thou take them away out of the world, but that Thou preserve them from evil. They are not of the world, as I also am not of the world. And not for them only do I pray, but for those also who through their word shall believe in me. Father, I will that where I am they also whom Thou hast given me may be with me, that they may see my glory which Thou hast given me, because Thou hast loved me before the foundation of the world. And I have made known Thy name unto them, and will make it

known, that the love wherewith Thou hast loved me may be in them and I in them." [1]

Yea, Lord, thus would I repeat Thy words, before losing myself in Thy loving embrace. Perhaps it is daring, but, for a long time, hast Thou not allowed me to be daring with Thee? Thou hast said to me, as the Prodigal's father to his elder son: *"All I have is thine."* [2] And therefore I may use Thy very own words to draw down favours from Our Heavenly Father on all who are dear to me.

My God, Thou knowest that I have ever desired to love Thee alone. It has been my only ambition. Thy love has gone before me, even from the days of my childhood. It has grown with my growth, and now it is an abyss whose depths I cannot fathom.

Love attracts love; mine darts towards Thee, and would fain make the abyss brim over, but alas! it is not even as a dewdrop in the ocean. To love Thee as Thou lovest me, I must make Thy Love mine own. Thus alone can I find rest. O my Jesus, it seems to me that Thou couldst not have overwhelmed a soul with more love than Thou hast poured out on mine, and that is why I dare ask Thee to love those Thou hast given me, even as Thou lovest me.

If, in Heaven, I find that Thou lovest them more than Thou lovest me, I shall rejoice, for I acknowledge that their deserts are greater than mine, but now, I can conceive no love more vast than that with which Thou hast favoured me, without any merit on my part.

.   .   .   .

Dear Mother, what I have just written amazes me. I had no intention of writing it. When I said: *"The words which Thou gavest me I have given unto them,"* I was thinking only of my little sisters in the novitiate. I am not able to teach missionaries, and the words I wrote for them were from the prayer of Our Lord: *"I do not ask that Thou shouldst take them out of the world; I pray also for them who through their word shall believe in thee."*

How could I forget those souls they are to win by their sufferings and exhortations?

[1] *Cf.* John xvii.   [2] Luke xv. 31.

But I have not told you all my thoughts on this passage of the Sacred Canticles: *"Draw me—we will run!"* Our Lord has said: *"No man can come to Me except the Father Who hath sent Me, draw him,"* [1] and later He tells us that *whosoever seeks shall find, whosoever asks shall receive, that unto him that knocks it shall be opened,* and He adds that whatever we ask the Father in His Name shall be given us. It was no doubt for this reason that, long before the birth of Our Lord, the Holy Spirit dictated these prophetic words: *"Draw me—we will run!"* By asking to be drawn, we desire an intimate union with the object of our love. If iron and fire were endowed with reason, and the iron could say: *"Draw me!"* would not that prove its desire to be identified with the fire to the point of sharing its substance? Well, this is precisely my prayer. I asked Jesus to draw me into the Fire of His love, and to unite me so closely to Himself that He may live and act in me. I feel that the more the fire of love consumes my heart, so much the more shall I say: *"Draw me!"* and the more also will souls who draw near me *run swiftly in the sweet odour of the Beloved.*

Yes, they will run—we shall all run together, for souls that are on fire can never be at rest. They may indeed, like St. Mary Magdalen, sit at the feet of Jesus, listening to His sweet and burning words, but, though they seem to give Him nothing, they give much more than Martha, who busied herself about many things. It is not Martha's work that Our Lord blames, but her over-solicitude; His Blessed Mother humbly occupied herself in the same kind of work when she prepared the meals for the Holy Family. All the Saints have understood this, especially those who have illumined the earth with the light of Christ's teaching. Was it not from prayer that St. Paul, St. Augustine, St. Thomas Aquinas, St. John of the Cross, St. Teresa, and so many other friends of God drew that wonderful science which has enthralled the loftiest minds?

"Give me a lever and a fulcrum on which to lean it," said Archimedes, "and I will lift the world."

What he could not obtain because his request had only a material end, without reference to God, the Saints have obtained in all its fulness. They lean on God Almighty's power itself and

[1] John vi. 44

their lever is the prayer that inflames with love's fire. With this lever they have raised the world—with this lever the Saints of the Church Militant still raise it, and will raise it to the end of time.

Dear Mother, I have still to tell you what I understand by the *sweet odour of the Beloved.* As Our Lord is now in Heaven, I can only follow Him by the footprints He has left—footprints full of life, full of fragrance. I have only to open the Holy Gospels and at once I breathe the perfume of Jesus, and then I know which way to run; and it is not to the first place, but to the last, that I hasten. I leave the Pharisee to go up, and full of confidence I repeat the humble prayer of the Publican. Above all I follow Magdalen, for the amazing, rather I should say, the loving audacity, that delights the Heart of Jesus, has cast its spell upon mine. It is not because I have been preserved from mortal sin that I lift up my heart to God in trust and love. I feel that even had I on my conscience every crime one could commit, I should lose nothing of my confidence: my heart broken with sorrow, I would throw myself into the Arms of my Saviour. I know that He loves the Prodigal Son, I have heard His words to St. Mary Magdalen, to the woman taken in adultery, and to the woman of Samaria. No one could frighten me, for I know what to believe concerning His mercy and His Love. And I know that all that multitude of sins would disappear in an instant, even as a drop of water cast into a flaming furnace.

It is told in the Lives of the Fathers of the Desert how one of them converted a public sinner, whose evil deeds were the scandal of the whole country. This wicked woman, touched by grace, followed the Saint into the desert, there to perform rigorous penance. But on the first night of the journey, before even reaching the place of her retirement, the bonds that bound her to earth were broken by the vehemence of her loving sorrow. The holy man, at the same instant, saw her soul borne by Angels to the Bosom of God.

This is a striking example of what I want to say, but these things cannot be expressed. Dearest Mother, if weak and imperfect souls like mine felt what I feel, none would despair of reaching the summit of the Mountain of Love, since Jesus does not ask for great deeds, but only for gratitude and self-surrender.

He says: "*I will not take the he-goats from out of thy flocks, for all the beasts of the forests are mine, the cattle on the hills and the oxen. I know all the fowls of the air. If I were hungry, I would not tell thee, for the world is Mine, and the fulness thereof. Shall I eat the flesh of bullocks, or shall I drink the blood of goats? Offer to God the sacrifice of praise and thanksgiving.*" [1]

This is all Our Lord claims from us. He has need of our love—He has no need of our works. The same God, Who declares that He has no need to tell us if He be hungry, did not disdain to beg a little water from the Samaritan woman. He was athirst, but when he said: "*Give me to drink,*" [2] He, the Creator of the Universe, asked for the love of His creature. He thirsted for love.

And this thirst of Our Divine Lord was ever on the increase. Amongst the disciples of the world, He meets with nothing but indifference and ingratitude, and alas! among His own, how few hearts surrender themselves without reserve to the infinite tenderness of His Love. Happy are we who are privileged to understand the inmost secrets of Our Divine Spouse. If you, dear Mother, would but set down in writing all you know, what wonders could you not unfold!

But, like Our Blessed Lady, you prefer to *keep all these things in your heart.*[3] To me you say that "*It is honourable to reveal and confess the works of God.*" [4] Yet you are right to keep silence, for no earthly words can convey the secrets of Heaven.

As for me, in spite of all I have written, I have not as yet begun. I see so many beautiful horizons, such infinitely varied tints, that the palette of the Divine Painter will alone, after the darkness of this life, be able to supply me with the colours wherewith I may portray the wonders that my soul descries. Since, however, you have expressed a desire to penetrate into the hidden sanctuary of my heart, and to have in writing what was the most consoling dream of my life, I will end this story of my soul, by an act of obedience. If you will allow me, it is to Jesus I will address myself, for in this way I shall speak more easily. You may find my expressions somewhat exaggerated, but I assure

[1] Ps. xlix. 9-14.
[2] John iv. 7.
[3] *Cf.* Luke ii. 19.
[4] Tob. xii. 7.

The vocation of a Priest! With what love, my Jesus, would I bear Thee in my hand, when my words brought Thee down from Heaven! With what love would I give Thee to souls! And yet, while longing to be a Priest, I admire and envy the humility of St. Francis of Assisi, and am drawn to imitate him by refusing the sublime dignity of the Priesthood. How reconcile these opposite tendencies? [1]

Like the Prophets and Doctors, I would be a light unto souls, I would travel to every land to preach Thy name, O my Beloved, and raise on heathen soil the glorious standard of Thy Cross. One mission alone would not satisfy my longings. I would spread the Gospel to the ends of the earth, even to the most distant isles. I would be a Missionary, not for a few years only, but, were it possible, from the beginning of the world till the consummation of time. Above all, I thirst for the Martyr's crown. It was the desire of my earliest days, and the desire has deepened with the years passed in the Carmel's narrow cell. But this too is folly, since I do not sigh for one torment; I need them all to slake my thirst. Like Thee, O Adorable Spouse, I would be scourged, I would be crucified! I would be flayed like St. Bartholomew, plunged into boiling oil like St. John, or, like St. Ignatius of Antioch, ground by the teeth of wild beasts into a bread worthy of God. [2]

With St. Agnes and St. Cecilia I would offer my neck to the sword of the executioner, and like Joan of Arc I would murmur the name of Jesus at the stake.

My heart thrills at the thought of the frightful tortures Christians are to suffer at the time of Anti-Christ, and I long to undergo them all. Open, O Jesus, the Book of Life, in which are written the deeds of Thy Saints: all the deeds told in that book I long to have accomplished for Thee. To such folly as this what answer wilt Thou make? Is there on the face of this earth a soul more feeble than mine? And yet, precisely because I am feeble, it has

[1] St. Francis of Assisi, out of humility, refused to accept the sublime dignity of the Priesthood, and remained a Deacon until his death. [ED.]

[2] An allusion to the beautiful words of the martyr St. Ignatius of Antioch, uttered when he heard the roar of the lions in the Roman arena. "I am the wheat of Christ; let me be ground by the teeth of the wild beasts, that I may become clean bread." [ED.]

delighted Thee to accede to my least and most child-like desires, and to-day it is Thy good pleasure to realise those other desires, more vast than the Universe. These aspirations becoming a true martyrdom, I opened, one day, the Epistles of St. Paul to seek relief in my sufferings. My eyes fell on the 12th and 13th chapters of the First Epistle to the Corinthians. I read that all cannot become Apostles, Prophets, and Doctors; that the Church is composed of different members; that the eye cannot also be the hand. The answer was clear, but it did not fulfil my desires, or give to me the peace I sought. *"Then descending into the depths of my nothingness, I was so lifted up that I reached my aim."* [1]

Without being discouraged I read on, and found comfort in this counsel: *"Be zealous for the better gifts. And I show unto you a yet more excellent way."* [2] The Apostle then explains how all perfect gifts are nothing without Love, that Charity is the most excellent way of going surely to God. At last I had found rest.

Meditating on the mystical Body of Holy Church, I could not recognise myself among any of its members as described by St. Paul, or was it not rather that I wished to recognise myself in all? Charity provided me with the key to my vocation. I understood that since the Church is a body composed of different members, the noblest and most important of all the organs would not be wanting. I knew that the Church has a heart, that this heart burns with love, and that it is love alone which gives life to its members. I knew that if this love were extinguished, the Apostles would no longer preach the Gospel, and the Martyrs would refuse to shed their blood. I understood that love embraces all vocations, that it is all things, and that it reaches out through all the ages, and to the uttermost limits of the earth, because it is eternal.

Then, beside myself with joy, I cried out: "O Jesus, my Love, at last I have found my vocation. My vocation is love! Yes, I have found my place in the bosom of the Church, and this place, O my God, Thou hast Thyself given to me: in the heart of the Church, my Mother, I will be LOVE! ... Thus I shall be all things: thus will my dream be realised. ..."

Why do I say I am beside myself with joy? This does not

[1] St. John of the Cross.   [2] 1 Cor. xii. 31.

convey my thought. Rather is it peace which has become my portion—the calm peace of the sailor when he catches sight of the beacon which lights him to port. O luminous Beacon of Love! I know how to come even unto Thee, I have found the means of borrowing Thy Fires.

I am but a weak and helpless child, yet it is my very weakness which makes me dare to offer myself, O Jesus, as victim to Thy Love.

In olden days pure and spotless holocausts alone were acceptable to the Omnipotent God. Nor could His Justice be appeased, save by the most perfect sacrifices. But the law of fear has given place to the law of love, and Love has chosen me, a weak and imperfect creature, as its victim. Is not such a choice worthy of God's Love? Yea, for in order that Love may be fully satisfied, it must stoop even unto nothingness, and must transform that nothingness into fire. O my God, I know it—*"Love is repaid by love alone."* [1] Therefore I have sought, I have found, how to ease my heart, by rendering Thee love for love.

"Use the riches that make men unjust, to find you friends who may receive you into everlasting dwellings." [2] This, O Lord, is the advice Thou gavest to Thy disciples after complaining that *"the children of this world are wiser in their generation than the children of light."* [3]

Child of light, as I am, I understood that my desires to be all things, and to embrace all vocations, were riches that might well make me unjust; so I set to work to use them for the making of friends. Mindful of the prayer of Eliseus when he asked the Prophet Elias for his double spirit, I presented myself before the company of the Angels and Saints and addressed them thus: "I am the least of all creatures. I know my mean estate, but I know that noble and generous hearts love to do good. Therefore, O Blessed Inhabitants of the Celestial City, I entreat you to adopt me as your child. All the glory that you help me to acquire, will be yours; only deign to hear my prayer, and obtain for me a double portion of the love of God."

O my God! I cannot measure the extent of my request, I should fear to be crushed by the very weight of its audacity. My only excuse is my claim to childhood, and that children do

---

[1] St. John of the Cross.   [2] *Cf.* Luke xvi. 9.   [3] Luke xvi. 8.

not grasp the full meaning of their words. Yet if a father or mother were on the throne and possessed vast treasures, they would not hesitate to grant the desires of those little ones, more dear to them than life itself. To give them pleasure they will stoop even unto folly.

Well, I am a child of Holy Church, and the Church is a Queen, because she is now espoused to the Divine King of Kings. I ask not for riches or glory, not even the glory of Heaven— that belongs by right to my brothers the Angels and Saints, and my own glory shall be the radiance that streams from the queenly brow of my Mother, the Church. Nay, I ask for Love. To love Thee, Jesus, is now my only desire. Great deeds are not for me; I cannot preach the Gospel or shed my blood. No matter! My brothers work in my stead, and I, a little child, stay close to the throne, and love Thee for all who are in the strife.

But how shall I show my love, since love proves itself by deeds? Well! the little child will strew flowers . . . she will embalm the Divine Throne with their fragrance, she will sing Love's Canticle in silvery tones. Yea, my Beloved, it is thus my short life shall be spent in Thy sight. The only way I have of proving my love is to strew flowers before Thee—that is to say, I will let no tiny sacrifice pass, no look, no word. I wish to profit by the smallest actions, and to do them for Love. I wish to suffer for Love's sake, and for Love's sake even to rejoice: thus shall I strew flowers. Not one shall I find without scattering its petals before Thee . . . and I will sing . . . I will sing always, even if my roses must be gathered from amidst thorns; and the longer and sharper the thorns, the sweeter shall be my song.

But of what avail to thee, my Jesus, are my flowers and my songs? I know it well: this fragrant shower, these delicate petals of little price, these songs of love from a poor little heart like mine, will nevertheless be pleasing unto Thee. Trifles they are, but Thou wilt smile on them. The Church Triumphant, stooping towards her child, will gather up these scattered rose leaves, and, placing them in Thy Divine Hands, there to acquire an infinite value, will shower them on the Church Suffering to extinguish its flames, and on the Church Militant to obtain its victory.

O my Jesus, I love Thee! I love my Mother, the Church;

I bear in mind that *"the least act of pure love is of more value to her than all other works together."* [1]

But is this pure love really in my heart? Are not my boundless desires but dreams—but foolishness? If this be so, I beseech Thee to enlighten me; Thou knowest I seek but the truth. If my desires be rash, then deliver me from them, and from this most grievous of all martyrdoms. And yet I confess, if I reach not those heights to which my soul aspires, this very martyrdom, this foolishness, will have been sweeter to me than eternal bliss will be, unless by a miracle Thou shouldst take from me all memory of the hopes I entertained upon earth. Jesus, Jesus! if the mere desire of Thy Love awakens such delight, what will it be to possess it, to enjoy it for ever?

How can a soul so imperfect as mine aspire to the plenitude of Love? What is the key of this mystery? O my only Friend, why dost Thou not reserve these infinite longings to lofty souls, to the eagles that soar in the heights? Alas! I am but a poor little unfledged bird. I am not an eagle, I have but the eagle's eyes and heart! Yet, notwithstanding my exceeding littleness, I dare to gaze upon the Divine Sun of Love, and I burn to dart upwards unto Him! I would fly, I would imitate the eagles; but all that I can do is to lift up my little wings—it is beyond my feeble power to soar. What is to become of me? Must I die of sorrow because of my helplessness? Oh, no! I will not even grieve. With daring self-abandonment there will I remain until death, my gaze fixed upon that Divine Sun. Nothing shall affright me, nor wind nor rain. And should impenetrable clouds conceal the Orb of Love, and should I seem to believe that beyond this life there is darkness only, that would be the hour of perfect joy, the hour in which to push my confidence to its uttermost bounds. I should not dare to detach my gaze, well knowing that beyond the dark clouds the sweet Sun still shines.

So far, O my God, I understand Thy Love for me. But Thou knowest how often I forget this, my only care. I stray from Thy side, and my scarcely fledged wings become draggled in the muddy pools of earth; then I lament *"like a young swallow,"* [2] and my lament tells Thee all, and I remember, O Infinite Mercy! that *"Thou didst not come to call the just, but sinners."* [3]

[1] St. John of the Cross.   [2] Isa. xxxviii. 14.   [3] Matt. iv. 15.

Yet shouldst Thou still be deaf to the plaintive cries of Thy feeble creature, shouldst Thou still be veiled, then I am content to remain benumbed with cold, my wings bedraggled, and once more I rejoice in this well-deserved suffering.

O Sun, my only Love, I am happy to feel myself so small, so frail in Thy sunshine, and I am in peace . . . I know that all the eagles of Thy Celestial Court have pity on me, they guard and defend me, they put to flight the vultures—the demons that fain would devour me. I fear them not, these demons, I am not destined to be their prey, but the prey of the Divine Eagle.

O Eternal Word! O my Saviour! Thou art the Divine Eagle Whom I love—Who lurest me. Thou Who, descending to this land of exile, didst will to suffer and to die, in order to bear away the souls of men and plunge them into the very heart of the Blessed Trinity—Love's Eternal Home! Thou Who, re-ascending into inaccessible light, dost still remain concealed here in our vale of tears under the snow-white semblance of the Host, and this, to nourish me with Thine own substance! O Jesus! forgive me if I tell Thee that Thy Love reacheth even unto folly. And in face of this folly, what wilt Thou, but that my heart leap up to Thee? How could my trust have any limits?

I know that the Saints have made themselves as fools for Thy sake; being "eagles," they have done great things. I am too little for great things, and my folly it is to hope that Thy Love accepts me as victim; my folly it is to count on the aid of Angels and Saints, in order that I may fly unto Thee with Thine own wings, O my Divine Eagle! For as long a time as Thou willest I shall remain—my eyes fixed upon Thee. I long to be allured by Thy Divine Eyes; I would become Love's prey. I have the hope that Thou wilt one day swoop down upon me, and, bearing me away to the Source of all Love, Thou wilt plunge me at last into that glowing abyss, that I may become for ever its happy Victim.

O Jesus! would that I could tell all *little souls* of Thine ineffable condescension! I feel that if by any possibility Thou couldst find one weaker than my own, Thou wouldst take delight in loading her with still greater favours, provided that she abandoned herself with entire confidence to Thine Infinite Mercy. But, O my Spouse, why these desires of mine to make known the secrets of Thy love? Is it not Thyself alone Who hast taught them to me, and canst Thou not unveil them to others? Yea, I know it, and this I implore Thee! . . .

I ENTREAT THEE TO LET THY DIVINE EYES REST UPON A VAST NUMBER OF LITTLE SOULS, I ENTREAT THEE TO CHOOSE, IN THIS WORLD, A LEGION OF LITTLE VICTIMS OF THY LOVE.

8. DANTE ALIGHIERI:
CANTOS XXXI, XXXII AND XXXIII OF THE *PARADISO*

¶DANTE was not read until comparatively recent years as a religious poet. The fourteenth and fifteenth centuries, for example, seem to have numbered him among the strictly secular writers. But to the nineteenth century he became "the central man of all the world" and the man in whom thirteen hundred silent years "found a voice." Gradually the stress was laid upon his doctrine and ethical views, for which he had created a symbolism of incomparable beauty and richness of texture. Accordingly, it is only proper that the three final cantos of the *Paradiso* should be included in a book which, like this, aims to provide glimpses of the world's spiritual masterpieces. The translation employed is that of the Rev. A. R. Bandini, published in San Francisco during 1931.

Having traveled through Hell, Purgatory and Heaven, the poet now envisages the ultimate splendour of the Saints and Angels in the company of God. The light which falls on these lines is intense, almost fierce. It is only to a limited extent the product of mystical reflection, but is rather the final spectacle unveiled before the intellect which has pondered the Divine mysteries to the end.*

---

* From Dante's *Paradiso*. Translated by the Rev. Albert R. Bandini. San Francisco: The People's Publishing Co., 1931.

CANTO XXXI
ARGUMENT

In the Empyrean. The Poet is in the interior of the Rose of Paradise: the leaves thereof are the Blessed Spirits on their thrones. Angels fly around and up and down. Beatrice leaves Dante and sits on her throne. Saint Bernard appears, instead, at the Poet's side. Vision of the light of the Virgin Mary.

THUS in the form of a white-colored rose
  The holy army spread before my sight—
  The one whom Christ as bride on Calvary
    chose;—

The other one who sees, the while in flight,
And sings the glory of their Beloved One
—The bounty, too, which gave to them such height—

(As bees that, swarming, drop for once upon
  The flowers, then again returning where
  Their labor is into sweet flavor spun),

Descended in the spacious flower, fair
  For wealth of many leaves; again then rose
  Up where their love has its abode for e'er.

Their face was all like flame that lusty glows;
  Golden their wings; the rest of such white hue
  That passed the limit of all earthly snows.

When down the flower, from tier to tier, they flew
  They offered of the peace and ardor sheer
  Which, fanning their white flanks, within they drew.

The spreading—twixt the flower's highest tier
  And what stood over—of such plenitude
  Of wings, made view and splendor no less clear;

Because the light divine doth so intrude
　　The universe (as this has aptness for't)
　　That by no object it can be withstood.

That full of joy, that safe and changeless court
　　With the new people thronged and with the old,
　　Did to one aim, with sight and love, resort.

O thou who give'st them peace, O light three-fold
　　Sparkling upon their sight, a gleaming One,
　　Look down from heaven and our storm behold!

If the Barbarians from such lands whereon
　　Helice hovers, wheeling every day—
　　Enamored still—in closeness to her son,

When seeing Rome were 'whelmed into dismay
　　At her great works, when Lateran did rise
　　Above all things that mortals could survey—

I, rapt from human things to godly assize,
　　From time's demesne to the eternal strand,
　　From Florence to a people just and wise,

By what a wonder was I not unmanned!
　　Forsooth, through wonder and through joy as well
　　Mute and unhearing, I loved there to stand.

And as a pilgrim cheered as he doth dwell
　　(His vow absolved) in the long-yearnèd fane,
　　—And how it was, already he thinks to tell;

Thus through the living light of that domain
　　I led my eyes and strolled from grade to grade,
　　Now up, now down, now circling 'round again.

I saw such aspects that to love persuade
　　Shining with their own smile and alien light,
　　And acts in every honesty arrayed.

How Paradise in general is dight
 Already I had surveyed the form entire,
 But stopping in no part to fix my sight.

And now I turned (moved by renewed desire)
 Since on a doubt which kept my mind oppressed
 I yearnèd from my Lady to enquire.

One thing I sought, another met my quest;
 Beatrice I thought to see, I saw instead
 An agèd man, robed like the glorious blest.

Upon his eyes and face was overspread
 A joy benign; in him the charity
 Of tender father plainly was imagèd.

And "Where is she?" such was my sudden cry.
 And he: "So that thy yearnings' end thou gain
 Moved me Beatrice from my place on high;

Upon the third of tiers thy vision train,
 Down from the top, and there thou shalt see her
 Upon the throne which her deserts obtain."

Answering not, I raised my eyes up there
 And saw my Lady and the crown she wore
 As she reflected the eternal glare.

From thunder's highest region there's no more
 Distance down to the range of human eye
 (Were one e'en sunk to deepest ocean floor)

As there Beatrice from my sight stood high.
 But that was of no hindrance, since her traits,
 Unfaded, came to me immediately.

—"O Lady in whom my hope invigorates,
 And who, for my welfare, didst not despise
 To leave thy foot's imprints within Hell's gates,

For all the things on which have gazed my eyes
    From thy most lavish aid and thy puissance
    The grace and strength in me I recognise.

From serfdom thou gave'st me deliverance
    Leading through every way, through every shift
    That could my steps on the long path advance.

Guard now in me thy most exalted gift,
    So that my soul, by thee restored, yet may
    Please thee when from its body set adrift."

Such was my prayer—and, so far away
    As seemed, her smiling gaze on me she bent,
    Then turned unto the fount of timeless day.

The holy Senior then: "To make th' intent
    Of this thy journey reach perfection's height
    (Wherefore by prayer and holy love I'm sent)

Over this garden wing thy vision's flight;
    Such view shall sharpen thy regard and spur
    Thy climb yet higher to the godly light.

And Heaven's Queen all graces will confer
    On us; She for whose love am all aflame
    I, Bernard, her most faithful follower."

As one who haply from Croatia came
    Yearning for our Veronica, and looks on
    Ne'er sated, thinking of its ancient fame—

But speaks within his thought, while it is shown:
    "Jesus, my Lord, true God, what here I see
    Is it a semblance truly like your own?"

Such like, I gazed upon the charity
    So bright, of him who in his worldly days
    Had tasted of that peace, in ecstasy.

He then began again: "O child of grace,
    This joyous state shall yet unknown remain
    To thee, if at this depth thou keep'st thy gaze.

But let thy eyes the farthest tier attain
    So that thou may'st perceive where sits the Queen
    To whom devoutly subject is this reign."

Upward I gazed: as in the matutine
    Horizon brightens all the orient
    More than the rim where the sunset is seen,

Thus, with my eyes as if in an ascent
    From vale to hill, I saw the edge extreme
    More than the other front with light besprent.

And as on earth, where one looks for the team
    Misled by Phaeton, doth the light increase
    And over either side less is the gleam,

In such a way that oriflamme of peace
    Shone brighter at midway, while on each side
    Softened the flame in similar degrees.

And at that central part, with wings oped wide
    Thousands of forms angelical, in way
    And splendor each distinguished, I descried.

And smiling on their songs and on their play
    A beauty there I saw, which filled the sight
    Of all the other saints, with joyous ray.

Could I in telling reach to such a height
    As in imagining, I would not dare
    Touch on the very least of that delight.

Bernard, as he perceived that I did stare
    Fixed and intent upon her warming fire
    With such a love his eyes turned unto her

That mine gazed on with even more desire.

CANTO XXXII

ARGUMENT

In the Empyrean. Bernard points out to Dante the main divisions of the Rose of Paradise and the most glorious personages having there their throne.

Fixed to his joy, the contemplating soul
    Let from his lips this holy sermon pour,
    Assuming willingly a doctor's rôle:

"The wound which Mary closed and soothèd o'er
    With balm, the One so beauteous at her feet
    Is she who opened it and pierced it sore.

'Mid those who have in the third tier their seat,
    Beneath that one—by Beatrice's throne—
    The ancient Rachel will thy vision meet.

Sarah, Rebecca, Judith and the one
    Whose great-grandson sang 'Miserere mei'
    That God his sin repented might condone,

From step to step thus sit thou may'st survey
    As I the proper name call at each row
    While through the rose's leaves I make my way.

Far as the seventh tier, and still below
    Therefrom, are women of the Jewish race
    Whose line athwart all leaves a mark doth show.

For, as the faith in Christ held in two ways
    Fixed its regard, these women are the wall
    Whereat is parted this divine staircase.

Upon this part wherein the flower with all
    Its leaves is ripened, those whose faith was aimed
    Unto the future Savior, have their stall.

Upon the other, where some voids are framed
    Within the semicircles, those abide
    Whom faith in Christ, already come, inflamed.

And as the glorious throne—upon this side—
    Of Heaven's Queen, and those on which they sit
    Who are beneath, make such a great divide,

Thus mighty John's own throne stands opposite:
    Who suffered desert, death by impious hands—
    Ever a saint—and for two years, the Pit.

Beneath him Francis marks that severance,
    Benedict and Augustine and the rest
    From tier to tier, down to this lowest stance.

Note how God's high decree is here expressed,
    Since Faith's two revelations shall complete,
    In balanced way, this garden of the blest.

Know, too, that downward from the leaves that meet—
    Midway—the length of the two straight partitions
    No merits truly one's own afford a seat;

Merits of others do, with some conditions:
    For these are spirits loosened from the shell
    Of flesh, ere they could grow to true volitions.

Of this their aspect doth quite clearly tell,
    And so the childish treble of their song
    If dost to them look sharp and listen well.

Yet doubtest thou and doubts impede thy tongue:
    But while such subtle thoughts thy mind occlude
    I shall resolve thy knots, albeit strong.

Within this realm, in all its amplitude,
    Cannot have place a casual happening
    (Even as hunger, thirst, or saddened mood)

For by eternal law is set each thing
　　Which hereabout thou see'st, to proper gauge
　　Answering as to finger doth a ring.

Therefore this people called at early age
　　To the true life, have not without a cause
　　Among themselves a varied privilege.

The King from whom this reign celestial draws
　　Of such a love and of such joy the prize
　　That none could wish for aught beyond its laws,

All minds that He created in the guise
　　Of His own joy, at will endows with grace
　　In various ways: let the effect suffice.

And clearly and directly this displays
　　The Holy Scripture telling of that pair
　　Whose wrath, e'en in the womb, was felt to blaze.

Hence following the color of the hair
　　Of granted grace, thus the Highest Light
　　Makes them the garland of their worth to wear.

Of their own deeds, therefore, regardless quite,
　　Through varied ranks they here receive their meed
　　For having differed in the primal sight.

During the early centuries, to lead
　　Unto salvation spirits innocent
　　Only of the faith of parents there was need;

After the primal ages were all spent
　　Then of the males unto the plumes unstained
　　By circumcision needed power was lent.

But when the time of grace at last was gained
　　Except when perfectly baptised in Christ
　　The innocents below must be constrained.

But now look on the face which more to Christ
 Is like: he only who becomes the knower
 Of that clear light has strength to gaze on Christ."

And over her I saw such gladness pour
 Brought by the holy minds—a wingèd host
 Created such that on those heights may soar—

That what so far to me had been disclosed
 Never held me so wondering, nor e'er
 To me God's semblance was so much exposed.

And from the love who first descended there
 AVE MARIA GRATIA PLENA—a cry
 Came while he spread his wings in front of her.

And to that chant divine rang a reply
 Up from that blessèd court, from every turn,
 And on all faces shone new clarity.

"O holy father, thou who dost not spurn,
 For me, to come this low and leave the place
 So sweet, where is thy seat by lot eterne,

Who is that Angel whose so festive gaze
 Is fixèd of our Queen into the eyes,
 So enamored that he look like flaming braise?"

Thus I invoked again the sermon wise
 Of him who fairer shone with Mary's glow
 As doth the star of morn with the sunrise.

"Whatever grace and gallantry may show
 In angel or in soul"—the father spake—
 "All is in him and we desire it so,

For it was he the chosen one to take
 The palm to Mary, when mortality
 The Son of God indued, for our own sake.

But as I shall proceed, let follow me
 Thy eyes—the great patricians to review
 Of this most just and pious Empery.

Those twain who sit up there, most happy shew
 Since closest to Augusta they were raised:
 Like roots they are from which this rose outgrew.

The one who leftward at her flank is placed
 The ancient father is whose palate bold
 Brought on the mortals such a bitter taste;

On the right flank thou see'st the father old
 Of Holy Church: by Christ into his hands
 The keys of this fair flower were gi'en to hold.

And he who saw, ere his deliverance
 All the distresses of the beauteous bride
 Won by the nails and by the piercing lance

Sits there by him; and by the other's side
 The leader under whom was fed with manna
 The ungrateful people, fickle, dour with pride.

Sitting to Peter opposite see Anna
 So happy in her daughter's countenance:
 Hardly she moves her eyes, singing Hosanna.

Against the greatest sire of men, there stands
 Lucia, she by whom thy Lady was sent
 When thou wert ruining with downward glance.

But since thy vision's time almost is spent
 Here we shall cease, as doth a tailor wise
 Who cuts the gown to fit the cloth's extent;

Let to the primal love be fixed our eyes
 That looking unto Him thou pierce the fire
 Blazing from him, far as thy power may rise.

But now indeed, lest haply thou retire
    Moving thy wings, while thinking to progress,
    'Tis meet by prayer her favor to require:

Favor from her who may thy striving bless:
    And that thy heart be with my words at one,
    With thy affection follow my address."

And he began this holy orison.

CANTO XXXIII
ARGUMENT

Saint Bernard prays to the Blessed Virgin that the grace of the final Vision be granted to Dante. The Poet is then enabled to pierce into the supreme mysteries: the Trinity and Unity of God and the Incarnation of the God and the Son.

"O Virgin Mother, daughter of thy Son;
    Humble, and higher than created thing,
    Point where th' Eternal Plan was fixèd on;

Thou art who didst to human nature bring
    Such nobleness, its Maker did not spurn
    To give Himself unto its fashioning.

Within thy womb anew the Love did burn
    Whose warmth beneficent has caused this rose
    To flower in this realm of peace eterne.

Thou art to us a torch of love that glows
    Like sun at noon: to mortals in their plight
    A fount of hope thou art that ceaseless flows.

Lady, so great thou art, such is thy might,
    Whoever craves for grace and seeks not thee,
    His hope, deprived of wings, attempts a flight.

Not only answers thy benignity
    Those who have asked; oft, of the spoken word
    Thou dost most liberally forestall the plea.

Pity is in thee, in thee misericord:
    In thee magnificence; whate'er we call
    Noble in creatures, all in thee is stored.

This man who from the lowest slough of all
    The universe has come so far and gazed
    Upon each mode of living spirital,

Now humbly begs of thee that he be graced
    With such a power that e'en to greater height
    Toward bliss supreme his vision may be raised.

And I who never burned for my own sight
    As now for his I do, all prayers tend
    To thee, and pray they may not be too slight,

So that thy prayers may strengthen him and rend
    The clouds which his mortality surround
    Unfolding thus to him the blissful end.

And after such a sight, O Queen God-crowned,
    Thou who for all thy wishes hast puissance,
    Again I pray—keep his affections sound.

Help him to conquer human circumstance:
    Beatrice and so many of the blest
    See how, with me, toward thee now fold their hands."

And now upon my advocate did rest
    The eyes beloved by God and honored high:
    Joy at the prayer devout they plainly expressed.

They gazed then on th' eternal radiancy
    In which—we must believe—cannot be sent
    With equal clearness, a created eye.

And at this time, since now was imminent
    The goal of all desires, I felt the fire—
    As it was meet—of my keen yearnings spent.

Bernard—that I should raise my vision higher
    Nodded and smiled; but I had sought that view,
    Of my own self fulfilling his desire.

Becoming pure, my sight was piercing through
    Deeper and deeper in the timeless ray
    Of Light excelse which in itself is true.

My vision passed, from henceforth, every way
    Of human tongue which to such sight must yield—
    And such excess doth memory dismay.

As one sees things which dreaming fancies build,
    And—the dream past—the emotion still is felt
    But memory to all the rest is sealed;

Such I; for to its end almost is spelt
    My vision, while 'tis yet distilled upon
    My heart the sweetness that from it has welled.

Thus is dissolved the snow beneath the sun;
    Thus on light leaves the Sibyl's oracle
    Was by the wind dispersèd here and yon.

O Light Supreme, who dost so highly excel
    All mortal concepts, grant my mind a trace
    Of that which then to me was visible.

And to my tongue give of such power the grace
    That of thy glory a spark at least I leave
    To those whom earth shall bear in future days.

If aught of it my memory can retrieve
    And voice it in my song (were it a mite)
    More of thy wonders mortals will conceive.

I think I had been wholly lost (so bright
    The living ray which did my vision meet)
    Had I from it turnèd aside my sight.

And I recall that, fearing that defeat,
    My gaze grew bolder that keen ray to bear
    Until it joined with the glory infinite.

O grace abundant, through which I did dare
    To cast my sight into the light eterne
    Exhausting all that I found visive there!

And gathered in its depth I did discern
    —In but one tome, love-bound—all that we see
    Throughout the Whole, whatever page we turn.

Accident, substance and each property
    Thereof, together in such way conflated
    That what I say naught but a flash can be.

Methinks that of this knot I contemplated
    The universal form, since with each word
    I say of this, my joy I feel dilated.

Yet only one point made more my memory blurred
    Than five and twenty centuries the emprise
    When Argo's shadow Neptune's wonder stirred.

Thus all my mind enraptured stood: its eyes
    Held fixèd and unswerving and intent,
    More ardent e'er, to look and to cognize.

Such one becomes in that envelopment
    That to a turning thence for other lure
    It is impossible e'er to consent,

Because the Good our will aims to procure
    All there is held; outside of it is found
    Defective what in it is whole and pure.

And now my words shall even shorter sound
    Than babe's who wets his tongue upon the breast—
    Even with what is still to memory bound.

A simple semblance only was manifest
    (Since nothing there is old and nothing new)
    Within the light where was my gaze addressed.

But keen yet more and more my vision grew
    The while I gazed; my changing made appear
    That single semblance altered in my view.

In that exalted light's profound and clear
    Subsistence, to my eyes three circles gleamed
    Of varied hue but closing equal sphere.

One from another did reflect and seemed
    Iris from Iris: fire-like the third ring
    Equally breathed hence and thence, I deemed.

How scant and feeble are my words to sing
    My concept: this—to what I there descried—
    For words of "smallness" sends me beggaring.

O light eternal who sole in thee dost bide,
    Sole know'st thyself: thus knowing and self-known
    Thou bring'st forth joyful love in inward tide!

That circulation which in Thee there shone
    Conceived within, like light that comes from light,
    After my eyes had gazed awhile thereon,

Within itself and of one color quite
    Bore—so methought—our human form designed,
    Wherefore all into that I fixed my sight.

As the geometer who with all his mind
    Strives for the circle's measure, gives great thought,
    But the principle needed fails to find:

Thus in that novel sight my wit was caught.
   I yearned to see how did the image fit
   Into the circle, how in it 'twas wrought;

But my own plumage this would not permit,
   Had not then struck my mind a radiance
   Which brought fulfilment of desire with it.

Here failed my lofty phantasy's puissance,
   While turned my will and my desire, as even
   As doth a wheel which moves all points at once,

The Love which sun and stars moves in the heaven.

II
SPIRITUAL COUNSEL

―――

1. THOMAS À KEMPIS:
FOURTH BOOK OF *THE IMITATION*
OF CHRIST

¶In all probability, *The Imitation of Christ* is the most widely read book ever published, if one excepts the Bible. It was written for men and women who wished to live apart from the world, in semi-retirement or in the cloister; and yet millions of lay persons have found it easy to adapt the counsel here given to their conduct. The *Imitation* has the advantage of being useful both as a manual to accompany meditation and as a prayer book. Most of the fourth book is reprinted here from what seems to the editor the best of all versions in English —that issued, with notes, and a learned introduction, by Canon C. Bigg (1898). Some of the notes have been conserved. The reader should notice that this translation, in addition to being accurate, preserves to a remarkable degree the rhythm and flavor of the original. As one helpful means, Canon Bigg retained the author's punctuation.

During 1441, Thomas à Kempis (c. 1380-1471) completed the manuscript of the *Imitation* but did not expressly declare that it was his own work. As a result, a number of critics have maintained that he was not the author and have suggested other names, particularly that of Gerson. To-day the evidence supporting Thomas's authorship appears so overwhelming that few dispute it. He was born near Cologne and eventually joined the Brethren of the Common Life, a community of lay-folk devoted to living apart from the world but bound by no vows.*

* From *The Imitation of Christ*. By Thomas à Kempis. Translated and edited by C. Bigg, D.D. London: Methuen and Co., 1898.

FOURTH BOOK

OF CHRIST'S SPEAKING INWARDLY TO THE
FAITHFUL SOUL

CHAPTER I

 *WILL hearken what the Lord God will speak in me.*[1]
Blessed is the soul which hears the Lord speaking within her: and receives from His mouth the word of consolation. Blessed are the ears that welcome the runlets of the Divine whisper:[2] and heed not the whisperings of this world. Blessed indeed are those ears that listen not to the voice which babbles without: but to the Truth which teaches within. Blessed are the eyes: which are shut to the outward, but open to the inward. Blessed are they that press into things within: and study to prepare themselves more and more by daily exercises, for the receipt of Heavenly secrets. Blessed are they who give themselves eagerly up to God: and shake themselves free from all worldly hindrance.

Consider this O my soul; and shut the door of thy sensual desires: that thou mayest hear what the Lord thy God shall speak in thee.

Thus saith thy Beloved. I am thy Salvation: thy Peace and thy Life. Keep thyself with Me: and thou shalt find peace. Let the transitory pass: seek the eternal. What are all temporal things; but a snare? and what can all creatures avail thee; if thou be forsaken by the Creator? Bid farewell therefore to all things, make thyself pleasing and faithful to thy Creator: that thou mayest lay hold of true blessedness.

[1] Psal. lxxxv. 8 (lxxxiv. 9)   [2] Job. iv. 12 (Vulgate).

THAT THE TRUTH SPEAKETH INWARDLY WITHOUT NOISE OF WORDS

CHAPTER II

SPEAK *Lord: for Thy servant heareth.*[1]

I am Thy servant: grant me understanding that I may know Thy testimonies.[2] Incline my heart to the words of Thy mouth:[3] let Thy speech distil as the dew.[4]

The children of Israel in times past said unto Moses. Speak thou unto us and we will hear; let not the Lord speak unto us: lest we die.[5] Not so Lord not so I beseech Thee: but rather with the prophet Samuel I humbly and earnestly entreat. Speak Lord for Thy servant heareth. Let not Moses speak unto me nor any of the prophets: but rather do Thou speak Lord God Inspirer and Enlightener of all prophets; for Thou alone without them canst perfectly instruct me: but they without Thee can profit nothing.

They indeed may sound forth words: but they cannot give the Spirit. Beautifully do they speak: but if Thou be silent they kindle not the heart. They teach the letter: but Thou openest the sense.[6] They bring forth mysteries: but Thou unlockest the meaning of sealed things. They declare Thy commandments: but Thou helpest to fulfil them. They shew the way: but Thou givest strength to walk in it.

What they do is all without: but Thou instructest and enlightenest the heart. They water outwardly: but Thou givest fruitfulness. They cry aloud in words: but Thou impartest understanding to the hearing.

Let not Moses therefore speak unto me but Thou O Lord my God the Eternal Truth: lest I die and prove unfruitful, if I be only warned outwardly and not kindled inwardly; lest the word turn to my condemnation if it be heard and not done, known and not loved: believed and not observed.

Speak therefore Lord for Thy servant heareth: for Thou hast

[1] Sam. iii. 10.
[2] Psal. cxix. (cxviii.) 125.
[3] Psal. lxxviii. (lxxvii.) 1.
[4] Deut. xxxii. 2.
[5] Ex. xx. 19.
[6] Luke xxiv. 45 (Vulgate).

the words of eternal life.[1] Speak Thou unto me to the partial comfort of my soul and to the perfect amendment of my life: and to Thy praise and glory and everlasting honour.

THAT THE WORDS OF GOD ARE TO BE HEARD WITH HUMILITY AND THAT MANY WEIGH THEM NOT

CHAPTER III

Son hear My words words most sweet: surpassing all knowledge of philosophers and wise men of this world. My words are Spirit and Life:[2] not to weighed by the understanding of man. They are not to be abused for complacent vanity; but heard in silence: and received with all humility and great affection.

And I said. Blessed is the man whom Thou shalt instruct O Lord: and shalt teach out of Thy Law. That Thou mayest give him rest from evil days:[3] and that he be not desolate upon earth.

I taught the Prophets from the beginning saith the Lord and cease not even to this day to speak to all: but many are deaf to My voice and hard. Most men listen to the world more readily than to God; they follow more readily the lust of their flesh: than the good pleasure of God. The world promises things temporal and little and is served with great avidity; I promise things high and eternal: and the hearts of men remain untouched. Who serves and obeys Me in all things so punctually; as the world and its lords are served? Blush Sidon saith the sea.[4] And if thou ask the cause: hear wherefore.

For a slender benefice men will run for miles: for eternal life few will once lift a foot from the ground. The poorest price is deemed worth effort, for a single coin at times there is shameful contention; for a vain matter and a light promise men shrink not from toil by day and night: but alas for an unchangeable good for a priceless reward, for the highest honour and endless glory men grudge even the least fatigue.

Blush therefore thou slothful and complaining servant; that

[1] John vi. 68.   [3] Psal. xciv. (xciii.) 12, 13.
[2] John vi. 63.   [4] Is. xxiii. 4.

they are found readier for destruction: than thou for life. They rejoice more in vanity: than thou in truth.

Sometimes indeed they are balked of their hope; but My promise fails no man: nor sends away empty him that trusts in Me. What I have promised I will give; what I have said I will fulfil: if only a man remain faithful in My love even to the end. I am the Rewarder of all good men: and the strong Approver of all devout men.

Write thou My words in Thy heart and meditate diligently on them: for in time of temptation they will be very needful. What thou understandest not when thou readest: thou shalt know in the day of visitation. In two ways I visit Mine elect: namely with temptation and with consolation. And daily I read two lessons to them; one in reproving their vices: another in exhorting them to the increase of virtues.

He that hath My words and despiseth them: hath One that shall judge him in the last day.[1]

A Prayer to Implore the Grace of Devotion

O Lord my God Thou art all my good. And who am I that I should dare to speak to Thee? I am Thy poorest little servant and a vile worm: far poorer and more contemptible than I can or dare express. Yet do Thou remember me Lord: because I am nothing, have nothing, and can do nothing. Thou alone art Good Just and Holy; Thou canst do all things,[2] Thou givest all fillest all:[3] only the sinner Thou leavest empty. Remember Thy mercies,[4] and fill my heart with Thy grace: Thou who wilt not that Thy handiwork should be empty.[5]

How can I bear with myself in this wretched life; unless Thy mercy and grace support me? Turn not Thy face away from me,[6] delay not Thy visitation; withdraw not Thy consolation: lest my soul become unto Thee as a waterless land.[6] Teach me Lord to do Thy will:[6] teach me to live worthily and humbly in Thy sight; for Thou art my Wisdom who knowest me as I am:

[1] John xii. 48.
[2] Job xliv. 2.
[3] Jer. xxiii. 24.
[4] Psal. xxv. (xxiv.) 6.
[5] Wisdom xiv. 5.
[6] Psal. cxliii. (cxlii.) 6-10.

and didst know me before the world was made and before I was born in the world.

THAT WE OUGHT TO LIVE IN TRUTH AND HUMILITY BEFORE GOD

CHAPTER IV

I

Son. Walk before Me in truth:[1] and seek Me ever in simplicity of thy heart. He that walks before Me in truth; shall be safe from the approach of harm: and the Truth shall set him free[2] from seducers and from the slanders of unjust men. If the Truth have made thee free thou shalt be free indeed:[3] and shalt not heed vain words of men.

Lord it is true. As Thou sayest, so I beseech Thee let it be with me. Let Thy Truth teach me; guard me: and keep me unto salvation at the last. Let it release me from all evil affection and inordinate love: and I shall walk with Thee in great freedom of heart.

II

I will teach thee saith the Truth what is right: and pleasing in My sight. Think on thy sins with great displeasure and grief: and never hold thyself in honour because of good works. In truth thou art a sinner: assailed and encompassed by many passions. Of thyself thou art ever drifting towards nothingness; quickly falling, quickly conquered: quickly confounded, quickly dissolved. Thou hast nought to boast of; but much reason to scorn thyself: for thou art far weaker than thou canst understand. Therefore let nothing seem great unto thee of all that thou doest. Let nothing seem great nothing precious and wonderful, nothing worthy of esteem; nothing high nothing truly praiseworthy and desirable: but that which is eternal. Let the eternal Truth delight thee above all things: and let thy utter unworthi-

---

[1] 1 Kings ii. 4: Wisdom i. 1.   [3] John viii. 36.
[2] John viii. 32.

ness be a constant grief unto thee. Fear nothing blame nothing flee nothing so anxiously, as thy vices and sins: which ought to discomfort thee more than any losses of earthly things.

Some walk not sincerely in My sight, but led by curiosity and pride wish to know My secrets and understand the high things of God: neglecting themselves and their salvation. These often fall into great temptations and sins through their pride and curiosity when I set myself against them. Fear the judgments of God: dread the wrath of the Almighty. Do not pry into the works of the Most High: but search diligently thine own iniquities what great faults thou hast committed: and how much good thou hast neglected.

Some carry their devotion only in books; some in images: some in outward signs and figures. Some have Me in their mouths: but little in their hearts.[1] Others there are who being enlightened in mind and purged in affection do always yearn for things eternal; grieve to hear of the things of earth, serve the needs of nature with sorrow: and these hear what the Spirit of Truth speaketh in them; for He teacheth them to despise earth, and love heaven: to neglect the world, and long for heaven all day and night.

OF THE WONDERFUL EFFECT OF DIVINE LOVE

CHAPTER V

I

I BLESS Thee Heavenly Father Father of my Lord Jesus Christ:[2] that Thou hast deigned to remember poor me. O Father of mercies and God of all comfort thanks be unto Thee: who sometimes with thy comfort refreshest me unworthy as I am of all comfort. I bless and glorify Thee alway with Thy only-begotten Son and the Holy Ghost the Comforter: for ever and ever.

Ah Lord God my Holy Lover, when Thou comest into my heart: all that is within me shall rejoice. Thou art my Glory:

[1] Is. xxix. 13: Matt. xv. 8: Mark vii. 6.
[2] 2 Cor. i. 3.

and the exultation of my heart. Thou art my Hope and Refuge: in the day of my trouble.[1]

But because I am still weak in love and imperfect in virtue: I need to be strengthened and comforted by Thee. Therefore visit me often and instruct me with holy discipline; set me free from evil passions: and heal my heart of all inordinate affections; that being cured and well cleansed within I may be made ready to love, brave to suffer, steady to persevere.

II

Love is a great thing, yea a great good; alone it makes every burden light: and bears evenly all that is uneven. For it carries a burden which is no burden; and makes all bitterness sweet and palatable.

The noble love of Jesus impels to great deeds: and arouses a constant desire for greater perfection. Love longs to soar: and will not be held down by things that are low. Love longs to be free, and estranged from all worldly affection: that its inner eye may not be dimmed; that it may not be caught by any temporal prosperity: or by any adversity cast down. Nothing is sweeter than Love; nothing braver, nothing higher nothing wider: nothing sweeter nothing fuller nor better in Heaven and in earth; because Love is born of God: and can only rest in God above all created things.

The lover flies runs and rejoices: he is free and cannot be held. He gives all for all: and has all in all; because he rests in One Highest above all things: from whom all good flows and proceeds. He regards not the gifts: but turns himself above all goods to the Giver. Love often knows no measure: but is fervent beyond all measure. Love feels no burden: counts no pains, exerts itself beyond its strength; talks not of impossibility: for it thinks all things possible and all permitted. It is therefore strong enough for all things; and it fulfils many things and warrants them to take effect: where he who loves not faints and lies down.

Love is watchful and sleeping slumbers not; though weary it is not tired, though hampered is not hampered, though alarmed is not affrighted: but as a lively flame and burning torch it forces

[1] Psal. lix. 16 (lviii. 17).

its way upwards and serenely passes through. If any man love: he knows what is the cry of this voice. A loud cry in the ears of God: is the glowing affection of a soul, which saith. My God my love: Thou art all mine, and I am all Thine.

Enlarge me in love; that with the inner mouth of my heart I may taste how sweet it is to love: and to be melted and bathed in love. Let me be held fast by Love: climbing above myself in ardent zeal and wonder. Let me sing the song of love, let me follow Thee my Beloved to the heights: let my soul spend itself in Thy praise exulting for love. Let me love Thee more than myself, and myself only for Thee, and in Thee all that love Thee truly: as the law of Love commandeth shining forth from Thee.

Love is swift sincere dutiful pleasant and delightful; brave patient faithful, prudent long-suffering manly: and never seeking itself. For where one seeks himself: there he falls from Love. Love is wary humble and upright; not soft nor fickle nor bent on vanities: sober chaste steady quiet and guarded in all its senses. Love is subject and obedient to prelates: to itself mean and despised, to God devout and thankful; trusting and hoping always in Him even when God is not sweet unto it: for without sorrow there is no living in love.

He that is not ready to suffer all and to resign himself to the will of the Beloved: is not worthy to be called a lover. A lover must welcome all hardship and bitterness for the sake of the Beloved: and not be turned away from Him by any rebuffs that may befall.

OF THE PROOF OF A TRUE LOVER

CHAPTER VI

I

Son thou art not yet a brave and discreet lover.

Why Lord?

Because for a light rebuff thou turnest back from thy purposes: and too eagerly seekest consolation. A brave lover stands firm in temptations: nor listens to the crafty persuasions of the Enemy.

As I please him in fair weather: so I displease not in foul. A discreet lover regards not so much the gift of his friend: as the love of the Giver. He counts the affection rather than the price: and sets the Beloved above all his gifts. A noble lover rests not in the gift: but in Me above every gift.

All is not lost, because at times thy heart is not stirred towards Me or My saints as thou wouldst. That good and sweet affection which thou sometimes feelest: is the effect of grace present, and a foretaste of thy heavenly home. But thou must not lean thereon too much: for it comes and goes. But to strive against the entrance of evil motions of the mind, and to scorn the promptings of the devil: is a sign of virtue and of great desert. Let no fancies from without therefore trouble thee: whatever the object that suggests them. Hold staunchly to thy purpose; and thy upright intention towards God.

Neither is it an illusion that at times thou art suddenly rapt into ecstasy: and presently returned unto the accustomed follies of thy heart. For these thou dost rather endure than pursue; and so long as thou mislike them and resist: it is merit and not perdition.

Know that the ancient Enemy doth try all means to thwart thy desire for good, and to empty thee from all devout exercises; to wit from the veneration of the saints from the devout commemoration of My Passion, from the salutary remembrance of sins, from the guard of thine own heart: and from the firm purpose of advancing in virtue. Many evil thoughts does he thrust upon thee, that he may cause in thee weariness and dread: to divert thee from prayer and holy reading. Humble confession he cannot abide: and if he could he would cause thee to cease from Communion.

Trust him not nor heed him: although he should often set snares of deceit for thee. Rebuke him with it: when he suggests evil and unclean thoughts. Say unto him. Away unclean Spirit, blush thou caitiff; most unclean art thou: that whisperest such things into mine ears. Begone thou wicked Seducer; thou shalt have no part in me: but Jesus shall be with me as a strong Warrior,[1] and thou shalt stand confounded. Rather would I die and bear any torment: than consent unto thee. Hold thy peace and be silent; I will hear thee no further: though thou shouldest trouble

[1] Jer. xx. 11.

me still more. The Lord is my Light and my Salvation: whom shall I fear? If a host should band together against me: my heart shall not fear? The Lord is my Helper: and my Redeemer.

II

Fight like a good soldier; and if at times thou fall through weakness, take again greater strength than before trusting in larger grace from Me: and take great heed of foolish conceit and of pride. Through this many are led into error: and fall at times into blindness almost past cure. Let the fall of the proud thus foolishly presuming on themselves: teach thee caution and constant humility.

OF HIDING GRACE UNDER THE GUARD OF HUMILITY

CHAPTER VII

Son. It is better for thee and safer to hide the grace of devotion: not to uplift thyself, nor to speak much thereof nor to prize it much; but rather to despise thyself: and to fear it as given to one unworthy. We should not cling to this affection: for it may quickly be changed to the contrary. Think when thou art in grace: how miserable and needy thou art without grace. Nor does thy progress in spiritual life, depend upon thy having the grace of comfort: but rather on thy humbly and resignedly and patiently enduring its withdrawal; so that thou dost not flag in prayer at such a time: nor suffer the rest of thy usual round of duties to fall wholly away; but rather cheerfully performest thy part to the best of thy power and understanding: and dost not wholly neglect thyself because of the dryness or anxiety of mind which thou feelest.

For there are many, who when it goes not well with them: straightway become impatient or slack. For the way of man is not always in his own power;[1] but God gives and comforts when He will and as He will and whom He will: as it shall please Him and no more.

[1] Jer. x. 23.

Some thoughtless ones have ruined themselves through the grace of devotion; because they wanted to do more than they could, not weighing the measure of their own littleness: but following the desire of their heart rather than the judgment of their reason. And because they ventured on greater things than God allowed: they quickly lost His grace. They who made themselves a nest in Heaven; [1] were abandoned to need and misery: that in abasement and poverty they might learn not to fly with their own wings: but to trust under My feathers. [2]

They that are yet novices and unskilled in the way of the Lord: unless they rule themselves by the counsel of the discreet, may easily be deceived and wrecked. And if they will rather follow their own fancy than trust to the experience of others; their end will be dangerous: if yet they will not be drawn away from their own conceit. Seldom do these who are wise in their own eyes: [3] submit humbly to be ruled by others. Better is a little wisdom with humility and a slender wit: than great treasures of learning with vain self-satisfaction. Better for thee to have little: than abound, in what may make thee proud.

He acts not discreetly, who gives himself over to joy: forgetting his former helplessness and the chastened fear of the Lord, which fears to lose the grace that has been given. Nor again is he virtuously minded; who in time of adversity or any heaviness yields too much to despair: and thinks and feels of Me less trustfully than he ought. He who in time of peace has been over secure: in time of war shall be often found too dejected and fearful. If thou couldst always remain humbly and modestly within thyself; and further couldst wisely curb and rule thy spirit: thou wouldst not fall so quickly into danger and offence.

It is good advice, that when the spirit of fervour is kindled: thou shouldest consider how it will be when that light departs. And when this happens, remember that the light may return again: which as a warning to thyself, and for Mine own glory I have withdrawn for a time. Such a trial is often more profitable: than if thou shouldest always have things prosper according to thy will. For a man's worthiness is not greater if he has more visions and comforts: or more skill in the Scriptures: or if he be placed in higher degree; but if he be grounded in true humility and full of

[1] Obadiah 4.   [2] Psal. xci. (xc.) 4.   [3] Rom. xi. 25.

divine charity: if God's honour be always his pure and single aim; if he think nothing of himself, and unfeignedly despise himself: and rejoice more to be despised and abased than honoured by others also.

OF LOW THOUGHTS OF OURSELVES IN THE SIGHT OF GOD

CHAPTER VIII

I WILL *speak unto my Lord: though I am but dust and ashes.*[1] If I think myself to be more; behold Thou standest against me, and my iniquities bear true witness: and I cannot gainsay it. But if I abase myself, and reduce myself to nothing: and shrink from all self-esteem, and grind myself to the dust that I am; Thy grace will be propitious to me and Thy light near unto my heart: and every shred of conceit shall be swallowed up in the valley of my nothingness and perish for ever. There Thou shewest me unto myself, what I am what I have been and whither I am come: for I am nothing and I knew it not.[2] If I be left to myself: behold I am nothing and all infirmity. But if Thou suddenly look upon me; I am forthwith made strong: and filled with new joy. And a great marvel it is, that I am so suddenly lifted up and so graciously embraced by Thee: who of mine own weight am always sinking down.

Thy love is the cause hereof freely preventing me, and supporting me in so many necessities; guarding me also from pressing dangers: and snatching me that I may tell the truth from evils out of number. For by loving myself amiss I lost myself;[3] and by seeking Thee alone and purely loving Thee I have found both myself and Thee: and for love have more utterly reduced myself to nought. Because Thou O Thou Sweetest dealest with me above all desert: and above all I dare hope or ask.

Blessed be Thou my God; for although I be unworthy of any benefits: yet Thy nobleness and infinite kindness never ceases to

[1] Gen. xviii. 27.
[2] Psal. lxii. 22 (Vulgate).
[3] John xii. 25: Matt. x. 39; xvi. 25: Mark viii. 35: Luke iv. 24: xvii. 33.

do good even to the ungrateful and to those who are turned away far from Thee. Turn Thou us unto Thee, that we may be thankful humble and devout: for Thou art our salvation, our courage and our strength.

THAT ALL THINGS ARE TO BE REFERRED UNTO GOD AS THEIR FINAL END

CHAPTER IX

Son. I ought to be thy supreme and final end: if thou desire to be truly blessed. By this intention thy affection will be purified: which is too often perversely warped to itself and created things. For if thou seekest thyself in any thing: immediately thou art faint and dry within. Refer therefore all things to Me as their Author: for I am He who gave them all. Think of them one by one as flowing from the Highest Good: and therefore unto Me as their source must all be traced.

From me the small and the great, the poor and the rich, as from a living fountain do draw the water of life;[1] and they that willingly and freely serve Me: shall receive grace for grace.[2] But he who glories without Me, or delights in any private good; shall not be stablished in true joy nor enlarged in his heart: but shall many ways be hindered and straitened. Thou shouldest therefore ascribe nothing of good to thyself: nor virtue to any man; but give all unto God: without whom man hath nothing. I gave all; I must have all given back again: and with great strictness do I require thanks.

This is the truth: whereby vain-glory is put to flight. And if heavenly grace enter in and true charity; there will be no envy, nor narrowness of heart: neither will private affection hold thee. For divine charity overcomes all things:[3] and enlarges all the powers of the soul. If thou art wise thou wilt rejoice in Me alone, wilt hope in Me alone; for none is good save God alone: who is to be praised above all things and in all to be blessed.

[1] John iv. 14: vii. 38.
[2] John i. 16.
[3] Matt. xix. 17: Luke xviii. 19.

THAT IT IS SWEET TO DESPISE THE WORLD AND SERVE GOD

CHAPTER X

I

Now I will speak again Lord and not be silent; I will say in the ears of my God, my Lord and my King: who is on high. O how great is the abundance of Thy sweetness Lord: which Thou hast laid up in secret for them that fear Thee.[1] But what art Thou to those who love Thee; what to those who serve Thee with their whole heart? Truly unspeakable is the sweetness of Thy contemplation: which Thou bestowest on them that love Thee. In this especially Thou hast shewed me the sweetness of Thy charity, that when I was not Thou madest me: when I went far astray from Thee, Thou broughtest me back again that I might serve Thee: and hast commanded me to love Thee.

O Fount of Love unceasing. What shall I say concerning Thee? How can I forget Thee; who hast deigned to remember me, even after I had wasted away and perished? Thou hast shewed mercy to Thy servant beyond all hope: and hast granted favour and friendship beyond all desert. What return shall I make to Thee for this grace? For it is not granted to all, to forsake all renounce the world: and assume the monastic life. Is it a great thing that I should serve Thee; whom all creation is bound to serve? It ought not to seem a great thing to me to serve Thee; but rather this appears great to me and wonderful: that Thou dost condescend to receive into Thy service one so poor and unworthy and to make him one with Thy beloved servants.

Behold all that I have and whereby I serve Thee: is Thine. And yet Thou servest me rather than I Thee.

Behold heaven and earth which Thou hast created for the service of man[2] wait upon Thee: and daily perform whatever Thou hast commanded. And this is little: Thou hast also appointed Angels in their orders to minister to man.[3] Yet is it more adorable

[1] Psal. xxxi. 19 (xxx. 20).
[2] Deut. iv. 19 (Vulgate).
[3] Heb. i. 14.

than all, that Thou Thyself hast deigned to serve man: and hast promised to give Thyself unto him.

What shall I give Thee for all these thousands of benefits? Would I could serve Thee all the days of my life. Would I were able for one single day to do Thee worthy service. Truly Thou art worthy of all service: all honour and eternal praise. Truly Thou art my Lord, and I Thy poor servant; who am bound to serve Thee with all my might: neither ought I ever to be weary of praising Thee. This is my wish this my desire: and whatsoever is wanting unto me, do Thou vouchsafe to supply.

II

It is great honour great glory to serve Thee: and despise all things for Thee. For they shall have great grace: who have willingly subjected themselves to Thy most holy thraldom. They who for Thy love have renounced all carnal delight: shall find the sweetest consolation of the Holy Ghost. They shall attain great freedom of mind; who for Thy Name's sake enter the narrow way: [1] and have cast aside all worldly care.

O pleasant and joyous bondage of God: by which a man is made truly free and holy. O sacred state of religious dependence; which makes man equal to Angels, pleasing to God, terrible to devils: and worthy to be commended of all the faithful. O welcome servitude and ever to be desired, in which the wage is the highest Good: and joy is attained which shall endure without end.

THAT THE DESIRES OF OUR HEARTS ARE TO BE EXAMINED AND MODERATED

CHAPTER XI

SON. It is needful for thee still to learn much more: which thou hast not yet well learned.

What is this Lord?

That thou frame thy desires wholly according to My good pleasure; and be not a lover of thyself: but an eager zealot of My will. Desires oft inflame thee and drive thee on with vehemence;

[1] Matt. vii. 14.

but do thou consider whether thou be moved for My honour or thine own advantage. If I be the cause: thou wilt be well content, whatsoever I shall ordain. But if there lurk in thee any self-seeking: behold this it is that hinders thee and weighs thee down.

Beware therefore thou lean not too much upon preconceived desire without asking My counsel; lest perhaps afterwards that repent or displease thee: which at first attracted thee and which thou didst eagerly pursue as being the best. For not every impulse which seems good is immediately to be followed: nor again is every painful impulse to be at once avoided. It is sometimes expedient to use the curb even in good endeavours and desires: lest through preoccupation thou incur distraction of mind; lest by want of self-government thou beget scandal unto others: or again by the contradiction of others thou suddenly lose temper and fall. Sometimes however thou must use violence and resist manfully thy sensual appetite; nor care what the flesh would or would not; but rather strive, that even against its will it may be subdued to the Spirit.[1] And it must be chastised and forced to bear the yoke, until it be ready for every thing; and learn to be content with little and find delight in simple things: and not murmur against any discomfort.

OF THE DISCIPLINE OF PATIENCE AND OF STRIVING AGAINST CONCUPISCENCE

CHAPTER XII

O LORD GOD as I see patience is very necessary for me; for many things in this life do happen to thwart us. For whatever plans I devise for my peace: my life cannot be without war and sorrow.

It is so Son. But My will is that thou seek not a peace which is free from temptations or feels no disturbance; but think that thou hast even then found peace: when thou art harassed by sundry tribulations, and tried by many crosses. If thou say that thou art not able to suffer much; how then wilt thou endure the fire of purgatory? Of two evils the less is always to be chosen. That

[1] 1 Cor. ix. 27.

thou mayest therefore escape eternal punishment in the future: strive to endure present evils calmly for God's sake.

Dost thou think that the men of this world suffer nothing or little? Thou wilt not find it so: though thou ask the most luxurious. But thou wilt say they have many delights and follow their own desires: and therefore they do not much weigh their afflictions. Be it so: grant that they have whatsoever they will. But how long dost thou think it will last? Behold the wealthy of this world shall consume away like smoke: [1] and there shall be no memory of their past joys. Yea while yet they are alive: they do not rest in them without bitterness and weariness and fear. For from the self-same thing from which they drink delight: oftentimes they receive the penalty of sorrow. Just it is, that having greedily sought and followed after pleasures: they should enjoy them not without shame and bitterness.

O how brief, how false: how intemperate and base are they all. Yet so drunken and blind are men that they understand it not: but like dumb beasts for the poor enjoyment of this transitory life they run upon the death of the soul.

Thou therefore son go not after thy lusts: but refrain thyself from thy will. [2] Delight thyself in the Lord: and He shall grant thee the petitions of thine heart. [3] For if thou desire true delight and to be more plentifully comforted by Me; behold in the contempt of all worldly things and in the cutting off of all base delights shall be thy blessing; and abundant consolation shall be rendered to thee. And the more thou withdrawest thyself from all solace of creatures: the sweeter and more powerful consolations shalt thou find in Me.

But at first thou shalt not without some sadness nor without toil of conflict attain unto them. Old inbred habits will rebel: but by a better habit shall it be entirely overcome. The flesh will murmur: but with fervency of spirit thou shalt bridle it. The Old Serpent will goad and embitter thee; but by prayer he shall be put to flight: moreover by useful employment thou shalt bar his main approach.

[1] Psal. lxxii. 12: xxxvi. 20 (Vulgate).
[2] Ecclesiasticus xviii. 30.
[3] Psal. xxxviii. (xxxvi.) 4.

OF THE OBEDIENCE OF ONE IN HUMBLE SUBJECTION AFTER THE EXAMPLE OF JESUS CHRIST

CHAPTER XIII

SON. He that endeavours to withdraw himself from obedience: withdraws himself from grace. And he who seeks his own: loses what all the brethren have. He that doth not cheerfully and freely submit himself to his superior; it is a sign that his flesh is not yet perfectly obedient unto him: but oftentimes kicks and murmurs. Learn therefore quickly to submit to thy superior: if thou desire to keep thine own flesh under the yoke. For the outward enemy is sooner overcome: if the inward man be not laid waste. There is no more troublesome or deadly enemy to the soul: than thou art unto thyself, if thou be not in harmony with the Spirit. It is indispensable that thou take up a true contempt for thyself: if thou desire to prevail against flesh and blood.[1]

Because as yet thou lovest thyself inordinately: therefore thou art afraid to resign thyself wholly to the will of others. And yet what great matter is it, if thou who art dust and nothing, subject thyself to a man for God's sake; when I the Almighty and the Most High who created all things of nothing humbly subjected Myself to man for thy sake? I became of all men the humblest and lowest: that thou mightest beat down thy pride with My humility.

O dust learn to obey; learn to humble thyself thou earth and clay: and to bow thyself down under the feet of all men. Learn to break thine own will: and to yield thyself to all subjection. Be fiercely hot against thyself, and suffer no pride to live in thee; but shew thyself so humble and so very small: that all may be able to walk over thee and tread thee down as the mire of the streets.

Vain man what hast thou to complain of: what canst thou answer foul sinner to them that upbraid thee; thou who hast so often offended God, and so many times deserved hell? But Mine eye spared thee; because thy soul was precious in My sight: that Thou mightest know My love and ever be thankful for My

[1] Eph. vi. 12.

benefits; and that thou mightest continually give thyself to true subjection and humility: and endure patiently the contempt which is thy due.

OF CONSIDERING THE SECRET JUDGMENTS OF GOD THAT WE BE NOT LIFTED UP FOR ANY GOOD

CHAPTER XIV

LORD Thou thunderest forth Thy judgments over me; Thou shakest all my bones with fear and trembling: and my soul is sore afraid. I stand astonished and I consider: that the Heavens are not pure in Thy sight.[1] If in Angels Thou didst find wickedness [2] and didst not spare them; what shall become of me? Stars fell from Heaven;[3] how then can I presume who am but dust? They whose works seemed laudable have fallen into the depths; and those who did eat the bread of Angels: I have seen delighting themselves with the husks of swine.[4]

There is therefore no sanctity if Thou O Lord withdraw Thine hand: no wisdom avails, if Thou cease to steer; no courage helps, if Thou cease to defend: no chastity is secure, if Thou do not protect it; no custody of our own avails, if Thy holy watchfulness be not over us. For left to ourselves we sink and perish: but if Thou visit us we are raised up and live. Truly we are unstable but through Thee we are strengthened: we grow cold, but by Thee we are enkindled.

O how humbly and meanly should I think of myself: how should I despise whatever good I seem to have. O how deeply should I abase myself beneath Thy unfathomable judgments Lord:[5] where I find myself to be nothing else, than Nothing and Nothing.

O unmeasurable weight; O shoreless sea: where I discover nothing of myself save only Nothing.

Where then is the hiding-place of glory; where the presumption of virtue? All vainglory is swallowed up, in the deep of Thy

---

[1] Job xv. 15.
[2] Job iv. 18.
[3] Rev. vi. 13: viii. 10.
[4] Psal. lxxviii. (lxxvii.) 25: Luke xv. 16.
[5] Psal. xxxvi. 6 (xxxv. 7).

judgments over me. What is all flesh in Thy sight? Shall the clay boast against Him that formeth it? [1] How can he be lifted up with vain words; whose heart is truly subject to God?

Not all the world can uplift him: whom the Truth hath subjected unto itself; neither shall he be moved though all tongues praise him: who hath settled his whole hope in God. For even they who speak, behold they all are nothing; for they will pass away with the sound of their words: but the Truth of the Lord remaineth for ever. [2]

IN EVERY THING WHICH WE DESIRE HOW WE OUGHT TO STAND AND WHAT WE OUGHT TO SAY

CHAPTER XV

Son. Say thou thus in every thing. Lord if this be pleasing unto Thee: so let it be. Lord if it be to Thy honour: in Thy Name let it be. Lord if Thou seest it expedient and approvest it to be good for me: then grant unto me that I may use it to Thine honour. But if Thou knowest it will hurt me and not tend to the health of my soul: take away from me any such desire.

For not every desire comes from the Holy Spirit: even though it seem unto a man right and good. It is difficult to judge truly, whether a good, or an evil spirit drive thee to desire this or that: or whether thou be moved by thine own spirit. Many have been deceived in the end: who at first seemed to be led by a good spirit.

Therefore whatever occurs to the mind as desirable, must always be desired and prayed for in the fear of God and with humility of heart: and chiefly thou must commit the whole matter to Me with resignation, and thou must say. Lord Thou knowest, what is best: let this or that be done and as Thou shalt please. Give what Thou wilt and how much Thou wilt: and when Thou wilt. Deal with me as Thou knowest and as best pleases Thee: and is most for Thy honour. Set me where Thou wilt: and deal with me freely in all things as Thou wilt. I am in Thy hand: spin me forward or spin me back. Behold I am Thy servant, ready for all;

[1] Is. xlv. 9: Jer. xviii. 6: Rom. ix. 20.
[2] Psal. cxvii. (cxvi.) 2.

for I desire not to live unto myself but unto Thee: and O that I could do it worthily and perfectly.

A Prayer that the Will of God may be fulfilled

O kind Jesus grant me Thy grace; that it may be with me and labour with me: and persevere with me even to the end. Grant that I may always desire and will: that which is to Thee more acceptable and more dear. Let Thy will be mine: and let my will ever follow Thine and perfectly agree with it. Let my yea and nay be one with Thine; and let me not be able to will or will not any thing: but what Thou willest or willest not.

Grant that I may die to all things that are in the world: and for Thy sake love to be contemned and unknown in this generation. Grant to me above all things that can be desired to rest in Thee: and in Thee to set my heart at peace. Thou art true peace of heart Thou alone art rest: out of Thee all things are hard and restless. In this peace, towards the Same: that is in Thee the one and Chief and Eternal Good I will sleep and rest. Amen.

THAT TRUE COMFORT IS TO BE SOUGHT IN GOD ALONE

CHAPTER XVI

WHATSOEVER I can desire or imagine for my comfort: I look for it not here, but hereafter. For if I might alone have all the comforts of the world and enjoy all its delights: it is certain that they could not long endure.

Wherefore O my soul thou canst not be fully comforted nor perfectly refreshed: except in God the Comforter of the poor and Sponsor of the humble. Wait a little while O my soul; wait for the divine promise: and thou shalt have abundance of all good things in heaven. If thou desire inordinately the things that are present: thou shalt lose those which are eternal and heavenly. Use temporal things: desire eternal. Thou canst not be satisfied with any temporal good: because thou art not created to enjoy them. Although thou shouldest possess all created goods, yet couldest thou not be happy nor blessed; but in God who created all things, stands thy whole blessedness and felicity: not such as is seen and praised by the foolish lovers of the world; but such as good and faithful servants of Christ wait for, and of which the spiritual and pure in heart: whose conversation is in heaven [1] sometimes have a foretaste.

Vain and brief is all human solace. Blessed and true is the solace: which is received inwardly from the Truth. A devout man bears every where about with him his own Comforter Jesus: and saith unto Him. Be Thou with me Lord Jesu in every place and time. Let this be my consolation: gladly to forego all human comfort. And if Thy consolation be wanting: let Thy will and just trial of me be unto me the greatest comfort. For Thou wilt not always be angry: neither wilt Thou threaten for ever. [2]

THAT ALL OUR ANXIETIES ARE TO BE PLACED ON GOD

CHAPTER XVII

SON. Suffer me to do with thee what I please: I know what is good for thee. Thou thinkest as man: thou judgest in many things as human inclination persuades thee.

Lord what Thou sayest is true. Greater is Thy anxiety for me: than all the care that I can take for myself. For he stands precariously: who casts not all his anxiety upon Thee. Lord if only my will may remain right and firm towards Thee: do with me whatsoever it shall please Thee. For it must needs be good: whatsoever Thou wilt do with me. If it be Thy will I should be in darkness blessed be Thou; and if it be Thy will I should be in light: be Thou again blessed. If Thou vouchsafe to comfort me be Thou blessed; and if Thou wilt have me afflicted: be Thou ever equally blessed.

Son, thus shouldest thou stand: if thou desire to walk with Me. Thou shouldest be as ready to suffer: as to rejoice. Thou shouldest as cheerfully be destitute and poor: as full and rich.

Lord, for Thy sake I will cheerfully suffer: whatever shall come on me with Thy permission. From Thy hand I will receive indifferently good and evil sweet and bitter joy and sorrow: and

[1] Phil. iii. 20.   [2] Psal. ciii. (cii.) 9.

for all that befalls me I will be thankful. Keep me safe from all sin: and I shall fear neither death nor hell. So as Thou dost not for ever cast me from Thee,[1] nor blot me out of the book of life: [2] whatever tribulation may come upon me shall not hurt me.

THAT TEMPORAL MISERIES MUST BE BORNE CALMLY AFTER THE EXAMPLE OF CHRIST

CHAPTER XVIII

Son. I came down from Heaven for thy salvation; I took upon Me thy miseries not necessity but charity drawing me thereto: that thou mightest learn patience, and bear temporal miseries without complaint. For from the hour of My birth, to My death on the cross: I was not without suffering of grief. I suffered great want of things temporal; I often heard many complaints against Me: I endured with calmness shame and revilings; for benefits I received ingratitude: for miracles blasphemies, for doctrine reproofs.

Lord, for that Thou wert patient in Thy lifetime, herein especially fulfilling the commandment of Thy Father; it is reason that I a miserable sinner should bear myself patiently according to Thy will: and for my soul's welfare carry the burden of this mortal life as long as Thou shalt choose. For although this present life is felt to be a burden: yet it is now by Thy grace made very meritorious, and by Thy example and the footsteps of Thy Saints more endurable and clearer to the weak; it is also much fuller of consolation than it was formerly under the old Law: when the gate of heaven remained shut, and even the way to heaven seemed darker; when so few cared to seek after the kingdom of heaven: moreover they who then were just and heirs of salvation could not enter into the heavenly kingdom before Thy Passion and the due atonement of Thy holy death.

O what thanks am I bound to render unto Thee: that Thou hast deigned to shew unto me and to all faithful people the right and the good way to Thine eternal kingdom. For Thy life is our way: and by holy patience we walk toward Thee who art our Crown.

[1] Psal. lxxvii. 7 (lxxvi. 8).   [2] Rev. iii. 5.

If Thou hadst not gone before us and taught us; who would care to follow? Alas how many would remain afar off and behind: if they saw not Thy noble example. Behold we are still cold though we have heard of Thy many miracles and doctrines; what would become of us if we had not so great Light whereby to follow Thee.

OF THE ENDURANCE OF INJURIES AND OF THE PROOF OF TRUE PATIENCE

CHAPTER XIX

WHAT sayest thou Son? Cease to complain: when thou considerest My Passion and that of other saints Thou hast not yet resisted unto blood.[1] It is but little which thou sufferest in comparison of those who suffered so much, who were so strongly tempted, so grievously afflicted: so many ways tried and harassed. Thou oughtest therefore to call to mind the heavier woes of others: that thou mayest the easier bear thy own small troubles. And if they seem unto thee not very small: then beware lest thy impatience be the cause of this also. However be they small or great: endeavour patiently to undergo them all.

The better thou disposest thyself to suffering: the more wisely thou doest and the ampler reward shalt thou receive; thou shalt also more easily endure: if both in mind and by habit thou art diligently prepared thereunto.

Do not say, I cannot bear these things at the hands of such an one; nor ought I to endure things of this sort, for he has done me great wrong, and charges me with things I never thought of: but of another I will cheerfully suffer, and as I shall see I ought to suffer. Such a thought is foolish, it takes not into account the virtue of patience, nor by whom it will be crowned: but weighs the persons and the injuries offered to itself.

He is not truly patient who will not suffer except so far as he thinks right: and from whom he pleases. But the truly patient man minds not by whom he is vexed whether by his prelate, or by an equal or by an inferior: by a good and holy man or by one that

[1] Heb. xii. 4.

is perverse and unworthy. But from every creature without distinction whatever and whenever annoyance befalls him, he takes it all thankfully from the hand of God and counts it great gain: for with God nothing however small if only it be suffered for God's sake can pass without reward.

Be thou therefore girded for the fight: if thou wilt have the victory. Without a conflict, thou canst not reach the crown of patience.[1] If thou wilt not suffer: thou art refusing to be crowned. But if thou desire to be crowned: fight manfully, endure patiently. Without toil there is no road to rest: nor without fighting can the victory be gained.

Lord make that possible to me by Thy grace: which by nature seems impossible. Thou knowest, that I can suffer but little: and that I am quickly cast down when a light opposition encounters me. For Thy Name's sake let every harassment of tribulation be made lovely and desirable to me: for to suffer and be disquieted for Thy sake, is very wholesome for my soul.

OF THE ACKNOWLEDGING OF OUR OWN INFIRMITY AND OF THE MISERIES OF THIS LIFE

CHAPTER XX

I WILL confess against myself mine own unrighteousness: I will confess my infirmity unto Thee O Lord.[2]

Oftentimes a small matter it is: that makes me sad and despondent. I resolve that I will act with courage; but when even a small temptation comes: I am in a great strait. Sometimes a very trifle it is: whence a great temptation arises. And while I think myself fairly safe when I least expect it: I sometimes find myself almost vanquished by a puff of wind.

Behold therefore Lord my lowness and my frailty which Thou knowest on every side; have mercy on me and draw me out of the mire lest I stick fast therein:[3] lest I remain utterly cast down. This it is that often strikes me backwards and confounds me in Thy sight: that I am so tottering and weak in resisting my pas-

[1] 2 Tim. ii. 5.
[2] Psal. xxxii. (xxxi.) 5.
[3] Psal. lxix. 14 (lxviii. 15).

sions. Although I do not altogether consent; yet their assaults are troublesome and grievous unto me: and it is very weary to live thus daily in strife. From whence my weakness becomes known unto me: that hateful fancies do always much more easily rush in than go away.

Most mighty God of Israel Thou zealous Lover of faithful souls O have respect unto the labour and sorrow of Thy servant: and stand by him in all that he undertakes.[1] Strengthen me with heavenly courage; lest the old man the wretched flesh not yet fully subdued to the Spirit get the dominion over me: against which it will be needful for me to fight, as long as breath remains in this miserable life.

Alas what kind of life is this: where tribulations and miseries are never wanting, where all is full of snares and enemies? For when one tribulation or temptation retreats another comes on; yea while the first conflict is yet enduring: many others come unexpected one after another. And how can a life be loved that hath so many embitterments; and is subject to so many calamities and miseries? How can it even be called a life; that begets so many deaths and plagues?

And yet it is loved: and many seek to delight themselves therein. Oftentimes the world is blamed for being deceitful and vain; and yet is it not easily renounced: because the desires of the flesh bear so great a sway. But some things draw us to love: others to despise. The lust of the flesh, the lust of the eyes and the pride of life,[2] draw us to the love of the world: but the pains and miseries that justly follow them, cause hatred and weariness of the world.

But alas evil pleasure overcomes the mind that is given up to the world; and he counts it a delight to be under thorns:[3] because he has neither seen nor tasted the sweetness of God and the inward loveliness of virtue. But they who perfectly despise the world, and study to live to God under holy discipline; these know well the divine sweetness promised to those who truly renounce: they also see more clearly, how grievously the world mistakes and is in many ways deceived.

[1] Josh. i. 9.   [2] 1 John ii. 16.   [3] Job xxx. 7.

THAT WE ARE TO REST IN GOD ABOVE ALL GOODS AND GIFTS

CHAPTER XXI

I

ABOVE all and in all O my soul thou shalt rest in the Lord alway: for He is the eternal Rest of the Saints.

Grant me O most sweet and loving Jesus to rest in Thee above all creatures; above all health and beauty, above all glory and honour: above all power and dignity, above all knowledge and subtilty; above all riches and arts, above all joy and gladness: above all fame and praise, above all sweetness and comfort; above all hope and promise, above all merit and desire: above all gifts and favours that Thou canst give and impart unto us; above all mirth and jubilation, that the mind can receive and feel: finally above Angels and Archangels and above all the heavenly host; above all things visible and invisible: and above all that Thou my God art not.

Because Thou O Lord my God art supremely good above all: Thou alone art most high Thou alone most powerful; Thou alone most sufficient, and most full: Thou alone most sweet and solacing, Thou alone most lovely and loving; Thou alone most noble and glorious above all things: in whom the sum of all good is united and perfect and ever has been and shall be; and therefore all beside Thyself is small and unsatisfying whatsoever Thou bestowest on me: or revealest of Thyself or promisest if Thou art not seen nor fully obtained. For my heart cannot truly rest nor be entirely contented, unless it rests in Thee:[1] and pass above all gifts, and all creatures.

II

O my beloved Bridegroom Jesu Christ Thou purest Lover Thou Lord of all creation; O that I had the wings of true freedom that I might flee away and rest in Thee.[2]

O when shall it be fully granted me to be at ease and see how

---

[1] Aug. *Conf.* i. 1.   [2] Psal. lv. 6 (liv. 7).

sweet Thou art O Lord my God? When shall I fully gather myself up into Thee: that for love of Thee I may not feel myself, but Thee alone above all sense and measure: in a manner not known to all.

But now I often sigh: and bear my infelicity with grief. Because many evils meet me in this vale of miseries which often trouble sadden and overcloud me; often hinder and distract, allure and entangle me: so that I can have no free access unto Thee, nor enjoy the sweet embraces which are ever ready for the blessed spirits.

Let my sighs move Thee and my manifold desolation here on earth: O Jesu Thou brightness of eternal glory. Thou comfort of the pilgrim soul. Heard of Thee is my voiceless tongue: and my silence speaketh unto Thee.

How long doth my Lord delay His coming? Let Him come unto me His poor one: and make me glad. Let Him put forth His hand: and save a poor wretch from every difficulty. Come come: for without Thee no day nor hour is joyful: for Thou art my joy and without Thee my table is empty.

A wretched creature am I and in manner imprisoned and loaded with fetters; until Thou refresh me with the light of Thy presence and grant me freedom: and shew a friendly countenance towards me.

Let others seek what they will instead of Thee; but for me nothing doth nor shall delight me: but Thou only my God my hope, my eternal salvation. I will not hold my peace nor cease to pray; until Thy grace return again: and Thou speak unto me within.

Behold here I am; behold I come unto thee: for thou hast called Me. Thy tears and the desire of thy soul: thy humiliation and thy contrition of heart have inclined and brought Me unto Thee.

And I said. Lord I have called Thee, and desired to enjoy Thee: being ready to refuse all things for Thy sake. For Thou first hast roused me: that I might seek Thee. Blessed be Thou therefore Lord: that hast shewed this goodness to Thy servant according to the multitude of Thy mercies.

What more hath Thy servant to say before Thee? he can but humble himself to the dust in Thy sight, ever mindful of his iniquity and vileness. For there is none like unto Thee: in all the wonders of heaven and earth. Thy works are very good; Thy judgments true: and by Thy providence the universe is governed. Praise therefore and glory be unto Thee O Wisdom of the Father; and let my mouth praise and bless Thee: my soul and all creation together.

OF THE REMEMBRANCE OF GOD'S MANIFOLD BENEFITS

CHAPTER XXII

OPEN Lord my heart in Thy law: and teach me to walk in Thy commandments. Grant me to understand Thy will; and with great reverence and diligent consideration to remember Thy benefits as well in general as in particular: that henceforward I may be able to give Thee thanks worthily.

But I know and confess: that I am not able even in the least point to give Thee due thanks and praise. I am less than the least of all Thy benefits; and when I consider Thine excellency: the greatness thereof makes my spirit faint.

All that we have in soul and in body, and whatsoever we possess without or within naturally or supernaturally are Thy benefits; and proclaim Thee bountiful merciful and good: from whom we have received all good things.

Although one have received more another less; yet all are Thine: and without Thee even the least blessing cannot be had.

He that has received the greater cannot boast of his own desert: nor uplift himself above others, nor triumph over the lesser; for he is the greatest and the best who ascribes least unto himself: and in rendering thanks is the most humble and devout. And he that thinks himself meanest of all and judges himself most unworthy: is fittest to receive the greater blessings.

But he that has received fewer: ought not to be out of heart nor complain, nor envy the richer; but rather he should fix his mind on Thee and exceedingly praise Thy goodness: for that Thou bestowest Thy gifts so bountifully, so freely and willingly without respect of persons.

All things come from Thee: and therefore in all Thou art to

be praised. Thou knowest what should be given to each; and why this man should have less and that more, it is not for us to judge but for Thee: who dost exactly mark each one's deserts.

Wherefore Lord God I count it even a great mercy not to have much of that which outwardly and in the opinion of men seems worthy of praise and glory: so that he who considers the poverty and meanness of his own person should be so far from feeling grief or sadness or despondency thereat; that he should rather take great comfort and be glad: because Thou O God hast chosen the poor and humble and the despised of this world, for Thy own familiar attendants.

Witnesses are Thy Apostles themselves: whom Thou hast made princes over all the earth.[1] And yet they lived in the world without complaint: so humble and simple so free from all malice and deceit; that they even rejoiced to suffer reproach for Thy name:[2] and what the world abhors they embraced with great affection.

When therefore a man loves Thee and recognises Thy benefits nothing ought so to rejoice him: as Thy will towards him and the good pleasure of Thine eternal appointment; and herewith he ought to be so contented and comforted: that he would as willingly be least as another would wish to be greatest; and as pacific and contented in the last place as in the first: as willing to be a despised cast-away of no name or fame, as to be preferred in honour before others and greater in the world. For Thy will and the love of Thy glory should outweigh all else; and comfort him more and please him better: than all the benefits which he hath received or may receive.

OF FOUR THINGS THAT BRING MUCH PEACE

CHAPTER XXIII

Son, now will I teach thee the way of peace and true freedom.
    Lord do as Thou sayest: for this is delightful to me to hear.
    Study son to do the will of another rather than thine own.
    Choose always to have less rather than more.

[1] Psal. xlv. 16 (xliv. 17).   [2] Acts v. 41.

Seek always the lowest place: and to be the inferior to every one.

Wish always and pray: that the will of God may be wholly fulfilled in thee.

Behold such a man enters the land of peace and rest.

Lord this brief discourse of Thine: contains within itself much perfection. It is small in speech: but full of meaning and rich in fruit. For if I could faithfully keep it: I should not be so easily disturbed. For as often as I feel myself restless and heavy: I find that I have gone back from this doctrine. But Thou who canst do all things and ever lovest the profit of my soul; increase in me Thy grace: that I may be able to fulfil Thy words, and to work out my salvation.

A Prayer against Evil Thoughts

Lord my God be not Thou far from me: my God have regard to help me;[1] for there have risen up against me various thoughts and great fears: afflicting my soul. How shall I pass through unhurt? how shall I break them to pieces?

I will go before thee saith He: and will humble the great ones of the earth. I will open the doors of the prison: and reveal unto thee hidden secrets.[2]

Do Lord as Thou sayest: and let all evil thoughts fly from Thy face. This is my hope my one only consolation, to flee unto Thee in every tribulation; to trust in Thee, to call upon Thee from my inmost heart: and to wait patiently for Thy consolation.

A Prayer for Mental Illumination

O good Jesu enlighten me with the shining of inner light: and remove away all darkness from the habitation of my heart. Repress Thou my many wandering thoughts: and break in pieces those temptations which violently assault me. Fight Thou strongly for me and vanquish the evil beasts,[3] I mean the alluring desires of the flesh; that peace may be obtained by Thy power:[4] and that Thine abundant praise may resound in Thy holy court that is in a pure conscience. Command the winds and tempests: say unto the

[1] Psal. lxxi. (lxx.) 12.   [3] 1 Cor. xv. 32: Titus i. 12.
[2] Is. xlv. 2, 3.   [4] Psal. cxxi. 7 (Vulgate).

sea Be still [1] and to the north wind Blow not: and there shall be a great calm. Send out Thy Light and Thy Truth [2] that they may shine upon the earth; for I am earth without form and void: [3] until Thou enlighten me. Pour forth Thy grace from above, sprinkle my heart with heavenly dew; supply streams of devotion, to water the face of the earth: that it may bring forth fruit good and excellent.

Lift Thou up my mind which is pressed down by a load of sins: and draw up my whole desire to things heavenly; that when I have tasted the sweetness of celestial happiness: it may be irksome to me to think about earthly things. Do Thou snatch me and deliver me from all fleeting comfort of created things: for no created thing can fully satisfy my desires or console.

Join Thou me to Thyself with an inseparable band of love; for Thou alone canst satisfy him that loves: and without Thee all things are futile.

OF AVOIDING CURIOUS ENQUIRY INTO OTHER MEN'S LIVES

CHAPTER XXIV

Son, be not curious: nor trouble thyself with idle anxieties. What is this or that to thee: follow thou Me. [4] For what is it to thee whether that man be such or such; or this man do or speak this or that? Thou needest not answer for others: but shalt give account for thyself. Why then dost thou entangle thyself?

Behold I know every one and see all things that are done beneath the sun; and I understand how it is with every one, what he thinks, what he wishes: and at what his intention aims. To Me therefore all things are to be left, but do thou keep thyself in good peace: and let the unquiet be as unquiet as they will. Whatsoever they have done or said shall come upon them: for Me they cannot deceive.

Care not for the shadow of a great name; nor for the familiar

[1] Psal. xliii. (xlii.) 3.
[2] Matt. viii. 26.
[3] Gen. i. 2.
[4] John xxi. 22.

friendship of many: nor for the private affection of men. For these things distract the heart: and greatly darken it.

Willingly would I speak My word and reveal My secrets unto thee; if thou wouldest diligently watch for My coming: and open unto Me the door of thine heart. Look to the future, and watch in prayer;[1] and in all things humble thyself.

WHEREIN FIRM PEACE OF HEART AND TRUE SPIRITUAL PROGRESS CONSISTETH

CHAPTER XXV

Son. I have spoken Peace I leave with you My peace I give unto you: not as the world giveth give I unto you.[2]

Peace is what all desire: but not all care for the things that pertain unto true peace. My peace is with the humble and gentle of heart.[3] In much patience shall thy peace be. If thou wilt hear Me and follow My voice: thou shalt enjoy much peace.

What then shall I do?

In every matter look to thyself what thou doest and what thou sayest; and direct thy whole intention unto this, that thou mayest please Me alone: and neither desire nor seek any thing besides Me; but of the words or deeds of others judge nothing hastily, neither do thou entangle thyself with things not committed unto thee: and thou wilt be little or seldom disturbed. But never to feel any disquiet, nor to suffer any trouble of heart or body; belongs not to this life: but to the state of eternal Rest.

Think not therefore that thou hast found true peace if thou feel no heaviness; nor that then all is well, if thou art vexed with no adversary: nor that to be perfect is to have all things happen according to thy desire; neither do thou then think highly of thyself, or account thyself to be specially beloved: if thou be in great devotion and sweetness; for not by these things is a true lover of virtue known: nor doth the progress and perfection of a man consist in these things.

Where then Lord is it to be found?

In surrendering thyself with all thy heart to the divine Will:

[1] 1 Pet. iv. 7.   [2] John xiv. 27.   [3] Matt. xi. 29.

not seeking thine own in great matters or in small, in time or in eternity; so that with unchanged countenance thou abide in thanksgiving, amid prosperity and adversity: weighing all things with equal balance.

If thou art so brave and patient in hope, that when inward comfort is withdrawn, thou prepare thy heart to suffer even greater things; and do not justify thyself as though thou oughtest not to suffer these afflictions or any so great: but justify Me in whatsoever I appoint and praise My Holy Name; then art thou walking in the true and right way of peace: and thou shalt have undoubted hope, to see My face again with exultation.

But if thou fully attain to contempt of thyself: know that thou shalt then enjoy abundance of peace as far as is possible for a sojourner like thee.

OF THE EXCELLENCY OF A FREE MIND WHICH IS SOONER GAINED BY HUMBLE PRAYER THAN BY READING

CHAPTER XXVI

I

LORD this is the work of a perfect man: never to relax his mind from thought of heavenly things; and amidst many cares to pass as it were without care, not as one who feels not, but by the privilege of a free mind: cleaving to no creature with inordinate affection.

II

I beseech Thee my most gracious God preserve me from the cares of this life lest I be too much entangled therein; from the many necessities of the body, lest I be ensnared by pleasure: from all obstacles to the soul, lest I be broken and overthrown by troubles. I speak not of those things which worldly vanity pursues with all its heart; but of those penal miseries which by the common curse of mortality weigh down and hinder the soul of Thy servant: that it cannot enter into the freedom of the Spirit so often as it would.

III

O my God Thou sweetness ineffable; turn into bitterness for me, all carnal comfort which draws me away from the love of things eternal: and in evil manner allures me to itself by the view of some present delightsome good. Let me not be overcome O Lord let me not be overcome by flesh and blood; let not the world and the brief glory thereof deceive me: let not the devil and his craft trip up my heels. Give me strength to resist; patience to endure: constancy to persevere.

Give me instead of all the comforts of the world the sweetest unction of Thy Spirit: and in place of carnal love pour in the love of Thy name.

Behold meat drink raiment, and other commodities for the sustenance of the body: are a burden to the fervent spirit. Grant me to use such refreshments moderately: not to be entangled with excessive desire.

It is not lawful to cast away all things: because nature must be sustained. But to require superfluities and those things that are more pleasurable the holy law forbids: for then the flesh would rebel against the Spirit. Herein I beseech Thee let Thy hand guide and teach me: that I may not exceed.

THAT IT IS PRIVATE LOVE WHICH MOST HINDERETH FROM THE CHIEFEST GOOD

CHAPTER XXVII

Son. Thou must give all for all: and nothing must be thine own. Know thou that the love of thyself doth thee more hurt: than anything in the world. According to the love and affection which thou bearest: everything doth more or less cleave to thee. If thy love be pure simple and well-ordered: thou shalt be free from the bondage of things. Covet not: what thou mayest not have. Have not: what thou mayest not have. Have not: what may hinder thee and rob thee of inward liberty.

Strange it is that thou committest not thyself wholly unto Me from the bottom of thy heart with all that thou canst desire or have. Why art thou wasted by vain grief; why wearied with superfluous cares? Stand to My good will: and thou shalt suffer no loss.

If thou seek this or that, and wouldest be here or there the better to enjoy thy own profit and pleasure: thou shalt never be in quiet, nor free from trouble of mind; for in every thing some flaw will be found: and in every place there will be one to cross thee.

Man's welfare then lies not in things outward that he gains or amasses: but in despising them and utterly rooting them out from the heart. And this thou must understand not only of income and wealth; but of seeking after honour also and the desire of vain praise: which all pass with the world.

No place is safe: if the spirit of fervour be wanting. Neither shall that peace long continue which is sought from without: if the state of thy heart have no sure foundation. That is unless thou stand stedfast in Me: thou mayest change but not better thyself. For when the chance arises and is taken: thou shalt find what thou didst flee from and more.

A PRAYER FOR A CLEAN HEART AND HEAVENLY WISDOM

Strengthen me O God by the grace of Thy Holy Spirit. Grant me power to be strengthened in the inner man [1] and to empty my heart of all useless care and anguish; not to be dragged about by various desires of anything mean or precious: but to look on all things as passing away, and on myself also as doomed to pass away with them; for nothing is lasting under the sun: where all is vanity and vexation of spirit.[2] O how wise is he that so considers them.

Lord grant me Heavenly wisdom that I may learn above all things to seek and to find Thee: above all things to taste and to love Thee: and to see all other things according to the rule of Thy wisdom as they are. Grant me prudence to avoid him that flatters me: and patience to endure him that contradicts me; because this is great wisdom, not to be blown about with every wind of words, nor to give ear to the false flattering siren: for thus we shall go on securely in the way we have begun.

[1] Eph. iii. 16.   [2] Eccles. i. 14: ii. 17, 26.

AGAINST THE TONGUES OF SLANDERERS

CHAPTER XXVIII

SON. Take it not hard if some think ill of thee: and speak what thou likest not to hear. Thou shouldest judge worse of thyself: and think no man weaker than thyself.

If thou dost walk inwardly: thou wilt not greatly heed words that pass. It is no small prudence to keep silence in an evil time and inwardly to turn thyself to Me: and not be troubled by the judgment of men.

Let not thy peace be in the tongues of men. For whether they construe thee well or ill: thou art not therefore another man. Where are true peace and true glory? are they not in Me? And he that neither desires to please men nor fears to displease them: shall enjoy much peace.

From inordinate love and vain fear: arise all disquietness of heart and distraction of the senses.

HOW WE OUGHT TO CALL UPON GOD AND TO BLESS HIM WHEN TRIBULATION IS UPON US

CHAPTER XXIX

BLESSED be Thy Name O Lord for ever: [1] for that it is Thy will that this temptation and tribulation should come upon me. I cannot escape it; but must needs flee to Thee: that Thou mayest help me and turn it to my good.

Lord, I am now in affliction; and my heart is ill at ease: for I am much troubled with this present suffering. And now Beloved Father what shall I say? I am caught amidst straits. Save Thou me from this hour. Yet therefore came I unto this hour, that Thou mayest be glorified: [2] when I shall have been greatly humbled and by Thee delivered. Let it please Thee Lord to deliver me: for poor wretch that I am what can I do; and whither shall I go without Thee? Grant me patience O Lord: once more.

[1] Psal. cxiii. (cxii.) 2.　　　　[2] John xii. 27, 28.

Help me my God; and I will not fear how grievously soever I be afflicted.

And now amidst these my troubles what shall I say?

Lord Thy will be done: [1] I have well deserved to be afflicted and weighed down. Certainly I ought to bear it; and O that I may bear it with patience: until the storm pass over and all be better. Yet Thy Almighty hand is able to take even this temptation from me; and to assuage the violence thereof that I utterly sink not: as oftentimes Thou has dealt with me in the past O my God my Mercy. And the harder it is to me: the easier to Thee is this change of the·right hand of the Most High. [2]

OF CRAVING THE DIVINE AID AND ASSURANCE OF RECOVERING GRACE

CHAPTER XXX

SON. I am the Lord that giveth strength in the day of tribulation. Come unto Me: when it is not well with Thee.

This is that which chiefly hinders heavenly consolation: that thou art slow in turning thyself unto prayer. For before thou dost earnestly beseech Me; thou seekest in the meanwhile many comforts: and refreshest thyself in outward things. And hence it comes to pass that all doth little profit thee; until thou mark that I am He who rescues them that hope in Me: and that out of Me there is no prevailing help; nor useful counsel: no nor lasting remedy. But now that the storm is past take courage, renew thy health in the light of My mercies; for I am at hand saith the Lord to restore all not only wholly: but abundantly and above measure.

Is anything hard to Me; or shall I be like one that saith and doeth not? Where is thy faith? Stand firmly, and with perseverance. Be long suffering, and brave: comfort will come to thee in due time. Wait, wait for Me: I will come and heal thee. [3]

It is temptation that vexeth thee: and a vain fear that affrighted thee. What doth anxiety about the chances of the future bring thee; but sorrow upon sorrow? Sufficient for the day is the evil

[1] Matt. xxvi. 42.   [2] Psal. lxxvi. 11 (Vulgate).   [3] Matt. viii. 7.

thereof.[1] It is a vain thing and unprofitable to be vexed or glad about the future: which perhaps will never come to pass. But it is human to be deluded by fancies like these; and a sign of courage as yet small: to be so easily drawn away by the suggestions of the Enemy. For so he may cozen and deceive thee he cares not whether it be by truth or by falsehood: nor whether he overthrow thee by love of the present, or fear of the future.

Let not therefore thy heart be troubled: neither let it fear.[2] Trust in Me: and have confidence in My mercy. When thou thinkest thyself farthest off from Me: oftentimes I am nearest. When thou countest almost all as lost: then oftentimes the greatest gain of reward is close at hand. All is not lost: when things fall crosswise.

Judge not by the feeling of the moment; brood not upon any grief come whence it may nor take it: as though all hope of lifting up thy head were gone. Think not thyself wholly left; although for a time I have sent thee tribulation: or even have withdrawn thy desired comfort. For this is the way to the Kingdom of Heaven. And without doubt it is more expedient for thee and all My servants that you be harassed with trials: than that you should have all things as you wish.

I know thy secret thoughts: for it is very expedient for thy salvation that thou be left sometimes without taste of sweetness; lest perhaps thou shouldest be uplifted with thy prosperous estate: and desire to please thyself in that which thou art not.

What I have given I can take away: and I can restore it again when I please. When I give it it is Mine: when I withdraw it I take not thine; for Mine is every good gift: and every perfect gift.[3]

If I send upon thee grief or any cross whatever: repine not, nor let thy heart fail thee; I can quickly raise thee up: and turn all thy heaviness into joy. Still I am righteous, and greatly to be praised: when I deal thus with thee. If thou art wise and seest truly: thou shouldest never mourn so dejectedly over thy trials; but rather rejoice and give thanks, yea count this thine especial joy: that I afflict thee with sorrows and do not spare.[4]

As the Father hath loved Me, I also loved you,[5] said I unto My

[1] Matt. vi. 34.   [3] James i. 17.   [5] John xv. 9.
[2] John xiv. 1, 27.   [4] Job vi. 10 (Vulgate).

beloved disciples: whom certainly I sent not forth to temporal joys but to great conflicts, not to honours, but to contempts: not to ease but to labours; not to rest: but to bring forth much fruit with patience.[1] Son, remember thou these words.

OF NEGLECTING ALL CREATURES THAT THE CREATOR MAY BE FOUND

CHAPTER XXXI

O LORD, sorely I need yet greater grace, if I am to reach that state: where neither man nor any creature shall be a hindrance unto me. For as long as any thing holds me back: I cannot freely take flight to Thee. Freely did he long to fly: who said. O that I had wings like a dove; and I will flee away and be at rest.[2]

What is more restful than the single eye? [3] and what more free than one that desires nothing upon earth? A man ought therefore to rise above all creatures and perfectly to forsake himself: and stand in ecstasy of mind and see that Thou the Creator of all things art in nothing like the creature. And unless a man be detached from all creatures: he cannot freely fix his mind upon the divine.

For that is why there are few contemplative men to be found: because few know how to isolate themselves wholly from perishing creatures. For this there is need of much grace: to lift up the soul, and carry it above itself. And unless a man be lifted up in spirit and freed from all creatures and united wholly unto God; whatsoever he knows, whatsoever he possesses: is of no great weight. For a long while shall he be small and grovel below: who thinks any thing great but the One only Infinite Eternal Good. And whatsoever is not God: is nothing, and ought to be accounted as nothing.

There is great difference, between the wisdom of an illuminated and devout man: and the knowledge of a learned and studious clerk. Far nobler is that learning which trickles down from above from the Divine influence: than that which is painfully amassed by the wit of man.

[1] Luke viii. 15.   [3] Matt. vi. 22.
[2] Psal. lv. 6 (liv. 7).

There are many that desire contemplation: but have no mind to practise what is required thereunto. It is also a great hindrance that men rest in symbols and sensible things: and take little care about perfect mortification.

I know not what it is, by what spirit we are led, or what we pretend we that seem to be called spiritual; that we take so much pains and are so full of anxiety about things transitory and mean: while we scarcely ever think of the inner life with full recollection of mind. Alas presently after brief recollection we rush out of doors: and weigh not our works with strict examination. We mind not where our affections lie: nor bewail the impurity of all our actions. For all flesh had corrupted his way: [1] and therefore did the great deluge follow. Since then our inward affection is much corrupted: the act ensuing the gauge of the lack of inner vigour, must needs be corrupted also.

From a pure heart comes the fruit of a good life. We ask how much a man has done: but with what virtue he does it is not so carefully weighed. We ask whether he is brave rich handsome clever a good writer, a good singer, a good labourer: how poor he is in spirit, how patient and meek, how devout and inward is seldom heard.

Nature regards the outward things of a man: grace turns itself to the inward. The one is often disappointed: the other trusts in God and is not deceived.

OF SELF-DENIAL AND RENOUNCING EVERY EVIL APPETITE

CHAPTER XXXII

SON thou canst not possess perfect freedom: unless thou wholly renounce thyself. All proprietors [2] and lovers of self are bound in fetters, all the covetous the inquisitive the gossipers, who seek

---

[1] Gen. vi. 12.

[2] *Proprietors*. They were monks who, under any pretence whatever, kept hold of their private property. Honorius III. laid them all under excommunication, and every Palm Sunday this decree was read in Chapter. Gerard Groot borrowed from St. Bernard the saying that "a religious man who possesses a farthing is not worth a farthing."

always what is pleasant not the things of Jesus Christ: and often devise and put together some building which will not stand. For all shall perish: that is not of God. Hold fast this short and pregnant saying. Forsake all and thou shalt find all; leave desire: and thou shalt find rest. Weigh this thoroughly in thy mind: and when thou hast fulfilled it thou shalt understand all things.

Lord, this is not the work of one day, nor children's sport: yea rather in this is included in brief all the perfection of the religious.

Son turn not away nor be cast down at once when thou hearest of the way of the perfect; but rather be challenged to higher things: at least to sigh after them in desire. Would it were so with thee and thou hadst advanced so far, as to be no longer a lover of thyself: but stand loyally at My beck, and at his whom I have appointed a father over thee; then shouldest thou exceedingly please Me: and all thy life would pass in joy and peace. Thou hast yet many things to abandon; which unless thou wholly resign up unto Me: thou shalt not attain to that which thou desirest.

I counsel thee to buy of Me gold tried in the fire that thou mayest become rich: [1] that is heavenly wisdom which treads under foot all things that are base. Set this above earthly wisdom: above all human and personal satisfaction.

I said thou shouldest buy mean things for things which among men are precious and high; for true heavenly wisdom seems very mean and small, and almost forgotten among men: as having no high thoughts of itself nor seeking to be magnified upon earth; many praise it with their lips, but in their life are far from it: yet is it the pearl of price [2] which is hidden from many.

OF INCONSTANCY OF HEART AND OF HAVING OUR FINAL INTENTION DIRECTED UNTO GOD

CHAPTER XXXIII

Son trust not to the feeling which is with thee now: it will quickly be changed into another. As long as thou livest thou art subject to change even against thy will; so that thou art found one while

---

[1] Rev. iii. xviii.   [2] Matt. xiii. 46.

merry another sad, one while quiet another troubled: now devout now indevout; now diligent now listless: now grave now frivolous. But he that is wise and well instructed in the Spirit standeth above these changeable things; not heeding what he feels in himself or which way the wind of instability blows: but so that the whole intention of his mind moves onwards to the right and wished for end. For thus he will remain one and the same and unshaken: with the single eye of his intention directed unceasingly towards Me amid all the shifts of circumstance. And the purer the eye of the intention is: the more steadily does a man make way through the veering blasts.

But in many the eye of a pure intention is dimmed: for the gaze is soon attracted to some pleasurable object which meets it: and it is rare to find one who is wholly free from the mole of self-seeking. So of old the Jews came to Bethany to Martha and Mary, not for Jesus' sake only: but that they might see Lazarus also.

The eye of our intention therefore must be purified that it may be single and right: and beyond all the various objects which may come between must be directed towards Me.

THAT GOD IS SWEET ABOVE ALL THINGS AND IN ALL THINGS TO HIM THAT LOVETH

CHAPTER XXXIV

BEHOLD my God and my all.

What can I wish more; and what happier thing can I long for?

O sweet and savoury word; to him that is who loveth the Word: not the world nor the things that are in the world.

My God and my all.

To him that understands enough is said: and to repeat it often is delightful to him that loveth. For when Thou art present all things are delightful: but when Thou art absent, all is wearisome. Thou makest quietness of heart and great peace: and festive joy. Thou makest us to think well of all things and in all to praise Thee: neither can any thing please long without Thee; but if it is to be pleasant and palatable: Thy grace must be present, and it must be seasoned with the seasoning of Thy Wisdom. If Thou art sweet, all is sweet: if Thou art not sweet; what can please?

But the wise men of the world and they to whom the flesh is sweet are poor in Thy sweet wisdom:[1] for in the world is utter vanity, and in the flesh is death. But they that follow Thee through contempt of worldly things and mortification of the flesh; are known to be truly wise: for they are translated from vanity to truth from flesh to spirit. To these God is sweet; and what good soever is found in creatures: they make the theme for praise of their Creator.

But great yea very great is the difference between the sweetness of the Creator and of the creature: of Eternity and of time: of Light uncreated and of light enlightened.

O Everlasting Light, surpassing all created luminaries: dart the beams of Thy brightness from above and penetrate all the corners of my heart. Purify, beatify, beautify and vivify my spirit with all its powers: that I may cleave unto Thee with transports of jubilation.

O for the coming of that blessed and desirable hour; when Thou wilt satisfy me with Thy Presence: and be unto me all in all. So long as this is not granted: neither will my joy be full. Still alas the old man lives in me: not wholly is he crucified, not perfectly is he dead. Still lusts he mightily against the Spirit, stirs up inward wars: nor suffers the kingdom of the soul to be in peace.

But Thou that rulest the power of the sea and stillest the tossing of its waves: arise and help me. Scatter the nations that delight in war: quell Thou them in Thy might; shew forth Thy wonderful works I beseech Thee: and let Thy right hand be glorified; for there is no other hope or refuge for me: save in Thee O Lord my God.

[1] In this passage there is a play on the two meanings of the verb *sapio*, which may signify either *to be sweet* or *to be wise*.

2. LORENZO SCUPOLI:
FROM *THE SPIRITUAL COMBAT*

¶Though hardly so well known in English-speaking countries as several other treatises on the spiritual life, *The Spiritual Combat* is certainly one of the clearest and best books of its kind ever written. It was introduced into France by St. Francis de Sales, who presumably received it from the author about 1590; and subsequently it became one of the great sources to which both saint and sinner turned for counsel. Notable are its practicality, its temperateness, and its profound understanding of human character. In not a few ways it offers advice now given in a different form and for a different reason by psychiatrists. The authorship of the book was long in dispute. Now it is by virtually unanimous consent attributed to Lorenzo Scupoli. The present translation follows that made with notable care and ability by the Rev. Thomas Barns and first published in 1909. Six chapters have been selected by the editor. Interested readers are referred to this edition for additional notes and a well-informed introduction.

Lorenzo Scupoli (baptised Francesco) was born in Otranto, Italy, during 1529. Of noble birth, he entered the Order of the Theatines when he was forty. He seems to have been an assiduous scholar, but was not admitted to the priesthood until 1577. Later on calumniators so undermined his reputation that he was degraded to the rank of a lay brother. But if his final years were spent in "solitude and silence," the humiliation sweetened rather than embittered his character. Scupoli lived to a ripe old age, dying in Naples during 1610. The reader will note that in appearing to address his work to a specific individual, the author was only following an established custom of his time.*

---

* From *The Spiritual Combat*. By Lorenzo Scupoli. Translated and edited by Thomas Barns, M.A. London: Methuen and Co., 1909.

CHAPTER XLIV

PRAYER

Of prayer

F distrust of ourselves, trust in God, and practice are as necessary in this combat as has been so far shown, above all prayer is necessary, for by it we are able to obtain not only those but all other good things from our Lord God.

For prayer is an instrument for obtaining all the graces which are showered down on us from that divine source of goodness and of love.

By prayer (if you use it aright) you will place a sword in the hand of God, so that He will fight and conquer for you.

And to make use of it aright there is need that you should be skilled, or that you should strive to be skilled in the following points.

First, That there should always be alive in you a true desire to serve His divine Majesty in all things, and in the way which is most pleasing to Him.

To kindle this desire in you, consider:

That God by His most marvellous excellences, His goodness, His majesty, His wisdom, His beauty, and His other infinite perfections, is above all else most worthy of being served and honoured.

That to serve you He has suffered and endured thirty-three years; and has healed and cured your festering wounds which were poisoned by the malignity of sin, not with oil, and wine, and pieces of lint, but with the precious drops which flowed from His most sacred veins, and with His flesh, torn in its purity by the scourges, the thorns, and the nails.

And besides this, think what this service means, since by it we become masters of ourselves, superior to the devil, and sons of God Himself.

Secondly, There must be in you a living faith and trust that the Lord wishes to give you all that you need for His service and for your good.

This holy trust is the vessel that the divine mercy fills with the treasures of His gifts, and the larger and the more ample it is the richer will prayer return to our own bosom.

And how can the Lord, who is unchangeable and almighty, fail to make us partakers of His gifts, when He Himself has commanded us to ask them of Him, and promises us also His Spirit if we ask It with faith and perseverance?

Thirdly, That you should draw near in prayer with the intention of being willing to do God's will alone, and not your own will, as well in asking as in obtaining what you ask; that is, that you should be moved to pray because God wishes it, and that you should desire to be heard only so far as He wills. In short, your intention ought to be to unite your will to the divine will, and not to draw God's will to your own.

And this because your will, since it is infected and spoiled by self-love, is frequently in error, and does not know what it asks; but the divine will is always united with ineffable goodness and can never err. And therefore it is the rule and the queen of all other wills, and deserves and wishes to be followed and obeyed by all.

And therefore such things as are in harmony with the good pleasure of God must always be asked. And if you are in doubt as to what such a thing is, you will ask it with the condition of wishing for it if the Lord wills that you should have it.

And those things which you know for certain are pleasing to Him, such as the virtues, you will ask more for the purpose of giving Him satisfaction and rendering service to Him than for any other end or purpose, however spiritual it may be.

Fourthly, That you should enter upon your prayer adorned with works corresponding to your requests, and that after prayer you should strive more than ever to make yourself fit for the grace and virtue you desire.

For the practice of prayer must be so accompanied by the practice of mastering ourselves that the one may follow circling round the other; for otherwise, to ask for any virtue and not to make an effort to have it would be nothing else than rather to tempt God.

Fifthly, That for the most part thanksgivings for benefits received should go before your requests, in this or in a similar way: "My Lord, who hast created and redeemed me by Thy goodness, and on occasions so innumerable that I myself do not know them, hast freed me from the hands of my enemies, help me now, and do not deny me what I ask of Thee, even though I have always been rebellious against Thee and ungrateful to Thee."

And if you are about to ask any particular virtue, and have at hand something which is trying you, with the view of practising that virtue do not forget to give Him thanks for the opportunity He has given you by it; for this is indeed no small benefit from Him.

Sixthly, Because prayer takes its force and power from inclining God to our desires by the goodness and mercy which are natural to Him, from the merits of the life and Passion of His only-begotten Son, and from the promise He has given us that He will hear us, you will conclude your requests with one or more of the following petitions: "Grant me this grace, O Lord, for Thine infinite pity's sake. May the merits of Thy Son obtain for me in Thy presence that which I ask of Thee. Remember Thy promises, O my God, and incline Thyself unto my prayer."

And sometimes you will also ask for gifts by the merits of the Blessed Virgin Mary and other saints, who have much power in the presence of God, and are much honoured by Him, because in this life they showed honour to His divine Majesty.

Seventhly, It is needful that you should persevere in prayer, because humble perseverance conquers the Invincible; for if the assiduity and importunity of the widow in the Gospel inclined the judge, who was full of all wickedness, to her requests (St. Luke xviii.), will it not have force to draw to our prayers the very fulness of all that is good?

And therefore, although after prayer the Lord may delay to come and hear us, and even may show signs that are unfavourable to us, yet go on praying and having a firm and living trust in His help, since there never lack in Him, indeed there abound in Him in more than infinite measure, all those things which are necessary to bring about other gifts.

And if the fault is not on your side, be assured indeed that you will always obtain all that you ask, or else what will be more useful to you, or indeed both these together.

And the more you seem to be repulsed, the more you should humble yourself in your own eyes, and considering your own unworthiness, with a steadfast thought of the mercy of God, you will always increase your trust in Him, and this being kept living and constant the more it is attacked, so much the more will it be pleasing to our Lord.

Render then thanks to Him always, recognising Him as good and wise and loving, no less when some things are denied you than if they are granted to you; remaining steadfast whatever happens, and joyful in a humble submission to His divine providence.

CHAPTER XLV

MENTAL PRAYER

What mental prayer is

MENTAL prayer is a lifting up of the mind to God with an actual or virtual request for that which is desired.

Actual prayer is offered when by words mentally uttered grace is asked for, in this or a similar way: "O Lord, my God, grant me this grace to Thy honour." Or in this way: "O my Lord, I believe that it is pleasing to Thee and that it is for Thy glory that I should ask for and should have this grace; fulfil then now Thy divine pleasure in me."

And when you are indeed attacked by enemies you will pray in this way: "Be ready, O my God, to help me, that I may not yield to my enemies"; or indeed: "My God, my refuge,[1] the strength of my soul, help me at once that I fall not."

And while the conflict lasts, continue also this method of prayer, always resisting manfully him who is fighting against you.

And when the fierceness of the warfare is past, turning to your Lord, present to Him the enemy who has fought against you, and your own weakness in resisting him, saying: "Behold, O my Lord, him who was created by the hands of Thy goodness, redeemed by Thy blood. Behold Thine enemy who has tried to take him from Thee and to devour him. To Thee, O my Lord, do I turn, in Thee alone do I trust, for Thou art almighty and good, and seest my weakness and my readiness apart from Thy aid to subject

[1] Ps. xlvi. (xlv.) 1.

myself willingly to him. Help me then, my hope, and the strength of my soul."

Virtual prayer is meant when the mind is lifted up to God to obtain some grace, showing Him our need without any other words or reasons.

For example, when I raise my mind to God, and there in His presence recognise that I am powerless to defend myself from evil and to do what is right, and inflamed with the desire to serve Him, humbly and faithfully waiting for His help, I gaze and gaze again on the Lord Himself.

And this knowledge thus gained, inflamed with desire or faith towards God is a prayer which virtually asks for what I need; and the clearer and more sincere this knowledge is, and the more inflamed the desire and the more living the faith, so much the more efficacious will be the prayer.

There is also another kind of virtual prayer which is more restrained, which consists in a simple glance of the mind to Godward, to the end that He may help us; and this glance is none else than a tacit remembrance and request for that grace which we have before asked for.

And take care that you learn aright this kind of prayer and make yourself familiar with it, because (as experience will show you) it is a weapon which you can easily have at hand in every opportunity and in every place, and is of more value and help than I can say.

CHAPTER XLVI

MEDITATION

Of prayer by way of meditation

IF you wish to pray for some length of time, for half an hour it may be, or even for a whole hour and more, you will join to your prayer the meditation on the Life and Passion of Jesus Christ, always applying His actions to that virtue which you desire.

For example, if you desire to obtain as a grace the virtue of patience, you will perchance take for meditation some points in the mystery of the scourging.

First, How, after the order given by Pilate, the Lord was dragged by the ministers of wickedness, with shouts and mockery, to the place appointed for the scourging.

Secondly, How He was stripped by them in haste and fury, and his flesh, in its spotless purity, left altogether exposed and naked.

Thirdly, How His innocent hands were bound together by a rough cord to the column.

Fourthly, How His body was altogether torn and lacerated by the scourges, so that streams of His divine blood ran down to the ground.

Fifthly, How blows upon blows falling in one and the same place, the wounds already made were always more and more irritated.

When you have thus set before you these or similar points of meditation that you may acquire patience, you will first of all apply your senses to feel as vividly as possible the most bitter anguish and the sharp pains which in each part of His most sacred Body, and in all together, your dear Lord endured.

Then you will pass to His most holy Soul, penetrating as far as possible the patience and meekness with which He bore so great afflictions, and yet not satisfying the hunger of suffering greater and more horrible torments for the honour of His Father and for our benefit.

Gaze then on Him, burning with a lively desire that you may bear your trouble, and see how, still turning to the Father, He prays for you that He may deign to give you grace to bear with patience the cross which is now tormenting you, and any other whatever.

And then, bending your will again and again that it may be willing to bear all with a patient mind, turn your mind again to the Father; and thanking Him first that of His pure love He has sent His only-begotten Son into the world to bear so many hard torments and to pray for us, ask of Him again the virtue of patience in virtue of the works and the prayers of His dear Son.

CHAPTER XLVII

MEDITATION AND PRAYER (*continued*)

Of another means of prayer by way of meditation

You will also be able to pray and to meditate in another way. When you have attentively considered the afflictions of the Lord, and seen in thought the readiness of mind with which He endured them, from the greatness of His troubles and from His patience you will pass to two other considerations: the one of His merit, the other of the satisfaction and the glory of the Eternal Father through the perfect obedience of His Son in the Passion.

And representing those two things to His divine Majesty, you will ask in virtue of them the grace which you desire.

And this you will be able to do not only in each mystery of the Passion of the Lord, but in every particular act, whether inward or outward, which He did in each mystery.

CHAPTER XLVIII

MEDITATION AND PRAYER (*continued*)

Of a method of prayer by the aid of the Blessed Virgin Mary

BESIDES the above there is another method of meditation and prayer, by the aid of the Blessed Virgin Mary, turning the mind first of all to the Eternal God, then to the Blessed Jesus, and lastly to the most glorious Mother herself.

Turning to God, consider two things: one, the delights which He of Himself took from eternity in Mary, before she had her being from nothing. The other, her virtues and actions after she was born into the world.

The delights you will meditate on in this way. Raise yourself on high in thought above all time and above every creature, and entering into the very eternity and mind of God, consider the pleasures which He of Himself took in the Blessed Virgin Mary; and amongst these having found God Himself, in virtue of them ask assuredly grace and strength for the destruction of your enemies, and in particular the one who is now attacking you.

Passing then to the consideration of the great and singular virtues and actions of the most Blessed Virgin herself, and presenting them sometimes all together, sometimes one by one to God, in virtue of them ask of His infinite goodness all that you need.

And then turning your mind to the Son, you will bring to His memory the Virgin's womb which bore Him for nine months; the reverence with which, after He was born, the Virgin adored Him and recognised Him as very Man and very God, her Son and her Creator; the eyes of pity with which she looked on Him in His poverty; the arms which embraced Him; the loving kisses with which she kissed Him; the milk with which she nourished Him, and the labours and anguish which she endured for Him in life and in death. And by virtue of those things you will do sweet violence to the divine Son that He may hear you.

Turning last of all to the most Blessed Virgin, call to her memory that by the eternal providence and goodness she was chosen as the Mother of grace and pity, and as our Advocate. And therefore, after her own Blessed Son, we have no surer and more powerful recourse than to her.

Moreover remind her of that truth which is written of her, and which rests on so very many miraculous effects, that there is never one who invokes her in faith but she has answered in her pity.

Finally, you will place before her the troubles of her only Son, which He bore for our salvation, praying her that she will obtain grace from Him that to His glory and honour they may have in you that result for which He bore them.

CHAPTER XLIX

MEDITATION AND PRAYER (continued)

Of some considerations why in faith and trust we should have recourse to the Blessed Virgin Mary

IF you wish to have recourse to the Blessed Virgin Mary in faith and trust in every need you have, you will be able to obtain it by the following considerations.

First, We know already by experience that all those vessels in which musk or some other precious liquor has been stored retain the scent of it though it be no longer there; and they retain it the more, the longer it has been there; and still more, if even in some way some of it has remained in them; even though musk, as well as every precious liquor, is of a virtue which is limited and restricted. As also one who is near a large fire retains its heat for some time, even though he be at some distance from the fire.

This being true, with what fire of love, with what sense of mercy and pity, shall we say that the heart of the Blessed Virgin Mary has been warmed and is full? Because for nine months she bore in her virgin's womb the Son of God, and always bears Him in her bosom and her heart, Him who is love and mercy and pity itself, her heart is full not merely of virtue which is limited and restricted, but of that which is infinite and without bounds.

So that, as one who draws near to a large fire cannot but receive of its heat; so, and much more, will everyone who is in need, and who draws near with humility and faith to the fire of love, of mercy, and of pity, which always burns in the heart of the Blessed Virgin Mary, receive help, favour, and grace in abundance; and so much the more if he frequently draws near to her in great faith and trust.

Secondly, No creature ever loved Jesus Christ so much, or was so much in harmony with His will, as His most Blessed Mother.

If then the Son of God Himself, who spent all His life and spent Himself wholly for the need of us sinners, has given us His Mother as our Mother and Advocate, that she may help us and be after Him a means of our salvation, how can she, our Mother and our Advocate, ever fail us, and become a rebel to her Son's will?

Run then, my daughter, with confidence in every need of yours to the most Blessed Mother, the Virgin Mary, for rich and blessed is this trust and safe the refuge you have in her, since she always brings forth grace and mercy in abundance.

CHAPTER L

MEDITATION AND PRAYER (*continued*)

*Of a method of meditation and prayer by the aid of the Angels
and all the Blessed*

THAT in this you may win the help and favour of the Angels and
the Saints in heaven, you will be able to use two methods.

One is that you should turn to the Eternal Father and present
to Him the love and the praises with which He is extolled by all
the heavenly Court, and the labours and pains which the Saints
have suffered on earth for love of Him; and by virtue of these
things you may ask of His divine Majesty all that you have
need of.

The other is that you should have recourse to these glorious
Spirits, as to those who not only desire our perfection but that we
should be set in a higher place than themselves, asking their
succour against all your vices and enemies, and also for their
defence of you when you are at the point of death.

And sometimes you will give yourself to the consideration of
the many and singular gifts which they have received from the
supreme Creator, stirring up in yourself a lively affection of love
and of joy towards them because they are rich in so many gifts,
as if indeed the gifts were your own.

Even you will rejoice more, if it is possible, that they have
them and not you, since such was the will of God, who for this
may be praised and thanked by them.

And to practise this with order and ease, you will be able to
divide the hosts of the Blessed through the days of the week in
this manner.

Sunday, you will take the Nine Choirs of Angels.

Monday: St. John the Baptist.

Tuesday: the Patriarchs and Prophets.

Wednesday: the Apostles.

Thursday: the Martyrs.

Friday: the Bishops with the other Saints.

Saturday: the Virgins with the other holy women.

But never omit on each day to have recourse frequently to the

Blessed Virgin Mary, the Queen of all the Saints, to your guardian Angel, to St. Michael the Archangel, and to all your patron Saints.

And each day pray the Blessed Virgin Mary, her Son, and the heavenly Father to grant you so great a favour as to give you as your chief patron and protector St. Joseph, the spouse of the Virgin, having then recourse to this Saint with prayers and with confidence that he will receive you under his protection.

Many things are told of this glorious Saint, and of the many favours which those have received from him who have held him in reverence, and have had recourse to him not only in their spiritual but also in their temporal wants, and particularly in directing the devout in the way of praying and meditating aright.

And if on the other Saints God sets so great a value, because when living amongst us they rendered Him obedience and honour, how much must we believe that he is held in esteem by Him, and how high a value in His presence the prayers of this most humble and most happy Saint must have, who was so honoured on earth by God Himself that He was willing to be subject unto him and to obey him and serve him as a father.

3. ST. FRANCIS DE SALES:

ON THE LOVE OF GOD

¶SAINT FRANCIS DE SALES (1567-1622) is usually remembered as
the author of the excellent *Introduction to a Devout Life,* which is
available in many editions. But since this treatise is to a great extent
based upon *The Spiritual Combat,* part of which is reprinted in the
present book, it seems advisable to offer a chapter of the treatise *On
the Love of God.* This suffered from neglect as a result of the
criticisms directed against it by Bossuet and of the use made of it
by the Quietists. In our time, however, these misunderstandings are
reckoned with all the other superseded errors of history, and this
treatise is enjoying a new vogue. Perhaps, indeed, it will soon be
considered the masterpiece of post-Tridentine mystical theology. The
sections here given constitute Book III of Dom Henry Benedict
Mackey's translation, first published in 1884.

Born in Savoy of aristocratic parents, Francis studied the humani-
ties in Paris and law in Padua. But since early experiences had led
him to make a vow of chastity, he decided, much against the will of
his father, to become a priest. The neighborhood of Annecy, where
he was stationed, had become in large measure Protestant, and as a
priest and later a bishop he threw himself with ardor into the work
of the Counter-Reformation. He was consecrated Bishop of Geneva
in 1602, and thereafter guided St. Jane Frances de Chantal,
foundress of the Institute of the Visitation. St. Francis was a
voluminous writer, whose work is distinguished for temperateness,
classic beauty and great charm.*

* From *Library of St. Francis de Sales,* Vol. II.   Edited by Rev. Henry
Benedict Mackey. London: Burns, Oates and Washbourne. N.D.

BOOK III

OF THE PROGRESS AND PERFECTION
OF LOVE

CHAPTER I

THAT HOLY LOVE MAY BE AUGMENTED STILL MORE AND MORE
IN EVERY ONE OF US

HE sacred Council of Trent assures us, that the friends of God, proceeding from virtue to virtue, are day by day renewed, that is, they increase by good works in the justice which they have received by God's grace, and are more and more justified, according to those heavenly admonitions; *He that is just let him be justified still: and he that is holy, let him be sanctified still.*[1] And: *Be not afraid to be justified even to death.*[2] *The path of the just, as a shining light, goeth forwards and increaseth even to perfect day.*[3] *Doing the truth in charity, let us in all things grow up in him who is the head, even Christ.*[4] And finally: *This I pray, that your charity may more and more abound in knowledge and in all understanding.*[5] All these are sacred words out of David, S. John, Ecclesiasticus, and S. Paul.

I never heard of any living creature whose growth was not bounded and limited, except the crocodile, who from an extremely little beginning never ceases to grow till it comes to its end, representing equally in this the good and the wicked: *For the pride of them that hate thee ascendeth continually,*[6] says the great king David; and the good increase as the break of day, from brightness to brightness. And to remain at a standstill is impossible; he that gains not, loses in this traffic; he that ascends not, descends upon this ladder; he that vanquishes not in this battle is vanquished: we live amidst the dangers of the wars which our enemies wage against us, if we resist not we perish; and we can-

[1] Apoc. xxii. 11.
[2] Eccles. xviii. 22.
[3] Prov. iv. 18.
[4] Eph. iv. 15.
[5] Phil. i. 9.
[6] Ps. lxxiii. 23.

not resist unless we overcome, nor overcome without triumph. For as the glorious S. Bernard says: "It is written in particular of man that *he never continueth in the same state;*[1] he necessarily either goes forward or returns backward. *All run indeed but one obtains the prize, so run that you may obtain.*[2] Who is the prize but Jesus Christ? And how can you take hold on him if you follow him not? But if you follow him you will march and run continually, for he never stayed, but continued his course of love and obedience until death and the death of the cross."

Go then, says S. Bernard; go, I say with him; go, my dear Theotimus, and admit no other bounds than those of life, and as long as it remains run after this Saviour. But run ardently and swiftly: for what better will you be for following him, if you be not so happy as to take hold of him! Let us hear the Prophet: *I have inclined my heart to do thy justifications for ever:*[3] he does not say that he will do them for a time only, but for ever, and because he desires eternally to do well, he shall have an eternal reward. *Blessed are the undefiled in the way, who walk in the law of the Lord.*[4] Accursed are they who are defiled, who walk not in the law of the Lord: it is only for the devil to say that he will *sit in the sides of the north.*[5] Detestable one, wilt thou *sit?* Ah! knowest thou not that thou art upon the way, and that the way is not made to sit down but to go in, and it is so made to go in, that going is called making way. And God speaking to one of his greatest friends says: *Walk before me and be perfect.*[6]

True virtue has no limits, it goes ever further; but especially holy charity, which is the virtue of virtues, and which, having an infinite object, would be capable of becoming infinite if it could meet with a heart capable of infinity. Nothing hinders this love from being infinite except the condition of the will which receives it, and which is to act by it: a condition which prevents any one loving God as much as God is amiable, as it prevents them from seeing him as much as he is visible. The heart which could love God with a love equal to the divine goodness would have a will infinitely good, which cannot be but in God. Charity then in us may be perfected up to the infinite, but exclusively; that is,

[1] Job xiv. 2.
[2] I Cor. ix. 24.
[3] Ps. cxviii. 112.
[4] *Ibid.* I.
[5] Is. xiv. 13.
[6] Gen. xvii. 1.

charity may become more and more, and ever more, excellent, yet never infinite. The Holy Ghost may elevate our hearts, and apply them to what supernatural actions it may please him, so they be not infinite. Between little and great things, though the one exceed the other never so much, there is still some proportion, provided always that the excess of the thing which exceeds be not an infinite excess: but between finite and infinite there is no proportion, and to make any, it would be necessary, either to raise the finite and make it infinite, or to lower the infinite and make it finite, which is impossible.

So that even the charity which is in our Redeemer, as he is man, though greater than Angels or men can comprehend, yet is not infinite of itself and in its own being, but only in regard to its value and merit, as being the charity of a divine Person, who is the eternal Son of the omnipotent Father.

Meanwhile it is an extreme honour to our souls that they may still grow more and more in the love of their God, as long as they shall live in this failing life: *Ascending by steps from virtue to virtue.*[1]

CHAPTER II

HOW EASY OUR SAVIOUR HAS MADE THE INCREASE OF LOVE

Do you see, Theotimus, that glass of water or that piece of bread which a holy soul gives to a poor body for God's sake; it is a small matter, God knows, and in human judgment hardly worthy of consideration: God, notwithstanding, recompenses it, and forthwith gives for it some increase of charity. The goat's-hair which was anciently presented to the Tabernacle was received in good part, and had place amongst the holy offerings; and the little actions which proceed from charity are agreeable to God, and have their place among merits. For as in Araby the Blest, not only the plants which are by nature aromatic, but even all the others, are sweet, gaining a share in the felicity of that soil; so in a charitable soul, not only the works which are excellent of their own nature, but also the little actions, smell of the virtue of holy love, and have a good odour before the majesty of God, who in

[1] Ps. lxxxiii. 6.

consideration of them increases charity. And I say God does it, because Charity does not produce her own increase as a tree does, which by its own virtue produces and throws out, one from another, its boughs: but as Faith, Hope and Charity are virtues which have their origin from the divine goodness, so thence also they draw their increase and perfection, not unlike bees, which, having their extraction from honey, have also their food from it.

Wherefore, as pearls are not only bred of dew but fed also with it, the mother-pearls to this end opening their shells towards heaven to beg, as it were, the drops which the freshness of the air makes fall at the break of day, so we, having received Faith, Hope and Charity from the heavenly bounty, ought always to turn our hearts and keep them turned towards it, thence to obtain the continuation and augmentation of the same virtues. "O, Lord," does holy Church our mother teach us to say, "give us the increase of faith, hope and charity." And this is in imitation of those that said to Our Saviour: *Lord increase our faith*,[1] and following the counsel of S. Paul, who assures us that: *God alone is able to make all grace abound in us*.[2]

It is God therefore that gives this increase, in consideration of the use we make of his grace, as it is written; *For he that hath*, that is, who uses well the favours received, *to him shall be given, and he shall abound*.[3] Thus is Our Saviour's exhortation practised: *Lay up to yourselves treasures in heaven:*[4] as though he said: add ever new good works to the former ones; for fasting, prayer and alms-deeds are the coins whereof your treasures are to consist. Now as amongst the treasures of the temple, the poor widow's mite was much esteemed, and as indeed, by the addition of many little pieces treasures become great, and their value increases, so the least little good works, even though performed somewhat coldly, and not according to the whole extent of the charity which is in us, are agreeable to God, and esteemed by him; in such sort that though of themselves they cannot cause any increase in the existing love, being of less force than it, yet the divine Providence, counting, and out of his goodness, valuing them, forthwith rewards them with increase of charity for the present, and assigns to them a greater heavenly glory for the future.

[1] Luke xvii. 5.
[2] 2 Cor. ix. 8.
[3] Matt. xiii. 12.
[4] Matt. vi. 20.

Theotimus, bees make the delicious honey which is their chief work; but the wax, which they also make, does not therefore cease to be of some worth, or to make their labour valuable. The loving heart ought to endeavour to bring forth works full of fervour, and of high value, that it may powerfully augment charity: yet if it bring forth some of lesser value, it shall not lose its recompense; for God will be pleased by these, that is to say he will love us ever a little more for them. Now God never loves a soul more without bestowing also upon her more charity, our love towards him being the proper, and special effect, of his love towards us.

The more attentively we regard our image in a looking-glass, the more attentively it regards us again; and the more lovingly God casts his gracious eyes upon our soul, which is made to his image and likeness, our soul in return, with so much the more attention and fervour is fixed upon the divine goodness, answering, according to her littleness, every increase which this sovereign sweetness makes of his divine love towards her. The Council of Trent says thus: "If any say that justice received is not preserved, yea that it is not augmented, by good works in the sight of God, but that works are only the fruits and signs of justification acquired, and not the cause of its increase, let him be anathema." Do you see, Theotimus, the justification wrought by charity is augmented by good works, and, which is to be noted, by good works without exception: for, as S. Bernard says excellently well on another subject, nothing is excepted where nothing is distinguished. The Council speaks of good works indifferently, and without reservation, giving us to understand, that not only the great and fervent, but also the little and feeble works cause the increase of holy Charity, but the great ones greatly, and the little much less.

Such is the love which God bears to our souls, such his desire to make us increase in the love which we owe to him. The divine sweetness renders all things profitable to us, takes all to our advantage, and turns all our endeavours, though never so lowly and feeble, to our gain.

In the action of moral virtues little works bring no increase to the virtue whence they proceed, yea, if they be very little, they impair it: for a great liberality perishes if it occupies itself in bestowing things of small value, and if liberality becomes niggardliness. But in the actions of those virtues which issue from God's mercy, and especially of charity, every work gives increase. Nor is it strange that sacred love, as King of virtues, has nothing either great or small which is not loveable, since the balm tree, prince of aromatic trees, has neither bark nor leaf that is not odoriferous: and what could love bring forth that were not worthy of love, or did not tend to love?

CHAPTER III

HOW A SOUL IN CHARITY MAKES PROGRESS IN IT

LET us make use of a parable, Theotimus, seeing that this method was so agreeable to the sovereign Master of the love which we are teaching. A great and brave King, having espoused a most amiable young princess, and having on a certain day led her into a very retired cabinet, there to converse with her more at his pleasure, after some discourse saw her by a certain sudden accident fall down as dead at his feet. Alas! he was extremely disturbed at this, and it well nigh put him also into a swoon; for she was dearer to him than his own life. Yet the same love that gave him this assault of grief, gave him an equal strength to sustain it, and set him into action to remedy, with an incomparable promptitude, the evil which had happened to the dear companion of his life. Therefore rapidly opening a sideboard which stood by, he takes a cordial-water, infinitely precious, and having filled his mouth with it, by force he opens the lips and the set teeth of his well-beloved princess, then breathing and spurting the precious liquor which he held in his mouth, into that of his poor lifeless one who lay in a swoon, and pouring what was left in the phial about the nostrils, the temples, and the heart, he made her return to herself and to her senses again; that done, he helps her up gently, and by virtue of remedies so strengthens and revives her, that she begins to stand and walk very quietly with him; but in no sort without his help, for he goes assisting and sustaining her by her arm, till at length he lays to her heart an *epithem* so precious and of so great virtue, that finding herself entirely restored to her wonted health, she walks all alone, her dear spouse not now sustaining her so much, but only holding her right hand softly between his, and his right arm folded over hers on to her bosom. Thus he went on treating her, and fulfilling to her in all this four most agreeable offices: for 1. He gave testimony that his heart was lovingly careful of her. 2. He continued ever a little nursing her. 3. If she had felt any touch of her former faintness he would have sustained her. 4. If she had lighted in any rough and difficult place in her walking he would have been her support and stay: and in accidents, or when she would make a little more haste, he raised her and powerfully succoured her. In fine he stayed by her with this heartfelt care till night approached, and then he assisted to lay her in her royal bed.

The soul is the spouse of Our Saviour when she is just; and because she is never just but when she is in charity, she is also no sooner spouse than she is led into the cabinet of those delicious perfumes mentioned in the Canticles. Now when the soul which has been thus honoured commits sin, she falls as if dead in a spiritual swoon; and this is in good truth a most unlooked-for accident: for who would ever think that a creature could forsake her Creator and sovereign good for things so trifling as the allurements of sin? Truly the heavens are astonished at it, and if God were subject to passions he would fall down in a swoon at this misfortune, as when he was mortal he died upon the cross for our redemption. But seeing it is not now necessary that he should employ his love in dying for us, when he sees the soul overthrown by sin he commonly runs to her succour, and by an unspeakable mercy, lays open the gates of her heart by the stings and remorses of conscience which come from the divers lights and apprehensions which he casts into our hearts, with salutary movements, by which, as by odorous and vital liquors, he makes the soul return to herself, and brings her back to good sentiments. And all this, Theotimus, God works in us without our action,[1] by his all-amiable Goodness which prevents us with its sweetness. For even as our bride, having fainted, would have died in her swoon, if the King had not assisted her; so the soul would remain lost in her sin if God prevented her not. But if the soul thus excited add her consent to the solicitation of grace, seconding the inspiration which prevents her, and accepting the required helps provided for by God; he will fortify her, and conduct her through various move-

---

[1] St. Augustine.

ments of faith, hope and penitence, even till he restore her to her true spiritual health, which is no other thing than charity. And while he thus makes her walk in the virtues by which he disposes her to this holy love, he does not conduct her only, but in such sort sustains her, that as she for her part goes as well as she is able, so he on his part supports and sustains her; and it is hard to say whether she goes or is carried; for she is not so carried that she goes not, and yet her going is such that if she were not carried she could not go. So that, to speak apostolically, she must say: I walk, *not I* alone, *but the grace of God with me.*[1]

But the soul being entirely restored to her health by the excellent *epithem* of charity which the Holy Ghost infuses into her heart, she is then able to walk and keep herself upon her feet of herself, yet by virtue of this health and this sacred *epithem* of holy love. Wherefore though she is able to walk of herself, yet is she to render the glory thereof to God, who has bestowed upon her a health so vigorous and strong: for whether the Holy Ghost fortify us by the motions which he enables our heart to make, or sustain us by the charity which he infuses into them, whether he succour us by manner of assistance in raising and carrying us, or strengthen our hearts by pouring into them fortifying and quickening love, we always live, walk, and work, in him and by him.

And although by means of charity poured into our hearts, we are able to walk in the presence of God, and make progress in the way of salvation, yet still it is the goodness of God which ever helps the soul to whom he has given his love, continually holding her with his holy hand; for so 1. He doth better make appear the sweetness of his love towards her. 2. He ever animates her more and more. 3. He supports her against depraved inclinations and evil habits contracted by former sins. 4. And finally, he supports her and defends her against temptations.

Do we not often see, Theotimus, that sound and robust men must be provoked to employ their strength and power well; and, as one would say, must be drawn by the hand to the work? So God having given us his charity, and by it the force and the means to gain ground in the way of perfection, his love does not permit him to let us walk thus alone, but makes him put himself upon the way with us, urges him to urge us, and solicits his heart to

[1] 1 Cor. xv. 10.

solicit and drive forward ours to make good use of the charity which he has given us, repeating often, by means of his inspirations, S. Paul's admonitions: *See that you receive not the grace of God in vain.*[1] *Whilst we have time let us work good to all men.*[2] *So run that you may obtain.*[3] So that we are often to think that he repeats in our ears the words which he used to the good father Abraham: *Walk before me and be perfect.*[4]

But principally the special assistance of God to the soul endowed with charity is required in sublime and extraordinary enterprises; for though charity, however weak it be, gives us enough inclination, and, as I think, enough power, to do the works necessary for salvation, yet, to aspire to and undertake excellent and extraordinary actions, our hearts stand in need of being pushed and raised by the hand and motion of this great heavenly lover; as the princess in our parable, although restored to health, could not ascend nor go fast, unless her dear spouse raised and strongly supported her. Thus S. Antony and S. Simeon Stylites were in the grace of God and charity when they designed so exalted a life; as also the B. Mother (S.) Teresa when she made her particular vow of obedience, S. Francis and S. Louis, when they undertook their journey beyond-seas for the advancement of God's glory, the Blessed Francis Xavier, when he consecrated his life to the conversion of the Indians, S. Charles, in exposing himself to serve the plague-stricken, S. Paulinus, when he sold himself to redeem the poor widow's child; yet still never would they have struck such mighty and generous blows, unless God, to that charity which they had in their hearts, had added special inspirations, invitations, lights and forces, whereby he animated and pushed them forward to these extraordinary exploits of spiritual valour.

Do you not mark the young man of the gospel, whom Our Saviour loved, and who, consequently, was in charity? Certainly, he never dreamed of selling all he had to give it to the poor, and following Our Saviour: nay though Our Saviour had given him such an inspiration, yet had he not the courage to put it into execution. For these great works, Theotimus, we need not only to be inspired, but also to be fortified, in order to effect what the

[1] 2 Cor. vi. 1.
[2] Gal. vi. 10.
[3] 1 Cor. ix. 24.
[4] Gen. xvii. 1.

inspiration inclines us to. As again, in the fierce assaults of extraordinary temptations, a special and particular presence of heavenly succour is absolutely necessary. For this cause holy church makes us so frequently cry out: "Excite our hearts O Lord:" "Prevent our actions by thy holy inspirations and further them with thy continual help:" "O Lord, make haste to help us:" and the like, in order by such prayers to obtain grace to be able to effect excellent and extraordinary works, and more frequently and fervently to do ordinary ones; as also more ardently to resist small temptations, and boldly to combat the greatest. S. Antony was assailed by a hideous legion of devils, and having long sustained their attacks, not without incredible pain and torment, at length saw the roof of his cell burst open, and a heavenly ray enter the breach, which made the black and darksome troop of his enemies vanish in a moment, and delivered him from all the pain of the wounds received in that battle; whence he perceived God's particular presence, and fetching a profound sigh towards the vision —"where wast thou, O good Jesus," said he, "where wast thou? Why wast thou not here from the beginning to have relieved my pain? It was answered him from above. Antony, I was here: but I awaited the event of thy combat: and since thou didst behave thyself bravely and valiantly, I will be thy continual aid." But in what did the valour and courage of this brave spiritual combatant consist? He himself declared it another time when, being set upon by a devil who acknowledged himself to be the spirit of fornication, this glorious saint after many words worthy of his great courage began to sing the 7th verse of the 117th Psalm: *The Lord is my helper: and I will look over my enemies.*

And Our Saviour revealed to S. Catharine of Sienna, that He was in the midst of her heart in a cruel temptation she had, as a captain in the midst of a fort to hold it; and that without His succour she would have been lost in that battle. It is the same in all the great assaults which our enemy makes against us: and we may well say with Jacob that it is *the angel that delivereth* us *from all evil,*[1] and may sing with the great King David: *The Lord ruleth me: and I shall want nothing. He hath set me in a place of pasture. He hath brought me up, on the water of refreshment: he hath converted my soul.* So that we ought often to repeat this

[1] Gen. xlviii. 16.

exclamation and prayer: *And thy mercy will follow me all the days of my life.*[1]

CHAPTER IV

OF HOLY PERSEVERANCE IN SACRED LOVE

Even as a tender mother, leading with her her little babe, assists and supports him as need requires, letting him now and then venture a step by himself in less dangerous and very smooth places, now taking him by the hand and steadying him, now taking him up in her arms and bearing him, so Our Lord has a continual care to conduct his children, that is such as are in charity; making them walk before him, reaching them his hand in difficulties, and bearing them himself in such travails, as he sees otherwise insupportable unto them. This he declared by Isaias saying: *I am the Lord thy God, who take thee by the hand, and say to thee: fear not, I have helped thee.*[2] So that with a good heart we must have a firm confidence in God, and his assistance, for if we fail not to second his grace, he will accomplish in us the good work of our salvation, which he also began, working in us *both to will and to accomplish,*[3] as the holy Council of Trent assures us.

In this conduct which the heavenly sweetness makes of our souls, from their entry into charity until their final perfection, which is not finished but in the hour of death, consists the great gift of perseverance, to which our Saviour attaches the greatest gift of eternal glory, according to his saying: *He that shall persevere unto the end, he shall be saved:*[4] for this gift is no other thing than the combination and sequence of the various helps, solaces and succours, whereby we continue in the love of God to the end: as the education, bringing up and supporting of a child is no other thing, than the many cares, aids, succours, and other offices necessary to a child, exercised and continued towards him till he grows to years in which he no longer needs them.

But the continuance of succours and helps is not equal in all those that persevere. In some it is short; as in such as were con-

[1] Ps. xxii.
[2] Is. xli. 13.
[3] Phil. ii. 13.
[4] Matt. x. 22.

verted a little before their death: so it happened to the Good Thief; so to that officer, who seeing the constancy of S. James made forthwith profession of faith, and became a companion of the martyrdom of this great Apostle; so to the blessed gaoler who guarded the forty martyrs at Sebaste, who seeing one of them lose courage, and forsake the crown of martyrdom, put himself in his place and became Christian, martyr and glorious all at once; so to the notary of whom mention is made in the life of S. Antony of Padua, who having all his life been a false villain yet died a martyr: and so it happened to a thousand others of whom we have seen and read that they died well, after an ill-spent life. As for these, they stand not in need of a great variety of succours, but unless some great temptation cross their way, they can make this short perseverance solely by the charity given them, and by the aids by which they were converted. For they arrive at the port without voyaging, and finish their pilgrimage in a single leap, which the powerful mercy of God makes them take so opportunely that their enemies see them triumph before seeing them fight: so that their conversion and perseverance are almost the same thing. And if we would speak with exact propriety, the grace which they received of God whereby they attained as soon the issue, as the beginning of their course, cannot well be termed perseverance, though all the same, because actually it holds the place of perseverance in giving salvation, we comprehend it under the name of perseverance. In others, on the contrary, perseverance is longer, as in S. Anne the prophetess, in S. John the Evangelist, S. Paul the first hermit, S. Hilarion, S. Romuald, S. Francis of Paula;—and they stood in need of a thousand sorts of different assistances, according to the variety of the adventures of their pilgrimage and the length of it.

But in any case, perseverance is the most desirable gift we can hope for in this life, and the one which, as the Council of Trent says, we cannot have but from the hand of God, who alone can assure him that stands, and help him up that falls: wherefore we must incessantly demand it, making use of the means which Our Saviour has taught us to the obtaining of it; prayer, fasting, alms-deeds, frequenting the sacraments, intercourse with the good, the hearing and reading of holy words.

Now since the gift of prayer and devotion is liberally granted to all those who sincerely will to consent to divine inspirations, it is consequently in our power to persevere. Not of course that I mean to say that our perseverance has its origin from our power, for on the contrary I know it springs from God's mercy, whose most precious gift it is, but I mean that though it does not come from our power, yet it comes within our power, by means of our will, which we cannot deny to be in our power: for though God's grace is necessary for us, to will to persevere, yet is this will in our power, because heavenly grace is never wanting to our will, and our will is not wanting to our power. And indeed according to the great S. Bernard's opinion, we may all truly say with the Apostle that: *Neither death, nor life, nor Angels, nor principalities, nor powers, nor things present, nor things to come, nor might, nor height, nor depth, nor any other creature, shall be able to separate us from the love of God, which is in Christ Jesus Our Lord.*[1] Yes, indeed, for no creature can take us away by force from this holy love; we only can forsake and abandon it by our own will, except for which there is nothing to be feared in this matter.

So, Theotimus, following the advice of the holy Council, we ought to place our whole hope in God, who will perfect the work of our salvation which he has begun in us, if we be not wanting to his grace: for we are not to think that he who said to the paralytic: *Go, and do not will to sin again:*[2] gave him not also power to avoid that willing which he forbade him: and surely he would never exhort the faithful to persevere, if he were not ready to furnish them with the power. *Be thou faithful until death,* said he to the bishop of Smyrna, *and I will give thee the crown of life.*[3] *Watch ye, stand fast in the faith, do manfully, and be strengthened. Let all your actions be done in charity.*[4] *So run that you may obtain.*[5] We must often then with the great King demand of God the heavenly gift of perseverance, and hope that he will grant it us. *Cast me not off in the time of old age; when my strength shall fail, do not thou forsake me.*[6]

[1] Rom. viii. 38-9.
[2] John v. 14.
[3] Apoc. ii. 10.
[4] I Cor. xvi. 13.
[5] I Cor. ix. 24.
[6] Ps. lxx. 9.

CHAPTER V

THAT THE HAPPINESS OF DYING IN HEAVENLY CHARITY IS A SPECIAL GIFT OF GOD

IN fine, the heavenly King having brought the soul which he loves to the end of this life, he assists her also in her blessed departure, by which he draws her to the marriage-bed of eternal glory, which is the delicious fruit of holy perseverance. And then, dear Theotimus, this soul, wholly ravished with the love of her well-beloved, putting before her eyes the multitude of favours and succours wherewith she was prevented and helped while she was yet in her pilgrimage, incessantly kisses this sweet helping hand, which conducted, drew and supported her in the way; and confesses, that it is of this divine Saviour that she holds her felicity, seeing he has done for her all that the patriarch Jacob wished for his journey, when he had seen the ladder to heaven. O Lord, she then says, thou wast with me, and didst guide me in the way by which I came. Thou didst feed me with the bread of thy sacraments, thou didst clothe me with the wedding garment of charity, thou hast happily conducted me to this mansion of glory, which is Thy house, O my eternal Father. Oh! what remains, O Lord, save that I should protest that thou art my God for ever and ever! Amen.

Thou hast held me by my right hand; and by thy will thou hast conducted me, and with thy glory thou hast received me.[1] Such then is the order of our journey to eternal life, for the accomplishment of which the divine providence ordained from all eternity the number, distinction and succession of graces necessary to it, with their dependence on one another.

He willed, first, with a true will, that even after the sin of Adam all men should be saved, but upon terms and by means agreeable to the condition of their nature, which is endowed with free-will; that is to say he willed the salvation of all those who would contribute their consent, to the graces and favours which he would prepare, offer and distribute to this end.

Now, amongst these favours, his will was that vocation should be the first, and that it should be so accommodated to our liberty

[1] Ps. lxxii. 24.

that we might at our pleasure accept or reject it: and such as he saw would receive it, he would furnish with the sacred motions of penitence, and to those who would second these motions he determined to give charity, those again who were in charity, he purposed to supply with the helps necessary to persevere, and to such as should make use of these divine helps he resolved to impart final perseverance, and the glorious felicity of his eternal love.

And thus we may give account of the order which is found in effects of that Providence which regards our salvation, descending from the first to the last, that is from the fruit, which is glory, to the root of this fair tree, which is Our Saviour's redemption. For the divine goodness gives glory after merits, merits after charity, charity after penitence, penitence after obedience to vocation, obedience to vocation after vocation itself, vocation after Our Saviour's redemption, on which rests all this mystical ladder of the great Jacob, as well at its heavenly end, since it rests in the bosom of the eternal Father, in which he receives and glorifies the elect, as also at its earthly end, since it is planted upon the bosom and pierced side of Our Saviour, who for this cause died upon Mount Calvary.

And that this order of the effects of Providence was thus ordained, with the same dependence which they have on one another in the eternal will of God, holy Church, in the preface of one of her solemn prayers, witnesses in these words: "O eternal and Almighty God, who are Lord of the living and the dead, and art merciful to all those who thou foreknowest will be thine by faith and good works:" as though she were declaring that glory, which is the crown and the fruit of God's mercy towards men, has only been ordained for those, of whom the divine wisdom has foreseen that in the future, obeying the vocation, they will attain the living faith which works by charity.

Finally, all these effects have an absolute dependence on Our Saviour's redemption, who merited them for us in rigour of justice by the loving obedience which he exercised even till death and the death of the cross, which is the root of all the graces which we receive; we who are the spiritual grafts engrafted on his stock. If being engrafted we remain in him, we shall certainly bear, by the life of grace which he will communicate unto us, the

fruit of glory prepared for us. But if we prove broken sprigs and
grafts upon this tree, that is, if by resistance we interrupt the
progress and break the connection of the effects of his clemency,
it will not be strange, if in the end we be wholly cut off, and be
thrown into eternal fire, as fruitless branches.

God, doubtless, prepared heaven for those only who he fore-
saw would be his. Let us be his then, Theotimus, by faith and
works, and he will be ours by glory. Now it is in our power to
be his: for though it be a gift of God to be God's, yet is it a gift
which God denies no one, but offers to all, to give it to such as
freely consent to receive it.

But mark, I pray you, Theotimus, how ardently God desires
we should be his, since to this end he has made himself entirely
ours, bestowing upon us his death and his life; his life, to exempt
us from eternal death, his death, to possess us of eternal life. Let
us remain therefore in peace and serve God, to be his in this
mortal life, and still more his in the eternal.

CHAPTER VI

THAT WE CANNOT ATTAIN TO PERFECT UNION WITH GOD IN THIS MORTAL LIFE

ALL the rivers flow incessantly, and, as the wise man says: *Unto
the place whence they come they return to flow again.*[1] The sea
which is the place whence they sprang, is also the place of their
final repose; all their motion tends no farther than to unite
themselves to their fountain. "O God," says S. Augustine, "thou
hast created my heart for thyself, and it can never repose but in
thee." *For what have I in heaven, and besides thee what do I
desire upon earth? Thou art the God of my heart, and the God
that is my portion for ever.*[2] Still the union which our heart
aspires to cannot attain to its perfection in this mortal life; we
can commence our loves in this, but we can consummate them
only in the other.

The heavenly Spouse makes a delicate expression of this. *I
found him whom my soul loveth*, says she, *I held him, and I will*

---

[1] Eccles. i. 7.   [2] Ps. lxxii. 25-6.

not let him go, till I bring him into my mother's house, and into the chamber of her that bore me.[1] She finds him, then, this well-beloved, for he makes her feel his presence by a thousand consolations; she holds him, for these feelings cause in her strong affections, by which she clasps and embraces him, protesting that she will never let him go,—O no! for these affections turn into eternal resolutions; yet she cannot consider that she kisses him with the nuptial kiss till she meet with him in her mother's house, which is the heavenly Jerusalem, as S. Paul says. But see, Theotimus, how this spouse thinks of nothing less than of keeping her beloved at her mercy as a slave of love; whence she imagines to herself that it is hers to lead him at her will, and to introduce him into her mother's happy abode; though in reality it is she who must be conducted thither by him, as was Rebecca into Sara's chamber by her dear Isaac. The spirit urged by amorous passion always gives itself a little advantage over what it loves; and the spouse himself confesses: *Thou hast wounded my heart, my sister, my spouse, thou hast wounded my heart with one of thy eyes, and with one hair of thy neck:*[2] acknowledging himself her prisoner by love.

This perfect conjunction then of the soul with God, shall only be in heaven, where, as the Apocalypse says, the Lamb's marriage feast shall be made. In this mortal life the soul is truly espoused and betrothed to the immaculate Lamb, but not as yet married to him: the troth is plighted, and promise given, but the execution of the marriage is deferred: so that we have always time, though never reason, to withdraw from it; our faithful spouse never abandons us unless we oblige him to it by our disloyalty and unfaithfulness. But in heaven the marriage of this divine union being celebrated, the bond which ties our hearts to their sovereign principle shall be eternally indissoluble.

It is true, Theotimus, that while we await this great kiss of indissoluble union which we shall receive from the spouse there above in glory, he gives us some kisses by a thousand feelings of his delightful presence: for unless the soul were kissed she would not be drawn, nor would she run in the odour of the beloved's perfumes. Whence, according to the original Hebrew text and the Seventy interpreters, she desires many kisses. *Let him kiss me,*

---

[1] Cant. iii. 4. [2] *Ibid.* iv. 9.

says she, *with the kisses of his mouth*. But because these little kisses of this present life all refer to the eternal kiss of the life to come, the sacred Vulgate edition has holily reduced the kisses of grace to that of glory, expressing the desires of the spouse in this manner: *Let him kiss me with the kiss of his mouth*,[1] as though she said: of all the kisses, of all the favours that the friend of my heart, or the heart of my soul has provided for me, ah! I only breathe after and aspire to this great and solemn marriage-kiss which remains for ever, and in comparison of which the other kisses deserve not the name of kisses, being rather signs of the future union between my beloved and me than union itself.

CHAPTER VII

THAT THE CHARITY OF SAINTS IN THIS MORTAL LIFE EQUALS, YEA SOMETIMES SURPASSES, THAT OF THE BLESSED

WHEN after the labours and dangers of this mortal life, good souls arrive at the port of the eternal, they ascend to the highest and utmost degree of love to which they can attain; and this final increase being bestowed upon them in recompense of their merits, it is distributed to them, not only in good measure, but *in a measure which is pressed down and shaken together and running over*,[2] as Our Saviour says; so that the love which is given for reward is greater in every one than that which was given for meriting.

Now, not only shall each one in particular have a greater love in heaven than ever he had on earth, but the exercise of the least charity in heaven, shall be much more happy and excellent, generally speaking, than that of the greatest which is, or has been, or shall be, in this failing life: for there above, all the saints incessantly, without any intermission, exercise love; while here below God's greatest servants, drawn away and tyrannized over by the necessities of this dying life, are forced to suffer a thousand and a thousand distractions, which often take them off the practice of holy love.

In heaven, Theotimus, the loving attention of the blessed is

[1] Cant. i. 1.   [2] Luke vi. 38.

firm, constant, inviolable, and cannot perish or decrease; their intention is pure and freed from all mixture of any inferior intention: in short, this felicity of seeing God clearly and loving him unchangeably is incomparable. And who would ever equal the pleasure, if there be any, of living amidst the perils, the continual tempests, the perpetual agitations and vicissitudes which have to be gone through on sea, with the contentment there is of being in a royal palace, where all things are at every wish, yea where delights incomparably surpass every wish!

There is then more content, sweetness and perfection in the exercise of sacred love amongst the inhabitants of heaven, than amongst the pilgrims of this miserable earth. Yet still there have been some so happy in their pilgrimage that their charity has been greater than that of many saints already enjoying the eternal fatherland: for certainly it were strange if the charity of the great S. John, of the Apostles and Apostolic men, were not greater, even while they were detained here below, than that of little children, who, dying simply with the grace of baptism, enjoy immortal glory.

It is not usual for shepherds to be more valiant than soldiers; and yet David, when a little shepherd, coming to the army of Israel, while he found every one more expert in the use of arms than himself, yet he was more valiant than all. So it is not an ordinary thing for mortals to have more charity than the immortals, and yet there have been some mortals, inferior to the immortals in the exercise of love, who, notwithstanding, have surpassed them in charity and the habit of love. And as, when comparing hot iron and a burning lamp, we say the iron has more fire and heat, the lamp more flame and light; so if we parallel a child in glory with S. John while yet prisoner, or S. Paul yet captive, we must say that the child in heaven has more brightness and light in the understanding, more flame and exercise of love in the will, but that S. John or S. Paul had even on earth more fire of charity, and heat of love.

CHAPTER VIII

OF THE INCOMPARABLE LOVE WHICH THE MOTHER OF GOD, OUR BLESSED LADY, HAD

BUT always and everywhere, when I make comparisons, I intend not to speak of the most holy virgin-mother, Our Blessed Lady. O my God—no indeed! For she is the daughter of incomparable dilection, the one only dove, the all-perfect spouse. Of this heavenly Queen, from my heart I pronounce this thought, amorous but true, that, at least towards the end of her mortal days, her charity surpassed that of the Seraphim, for *many daughters have gathered together riches: thou hast surpassed them all.*[1] The Saints and Angels are but compared to stars, and the first of them to the fairest of the stars: but she is fair as the moon, as easy to be chosen and discerned from all the Saints as the sun from the stars. And going on further I think again that as the charity of this Mother of love excels in perfection that of all the Saints in heaven, so did she exercise it more perfectly, I say even in this mortal life. She never sinned venially, as the church considers; she had then no change nor delay in the way of love, but by a perpetual advancement ascended from love to love. She never felt any contradiction from the sensual appetite, and therefore her love, as a true Solomon, reigned peaceably in her soul and made all its acts at its pleasure. The virginity of her heart and body was more worthy and honourable than that of the Angels. So that her spirit, not divided or separated, as S. Paul says, *was solicitous for the things that belong to the Lord how* it *might please God.*[2] And, in fine, maternal love, the most pressing, the most active and the most ardent of all, what must it not have worked in the heart of such a Mother and for the heart of such a Son?

Ah! do not say, I pray you, that this virgin was subject to sleep; no, say not this to me, Theotimus: for do you not see that her sleep is a sleep of love? So that even her spouse wishes that she should sleep as long as she pleases. Ah! take heed, *I adjure you*, says he, *that you stir not up nor make the beloved to awake till she please.*[3] No, Theotimus, this heavenly Queen

[1] Prov. xxxi. 29.   [2] 1 Cor. vii. 32.   [3] Cant. ii. 7.

never slept but with love, since she never gave repose to her precious body, but to reinvigorate it, the better afterwards to serve her God, which is certainly a most excellent act of charity. For, as the great S. Augustine says, charity obliges us to love our bodies properly, insomuch as they are necessary to good works, as they make a part of our person, and as they shall be sharers in our eternal felicity. In good truth, a Christian is to love his body as a living image of Our Saviour incarnate, as having issued from the same stock, and consequently belonging to him in parentage and consanguinity; especially after we have renewed the alliance, by the real reception of the divine body of Our Redeemer, in the most adorable sacrament of the Eucharist, and when by Baptism, Confirmation and other Sacraments we have dedicated and consecrated ourselves to the sovereign goodness.

But as to the Blessed Virgin,—O God, with what devotion must she have loved her virginal body! Not only because it was a sweet, humble, pure body, obedient to divine love, and wholly embalmed with a thousand sweetnesses, but also because it was the living source of Our Saviour's, and belonged so strictly to him, by an incomparable appurtenance. For which cause when she placed her angelic body in the repose of sleep: Repose then now, would she say, O Tabernacle of Alliance, Ark of Sanctity, Throne of the Divinity, ease thyself a little of thy weariness, and repair thy forces, by this sweet tranquillity.

Besides, dear Theotimus, do you not know that bad dreams, voluntarily procured by the depraved thoughts of the day, are in some sort sins, inasmuch as they are consequences and execution of the malice preceding? Even so the dreams which proceed from the holy affections of our waking time, are reputed virtuous and holy. O God! Theotimus, what a consolation it is to hear S. Chrysostom recounting on a certain day to his people the vehemence of his love towards them. "The necessity of sleep," said he, "pressing our eyelids, the tyranny of our love towards you excites the eyes of our mind: and many a time while I sleep methinks I speak unto you, for the soul is wont to see in a dream by imagination what she thinks in the daytime. Thus while we see you not with the eyes of the flesh, we see you with the eyes of charity." O sweet Jesus! what dreams must thy most holy Mother have had when she slept, while her heart watched? Did she not dream that she had thee yet in her womb, or hanging at her sacred breasts and sweetly pressing those virginal lilies? Ah! what sweetness was in this soul. Perhaps she often dreamed that as Our Saviour had formerly slept in her bosom, as a tender lambkin upon the soft flank of its mother, so she slept in his pierced side, as a white dove in the cave of an assured rock: so that her sleep was wholly like to an ecstasy as regards the spirit, though as regards the body it was a sweet and grateful unwearying and rest. But if ever she dreamed, as did the ancient Joseph, of her future greatness,—when in heaven she should be *clothed with the sun, crowned with stars and having the moon under her feet*,[1] that is, wholly environed with her Son's glory, crowned with that of the Saints, and having the universe under her—or if ever, like Jacob, she saw the progress and fruit of the redemption made by her Son, for the love of the angels and of men;—Theotimus, who could ever imagine the immensity of so great delights? O what conferences with her dear child! What delights on every side!

But mark, I pray you, that I neither say nor mean to say that this privileged soul of the Mother of God was deprived of the use of reason in her sleep. Many are of opinion that Solomon in that beautiful dream, though really a dream, in which he demanded and received the gift of his incomparable wisdom, had the true use of his free-will, on account of the judicious eloquence of the discourse he made, of his choice full of discretion, and of the most excellent prayer which he used, the whole without any mixture of inconsistency or distraction of mind. But how much more probability is there then that the mother of the true Solomon had the use of reason in her sleep, that is to say, as Solomon himself makes her say, that her heart watched while she slept? Surely it was a far greater marvel that S. John had the exercise of reason in his mother's womb, and why then should we deny a less to her for whom, and to whom, God did more favours, than either he did or ever will do for all creatures besides?

To conclude, as the precious stone, *asbestos*, does by a peerless propriety preserve for ever the fire which it has conceived, so

[1] Gen. xxxvii.; Apoc. xii. 1.

the Virgin Mother's heart remained perpetually inflamed with the holy love which she received of her Son: yet with this difference, that the fire of the asbestos, as it cannot be extinguished, so it cannot be augmented, but the Virgin's sacred flames, since they could neither perish, diminish, nor remain in the same state, never ceased to take incredible increase, even as far as heaven the place of their origin: so true it is that this Mother is the *Mother of fair love*, that is, as the most amiable, so the most loving, and as the most loving, so the most beloved Mother of this only Son; who again is the most amiable, most loving, and most beloved Son of this only Mother.

CHAPTER IX

A PREPARATION FOR THE DISCOURSE ON THE UNION OF THE BLESSED WITH GOD

THE triumphant love which the blessed in heaven exercise, consists in the final, invariable and eternal union of the soul with its God. But this union—what is it?

By how much more agreeable and excellent are the objects our senses meet with, so much more ardently and greedily they give themselves to the fruition of them. By how much more fair, delightful to the view, and duly set in light they are, so much the more eagerly and attentively does the eye regard them: and by how much more sweet and pleasant voices or music are, so much the more is the attention of the ear drawn to them. So that every object exercises a powerful but grateful violence upon the sense to which it belongs, a violence more or less strong as the excellence is greater or less; provided always that it be proportionable to the capacity of the sense which desires to enjoy it; for the eye which finds so much pleasure in light cannot, however, bear an extreme light, nor fix itself upon the sun, and be music never so sweet, if loud and too near, it importunes and offends our ears. Truth is the object of our understanding, which consequently has all its content in discovering and knowing the truth of things; and according as truths are more excellent, so the understanding applies itself with more delight and attention to the consideration of them. How great was the pleasure, think you, Theotimus, of those ancient philosophers who had such an excellent knowledge of so many beautiful truths of Nature? Verily they reputed all pleasures as nothing in comparison with their well-beloved philosophy, for which some of them quitted honours, others great riches, others their country: and there was such a one as deliberately plucked out his eyes, depriving himself for ever of the enjoyment of the fair and agreeable corporal light, that he might with more liberty apply himself to consider the truth of things by the light of the spirit. This we read of Democritus: so sweet is the knowledge of truth! Hence Aristotle has very often said that human felicity and beatitude consists in wisdom, which is the knowledge of the eminent truths.

But when our spirit, raised above natural light, begins to see the sacred truths of faith, O God! Theotimus, what joy! The soul melts with pleasure, hearing the voice of her heavenly spouse, whom she finds more sweet and delicious than the honey of all human sciences.

God has imprinted upon all created things his traces, trail, or footsteps, so that the knowledge we have of his divine Majesty by creatures seems no other thing than the sight of the feet of God, while in comparison of this, faith is a view of the very face of the divine Majesty. This we do not yet see in the clear day of glory, but as it were in the breaking of day; as it happened to Jacob near to the ford of Jaboc; for though he saw not the angel with whom he wrestled, save in the weak light of daybreak, yet this was enough to make him cry out, ravished with delight: *I have seen God face to face, and my soul has been saved.*[1] O! how delightful is the holy light of faith, by which we know, with an unequalled certitude, not only the history of the beginning of creatures, and their true use, but even that of the eternal birth of the great and sovereign divine Word, for whom and by whom all has been made, and who with the Father and the Holy Ghost is one only God, most singular, most adorable, and blessed for ever and ever! Amen. Ah! says S. Jerome to his Paulinus: "The learned Plato never knew this, the eloquent Demosthenes was ignorant of it." *How sweet are thy words,*

[1] Gen. xxxii. 30.

O Lord, to my palate, said that great king, *more than honey to my mouth!* [1] *Was not our burning within us, whilst he spoke in the way?* [2] said those happy pilgrims of Emmaus, speaking of the flames of love with which they were touched by the word of faith. But if divine truths be so sweet, when proposed in the obscure light of faith, O God, what shall they be when we shall contemplate them in the light of the noonday of glory!

The Queen of Saba, who at the greatness of Solomon's renown had left all to go and see him, having arrived in his presence, and having heard the wonders of the wisdom which he poured out in his speeches, as one astonished and lost in admiration, cried out that what she had learnt by hearsay of this heavenly wisdom was not half the knowledge which sight and experience gave her.

Ah! how beautiful and dear are the truths which faith discovers unto us by hearing! But when having arrived in the heavenly Jerusalem, we shall see the great Solomon, the King of Glory, seated upon the throne of his wisdom, manifesting by an incomprehensible brightness the wonders and eternal secrets of his sovereign truth, with such light that our understanding will actually see what it had believed here below—Ah! then, dearest Theotimus, what raptures! what ecstasies! what admiration! what love! what sweetness! No, never (shall we say in this excess of sweetness) never could we have conceived that we should see truths so delightsome. We believed indeed all the glorious things that were said of thee, *O great city of God*, but we could not conceive the infinite greatness of the abysses of thy delights.

CHAPTER X

THAT THE PRECEDING DESIRE WILL MUCH INCREASE THE UNION OF THE BLESSED WITH GOD

THE desire which precedes enjoyment, sharpens and intensifies the feeling of it, and by how much the desire was more urgent and powerful, by so much more agreeable and delicious is the possession of the thing desired. Oh! my dear Theotimus, what

[1] Ps. cxviii. 103. [2] Luke xxiv. 32.

pleasure will man's heart take in seeing the face of the Divinity, a face so much desired, yea a face the only desire of our souls? Our hearts have a thirst which cannot be quenched by the pleasures of this mortal life, whereof the most esteemed and highest prized if moderate do not satisfy us, and if extreme suffocate us. Yet we desire them always to be extreme, and they are never such without being excessive, insupportable, hurtful. We die of joy as well as of grief: yea, joy is more active to ruin us than grief. Alexander, having swallowed up, in effect or in hope, all this lower world, heard some base fellow say, that there were yet many other worlds, and like a little child, who will cry if one refuse him an apple, this Alexander, whom the world styles the great, more foolish notwithstanding than a little child, began bitterly to weep, because there was no likelihood that he should conquer the other worlds, not having as yet got the entire possession of this. He that did more fully enjoy the world than ever any other did, is yet so little satisfied with it that he weeps for sorrow that he cannot have the other worlds which the foolish persuasion of a wretched babbler made him imagine to exist. Tell me, I pray you, Theotimus, does he not show that the thirst of his heart cannot be slaked in this life, and that this world is not sufficient to quench it? O wonderful yet dear unrest of man's heart! Be, be ever, my soul, without any rest or tranquillity on this earth, till thou shalt have met with the fresh waters of the immortal life and the most holy Divinity, which alone can satisfy thy thirst and quiet thy desire.

Now, Theotimus, imagine to yourself with the Psalmist, that hart which, hard set by the hounds, has neither wind nor legs; how greedily he plunges himself into the waters which he panted after, and with what ardour he rolls into and buries himself in that element. One would think he would willingly be dissolved and converted into water, more fully to enjoy its coolness. Ah! what a union of our hearts shall there be with God there above in heaven, where, after these infinite desires of the true good never assuaged in this world, we shall find the living and powerful source thereof. Then, truly, as we see a hungry child closely fixed to his mother's breast, greedily press this dear fountain of most desired sweetness, so that one would think that either it would thrust itself into its mother's breast, or else suck and draw all that breast into itself; so our soul, panting with an extreme thirst for the true good, when she shall find that inexhaustible source in the Divinity,—O good God! what a holy and sweet ardour to be united and joined to the plentiful breasts of the All-goodness, either to be altogether absorbed in it, or to have it come entirely into us!

CHAPTER XI

OF THE UNION OF THE BLESSED SPIRITS WITH GOD, IN THE VISION OF THE DIVINITY

WHEN we look upon anything, though it is present to us, it is not itself united to our eyes, but only sends out to them a certain representation or picture of itself, which is called its *sensible species*, by means of which we see. So also when we contemplate or understand anything, that which we understand is not united to our understanding otherwise than by another representation and most delicate and spiritual image, which is called *intelligible species*. But further, these species, by how many windings and changes do they get to the understanding! They arrive at the exterior senses, thence pass to the interior, then to the imagination, then to the active understanding, and come at last to the passive understanding, to the end that passing through so many strainers and under so many files they may be purified, subtilised and perfected, and of sensible become intelligible.

Thus, Theotimus, we see and understand all that we see and understand in this mortal life, yea even things of faith; for, as the mirror contains not the thing we see in it but only the representation and species of it (which representation, stayed by the mirror, produces another in the beholding eye), so the word of faith does not contain the things which it announces, but only represents them, and this representation of divine things which is in the word of faith produces another representation of them, which our understanding, helped by God's grace, accepts and receives as a representation of holy truth, and our will takes delight in it, and embraces it, as an honourable, profitable, lovely and excellent truth. Thus the truths signified in God's word are

by it represented to the understanding as things expressed in the
mirror are by the mirror represented to the eye: whence the
great Apostle said that to believe is to *see as in a glass*.[1]

But in heaven, Theotimus,—Ah, my God, what a favour!—
The Divinity will unite itself to our understanding without the
mediation of any species or representation at all, but it will itself
apply and join itself to our understanding, making itself in such
sort present unto it, that that inward presence shall be instead
of a representation or species. O God! what sweetness shall it
be for man's understanding to be united for ever to its sovereign
object, receiving not its representation but its presence, not the
picture or species, but the very essence of its divine truth and
majesty. We shall be there as most happy children of the divinity,
and shall have the honour to be fed with the divine substance
itself, taken into our soul by the mouth of our understanding,
and what surpasses all sweetness is, that as mothers are not
contented with feeding their babes with their milk, which is their
own substance, if they do not also put the breast into their mouth,
that these may receive their substance, not in a spoon or other
instrument, but even in, and by this same substance (so that this
maternal substance serves as well for food, as for a conduit to
convey it to the dear little suckling);—so God our Father is
not contented to make us receive his proper sustenance in our
understanding, that is, to make us see his divinity, but by an
abyss of his sweetness, wills himself to apply his substance to
our soul, to the end that we may no longer understand it by
species or representation but in itself and by itself; so that his
fatherly and eternal substance is both species and object to our
understanding. Then these divine promises shall be fulfilled in
an excellent manner: *I will lead her into the wilderness, and I
will speak to her heart*,[2] and give her suck. *Rejoice with Jerusalem
and be glad with her. That you may suck and be filled with the
breasts of her consolations, that you may milk out, and flow with
delights from the abundance of her glory: you shall be carried
at the breasts, and upon the knees they shall caress you*.[3]

Infinite bliss, Theotimus, and one which has not been promised
only, but of which we have a pledge in the Blessed Sacrament,
that perpetual feast of Divine Grace. For in it we receive the

[1] Cor. xiii. 12.   [2] Osee. ii. 14.   [3] Is. lxvi. 10, 11, 12.

blood of Our Saviour in his flesh, and his flesh in his blood; his blood being applied unto us by means of his flesh, his substance by his substance to our very corporal mouth; that we may know that so he will apply unto us his divine essence in the eternal feast of his glory. True it is, this favour is done unto us here really but covertly, under Sacramental species and appearances, whereas in heaven, the Divinity will give himself openly, and we shall see him face to face as he is.

CHAPTER XII

OF THE ETERNAL UNION OF THE BLESSED SPIRITS WITH GOD, IN THE VISION OF THE ETERNAL BIRTH OF THE SON OF GOD

O HOLY and Divine Spirit, eternal Love of the Father and the Son, be propitious to mine infancy. Our understanding then shall see God, Theotimus; yes, it shall see God Himself face to face, contemplating with a view of true and real presence, the divine essence Itself, and in It, the infinite beauties thereof, all-power, all-goodness, all-wisdom, all-justice, and the rest of this abyss of perfections.

It shall see clearly then, shall this understanding, the infinite knowledge which God the Father had from all eternity of His own beauty, for the expression of which in Himself, He pronounced and said eternally the Word, the *Verbum*, or the most singular and most infinite speech and diction, which, comprising and representing all the perfection of the Father, can be but one same God, entirely one with Him, without division or separation. We shall thus then see that eternal and admirable generation of the Divine Word and Son, by which He was eternally born to the image and likeness of the Father, a lively and natural image and likeness, not representing any accidents or external thing; since in God all is substance, nor can there be any accident, all is interior, nor can there be any exterior; but an image representing the proper substance of the Father so perfectly, so naturally, so essentially and substantially, that therefore it can be no other thing than the same God with Him, without distinction or difference at all either in essence or substance, and with only the distinction of Persons. For how could this Divine Son be the true, truly perfect and truly natural image, resemblance and figure of the infinite beauty and substance of the Father, if this image did not represent absolutely to the life and according to nature, the infinite perfections of the Father? And how could it infinitely represent infinite perfections if it were not itself infinitely perfect? And how could it be infinitely perfect if it were not God, and how could it be God if it were not one same God with the Father?

This Son then, the infinite image and figure of His infinite Father, is with His Father one sole, most unique, and infinite God, there being no difference of substance between Them, but only the distinction of persons. This distinction of persons, as it is certainly required, so also it is absolutely sufficient, to effect that the Father pronounces, and the Son is the Word pronounced; that the Father speaks, and the Son is the Word, or the diction; that the Father expresses, and the Son is the image, likeness or figure expressed, and, in short, that the Father is Father, and the Son, Son—two distinct persons, but one only Essence or Divinity; so that God Who is sole is not solitary, for He is sole in His most singular and simple Deity, yet is not solitary, because He is Father and Son in two persons. O Theotimus, what joy, what jubilee to celebrate this eternal birth, kept *in the brightness of the Saints*,[1] to celebrate it in seeing it, and to see it in celebrating it!

The most sweet S. Bernard, as yet a little boy at Chastillon-sur-Seine, was waiting in Church on Christmas night for the divine office to begin, and whilst waiting the poor child fell into a light slumber, during which (O God, what sweetness!) he saw in spirit, yet in a vision very distinct and clear, how the Son of God, having espoused human nature, and becoming a little child in His Mother's most pure womb, was with a humble sweetness mingled with a celestial majesty, virginally born of her:—*As a bridegroom coming out of his bride-chamber:*[2]—a vision, Theotimus, which so replenished the loving heart of the little Bernard with gladness, jubilation and spiritual delights, that he had all his life an extreme sense of it, and therefore, though afterwards as a sacred bee he ever culled out of all the

---

[1] Ps. cix. 3.   [2] Ps. xviii. 6.

divine mysteries the honey of a thousand sweet and heavenly consolations, yet had he a more particular sweetness in the solemnity of the Nativity, and spoke with a singular relish of this birth of his Master. But Ah! I beeseech thee, Theotimus, if a mystical and imaginary vision of the temporal and human birth of the Son of God, by which he proceeded man from a woman, virgin from a virgin, ravishes and so highly delights a child's heart, what shall it be when our spirits, gloriously illuminated with the light of glory, shall see this eternal birth by which the Son proceeds, God from God, Light from Light, true God from true God, divinely and eternally! Then shall our spirit be joined by an incomprehensible complacency to this object of delight, and by an unchangeable attention remain united to it for ever.

CHAPTER XIII

OF THE UNION OF THE BLESSED WITH GOD IN THE VISION OF THE PRODUCTION OF THE HOLY GHOST

THE eternal Father, seeing the infinite goodness and beauty of His own essence, so perfectly, essentially and substantially expressed in His Son, and the Son seeing reciprocally that His same essence, goodness and beauty is originally in His Father as in its source and fountain, ah! can it possibly be that this Divine Father and His Son should not mutually love one another with an infinite love, since Their will by which They love, and Their goodness for which They love are infinite in each of Them.

Love not finding us equal, equalizes us, not finding us united, unites us. Now the Father and the Son finding Themselves not only equal and united, but even one same God, one same goodness, one same essence and one same unity, how much must They needs love one another. But this love does not act like the love which intellectual creatures have amongst themselves, or towards their Creator; for created love is exercised by many and various movements, aspirations, unions and joinings which immediately succeed one another, and make a continuation of love with a grateful vicissitude of spiritual movements, but the divine love of the eternal Father towards His Son is practised in one only spiration *(souspir)* mutually from Them both, Who in this sort remain united and joined together. Yes, Theotimus; for the goodness of the Father and Son being but one sole most perfectly singular goodness, common to Them both, the love of this goodness can be but one only love; for though there be two lovers, to wit, the Father and the Son, yet seeing it is only Their most singular goodness common to Them both which is loved, and Their most unique will which loves, it is therefore but one love exercised by one amorous spiration. The Father breathes this love and so does the Son; but because the Father only breathes this love by means of the same will and for the same goodness which is equally and singularly in Him and His Son: the Son again only breathes this spiration of love for this same goodness and by this same will,—therefore this spiration of love is but one spiration, or one only spirit breathed out by two breathers.

And because the Father and the Son Who breathe, have an infinite essence and will by which They breathe, and because the goodness for which They breathe is infinite, it is impossible Their breathing should not be infinite; and forasmuch as it cannot be infinite without being God, therefore this Spirit breathed from the Father and the Son is true God: and since there neither is, nor can be, more than one only God, He is one only true God with the Father and the Son. Moreover, as this love is an act which proceeds mutually from the Father and the Son, it can neither be the Father, nor the Son, from whom it proceeds, though it has the same goodness and substance of the Father and the Son, but must necessarily be a third person, Who with the Father and the Son is one only God. And because this love is produced by manner of breathings or spirations, it is called the Holy Spirit.

Now, Theotimus, King David, describing the sweetness of the friendship of God's servants, cries out: *Behold how good and how pleasant it is for brethren to dwell together in unity: like the precious ointment on the head, that ran down upon the beard, the beard of Aaron, which ran down to the skirt of his garment: as the dew of Hermon, which descendeth upon Mount Sion.*[1]

But, O God! if human friendship be so agreeably lovely, and

[1] Ps. cxxxii.

spread so delicious an odour on them that contemplate it, what shall it be, my well-beloved Theotimus, to behold the sacred exercise of mutual love between the eternal Father and the Son. S. Gregory Nazianzen recounts that the incomparable love which existed between him and S. Basil the Great was famous all through Greece, and Tertullian testifies, that the Pagans admired the more than brotherly love which reigned amongst the primitive Christians. Oh! with what celebration and solemnity, with what praises and benedictions, should be kept, with what admirations should be honoured and loved, the eternal and sovereign friendship of the Father and the Son! What is there to be loved and desired if friendship is not? And if friendship is to be loved and desired, what friendship can be so in comparison with that infinite friendship which is between the Father and the Son, and Which is one same most sole God with them? Our heart, Theotimus, will sink lost in love, through admiration of the beauty and sweetness of the love, that this eternal Father and this incomprehensible Son practise divinely and eternally.

CHAPTER XIV

THAT THE HOLY LIGHT OF GLORY WILL SERVE FOR THE UNION OF THE BLESSED SPIRITS WITH GOD

THE created understanding then shall see the divine essence, without any medium of species or representation; yet not without a certain excellent light which disposes, elevates, and strengthens it, to raise its view so high, and to an object so sublime and resplendent. For as the owl has a sight strong enough to bear the sombre light of a clear night, but not strong enough to stand the mid-day light, which is too brilliant to be borne by eyes so dim and weak; so our understanding, which is strong enough to consider natural truths by its discourse, yea even the supernatural things of grace by the light of faith, is not yet able, by the light of either nature or faith, to attain unto the view of the divine substance in itself. Wherefore the sweetness of the eternal wisdom determined not to apply His essence to our understanding till He had prepared, strengthened and fitted it to receive a sight so eminent, and so disproportionate to its natural condition as is the view of the Divinity. So the sun, the sovereign object of our corporal eyes amongst natural things, does not present itself unto our view without sending first its rays, by means whereof we may be able to see it, so that we only see it by its light. Yet there is a difference between the rays which the sun casts upon our corporal eyes and the light which God will create in our understandings in heaven: for the sun's rays do not fortify our corporal eyes when they are weak and unable to see, but rather blind them, dazzling and counfounding their infirm vision: whereas, on the contrary, this sacred light of glory, finding our understandings unapt and unable to behold the Divinity, raises, strengthens and perfects them so excellently, that by an incomprehensible marvel they behold and contemplate the abyss of the divine brightness in itself with a fixed and direct gaze, not being dazzled or beaten back by the infinite greatness of its splendour.

In like manner, therefore, as God has given us the light of reason, by which we may know Him as Author of nature, and the light of faith by which we consider Him as source of grace, so will He bestow upon us the light of glory by which we shall contemplate Him as the fountain of beatitude and eternal life: but a fountain, Theotimus, which we shall not contemplate afar off as we do now by faith, but which we shall see by the light of glory while plunged and swallowed up in it.

Divers, who, fishing for precious stones, go down into the water, take oil, says Pliny, in their mouths, that by scattering it, they may have more light to see in the waters where they swim. Theotimus, a blessed soul having entered and plunged into the ocean of the divine essence, God will pour into its understanding the sacred light of glory, which will enlighten it in this abyss of inaccessible light, that so by the light of glory we may see the light of the Divinity. *For with Thee is the fountain of life; and in Thy light we shall see light.*[1]

[1] Ps. xxxi. 10.

CHAPTER XV

THAT THERE SHALL BE DIFFERENT DEGREES OF THE UNION OF THE BLESSED WITH GOD

Now this light of glory, Theotimus, shall be the measure of the sight and contemplation of the Blessed; and according as we shall have less or more of this holy splendour, we shall see more or less clearly, and consequently with more or less happiness, the most holy Divinity, which as it is beholden diversely so it will make us diversely glorious. All the spirits indeed in this heavenly Paradise see all the divine essence, yet it is not seen and cannot be seen entirely by any one of them or by all of them together. No, Theotimus, for God being most singularly one, and most simply indivisible, we cannot see Him without seeing Him all: but being infinite, without limit, without bounds or measure at all in His perfection, there neither is, nor can be, any capacity out of Himself which can ever totally comprehend or penetrate the infinity of His goodness, infinitely essential and essentially infinite.

This created light of the visible sun, which is limited and finite, is in such sort all seen by those that behold it that it is never totally seen by any one of them nor by all together. It is in a manner so with all our senses. Amongst many that hear excellent music, though all of them hear it all, yet some hear it not so well, nor with so much delight as others, according as their ears are more or less delicate. The manna was all tasted by each one that ate it, yet differently, according to the different appetites of those who ate it, and was never wholly tasted, for it had more tastes of different kinds than the Israelites had varieties of tasting power. Theotimus, we shall see and taste in heaven all the Divinity, but no one of the Blessed nor all together shall ever see or taste it totally. This infinite Divinity shall still have infinitely more excellences than we sufficiency and capacity; and we shall have an unspeakable content to know that after we have satiated all the desires of our heart, and fully replenished its capacity in the fruition of the infinite good which is God, nevertheless there will remain in this infinity, infinite perfections to be seen, enjoyed and possessed, which His divine Majesty knows and sees, it alone comprehending itself.

So fishes enjoy the incredible vastness of the ocean; but not any fish, nor yet all the multitude of fishes, ever saw all the shores of the sea or wetted their fins in all its waters. Birds sport in the open air at their pleasure, but not any bird, nor yet all the flocks of birds together, did ever beat with their wings all the regions of the air, or arrive at the supreme region of the same. Ah! Theotimus, our souls shall freely and according to the full extent of their wishes swim in the ocean and soar in the air of the Divinity, rejoicing eternally to see that this air is so infinite, this ocean so vast, that it cannot be measured by their wings, and that enjoying without reserve or exception all this infinite abyss of the Divinity, yet shall they never be able to equalize their fruition to this infinity, which remains still infinitely infinite beyond their capacity.

And at this the Blessed Spirits are ravished with two admirations, first for the infinite beauty which they contemplate, secondly for the abyss of the infinity which remains to be seen in this same beauty. O God! how admirable is that which they see! But, O God! how much more admirable is that which they see not! And yet, Theotimus, since the most sacred beauty which they see is infinite, it entirely satisfies and satiates them, and being content to enjoy it according to the rank which they hold in heaven, because God's most amiable providence has so determined, they convert the knowledge they have of not possessing and of not being able totally to possess their object, into a simple complacency of admiration, in which they have a sovereign joy to see that the beauty they love is so infinite that it cannot be totally known but by itself. For in this consists the Divinity of this infinite beauty or the beauty of this infinite Divinity.

4. ANONYMOUS:

CHAPTERS I-VII OF *THE CLOUD OF UNKNOWING*

¶ENGLAND during the fourteenth century—age of Chaucer and Langland—was the home of several mystics, whose contemplative lives were in sharp contrast with the tumult of the age. Among them there is none whose writings are now held in such esteem as the anonymous author of *The Cloud of Unknowing* and other treatises. Seven texts in all are attributed to him and these have been published by Edmund Gardner (1921). The present version (seven chapters are offered here) is based upon the excellent edition of Dom Justin McCann (1924). To his volume the reader who desires a commentary on the present text may turn with the certainty that he will be rewarded.

The author of *The Cloud of Unknowing* was deeply influenced by the writing of Dionysius, the pseudo-Areopagite, whose *Mystical Theology* he translated and whose doctrine he skilfully adapted to his own use. The "cloud" is that state of abstractedness from the common things of earth in which the contemplative seeks to gain awareness of the Divine Being, whose existence must remain incomprehensible otherwise. What this concept involves is set forth in strong and lucid English which, even when modernized, keeps a real effectiveness and charm. Modern English and American interest in mysticism is in large measure traceable to concern with this and several books.*

* From *The Cloud of Unknowing and Other Treatises*. Edited by Dom Justin McCann. New York: Benziger Brothers, 1924.

THE FIRST CHAPTER

OF FOUR DEGREES OF CHRISTIAN MEN'S LIVING; AND OF THE
COURSE OF HIS CALLING THAT THIS BOOK WAS MADE UNTO

HOSTLY friend in God, thou shalt well understand that I find, in my rough way of beholding four degrees of Christian men's living, and they be these: *Common, Special, Singular,* and *Perfect.* Three of these may be begun and ended in this life; and the fourth may by grace be begun here, but it shall ever last without end in the bliss of heaven. And right as thou seest how they be set here in order, each after other, first *Common, then Special, after Singular, and last Perfect:* right so me thinketh that in the same order and in the same course hath our Lord of his great mercy called thee and led thee unto him by the desire of thine heart.

For first thou knowest well, that when thou wert living in the *common* degree of Christian men's living in company of thy worldly friends, it seemeth to me that the everlasting love of his Godhead, through the which he made thee and wrought thee when thou wert nought, and then bought thee with the price of his precious blood when thou wert lost in Adam, might not suffer thee to be so far from him in form and degree of living. And therefore he kindled thy desire full graciously, and fastened by it a leash of a lovely [1] longing, and led thee by it into a more *special* state and form of living, to be a servant of the special servants of his; where thou mightest learn to live more specially and more ghostly in his service than thou didst, or mightest do, in the common degree of living before.

And what more? Yet it seemeth that he would not leave thee thus lightly, for the love of his heart, the which he hath evermore had unto thee since thou wert aught. But what did he? Seest thou not how sweetly and how graciously he hath privily pulled thee to the third degree and manner of living, the which is called *singular?* In the which solitary form and manner of living thou mayest learn to lift up the foot of thy love, and to step towards

[1] Loving.

that state and degree of living that is *perfect*, and the last state of all.

THE SECOND CHAPTER

A SHORT STIRRING TO MEEKNESS AND TO THE WORK OF THIS BOOK

LOOK up now, thou weak wretch, and see what thou art. What art thou, and how hast thou merited thus to be called by our Lord? What weary wretched heart and sleeping in sloth is that, the which is not wakened with the drawing of this love and the voice of this calling? Beware now in this while of thine enemy; and hold thyself never the holier nor the better, for the worthiness of this calling and for the singular form of living that thou art in; but the more wretched and cursed, unless thou do that in thee is goodly, by grace and by counsel,[1] to live according to thy calling. And insomuch thou shouldst be more meek and loving to thy ghostly Spouse, in that he, that is the Almighty God, King of kings and Lord of lords, would meek himself so low unto thee, and, among all the flock of his sheep, so graciously would choose thee to be one of his specials, and then set thee in the place of pasture, where thou mayest be fed with the sweetness of his love, in earnest of thine heritage the kingdom of heaven.

Do on then fast, I pray thee. Look now forwards and let the backwards be. And see what thou lackest and not what thou hast; for that is the readiest getting and keeping of meekness. All thy life now must all ways stand in desire, if thou shalt advance in degree of perfection. This desire must all ways be wrought in thy will, by the hand of Almighty God and thy consent. But one thing I tell thee: he is a jealous lover and suffereth no fellowship, and he liketh not to work in thy will unless he be only with thee by himself. He asketh no help but only thyself. He wills thou do but look upon him and let him alone. And keep thou the windows and the door from flies and enemies assailing. And if thou be willing to do this, thou needest but meekly to set upon him with prayer, and soon will he help thee. Set on then: let

---

[1] The advice of a confessor, or the confessor or director himself.

me see how thou bearest thee. He is full ready, and doth but abide thee. But what shalt thou do, and how shalt thou set on?

THE THIRD CHAPTER

HOW THE WORK OF THIS BOOK SHALL BE WROUGHT, AND OF THE WORTHINESS OF IT BEFORE ALL OTHER WORKS

LIFT up thine heart unto God with a meek stirring of love; and mean himself and none of his goods. And thereto look that thou loathe to think on aught but himself, so that nought work in thy mind nor in thy will but only himself. And do that in thee is to forget all the creatures that ever God made and the works of them, so that thy thought or thy desire be not directed or stretched to any of them, neither in general nor in special. But let them be, with a seemly recklessness,[1] and take no heed of them.

This is the work of the soul that most pleaseth God. All saints and angels have joy of this work and hasten them to help it with all their might. All fiends be mad when thou dost thus, and try for to defeat it in all that they can. All men living on earth be wonderfully helped by this work, thou knowest not how. Yea, the souls in purgatory are eased of their pains by virtue of this work. Thou thyself art cleansed and made virtuous by no work so much. And yet it is the lightest work of all, when a soul is helped with grace in sensible list; and soonest done. But else it is hard and wonderful for thee to do.

Cease not, therefore, but travail therein till thou feel list. For at the first time when thou dost it, thou findest but a darkness, and as it were a *cloud of unknowing*, thou knowest not what, saving that thou feelest in thy will a naked intent unto God. This darkness and this cloud, howsoever thou dost, is betwixt thee and thy God, and hindereth thee, so that thou mayest neither see him clearly by light of understanding in thy reason, nor feel him in sweetness of love in thine affection. And therefore shape thee to bide in this darkness as long as thou mayest, evermore crying after him whom thou lovest. For if ever thou shalt see him or

---

[1] Heedlessness, carelessness.

feel him, as it may be here, it must always be in this cloud and in this darkness. And if thou wilt busily travail as I bid thee, I trust in his mercy that thou shalt come thereto.

THE FOURTH CHAPTER

OF THE SHORTNESS OF THIS WORK, AND HOW IT MAY NOT BE COME TO BY NO CURIOSITY OF WIT, NOR BY IMAGINATION

BUT for this, that thou shalt not err in this working, and ween that it be otherwise than it is, I shall tell thee a little more thereof, as me thinketh.

This work asketh no long time ere it be once truly done, as some men ween; for it is the shortest work of all that man may imagine. It is never longer nor shorter than is an atom; the which atom, by the definition of true philosophers in the science of astronomy, is the least part of time. And it is so little that, for the littleness of it, it is indivisible and nearly incomprehensible. This is that time of the which it is written: *All the time that is given to thee, it shall be asked of thee how thou hast spent it.* And a right thing it is that thou shouldst give account of it. For it is neither longer nor shorter, but exactly equal to one single stirring that is within in the principal working power of thy soul, the which is thy will. For even so many willings or desirings— no more nor no fewer—may be and are in one hour in thy will, as are atoms in one hour. And if thou wert reformed by grace to the first state of man's soul, as it was before sin, then shouldst thou evermore be lord of that stirring or of those stirrings. So that none should go amiss, but all should stretch unto the sovereign desirable, and unto the highest willable thing, the which is God.

For he is even meet to our soul by measuring of his Godhead; and our soul is even meet unto him by the worthiness of our creation to his image and likeness. And he by himself without more, and none but he, is sufficient to the full, and much more, to fulfil the will and the desire of our soul. And our soul, by virtue of this reforming grace, is made sufficient to the full to comprehend all him by love, the which is incomprehensible to all created knowing powers, as is angel or man's soul. He is incomprehensible, I mean, by their knowing and not by their loving. And therefore I call them in this case knowing powers.

But see. All reasonable creatures, angel and man, have in them, each one by himself, one principal working power, the which is called a knowing power, and another principal working power, the which is called a loving power. Of the which two powers, to the first, the which is a knowing power, God who is the maker of them is evermore incomprehensible; but to the second, the which is the loving power, he is, in every man diversely, all comprehensible to the full. Insomuch that one loving soul alone in itself, by virtue of love, may comprehend in itself him who is sufficient to the full—and much more, without comparison— to fill all the souls and angels that may be. And this is the endless marvellous miracle of love, the working of which shall never have end, for ever shall he do it, and never shall he cease for to do it. See, whoso by grace see may; for the feeling of this is endless bliss, and the contrary is endless pain.

And therefore whoso were reformed by grace thus to continue in heeding all the stirrings of his will, should never be in this life—as he may not be without these stirrings in nature—without some taste of the endless sweetness; nor in the bliss of heaven without the full food. And therefore have no wonder that I stir thee to this work. For this is the work, as thou shalt hear afterward, in the which man should have continued if he never had sinned. And to this working was man made, and all things for man, to help him and further him thereto. And by this working shall man be repaired again. And for want of this working a man falleth evermore deeper and deeper into sin, and further and further from God. And by heeding and continual working in this work alone, without more, a man riseth evermore higher and higher from sin, and nearer and nearer unto God.

And therefore take good heed unto time, how thou spendest it; for nothing is more precious than time. In one little time, as little as it is, may heaven be won and lost. A token it is that time is precious: for God, that is giver of time, giveth never two times together, but each one after other. And this he doth because he would not reverse the order or the appointed course in the causes of his creation. For time is made for man, and not man for time.

And therefore God, who is the ruler of nature, would not in his giving of time go before the stirring of nature in man's soul; the which stirring is even according to one time only. So that man shall have no excuse against God in the Doom, and at the giving account of the spending of time, saying thus: "Thou givest two times at once, and I have but one stirring at once."

But sorrowfully thou sayest now: "How shall I do? And if it be true what thou sayest, how shall I give account of each time severally; I that unto this day, being now four-and-twenty years of age, have never taken heed of time? If I would now amend it, thou knowest well, by very reason of thy words written before, how it may not be according to the course of nature or of common grace, that I should be able to heed any more times, or make satisfaction for any more, than for those that be to come. Yea, and moreover well I know by very experience, that of those that be to come I shall in no wise, for abundance of frailty and slowness of spirit, be able to heed one in a hundred. So that I am verily confounded by these reasons. Help me now, for the love of Jesu!"

Right well hast thou said "for the love of Jesu." For in the love of Jesu there shall be thine help. Love is such a power that it maketh all things to be shared. Therefore love Jesu, and all thing that he hath it is thine. He by his Godhead is maker and giver of time. He by his Manhood is the true heeder of time. And he, by his Godhead and his Manhood together, is the truest judge and the asker of account of the spending of time. Knit thee therefore to him, by love and by belief; and then by virtue of that knot thou shalt be common partaker with him and with all that by love so be knitted unto him; that is to say, with our Lady Saint Mary, that full was of all grace in heeding of time, with all the angels of heaven that never may lose time, and with all the saints in heaven and on earth, that by the grace of Jesus heed time full justly in virtue of love.

Lo! here lieth comfort; understand thou wisely and pick thee some profit. But of one thing I warn thee beyond all other: I cannot see who may truly claim fellowship thus with Jesu and his just Mother, his high angels and also with his saints, unless he be such a one as doth that in him is, with the help of grace, in heeding of time. So that he be seen to be of profit on his part,

so little as it is, unto the fellowship; as each one of them is
on his.

And therefore take heed to this work and to the marvellous
manner of it within in thy soul. For if it be truly conceived, it
is but a sudden stirring, and as it were unadvised, speedily spring-
ing unto God as a sparkle from the coal. And it is marvellous to
number the stirrings that may be in one hour wrought in a soul
that is disposed to this work. And yet in one stirring of all these
it may have suddenly and perfectly forgotten all created things.
But fast after each stirring, through the corruption of the flesh,
it falleth down again to some thought, or to some done or undone
deed. But what matter? For fast after, it riseth again as suddenly
as it did before.

And here may men shortly conceive the manner of this working, and clearly know that it is far from any fantasy, or any false
imagination, or quaint [1] opinion; the which be caused, not by
such a devout and a meek blind stirring of love, but by a proud,
curious and an imaginative wit. Such a proud, curious wit must
always be borne down and stiffly trodden under foot, if this work
shall truly be conceived in purity of spirit. For whoso heareth
this work either read or spoken, and weeneth that it may or should
be come to by travail in their wits, and therefore sit and seek in
their wits how it may be: in this curiosity they travail their imagination peradventure against the course of nature, and they feign
a manner of working the which is neither bodily nor ghostly.
Truly this man, whatsoever he be, is perilously deceived. Insomuch, that unless God of his great goodness show his merciful
miracle, and make him soon to leave work and meek him to the
counsel of proved workers, he shall fall either into frenzies, or
else into other great mischiefs of ghostly sins and devils' deceits;
through the which he may lightly be lost, both life and soul,
without any end. And therefore for God's love beware in this
work, and travail not in thy wits nor in thy imagination in nowise:
for I tell thee truly, it may not be come to by travail in them;
and therefore leave them and work not with them.

And ween not, because I call it a darkness or a cloud, that it
is any cloud congealed of the vapours that fly in the air, or any
darkness such as in thine house on nights, when the candle is out.

[1] Clever, ingenious.

For such a darkness and such a cloud mayest thou imagine with curiosity of wit, for to bear before thine eyes in the lightest day of summer; and also contrariwise in the darkest night of winter thou mayest imagine a clear shining light. Let be such falsehoods; I mean not thus. For when I say darkness, I mean a lacking of knowing: as all things that thou knowest not, or hast forgotten, is dark to thee; for thou seest it not with thy ghostly eye. And for this reason it is called, not a cloud of the air, but a *cloud of unknowing;* which is betwixt thee and thy God.

THE FIFTH CHAPTER

THAT IN THE TIME OF THIS WORK ALL THE CREATURES THAT EVER HAVE BEEN, BE NOW, OR EVER SHALL BE, AND ALL THE WORKS OF THE SAME CREATURES, SHOULD BE HID UNDER THE CLOUD OF FORGETTING

AND if ever thou shalt come to this cloud and dwell and work therein as I bid thee, thou must, as this *cloud of unknowing* is above thee, betwixt thee and thy God, right so put a *cloud of forgetting* beneath thee, betwixt thee and all the creatures that ever be made. Thou thinkest, peradventure, that thou art full far from God, because this *cloud of unknowing* is betwixt thee and thy God; but surely, if it be well conceived, thou art full further from him when thou hast no *cloud of forgetting* betwixt thee and all the creatures that ever be made. As oft as I say "all the creatures that ever be made," so oft do I mean, not only the creatures themselves, but also all the works and the conditions of the same creatures. I except not one creature, whether they be bodily creatures or ghostly; nor yet any condition or work of any creature, whether they be good or evil. But, to speak shortly, all should be hid under the *cloud of forgetting* in this case.

For although it be full profitable sometimes to think of certain conditions and deeds of some certain special creatures, nevertheless in this work it profiteth little or nought. Because mind [1] or thinking of any creature that ever God made, or of any of their

[1] Besides its present meaning, "mind" in Middle English has the sense of "remembrance," which survives in "month's mind."

deeds either, is a manner of ghostly sight; for the eye of thy soul is opened on it and close fixed thereupon, as the eye of a shooter is upon the prick [1] that he shooteth to. And one thing I tell thee, that everything that thou thinkest upon is above thee for the time and betwixt thee and thy God. And insomuch thou art the further from God, that aught is in thy mind but only God.

Yea—and if it be courteous and seemly to say—in this work it profiteth little or nought to think of the kindness or the worthiness of God, nor on our Lady, nor on the saints or angels in heaven, nor yet on the joys of heaven: that is to say, with a special beholding [2] to them, as though thou wouldst by that beholding feed and increase thy purpose. I trow that on nowise it should help in this case and in this work. For although it be good to think upon the kindness of God, and to love him and praise him for it: yet it is far better to think upon the naked being of him, and to love him and praise him for himself.

THE SIXTH CHAPTER

A SHORT CONCEIT OF THIS WORK, TREATED BY QUESTION

But now thou askest me and sayest: "How shall I think on himself, and what is he?" Unto this I cannot answer thee, except to say: "I know not."

For thou hast brought me with thy question into that same darkness, and into that same *cloud of unknowing*, that I would thou wert in thyself. For of all other creatures and their works —yea, and of the works of God himself—many a man through grace hath fulness of knowing, and well can he think of them; but of God himself can no man think. And therefore I would leave all that thing that I can think, and choose to my love that thing that I cannot think. For why, he may well be loved, but not thought. By love may he be gotten and holden; but by thought never. And therefore, although it be good sometime to think on the kindness and the worthiness of God in special, and although it be a light and a part of contemplation; nevertheless in this work it shall be cast down and covered with a *cloud of forgetting*.

[1] Mark, target.   [2] Consideration, regard.

And thou shalt step above it stalwartly, but listily, with a devout and a pleasing stirring of love, and try to pierce that darkness above thee. And smite upon that thick *cloud of unknowing* with a sharp dart of longing love; and go not thence for aught that befalleth.

THE SEVENTH CHAPTER

HOW A MAN SHALL BEAR HIMSELF IN THIS WORK AGAINST ALL THOUGHTS, AND ESPECIALLY AGAINST ALL THOSE THAT ARISE FROM HIS OWN CURIOSITY, FROM LEARNING, AND FROM NATURAL WIT

AND if any thought rise and will press all ways above thee, betwixt thee and that darkness, and ask thee saying: "What seekest thou, and what wouldst thou have?" say thou, that it is God that thou wouldst have. "Him I covet, him I seek, and nought but him."

And if he ask thee: "What is that God?" say thou, that it is God that made thee and bought thee, and that graciously hath called thee to thy degree. "And in him," say, "thou hast no skill." And therefore say: "Go thou down again"; and tread him fast down again with a stirring of love, although he seem to thee right holy, and seem to thee as if he would help thee to seek him. For peradventure he will bring to thy mind divers full fair and wonderful points of his kindness, and say that he is full sweet and full loving, full gracious and full merciful. And if thou wilt hear him, he coveteth no better; for at the last he will thus chatter ever more and more till he bring thee lower, to the thought of his passion.

And there will he let thee see the wonderful kindness of God; and if thou listen to him, he desireth nought better. For soon after he will let thee see thine old wretched living; and peradventure, in seeing and thinking thereof, he will bring to thy mind some place that thou hast dwelt in before this time. So that at the last, ere ever thou knowest, thou shalt be scattered thou knowest not where. The cause of this scattering is: that first thou didst wilfully listen to that thought, and then thou didst answer him, receive him, and let him have his way.

And yet, nevertheless, the thing that he said was both good and holy. Yea, and so holy, that whatever man or woman weeneth to come to contemplation without many such sweet meditations beforehand of their own wretchedness, the passion, the kindness, the great goodness and the worthiness of God, surely he shall err and fail of his purpose. And yet, a man or woman that hath long time been practised in these meditations, must nevertheless leave them, and put them and hold them far down under the *cloud of forgetting*, if ever he shall pierce the *cloud of unknowing* betwixt him and his God.

And therefore, when thou purposest thee to this work, and feelest by grace that thou art called by God, lift up thine heart unto God with a meek stirring of love. And mean God that made thee, and bought thee, and that graciously hath called thee to thy degree: and receive none other thought of God. And yet not all these, except thou desirest; for a naked intent directed unto God, without any other cause than himself, sufficeth wholly.

And if thou desirest to have this intent lapped and folden in one word, so that thou mayest have better hold thereupon, take thee but a little word of one syllable, for so it is better than of two; for the shorter the word, the better it accordeth with the work of the spirit. And such a word is this word GOD or this word LOVE. Choose whichever thou wilt, or another: whatever word thou likest best of one syllable. And fasten this word to thine heart, so that it may never go thence for anything that befalleth.

This word shall be thy shield and thy spear, whether thou ridest on peace or on war. With this word, thou shalt beat on this cloud and this darkness above thee. With this word, thou shalt smite down all manner of thought under the *cloud of forgetting*. Insomuch, that if any thought press upon thee to ask thee what thou wouldst have, answer with no more words but with this one word. And if he offer of his great learning to expound to thee that word and to tell thee the conditions of that word, say to him that thou wilt have it all whole, and not broken nor undone. And if thou wilt hold fast to this purpose, be thou sure that that thought will no while bide. And why? Surely because thou wilt not let him feed himself on such sweet meditations of God touched before.

5. BLESSED JOHN RUYSBROECK:
CHAPTER XII OF *LOVE'S GRADATORY*

¶THE Netherlands produced a numerous body of mystical writers during the late Middle Ages. Of these the Blessed John Ruysbroeck was perhaps the most influential. Born in 1293, he began at an early age to prepare for life in religion and was ordained to the priesthood when he was twenty-four. Thereupon he gained considerable repute as a controversialist and a spiritual director, but retired to the hermitage of Groenendael with some friends and established a contemplative community. Here Ruysbroeck continued to write, though there is great uncertainty as to when his various treatises were completed. He died in 1381.

It is impossible to set forth here the characteristics of Ruysbroeck's mystical teaching. His works tend to stress—perhaps occasionally to overemphasize—the unity of God and man aimed at by contemplatives. The common statement that he was an unlettered man is incorrect, but one gathers that he was prone to assign learning to a very subordinate place in the scale of values. The selection which follows is taken from *Love's Gradatory*, which was translated into English by Mother St. Jerome.*

---

* From *Love's Gradatory*. By Blessed John Ruysbroeck. Translated by Mother St. Jerome. New York: Benziger Brothers. N.D.

LOVE'S GRADATORY

That with quadruple harmony
And all mellifluous melody,
In Heaven resounds eternally.

OF CELESTIAL MELODIES

UR Heavenly Father called us from all eternity, elected us in His Beloved Son, and wrote our names with the finger of His Love in the living book of eternal Wisdom, therefore we should respond with all our power in constant Reverence and Veneration. Thus commences every song of Angels and men, never to cease.

The first method of Celestial Song is love of God and men, the which to teach us God sent His Son. Whoso knows not this method cannot enter the heavenly Choir, since having neither knowledge nor the vestment of Grace he must remain everlastingly without.

Jesus Christ, the Soul's Lover, at the moment of His Conception in the chaste womb of His Virgin Mother, chanted in spirit the Glory and Honour of His Heavenly Father, peace and rest to men of goodwill; and on that night in which He was born of the Virgin Mother the Angels sang the same sweet refrain. The Church recalls it when she, in her turn, sings it, especially on these two Festivals. Love of God and love of man for God and in God, what can be hymned of more sublime or more joyous in Heaven or on earth, since the form and meaning of this song are infused by the Holy Spirit?

The Christ, our Choir Master and Precentor, intoned it from the beginning, and will intone eternally for us this hymn of love and endless felicity. Then, in our turn, with all our might, we shall sing with Him, both here below and in the midst of the Choir of the Glory of God. Thus Love, pure and without pretence, is the common song we must all learn in order to take part in the Choir of Angels and Saints in the Kingdom of God; for Love is the root and cause of all interior virtues, the true ornament and adornment of all exterior good work. Love lives of itself, and is its own recompense; in its action it cannot be deceived, for there the Christ has gone before Who taught us to love, and lives in love with all who are His, for us to imitate Him, if we wish to be happy with Him, and attain Salvation. Such is the first method of Celestial Song that the Wisdom of God teaches His obedient disciples by the intervention of the Holy Spirit.

Next comes the second method of Celestial Song, which is unpretentious Humility, that none can raise or abase. In this really consists the root and sure foundation of all virtue and the whole spiritual edifice; this, too, constitutes the measure, key, and finale of all heavenly Song, for it is the mantle and ornament of Love, the sweetest voice that can sing before the face of God. The chords are so graceful and attractive that they draw the Wisdom of God even into our human nature, as when Mary said: "Behold the servant of the Lord, be it unto me according to thy word." [1] God was so completely won that He willed the Eternal Wisdom to take flesh in the womb of the Virgin.

Thus the highest height became lowliness, since the Son of God humbled Himself and took upon Him the form of a slave, so as to raise us to the image of the Godhead. He humiliated Himself, placing Himself lower than all, despising Himself through desire to serve us even unto death.

If you wish to resemble and follow Him there where is sung the hymn of sincere Humility, you must also deny and despise self, love and desire contempt, disdain, and neglect from others, for true Humility is insensible to what flatters or pains, to honour or shame, to all that is not itself. It is the highest gift and the loveliest jewel that God can bestow on the loving Soul, outside of Himself, the plenitude of every Grace and gift; whoso dwells with it becomes one with it, and finds everlasting Peace.

The third method of Celestial Song consists in renouncing self-will and everything belonging to self, abandoning all to the most dear Will of God and bearing submissively all He sees fit to impose. And though Nature, bowed under the cross, following our Lord even unto death, suffers pain, the spirit that willingly makes such an offering is joyous. Nature weeps and complains of the heavy burden it bears, but hereafter there will be joy in

[1] St. Luke i. 38.

the Glory of God, when Jesus shall wipe away all tears, showing us how by His Precious Blood He bought us of His Father by paying the price of death. Then shall we sing with Him this sweet melody, merited by voluntary suffering, and belonging to men, not to Angels. The greater the martyrdom, labour, and suffering, so much greater, too, will be the Glory, recompense, and honour. The Christ, our Precentor, constrains us to sing this hymn, for He is King and Prince of all suffering willingly endured for the love and honour of God, and His voice is so rich, so sonorous, it is the perfection of science in heavenly Song, its tones, keys, and varied harmonies. With Him we shall all sing, thanking and praising His Heavenly Father Who Sent Him to us.

As it behoved the Christ to suffer and thus to enter into His Glory, so it behoves us, too, to suffer gladly, so as to be like unto Him, and to follow Him into the glory of the Father, with Whom He is one in the fruition of the Holy Ghost, there to sing His praise in the Name of our Lord Jesus Christ, each one personally, in spirit, according to our merits and dignity before God.

Finally, the fourth method of Celestial Song, the most interior, noble, and highest, consists in deliquescence in the Praise of God.[1]

Our heavenly Father is at the same time covetous and liberal. On His beloved who walk before His Face and are elevated in the Spirit, He bestows liberally His gifts and blessings, but expects in return that each render thanks, praise and good works in the measure in which He has endowed him, both exteriorly and interiorly. For Divine Grace is not given uselessly, nor in vain; if we make use of it the flow is ceaseless, giving all that we need, claiming in return from us all that we can give, and from these

---

[1] Above the love of God and our neighbour, true Humility and complete renouncement of self-will, Blessed John Ruysbroeck places the confession of absolute powerlessness to praise God as He deserves. This he calls a mystical fainting in the Praise of God. This acknowledgement of powerlessness comes from the Divine exigency claiming more than we are capable of giving. Under the influence of Grace our supernatural activity can well lead us to the union with God, which the author names *intermedium*, but the union *without intervention of a medium*, goes beyond our force and is the work of God alone. The first kind of union has a *likeness with God*, but the second is the very image of God, graven in the substance of the Soul and constitutes the *living Unity* with God. In one, the Soul operates continually with the help of the Holy Spirit; in the other, the Soul enjoys and reposes in Him.

reciprocal gifts springs the practice of every virtue, without fear of error.

But that which goes beyond all works and the exercise of all Virtues, our heavenly Father teaches to those who are especially dear to Him; thus in His gifts and in His exigency He shows Himself not only liberal and covetous, but covetousness and liberality itself. He wills to give Himself to us entirely, Himself and all that He is, but in return He claims the full donation of ourselves to Him, with all that we are or can be. His will and intention is that we should be entirely His, as He is altogether ours; each, however, remaining what they are, for we cannot become Divine, but can be united to God both by an intermedium and without an intermedium. We are united to Him by means of His Grace and our good works, and this mutual Love, thus constituted, results in His being in us and we in Him, submissive to His influence even to the point of having but one only will with Him for all good. For His Spirit and Grace operate in every good work far more than our own action; and the Grace he bestows, with the love we render Him, elaborates a work in which He and we co-operate together of common accord. Our love for God is, indeed, the highest and noblest work of which we can conceive between God and self. The Divine Spirit, on His side, requires of our spirit that we should love and thank God and sing the praises due to His supreme dignity and majesty; it is in this that all loving Souls in Heaven as on earth fall short. They are consumed with this desire and fall powerless before the infinite Majesty of God; His Grace is there perfected with every virtue. But it is possible to be united to God without an intermedium, above Grace and beyond all Virtue, for independently of any medium, we have received the image of God in the living substance of the Soul, and thus established union with God without an intermedium; not by becoming God, but by remaining always like Him, He living in us and we in Him, through Grace and good works.

We are then united to God without medium and beyond all Virtue, bearing His image impressed on the very summit of our created nature; nevertheless, we remain like Him and united to Him by means of His Grace and our good works; being like unto Him in Grace and Glory, one with Him in our eternal image or ideal. Living union with God is in our very essence; we cannot understand nor attain to it, nor seize it. It baffles our strength and requires us to be one with God without an intermediary, although this cannot be accomplished alone. We can, indeed, follow after God so far as to attain to the state of emptiness of self; once in this state the Holy Spirit makes His dwelling in the Soul, reposing there with all His gifts. He bestows His graces and gifts on all our powers, asking in return love, thanksgiving, and praise. He inhabits in our essence, claiming from us freedom from self, love and union with Him above all Virtue. Consequently we cannot remain in self with our good works, nor above self with God, in a state of vacuum, in which consists the most intimate action of Love. The Spirit of the Lord within is an eternal operation of God, Who wills that we correspond continually in order to become like unto Him. But He is also repose and fruition of the Father and the Son and all His beloved, in everlasting inaction. This fruition is above works and we cannot comprehend it; works remaining always below fruition we cannot introduce them into that condition. When we act, we always lack something, not being able to love God sufficiently, but in enjoying, we attain satisfaction; we are then all that we desire. Such is the fourth method of Celestial Song, the noblest that can be chanted in Heaven or on earth.

You should know, however, that neither God, nor the Angels, nor Souls, sing with a corporeal voice, since they are spirits, having neither ears, nor mouth, nor tongue, nor throat, to form a note. The Holy Scriptures say well that God spoke to Abraham and Moses, to the Patriarchs and Prophets in many ways with sensible words, before He took upon Himself human nature. Holy Church, in her turn, attests that the Angels sing everlastingly and ceaselessly, "*Sanctus, Sanctus, Sanctus.*" Again, the Angel Gabriel brought to Our Lady the message that she should conceive the Son of God, by virtue of the Holy Spirit; Angels sang while bearing the soul of St. Martin to Heaven, and Angels daily delighted Mary Magdalen by their singing. It would seem, then, that good and bad spirits and disembodied Souls can appear to men in what form they like, as far as it pleases God to allow; but in the next life this is unnecessary, for then we shall contemplate with the eyes of the intelligent the Glory of God and of all

Angels and Saints in general, at the same time as the special Glory and recompense of each in particular, in every delectable way.

But at the last day, at the Judgment of God, when we rise again with glorious bodies, in the power of the Lord, these bodies will be white and resplendent as the snow, more brilliant than the sun, more transparent than crystal, and each one will have a special mark of honour and glory, according to the support and endurance of torments and sufferings, willingly and freely borne to the honour of God. For all things shall be regulated and recompensed according to the Wisdom of God and the nobility of our works; and the Christ, our Precentor and Choir-Master, shall sing with His sweet triumphant voice an eternal canticle to the Praise and Glory of the Heavenly Father. We also shall sing the same hymn, with joyous spirit and clear voice, eternally without end. The happiness and glory of the Soul shall be reflected in our senses and members, as we contemplate one the other with glorified vision, hearing, speaking, and chanting the Praise of our Lord with unfailing voice. The Christ will serve us and show us His illuminated Visage and glorious Body bearing the marks of love and fidelity printed on them.

We shall, too, contemplate the glorified bodies of the Just, clothed in numberless marks of love, spent in the service of God since the beginning of the world; and our sensitive life shall be filled, exteriorly and interiorly, with the Glory of God; the heart full of life burning with ardent love of God, the powers of the Soul resplendent with Glory, ornamented with the gifts of God and the practice of all virtue on earth.

Finally, and beyond all else, ravished out of self into the Glory of God, without limit, incomprehensible, immense, we are to enjoy Him for ever and ever.

The Christ in His human nature shall lead the Choir on the right, for He is the highest and most sublime creation of God, and to this Choir belong all who live in Him and He in them. The other Choir is the angelic, for although they are by Nature the more noble, we have been dowered in a more sublime fashion in Jesus Christ, with Whom we are one. He shall be the supreme Pontiff in the midst of the Choir of Angels and men before the throne of the sovereign Majesty of God, and will offer and renew before His heavenly Father, God Almighty, all offerings that were ever presented by Angels and men, fixed in the Glory of God for ever and ever.

Thus, then, shall our bodies and senses by which we serve God now be glorified and beatified, like unto the glorious Body of the Christ; that Body in which He served God and man. Our Souls, by which we now and always love, thank, and praise God, will then be blessed and glorious spirits, like to the blessed and glorious Soul of the Christ, the Angels and all spirits who love, praise, and bless God; and through the Christ we shall be ravished in God to be with Him in fruition and eternal Beatitude. And thus I end the fifth step of the Celestial Ladder.

6. BLAISE PASCAL:

FROM THE *PENSÉES*

¶FEW books have been more passionately read and discussed than Pascal's *Pensées* which in the strict sense is not a book at all. On November 23, 1654, Pascal (who was then 31, having been born in 1623) met with a religious experience which he described on a note of paper which he thereafter wore sewn into his coat. Six years later he acted upon this experience by conceiving the plan of a great book which was to form a complete apology for the Christian faith. This he did not live to finish. But when he died in 1662 he left the voluminous, incisive notes or "thoughts" which constitute the book as we know it. In one respect this incompleteness is valuable. It enables us to see how the mind of Pascal, of whose mathematical and literary genius there can be no doubt, studied the great problem before him. Since he was neither a theologian nor a trained philosopher, he reasoned in his own way and often with startling effectiveness and originality. As a consequence the *Pensées* have always appealed very particularly to literary men.

The history of the text is somewhat stormy. In preparing the original (1670) edition, Pascal's literary executors bungled so badly that the work was almost rendered useless. It was really not until 1897, when Brunschvig began publishing his monumental edition, that it was possible to follow the trend of Pascal's thought. Very likely the best English translation is that by William Finlayson Trotter, which is followed rather closely in the present selection. "The Fundamentals of the Christian Faith" forms the eighth section of the *Pensées*.*

---

* From Pascal's *Pensées*. Translated by William Finlayson Trotter. London: J. N. Dent and Sons, 1904.

THE FUNDAMENTALS OF THE CHRISTIAN FAITH

555

 EN blaspheme what they do not know. The Christian religion consists in two points. It is of equal concern to men to know them, and it is equally dangerous to be ignorant of them. And it is equally of God's mercy that He has given indications of both.

And yet they take occasion to conclude that one of these points does not exist, from that which should have caused them to infer the other. The sages who have said there is only one God have been persecuted, the Jews were hated, and still more the Christians. Thy have seen by the light of nature that if there be a true religion on earth, the course of all things must tend to it as to a centre.

The whole course of things must have for its object the establishment and the greatness of religion. Men must have within them feelings suited to what religion teaches us. And, finally, religion must so be the object and centre to which all things tend, that whoever knows the principles of religion can give an explanation both of the whole nature of man in particular, and of the whole course of the world in general.

And on this ground they take occasion to revile the Christian religion, because they misunderstand it. They imagine that it consists simply in the worship of a God considered as great, powerful, and eternal; which is strictly deism, almost as far removed from the Christian religion as atheism, which is its exact opposite. And thence they conclude that this religion is not true, because they do not see that all things concur to the establishment of this point, that God does not manifest Himself to men with all the evidence which He could show.

But let them conclude what they will against deism, they will conclude nothing against the Christian religion, which properly consists in the mystery of the Redeemer, who, uniting in Himself the two natures, human and divine, has redeemed men from the corruption of sin in order to reconcile them in His divine person to God.

The Christian religion, then, teaches men these two truths; that there is a God whom men can know, and that there is a corruption in their nature which renders them unworthy of Him. It is equally important to men to know both these points; and it is equally dangerous for man to know God without knowing his own wretchedness, and to know his own wretchedness without knowing the Redeemer who can free him from it. The knowledge of only one of these points gives rise either to the pride of philosophers, who have known God, and not their own wretchedness, or to the despair of atheists, who know their own wretchedness, but not the Redeemer.

And, as it is alike necessary to man to know these two points, so is it alike merciful of God to have made us know them. The Christian religion does this; it is in this that it consists.

Let us herein examine the order of the world, and see if all things do not tend to establish these two chief points of this religion: Jesus Christ is the end of all, and the centre to which all tends. Whoever knows Him knows the reason of everything.

Those who fall into error err only through failure to see one of these two things. We can then have an excellent knowledge of God without that of our own wretchedness, and of our own wretchedness without that of God. But we cannot know Jesus Christ without knowing at the same time both God and our own wretchedness.

Therefore I shall not undertake here to prove by natural reasons either the existence of God, or the Trinity, or the immortality of the soul, or anything of that nature; not only because I should not feel myself sufficiently able to find in nature arguments to convince hardened atheists, but also because such knowledge without Jesus Christ is useless and barren. Though a man should be convinced that numerical proportions are immaterial truths, eternal and dependent on a first truth, in which they subsist, and which is called God, I should not think him far advanced towards his own salvation.

The God of Christians is not a God who is simply the author of mathematical truths, or of the order of the elements; that is the view of heathens and Epicureans. He is not merely a God who exercises His providence over the life and fortunes of men to bestow on those who worship Him a long and happy life. That was the portion of the Jews. But the God of Abraham, the God of Isaac, the God of Jacob, the God of Christians, is a God of love and of comfort, a God who fills the soul and heart of those whom He possesses, a God who makes them conscious of their inward wretchedness, and His infinite mercy, who unites Himself to their inmost soul, who fills it with humility and joy, with confidence and love, who renders them incapable of any other end than Himself.

All who seek God without Jesus Christ, and who rest in nature, either find no light to satisfy them, or come to form for themselves a means of knowing God and serving Him without a mediator. Thereby they fall either into atheism, or into deism, two things which the Christian religion abhors almost equally.

Without Jesus Christ the world would not exist; for it should needs be either that it would be destroyed or be a hell.

If the world existed to instruct man of God, His divinity would shine through every part in it in an indisputable manner; but as it exists only by Jesus Christ, and for Jesus Christ, and to teach men both their corruption and their redemption, all displays the proofs of these two truths.

All appearance indicates neither a total exclusion nor a manifest presence of divinity, but the presence of a God who hides Himself. Everything bears this character.

... Shall he alone who knows his nature know it only to be miserable? Shall he alone who knows it be alone unhappy?

... He must not see nothing at all, nor must he see sufficient for him to believe he possesses it; but he must see enough to know that he has lost it. For to know of his loss, he must see and not see; and that is exactly the state in which he naturally is.

... Whatever part he takes, I shall not leave him at rest. ...

556

... It is then true that everything teaches man his condition, but he must understand this well. For it is not true that all reveals God, and it is not true that all conceals God. But it is at the same time true that He hides Himself from those who tempt Him, and that He reveals Himself to those who seek Him, because men are both unworthy and capable of God; unworthy by their corruption, capable by their original nature.

557

What shall we conclude from all our darkness, but our unworthiness?

558

If there never had been any appearance of God, this eternal deprivation would have been equivocal, and might have as well corresponded with the absence of all divinity, as with the unworthiness of men to know Him; but His occasional, though not continual, appearances remove the ambiguity. If He appeared once, He exists always; and thus we cannot but conclude both that there is a God, and that men are unworthy of Him.

559

We do not understand the glorious state of Adam, nor the nature of his sin, nor the transmission of it to us. These are matters which took place under conditions of a nature altogether different from our own, and which transcend our present understanding.

The knowledge of all this is useless to us as a means of escape from it; and all that we are concerned to know, is that we are miserable, corrupt, separated from God, but ransomed by Jesus Christ, whereof we have wonderful proofs on earth.

So the two proofs of corruption and redemption are drawn from the ungodly, who live in indifference to religion, and from the Jews who are irreconcilable enemies.

560

There are two ways of proving the truths of our religion; one by the power of reason, the other by the authority of him who speaks.

We do not make use of the latter, but of the former. We do not say, "This must be believed, for Scripture, which says it, is divine." But we say that it must be believed for such and such a reason, which are feeble arguments, as reason may be bent to everything.

561

There is nothing on earth that does not show either the wretchedness of man, or the mercy of God; either the weakness of man without God, or the strength of man with God.

562

It will be one of the confusions of the damned to see that they are condemned by their own reason, by which they claimed to condemn the Christian religion.

563

The prophecies, the very miracles and proofs of our religion, are not of such a nature that they can be said to be absolutely convincing. But they are also of such a kind that it cannot be said that it is unreasonable to believe them. Thus there is both evidence and obscurity to enlighten some and confuse others. But the evidence is such that it surpasses, or at least equals, the evidence to the contrary; so that it is not reason which can determine men not to follow it, and thus it can only be lust or malice of heart. And by this means there is sufficient evidence to condemn, and insufficient to convince; so that it appears in those who follow it, that it is grace, and not reason, which makes them follow it; and in those who shun it, that it is lust, not reason which makes them shun it.

Vere discipuli, vere Israëlita, vere liberi, vere cibus.

564

Recognise, then, the truth of religion in the very obscurity of religion, in the little light we have of it, and in the indifference which we have to knowing it.

565

We understand nothing of the works of God, if we do not take as a principle that He has willed to blind some, and enlighten others.

566

The two contrary reasons. We must begin with that; without that we understand nothing, and all is heretical; and we must even add at the end of each truth that the opposite truth is to be remembered.

567

Objection. The Scripture is plainly full óf matters not dictated by the Holy Spirit.—*Answer.* Then they do not harm faith.—*Objection.* But the Church has decided that all is of the Holy Spirit.—*Answer.* I answer two things: first, the Church has not so decided; secondly; if she should so decide, it could be maintained.

Do you think that the prophecies cited in the Gospel are related to make you believe? No, it is to keep you from believing.

568

Canonical.—The heretical books in the beginning of the Church serve to prove the canonical.

569

To the chapter on the *Fundamentals* must be added that on *Typology* touching the reason of types: why Jesus Christ was prophesied as to His first coming; why prophesied obscurely as to the manner.

570

The reason why. Types.—[They had to deal with a carnal people and to render them the depositary of the spiritual covenant.] To give faith to the Messiah, it was necessary there should have been precedent prophecies, and that these should be conveyed by persons above suspicion, diligent, faithful, unusually zealous, and known to all the world.

To accomplish all this, God chose this carnal people, to whom He entrusted the prophecies which foretell the Messiah as a deliverer, and as a dispenser of those carnal goods which this people loved. And thus they have had an extraordinary passion for their prophets, and, in sight of the whole world, have had charge of these books which foretell their Messiah, assuring all nations that He should come, and in the way foretold in the books, which they held open to the whole world. Yet this people, deceived by the poor and ignominious advent of the Messiah, have been His most cruel enemies. So that they, the people least open to suspicion in the world of favouring us, the most strict and most zealous that can be named for their law and their prophets, have kept the books incorrupt. Hence those who have rejected and crucified Jesus Christ, who has been to them an offence, are those who have charge of the books which testify of Him, and state that He will be an offence and rejected. Therefore they have shown it was He by rejecting Him, and He has been alike proved both by the righteous Jews who received Him, and by the unrighteous who rejected Him, both facts having been foretold.

Wherefore the prophecies have a hidden and spiritual meaning, to which this people were hostile, under the carnal meaning which they loved. If the spiritual meaning had been revealed, they would not have loved it, and, unable to bear it, they would not have been zealous of the preservation of their books and their ceremonies; and if they had loved these spiritual promises, and had preserved them incorrupt till the time of the Messiah, their testimony would have had no force, because they had been his friends.

Therefore it was well that the spiritual meaning should be concealed; but, on the other hand, if this meaning had been so hidden as not to appear at all, it could not have served as a proof of the Messiah. What then was done? In a crowd of passages it has been hidden under the temporal meaning, and in a few has been clearly revealed; besides that the time and the state of the world have been so clearly foretold that it is clearer than the sun. And in some places this spiritual meaning is so clearly expressed, that it would require a blindness like that which the flesh imposes on the spirit when it is subdued by it, not to recognise it.

See, then, what has been the prudence of God. This meaning is concealed under another in an infinite number of passages, and in some, though rarely, it is revealed; but yet so that the passages in which it is concealed are equivocal, and can suit both meanings; whereas the passages where it is disclosed are unequivocal, and can only suit the spiritual meaning.

So that this cannot lead us into error, and could only be misunderstood by so carnal a people.

For when blessings are promised in abundance, what was to prevent them from understanding the true blessings, but their covetousness, which limited the meaning to worldly goods? But those whose only good was in God referred them to God alone. For there are two principles, which divide the wills of men, covetousness and charity. Not that covetousness cannot exist along with faith in God, nor charity with worldly riches; but covetousness uses God, and enjoys the world, and charity is the opposite.

Now the ultimate end gives names to things. All which prevents us from attaining it, is called an enemy to us. Thus the creatures, however good, are the enemies of the righteous, when they turn them away from God, and God Himself is the enemy of those whose covetousness He confounds.

Thus as the significance of the word "enemy" is dependent on the ultimate end, the righteous understood by it their passions, and the carnal the Babylonians; and so these terms were obscure only for the unrighteous. And this is what Isaiah says: *Signa legem in electis meis,* and that Jesus Christ shall be a stone of stumbling. But, "Blessed are they who shall not be offended in him." Hosea, *ult.,* says excellently, "Where is the wise? and he shall understand what I say. The righteous shall know them, for the ways of God are right; but the transgressors shall fall therein."

571

Hypothesis that the apostles were impostors.—The time clearly, the manner obscurely.—Five typical proofs.

$$2000 \begin{cases} 1600 \text{ prophets.} \\ 400 \text{ scattered.} \end{cases}$$

572

Blindness of Scripture.—"The Scripture," said the Jews, "says that we shall not know whence Christ will come (John vii, 27, and xii, 34). The Scripture says that Christ abideth for ever, and He said that He should die." Therefore, says Saint John, they believed not, though He had done so many miracles, that the word of Isaiah might be fulfilled: "He hath blinded them," etc.

573

Greatness.—Religion is so great a thing that it is right that those who will not take the trouble to seek it, if it be obscure, should be deprived of it. Why, then, do any complain, if it be such as can be found by seeking?

574

All things work together for good to the elect, even the obscurities of Scripture; for they honour them because of what is divinely clear. And all things work together for evil to the rest of the world, even what is clear, for they revile such, because of the obscurities which they do not understand.

575

The general conduct of the world towards the Church: God willing to blind and to enlighten.—The event having proved the divinity of these prophecies, the rest ought to be believed. And thereby we see the order of the world to be of this kind. The miracles of the Creation and the Deluge being forgotten, God sends the law and the miracles of Moses, the prophets who prophesied particular things; and to prepare a lasting miracle, He prepares prophecies and their fulfilment; but, as the prophecies could be suspected, He desires to make them above suspicion, etc.

576

God has made the blindness of this people subservient to the good of the elect.

577

There is sufficient clearness to enlighten the elect, and sufficient obscurity to humble them. There is sufficient obscurity to blind the reprobate, and sufficient clearness to condemn them, and make them inexcusable.—Saint Augustine, Montaigne, Sébond.

The genealogy of Jesus Christ in the Old Testament is intermingled with so many others that are useless, that it cannot be distinguished. If Moses had kept only the record of the ancestors of Christ, that might have been too plain. If he had not noted that of Jesus Christ, it might not have been sufficiently plain.

But, after all, whoever looks closely sees that of Jesus Christ expressly traced through Tamar, Ruth, etc.

Those who ordained these sacrifices, knew their uselessness; those who have declared their uselessness, have not ceased to practise them.

If God had permitted only one religion, it had been too easily known; but when we look at it closely, we clearly discern the truth amidst this confusion.

The premiss.—Moses was a clever man. If, then, he ruled himself by his reason, he would say nothing clearly which was directly against reason.

Thus all the very apparent weaknesses are strength. Example: the two genealogies in Saint Matthew and Saint Luke. What can be clearer than that this was not concerted?

578

God (and the Apostles), foreseeing that the seeds of pride would make heresies spring up, and being unwilling to give them occasion to arise from correct expressions, has put in Scripture and the prayers of the Church contrary words and sentences to produce their fruit in time.

So in morals He gives charity, which produces fruits contrary to lust.

579

Nature has some perfections to show that she is the image of God, and some defects to show that she is only His image.

580

God prefers rather to incline the will than the intellect. Perfect clearness would be of use to the intellect, and would harm the will. To humble pride.

581

We make an idol of truth itself; for truth apart from charity is not God, but His image and idol, which we must neither love nor worship; and still less must we love or worship its opposite, namely, falsehood.

I can easily love total darkness; but if God keeps me in a

state of semi-darknes, such partial darkness displeases me, and, because I do not see therein the advantage of total darkness, it is unpleasant to me. This is a fault, and a sign that I make for myself an idol of darkness, apart from the order of God. Now only His order must be worshipped.

582

The feeble-minded are people who know the truth, but only affirm it so far as consistent with their own interest. But, apart from that, they renounce it.

583

The world exists for the exercise of mercy and judgment, not as if men were placed in it out of the hands of God, but as hostile to God; and to them He grants by grace sufficient light, that they may return to Him, if they desire to seek and follow Him; and also that they may be punished, if they refuse to seek or follow him.

584

That God has willed to hide Himself.—If there were only one religion, God would indeed be manifest. The same would be the case, if there were no martyrs but in our religion.

God being thus hidden, every religion which does not affirm that God is hidden, is not true; and every religion which does not give the reason of it, is not instructive. Our religion does all this: *Vere tu es Deus absconditus.*

585

If there were no obscurity, man would not be sensible of his corruption; if there were no light, man would not hope for a remedy. Thus, it is not only fair, but advantageous to us, that God be partly hidden and partly revealed; since it is equally dangerous to man to know God without knowing his own wretchedness, and to know his own wretchedness without knowing God.

586

This religion, so great in miracles, saints, blameless Fathers, learned and great witnesses, martyrs, established kings as David, and Isaiah, a prince of the blood, and so great in science, after having displayed all her miracles and all her wisdom, rejects all this, and declares that she has neither wisdom nor signs, but only the cross and foolishness.

For those, who, by these signs and that wisdom, have deserved your belief, and who have proved to you their character, declare to you that nothing of all this can change you, and render you capable of knowing and loving God, but the power of the foolishness of the cross without wisdom and signs, and not the signs without this power. Thus our religion is foolish in respect to the effective cause, and wise in respect to the wisdom which prepares it.

587

Our religion is wise and foolish. Wise, because it is the most learned, and the most founded on miracles, prophecies, etc. Foolish, because it is not all this which makes us belong to it. This makes us indeed condemn those who do not belong to it; but it does not cause belief in those who do belong to it. It is the cross that makes them believe, *ne evacuata sit crux*. And so Saint Paul, who came with wisdom and signs, says that he has come neither with wisdom nor with signs; for he came to convert. But those who come only to convince, can say that they come with wisdom and with signs.

III

ENGLISH MYSTICISM AND DIVINITY

===

1. LANCELOT ANDREWES:
SERMON ON THE NATIVITY

¶ Of Lancelot Andrewes, once chaplain to Queen Elizabeth, and Bishop of Winchester under James I, little enough was popularly known until quite recently. It is one of the services of Mr. T. S. Eliot to the criticism of English letters that he has spoken forcefully in behalf of a theologian and writer whose name surely belongs among those of the greatest Anglican divines. Andrewes was, to be sure, a man of remarkable learning, whose subtlety occasionally dazzles the reader of our time and leads him to suspect conceits where there is question only of careful distinctions. Born in 1555 and educated at Oxford and Cambridge, he died in 1626.

The present sermon is one of sixteen preached on various Christmas days. It happens to be one of Bishop Andrewes's last addresses, having been delivered in 1623. The text here used is, excepting for a few curtailments, that of the original edition. Since the author, who was definitively a traditionalist, relied upon the Vulgate, the Latin phrasing has been for the most part retained.*

---

* From *Seventeen Sermons on the Nativity*. By Lancelot Andrewes. London: Griffith, Farren, Okeden and Welsh. N.D.

OF THE NATIVITY

That in the dispensation of the fulness of the times, He might gather together into one all things, both which are in Heaven, and which are in earth, even in Christ. EPHESIANS i. 10.

IN DISPENSATIONE PLENITUDINIS TEMPORUM, INSTAURARE OMNIA, IN CHRISTO, QUÆ IN CŒLIS, ET QUÆ IN TERRA SUNT, IN IPSO

EEING the text is of seasons, it would not be out of season itself. And though it never be out of season to speak of Christ, yet even Christ hath His seasons. "Your time is always," (John vii, 6), saith He, so is not Mine; I have My seasons. One of which seasons is this, the season of His birth, whereby all were "recapitulate in Heaven and earth," which is the season of the text. And so, this a text of the season.

There is for the most part in each text some one predominant word. That word in this is the word ἀνακεφαλαιώσασθαί, here turned "gathering together into one again." To know the nature and full force of it, we may consider it three ways: 1. as it is properly taken: 2. as it is extended; 3. as it is derived.

1. As it is taken properly. So it signifies "to make the foot of an account." We call it the foot, because we write it below at the foot. They of old writ theirs above, over the head, and so called it the sum in the top.

2. As it is extended. So it is "the short recapitulation of a long chapter," the compendium of a book or of some discourse. These are all like the foot of an account, and are usually called the sum of all that hath been said.

3. As it is derived. So shall we have the native sense of it. It comes of κεφάλιον, and that of κεφαλὴ, Greek for 'a head.' Best expressed in the word 'recapitulate;' that is, to reduce all to a head. Each of these is a gathering together into one, as we read. Which of the three you take, nay take them all three, you cannot do amiss. They be all true, all tend to edify. Christ is the 1. sum of our account, 2. the shutting up of our discourse,

3. "the Head of the body" (Col. i. 18, and Eph. iv. 15, 16) mystical whereto this gathering here is. We shall make no good audit without Him; no, nor good apology. Whatsoever be the premises, with Christ we must conclude. As we do the year with Christmas, so conclude all with *in Christo*.

The old division is—*ut res, ita tempora rerum.* Here it holds, here are both seasons and things; things for seasons, and seasons for things.

I. Two parts here be. 1. Seasons, first; seasons, more than one. 2. Here is a fulness of them. 3. Here is a dispensation of that fulness. 4. And that by God; "that He," that is God—"that in the dispensation of the fulness of times He might." This is the first part.

II. The "things." For first, here are "all things; things in Heaven, things on earth"—all in both. 2. Of these, a collection or gathering them all together; or rather, a recollection or gathering them together again. 3. A gathering them all into one; all into one κεφάλιον, one "sum;" or all to one κεφαλὴ, one "head." And these two are one, and that one is Christ.

You observe, that as the things answer the seasons, and the seasons them, so doth the fulness answer the gathering, and the gathering it. 1. To fill the seasons, to make a fulness of them, here is a gathering. 2. A gathering whereof? Of all in Heaven, and all on earth—a great gathering sure, and able to fill the seasons full up to the brim. 3. But this is not a gathering at the first hand, but a gathering again, that is, a-new at second-hand. 4. A gathering whereto? "To one"—one, either one sum, or one head, both are in the body of the word, and these two are one, and that one is Christ. 5. A gathering, how? that is in the word too: by way of contracting or recapitulation. 6. And when? When God dispensed it; and that is at Christ's birth. 7. Now last, what we are the better by this gathering, what fruit we gather by or from it, what our share is in this sum, which is *summa dividenda.* 8. And then how we may be the better for it, if we divide as God, and when God did it. 9. As God, gather things in Heaven first. 10. When God, and that is this season of the year, the gathering time with God and with us. So shall we dispense the season well.

Find the things, they will bring you to the season; find the fulness of things, you shall find the fulness of seasons. Find the gathering, you shall find the fulness; find Christ, and you shall find the gathering, for the gathering is full and whole in Christ. So, upon the point, find Christ and find all. And this is the first day we can find Him; for this day was He born, and so first to be found by us.

We have heretofore dealt with "the fulness of time;" and now are we to deal with the fulness of season. Time and season are two, and have in all tongues two different words to shew they differ. In Hebrew, ימו and עת ; in Greek χρόνος and καιρός; in Latin, *tempus and tempestivum*.

And differ they do as much as a time, and a good time. It is time alway, all the year long; so is it not season, but when the good time is. Time is taken at large, any time. Season not so, but is applied to that with which it suits, or for which it serves best. Here it is applied to gathering, the season of gathering.

These seasons be καιρῶν in the plural; for, 'as the things to be gathered are many, so are the seasons wherein they are to be gathered, many likewise.' Each, his several season to be gathered in.

Now, as 'the things,' *res*, have their autumn of maturity, so *tempora*, 'the seasons' have their fulness, and when the things are ripe and ready to be gathered, then is the season full.

Now of these seasons and their fulness there is "a dispensation," an *œconomia*, the word in the text, which is a word of husbandry; a great part whereof consisteth in the skill of seasons, of taking them when they come, allotting the thing to the season, and the season to it.

Which dispensation is here ascribed to God; that He, that is, that God "in Whose hands our times are," saith the Psalm, and our seasons, (Psa. civ. 27, 28; cxlv. 15, 16), both. He that can make them full by giving us kindly seasons, or empty by making them unseasonable, and having made them full is to dispose of them of very right. There is none of these but is sensible in the course of the year, in things upon earth.

But are there seasons for the things on earth and their fulness, and are there not also seasons for the things in Heaven and for the filling of them? All for relief of the bodily wants here below, none for the supply of spiritual necessities above? All for the body, and never a season for the soul? If we allow them to the world, shall we not to the Church, ἀνακεφαλαίωσις or 'abridgment' of the world? If it be sensible in the natural things, though not so easily discerned, yet it is as certain in the main revolution of *annus magnus*, 'the great periodical year' of the world's endurance.

It can never enter into any man to think that the great *Œconomus* or 'Steward of this great household,' the world, should so far forget himself, but if for all matters He "had appointed a season," (Eccl. iii. 1), then for the greatest matter. If for every purpose under Heaven, then for the highest purpose of all, that as we see concerneth all the things in Heaven and earth both. Above *salus populi* this *salus mundi*, 'the saving the whole world.' Shall not these have their seasons, and the seasons their fulness there, and that fulness the due dispensation of all other most worthy of God, the greatest work of the greatest Person? Set this down then to begin with: there are seasons, as in our common year of twelve months, so in the great year, whereof every day is a year by Daniel's, nay, "a thousand years," (2 Pet. iii. 8), by St. Peter's calculation.

And which be the seasons, and when, in the common year? Our Saviour sets them down. 1. The season "when the earth bringeth forth the blade," (Mark iv. 28); 2. when "the stalk;" 3. when "the ear;" 4. when "the full corn in the ear." And when the ear is full, and full ripe, the season is full; then is the season of fulness, the fulness of season. Then "the reaper fills his hand, and he that bindeth up the sheaves his bosom." (Psa. cxxix. 7). "Then are the barns filled with plenty, and the presses run over with new wine." (Prov. iii. 10.) And when all is full, then to gathering we go.

Such like seasons do we find *in anno magno*. 1. The time of nature, all in the blade; 2. of Moses, in the stalk; 3. of the Prophets, in the ear, 4. And when the full corn? When but at this great gathering here mentioned? When all in Heaven, and all in earth gathered, that I think was the fulness of things, *plenitudo rerum;* and the fulness of seasons, *plenitudo temporum*, may be allowed for it.

II. This sets us over to the second part, from the seasons to the things; from the fulness of seasons to the gathering of things. And first, whereof, of what things? Of "even all." "All;" and to shew the extent of it, subdivided into "all in Heaven, all in earth;" and that I trow is "all." It was not amiss he should thus sever them, and express things in Heaven by name; else we should little have thought of gathering things there so high. No farther than earth, we; there is all our gathering, and there only. The Apostle points up to Heaven—*sursum corda*, "to lift up our hearts, to set our affections on things there above," (Col. iii. 1, 2), to gather them. There is a gathering of them also.

Of which gathering into one, I know not what the things in Heaven have—the things on earth I am sure have good cause to be glad. In Heaven is all good, and nothing but good. In earth, to say the least, there is much evil. Yet upon the reckoning, Heaven is like to come by the loss; we on earth are sensibly gainers by it. It is a good hearing for us, that both these shall be thus gathered together. For if Heaven and earth be so gathered, it is that Heaven may advance earth higher; and no meaning, that earth should draw it down hither.

But well: between them both here is a great gathering toward, well expressed by the Apostle in the terms of a sum. For it is *summa summarum*, 'a sum indeed;' Heaven and earth, and the fulness of them both.

All these to be gathered, and well. Gathering God favours, for it ends in unity, to gather into one; and unity God loves, Himself being *principalis unitas*. God favours it sure, Himself is the gatherer. Scattering God favours not; that tends to division, and division upon division. Gathering is good for us; unity preserves, division destroys. The kite, he scatters; the hen, how fain would she gather!

But stay awhile, and take with us what kind of gathering. It is not κεφαλαίωσις, 'a gathering;' but ἀνακεφαλαίωσις, "a gathering together again." We must not lose ἀνά, there is force in it. It is not a collection, but a recollection. *Re* imports it is a new collection again, the second time. You see it in *recall, return, reduce*; that is, to call, turn, bring back again.

Now our rule is, ἀνά ever presupposeth ἀπὸ. Ἀνακεφαλαίωσις presupposeth ἀοπκεφαλαίωσις: that is, a returning to implies a departing from: "a gathering together again," a scattering in sunder before; "a dispensation," a dissipation. So a dissipation, a departure, a scattering there had been.

Yet one degree more. Ἀπὸ, that is 'from,' ever implies σὺν, that is a former being 'with.' One cannot be said to be gone from, that was never with; or to fall out, that was never in: one cannot be said to be so again, that was never so before. So then together we were first; and in sunder we fell after. Which falling in sunder required an ἀνὰ to bring us together again, to restore us to that the second time that we had before lost, to our former estate. It is St. Peter's word "restoring," (Acts iii. 21), the same with St. Paul's "gathering together again" here.

Now these three set forth unto us our threefold estate. 1. 'Together,' σὺν, our first original, which we had in Adam, while he stood with God together. 2. 'In sunder,' ἀπὸ,—there came our misery, by Adam's not keeping his first estate, but scattering from God. 3. But then comes ἀνὰ about, and makes all well again, by bringing us where we were at the first. There was a former capitulation—the articles were broken: then came this recapitulation here anew. An account was cast, but it was mis-cast, and so it is here cast new over again.

But when all is done, ἀνὰ is it we must hold by. The first is gone, all perished by being scattered from. All must be recovered by being gathered to again. Our Separation, our ruin; our reparation, our ἀνὰ, our 'gathering again;' and not ours alone, but *salus mundi*, of "all in Heaven all in earth."

But this we may see by the way, 1. what case all were in; 2. what case all are in still, that lie loose and ungathered, and whom ἀνὰ hath not recollected again.

We see what and how gathered. Now the next point is, whereto? Into one. Every thing that is gathered is so. But there is more ones than one. One heap, as of stones; one flock, as of sheep; one pile, as of materials of a building. All are good; but to take the word in the native sense, the gathering here is either to one κεφάλαιον, "one sum," as many number; or to go nearer, to one κεφαλὴ, "one head," as many members—and that is it the Apostle pursueth to the chapter's end. Both these, sum and head, are in the body of the word κεφάλαιον, and they both serve and suit well. The body: the head is as it were the sum of all; all 1. sense, 2. motion, 3. speech, 4. understanding, all recapitulate into the head. This of head or sum fitteth it best. For to speak properly, many heaps, flocks, piles there may be; heads there can be but one. And so of a sum, but one true sum, were there never so many so divers ways cast.

So then into one, that is not enough; it is not co-adunation will serve. It is recapitulation, and in that word there is *caput*; it is ἀνακεφάλαίωσις, and in that word there is κεφαλὴ, such a reducing all to one, as that one be the head. A headless gathering the Apostle cannot skill of. And indeed, say there were an entire body, and every member in his right place, and all strictly knit together, yet if the head should hap to be away, as good the members all in sunder, for all were to no purpose. So, a head or nothing.

This gathering then, you see, is to the chief member, to the member that wears the crown. Thither, upward, the true gathering goes. There is an union downwards, as of Samson's foxes, that were together by the tails, (Judges xv. 4); that is not the right, but by the head. The oxen that plough are joined together by the head; the foxes that are tied by the tails, they set all on fire. The unity of the head God send us! that is the true unity.

And yet are we not where we should. We may gather upward too, and make a head, and not the right head. That to a head is not enough, if it fall out to be a wrong head, suppose Romely's son. (Isa. vii. 9.) Do but paint, saith the Poet, anybody with a wrong head, it will but move laughter and scorn. The right, the own head it would be. A strange head will not suit, nor do us any stead. The right head then.

And which is the right head he adds? *Recapitulati in Christo*— it is Christ. There, lo, is the right head now. To That let all gather.

And now we are arrived at Christ, we are where we should, our gathering is at the best. All in Heaven, all in earth, gathered together, together again—again into one, one sum whereof Christ is the foot, one body whereof Christ is the Head. Gather then, and be gathered to Him; gather then, and be gathered with Him. "He that gathereth not with Him scattereth." (Luke xi. 23.)

And so were all, all scattered without Christ, till He came with His ἀνὰ, and got them again together. The seasons were all empty, the things all on heaps.

Things in Heaven from things in earth—Angels with "drawn

swords at men." (Gen. iii. 24.) Things on earth from things in Heaven—men at but the sight of an Angel ready to fall down dead. (Judges xiii. 22.) The members from the head, the head from the members, the members one from another: neither union with the head, nor among themselves. It was sin that divided between God and them, and divided once and divided ever, divided *in semper divisibilia*, 'till they were quite past all division;' no longer divided now, but even scattered. The case of the world then.

Scattered on point of religion. Gods scattered all over, "as many gods as cities." (Jer. ii. 28.) All the hosts of Heaven, all the beasts and creeping things of the earth.

Scattered in point of morality or moral philosophy. I know not how many scattered opinions Augustine reckons *de Summo Bono*, the chief point of all.

The Jews scattered from the Gentiles, and the Gentiles from the Jews—a main wall between. (Eph. ii. 14.)

The Gentiles scattered from themselves grossly; all in fractions, they. Nothing of a body, never a head; and yet many heads, but never a right one among them all.

No, not the Jews themselves; for "the Tabernacle of David" was then down, and the ruins of it scattered into many sects, as the Prophet Amos complains, (Amos ix. 11), and St. James allegeth it out of him. (Acts xv. 16.) In a word, the whole world then was but a mass of errors, a chaos of confusion, *Tohu* and *Bohu*; "empty and void" (Gen. i. 2) of all saving grace or truth. Well likened to them that were scattered at the tower of Babel, where no man understood another, (Gen. xi. 7); or to the people that were "scattered all over the land of Egypt to gather stubble, to pick up straws." (Exodus v. 12.) All then wandering hither and thither, and seeking "death in the error of their life." (Wisd. i. 12.) By all which you see what need there was of this gathering, this ἀναϰεφάλαίωσις.

Now then if, "for the divisions of Reuben, there were great thoughts of heart," (Judges v. 15), as it is in Deborah's song, for but one tribe scattered from the rest, shall there be no thought or course taken for these, such, so general, so many, not divisions but plain dispersions, scattering all abroad? Great pity that all these should lie thus loose and ungathered, as if they were not worth the taking up. He that in John vi. took order for the broken meat, for the fragments, willed them to be gathered ἵνα μή τι ἀπόληται, "that nothing might be lost," (John vi. 12)—no, not of them, He certainly were no good *Œconomus* if He would let all these be lost for lack of gathering.

But could not this gathering be *absque Christo,* in some other? It appears no. Seasons there were more than one, but all empty; proffers were made in them, but nothing full, nor anything near full. A season of the Law unwritten. Then came the Patriarchs. But they had much ado to keep themselves from scattering; they gathered none.

A season of the Law written. Then the Priests and Levites; but the gathering little the fuller for them.

Then came all the Prophets, to no great purpose they neither; some few proselytes they made, that was all. But in the end, all these, as they in the parable of the wounded man, "passed by, looked on him," but let him lie; little was done till the good Samaritan came. (Luke x. 31, 32.) The things in heaven and earth, the generality of them so, in not much better case for all these, could not be recapitulate in the Patriarchs, Moses, the Prophets. So that to this plunge it was come, that the Psalmist even asked God, "Wherefore hast Thou made all men for nought?" (Ps. lxxxix. 47.) It was for Him to come, *Qui venturus erat.* (Heb. x. 37.)

It was time, more than time, when that which was the only known way, when one was scattered from God, how to gather him to God again, which was, "Let Him smell a sacrifice," (1 Sam. xxvi. 19)—when that grew out of season, when that failed. And that it did. "Sacrifice, burnt-offering, burnt-offerings for sin," (sin that made all the scattering), *noluisti,* that is plain, "Thou wouldst not"—it is Christ now speaketh—"Then said I, Lo, I come." (Psa. xl. 6.) I, of Whom it is written, "in the top or front of the book, that I should fulfil Thy will," and gather these together again; "lo, I come to do it."

By this *Ecce venio* of His a way was found, those that were thus distracted and scattered before, how to bring them together again. What way was that? It follows in the same place what He meant by *Ecce venio.* He goes it over again; "No sacrifice Thou wouldst;"—no: "but a body hast Thou ordained Me." (Psa.

xl. 6.) The incorporating Christ, the ordaining Him a body, that is the "new and living way, through the veil, that is His flesh." (Heb. x. 20.) With that He comes this day, and gathers all again.

How, or in what manner that? The manner is set down in the word by way of recapitulation. We are not to conceive there was such "a great sheet," as St. Peter saw, "let down from Heaven," (Acts x. 11), and that all these were put into it and so gathered. No, it was *recapitulando,* 'by reducing to less room,' as we do many diffused matters to a few heads, as we contract great maps to a small compass, as great plots to a small module; for that is properly to recapitulate.

If then we be to proceed by way of recapitulation, then are we to reduce all to heads. So let us reduce these things to these two heads; 1. First, Heaven, and all in it, to God; earth, and all in it, to man. Gather these two into one, and there is the ἀνακεφαλαίωσις in short. To conceive it the better, you shall understand this was on a good way one-ward, before. You have heard man called the little world, the ἀνακεφαλαίωσις of the great one, a compendium of all the creatures. And so he is of both. He participates with the Angels, and so with things in Heaven, by his soul; he participates with the elements, and so with things on earth, by His body. That to the making of man's body there went a piece of every of the creatures. So there was in man a kind of recapitulation before.

But that was not full, yet lacked there one thing. All in Heaven were not gathered into man. Of God we say, *Qui es in Cœlis.* He was one of the things in Heaven, and He was out all the while. But if He could be gathered in too, then were it a full gathering indeed. All in Heaven recapitulate into One, that is God; all in earth recapitulate into one, that is man. Gather these two now, and all are gathered, all the things in either. And now at this last great recollection of God and man, and in them of Heaven and earth, and in them of all in Heaven and earth, are all recapitulate into the unity of One entire Person. And how? Not so as they were gathered at first; not as the κεφαλαίωσις, 'the first gathering,' so the ἀνακεφαλαίωσις, 'the second gathering.' When things were at the best, God and man were two in number; now God and man are but one Christ. So the gathering nearer than before, so surer than before, so every way better than before.

In man there was one-ward an abridgment of all the rest. Gather God and him into one, and so you have all. There is nothing, not anything, in Heaven or earth left out. Heaven is in and earth, the creatures in Heaven and earth, the Creator of Heaven and earth. All are in now; all reconciled, as it were, in one mass, all cast into one sum; recapitulate indeed truly and properly.

Herein is the fulness, that God Himself comes into this κεφαλαιον. The Apostle, where the Psalm saith, "He hath put all things in subjection under His feet;" it is "manifest," saith the Apostle, "that He was excepted That so put them under. (1 Cor. xv. 27.) But here it is manifest, say we, that He is not excepted that did gather; but He the very Collector is in this collection Himself and all.

For "God was in Christ reconciling the world." (2 Cor. v. 19.) "The world," that is all things, all in Heaven, all in earth. And in Christ did "dwell the fulness of the Godhead bodily," (Col. ii. 9), when He did so "reconcile them in the body of His flesh." (Col. i. 21, 22.) In a word, certain it is that by virtue of this recapitulation we are one with Christ, Christ as man. God is one with Christ—Christ as God. So in Christ God and man are one. And there is good hope they that are one, will soon be at one; where unity is, union will be had with no great ado.

And even besides this there is yet another recapitulation; that well might it have that name. For if you mark it, it is not recapitation, but recapitulation; and that comes of *capitulum*, which is a diminutive. So was it: *Verbum in principio*, "the eternal," mighty, great "Word" became *Verbum abbreviatum*, (Rom. x. 8), as the Apostle saith, to bring this to pass. He that "the Heavens are but His span," (Isa. xl. 12), abbreviate into a child of a span long; He that *Caput*, "the Head" of men and Angels, principalities, and powers, became *Capitulum;* He that Κεφαλὴ, Κεφάλαιον, 'a little diminutive Head.' Head? Nay, became the Foot, *Pes computi* the text is, 'the Foot, the lowest part of the account,' and of the lowest account.

And now, because we are in seasons, we speak of seasons. When was this, at what season of the year? when was it that He was so *capite minutus?* Sure never less, never so little, never so minorated, so minimated, I am sure, as now. When was *Ecce venio* fulfilled? We may know that by all the four Sundays in Advent now past, that to-day it is *Ecce venio*. His coming the Psalm expounds by ordaining Him a body, (Ps. xl. 7); a body there was ordained Him in the womb, but to us things are when they appear. That though the Word were made flesh before, yet God was not "manifested in the flesh," came not and "dwelt among us," (John i. 14), visibly to be seen till this day. So that if you ask of *in Christo*, what or when? *In Christo nato*, then was this gathering of things in Heaven and earth.

And in sign it was then, look there comes a choir of Angels down, (Luke ii. 13), there comes a new star forth to represent the things in Heaven, there comes together a sort of shepherds, and there is gathering to them a troop of great princes from the East (Matt. ii. 1) to represent the things on earth, which consist, as these do, of high and low, noble and base, wise and simple; all to celebrate, and make shew of this gathering, of this great πλήρωμα into this small κεφάλαιον. And in their Heavenly hymn (Luke ii. 14) there is mention of this gathering; *in excelsis*, and *in terris* set together, as if all in both were now in full and perfect harmony.

Now when the seasons had travailed with, at last brought forth Him That was the best thing they had, or should ever bring forth, then were they at the best. When "Him in Whom it pleased the Father all fulness should dwell," then were they at the full. The gathering of the things so full as it made *plenitudo rerum*, the gathering of the seasons so full as it made *plenitudo temporum*. And so have we brought both parts, seasons and things together.

The sum is at the foot, the oration at the period, the building at the head-stone, the tide at the full; "the fulness of the Gentiles" (Rom. xi. 25) are come into His Church, "which is His body, the fulness of Him that filleth all in all." (Eph. i. 23.)

But why God in the dispensation of the seasons did so order that at such a year of the world, such a month of the year, such a day of the month, this should fall out just, this is more than I dare take upon me to define. But this I may, that the Christian world hath ever observed divers good congruities of this feast with this text.

The text is of a recapitulation; the feast is so. Twelve months recapitulate to twelve days. Six for the old, in six days was the creation of the old. And when "the old things are past," as many for the new; for "behold all things are new," and "if any be in Christ he is a new creature." (2 Cor. v. 17.) Both these recapitulate in one season equally divided. Equally divided between both, yet so as the days of the last are set before the first, that so *erunt novissimi primi* (Matt. xix. 30) is verified even of the season, and the last first there also.

The text is of a gathering, and that falls fit with the season, and giveth us great cause to admire the high wisdom of God in the dispensation of seasons; that now at this season, when we gather nothing, when nothing groweth to be gathered, there should be a gathering yet and a great one; nay, the greatest gathering that ever was or will be; and so by that means, the poorest and emptiest season in nature become the fullest and richest in grace.

Now we do ourselves in effect express as much as this comes to. For we also make it a season of gathering together, of neighbourly meetings and invitations. Wherein we come together, and both ourselves have, and we make each other partakers of, what we have gathered all the year before.

In which sense also we may call it the season of dispensation; in that we then dispense the blessing God hath sent us, and that is in good house-keeping and hospitality.

And if you will, of fulness too. For the most part do then use to be better filled, and with better fare that are not so full again all the year beside. That one may truly say, there is more fulness in this season than any other. And so it is the season of fulness then; for the "hungry are then filled with good things," (Ps. cvii. 9), then of all the seasons of the year.

And last, there is in the text, and it is the main word in the text, ἀνακεφαλαίωσις, which in the primitive sense is the making the foot of an account; which agreeth well with the foot of the year, for at the foot of the leaf sums used to be set. Set it at the head, or set it at the foot, it is the foot of the old, and the head of the new, and so the fittest season to celebrate it in. For be it head, or be it foot, Christ it is. So recapitulation or gathering, fulness or dispensation, or summing all up, the text is seasonable.

But these I have spoke of are of things on earth. Were it not to be wished, we would endeavour to have some fruition, and to gather some fruit for the Heavenly part from this gathering, this summing up of Christ's?

Christ is but κεφάλαιον, 'a short sum;' but there is in Him πλήρωμα, "a fulness of all." Christ is but the contents of a chapter, some three or four lines, but a great long chapter follows, long and large. For what shall you see in this Shulamite, (Cant. vi. 13), but *chorus castrorum*, legions, whole armies of good things to gather. Such, so great a sum, as twelve days will not serve to cast them up. But yet somewhat let us gather, that the seasons being full, we ourselves be not sent empty away.

The time fails; I will therefore name but one, and that the main word of the text, ἀνακεφαλαίωσις, which referreth properly to 'the making up an account.' The Fathers taking the verse into their considerations, pitch upon it; as St. Jerome, who thinks it chosen of purpose to that end. But the word and thing both we may have good use of, seeing we all are to be accountants, *redde rationem* (Luke xvi. 2), said to us all, seeing to an account we must all come.

And thus he followeth it, goes no farther than the text for the particulars of our account, makes them consist of *quæ in Cœlis* and *quæ in terris*. Which two, as they are principally taken for the creatures in both, so may they also, and not amiss, be taken for the things done in them both; specially our gatherings in them referring to either.

Things in Heaven to stand for our good deeds, our alms, fasts, and prayers, that "ascend up thither"—the Angel tells Cornelius so, (Acts x. 4)—and "will receive us up thither into everlasting tabernacles." Of which, gather we as many as we can all our life long.

As for these on earth, we gather but too fast; meaning our evil deeds, which smell of the earth whence they are, and where they were done.

Now when we come to give up our account, it should seem by the word ἀνά, we had cast them once before and cast them false, that we must to it again, and see if we can find our sums right. There is no danger but in casting our *quæ in Cœlis*, our good, lest we cast them over; and our *quæ in terris*, our bad, lest them we cast under. The other way the error is nothing so perilous.

Our *quæ in Cœlis*, our good, howsoever our new auditors cast them so as they find God in their debt, for that we have laid out more than ever God required, I doubt will not prove so at the audit. But of our *quæ in terris*, our evil, there is no great fear of overcasting them, their sum will rise but too high if we deceive not ourselves.

But whether it be of both, we shall find ourselves wrong in both, if they be not recapitulate *in Christo*. For our *quæ in Cœlis*; having done all we can, Christ bids us say, *servi inutiles sumus*, (Luke xvii. 10); and so we must say then, and what account can be made of *inutile?* Having suffered all we can, *non sunt condignæ*, (Rom. viii. 18), saith St. Paul; so both come not home. The good Centurion, he that "built the Synagogue," (Luke vii. 5), nay then St. John Baptist himself, (Luke iii. 16), both cast themselves to a *non sum dignus*, even the best of our nature. That when we have done we must begin again, and cast and cast till we be weary, unless we cast in Christ; fail still, unless our total of *quæ in Cœlis* be recapitulate *in Christo*.

But then come to the other account of *quæ in terris*; to that there is our fulness, and the fulness of our seasons. Many a broken reckoning shall we find there, such surd numbers, such fractions we shall meet with, we shall not tell how or when to get through, we shall want counters. They are so infinite and intricate withal, that I fear we shall be found in a mighty arrear, a huge debt of thousands and "ten thousands of talents," (Matt. xviii. 24); we shall not tell which way to turn us, nor which way to satisfy it, though all we have were sold, and we ourselves too. To balance this account, Christ is most needful; for *summis conjunctis*, 'cast both these together,' and Job being our auditor, he finds we shall not be able to "answer God one for a thousand," (Job ix. 3), that he can charge us with. *Sine me nihil potestis facere*, (John xv. 5), if ever, we shall find in this most true. For gather Heaven and earth, and all that is in them altogether, and leave Him out, they will never be able to make our discharge, nor the best auditor of them all.

But He out of the fulness of His satisfactions can relieve us that way, to take off, or strike off, a great part of our *onus*. And He can cast in of the fulness of His merits to make up that is found *minus habens*, or defective in ours that way. For the short is, He is both *Pes and Caput computi*, the Κεφαλὴ, and the

Κεφάλαιον; He is called both in the text. His ἀνακεφαλαίωσις must help us if ever we come to our audit.

But foreseen, that this be no hindrance to our gathering. No: gathering we must be still those of Heaven, spiritual; and turn as much of our earthly as we can into them. And still order the matter so, as "while we have time we be doing good." (Gal. vi. 10.) We shall but evil sum up all in Christ, if we have no particulars to raise our sum of, if we have nothing but what is out of Christ to recapitulate in Christ. To gather, I say, else are we like to have but an empty season of it.

And even to begin now to imitate God in His time when, and in His order how. His time: this is the time, God made His in; now we to take the same time to fall on gathering. His order: this is the order God made His by; He began with Heavenly things, we to keep the same order, follow His method, begin where He begins, begin with the things that have the priority of place in the text, begin with them; make *Regnum Ejus* our *primum quærite*, (Matt. vi. 33), and the things that pertain to it. And not pervert God's order, and be so wholly given to the fulness of the things on earth, that we fall to them first. Nay, I pray God it be not first, and last and all. We shall the better dispense the season, if we gather to prayers, to God's word; if we begin with them, if with the dispensation of His holy mysteries gather to that specially.

For there we do not gather to Christ or of Christ, but we gather Christ Himself; and gathering Him we shall gather the tree and fruit and all upon it. For as there is a recapitulation of all in Heaven and earth in Christ, so there is a recapitulation of all in Christ in the holy Sacrament. You may see it clearly: there is in Christ the Word eternal for things in Heaven; there is also flesh for things on earth. Semblably, the Sacrament consisteth of a Heavenly and of a terrene part, (it is Irenæus' own words); the Heavenly—there the word too, the abstract of the other; the earthly—the element.

And in the elements, you may observe there is a fulness of the seasons of the natural year; of the corn-flour or harvest in the one, bread; of the wine-press or vintage in the other, wine. And in the heavenly, of the "wheat-corn," (John xii. 24), whereto He compareth Himself—bread, even "the living Bread" (or,

"Bread of life"), "that came down from Heaven," (John vi. 50, 51); the true Manna, whereof we may gather each his gomer. And again, of Him, the true Vine as He calls Himself, (John xv. 1.)—the blood of the grapes of that Vine. Both these issuing out of this day's recapitulation, both in *corpus autem aptasti Mihi*, (Ps. xl. 6), of this day.

And the gathering or vintage of these two in the blessed Eucharist, is, as I may say a kind of hypostatical union of the sign and the thing signified, so united together as are the two natures of Christ. And even from this Sacramental union do the Fathers borrow their resemblance, to illustrate by it the personal union in Christ; I name Theodoret for the Greek, and Gelasius for the Latin Church, that insist upon it both, and press it against Eutyches. That even as in the Eucharist neither part is evacuate or turned into the other, but abide each still in his former nature and substance, no more is either of Christ's natures annulled, or one of them converted into the other, as Eutyches held, but each nature remaineth still full and whole in his own kind. And backwards; as the two natures in Christ, so the *signum* and *signatum* in the Sacrament, *e converso*. And this latter device, of the substance of the bread and wine to be flown away and gone, and in the room of it a remainder of nothing else but accidents to stay behind, was to them not known, and had it been true, had made for Eutyches and against them. And this for the likeness of union in both.

Now for the word "gathering together in one." It is well known the holy Eucharist itself is called *Synaxis*, by no name more usual in all antiquity, that is, a 'collection or gathering.' For so it is in itself; for at the celebration of it, though we gather to prayer and to preaching, yet that is the principal gathering the Church hath, which is itself called a "collection" (Heb. x. 25) too by the same name from the chief; for "where the body is there the eagles will be gathered," (Luke xvii. 37), and so one *Synaxis* begets another.

And last, there is a "dispensation"—that word in it too, that most clearly. For it is our office, we are styled by the Apostle "dispensers of the mysteries of God," (1 Cor. iv. 1); and in and by them, of all the benefits that came to mankind by this dispensation in the fulness of season of all that are recapitulate in Christ.

Which benefits are too many to deal with. One shall serve as the sum of all; that the very end of the Sacrament is to gather again to God and His favour, if it happen, as oft it doth, we scatter and stray from Him. And to gather us as close and near as *alimentum alito*, that is as near as near may be.

And as to gather us to God, so likewise each to other mutually; expressed lively in the symbols of many grains into the one, and many grapes into the other. The Apostle is plain that we are all "one bread and body, so many as are partakers of one bread," (1 Cor. x. 17), so moulding us as it were into one loaf together. The gathering to God refers still to things in Heaven, this other to men to the things in earth here. All under one head by the common faith; all into one body mystical by mutual charity. So shall we well enter into the dispensing of this season, to begin with.

And even thus to be recollected at this feast by the Holy Communion into that blessed union, is the highest perfection we can in this life aspire unto. We then are at the highest pitch, at the very best we shall ever attain to on earth, what time we newly come from it; gathered to Christ, and by Christ to God; stated in all whatsoever He hath gathered and laid up against His next coming. With which gathering here in this world we must content and stay ourselves, and wait for the consummation of all at His coming again. For there is an *Ecce venio* (Rev. xxii. 12) yet to come.

This gathering thus here begun, it is to take end and to have the full accomplishment at the last and great gathering of all, (Matt. xxv. 32), which shall be of the quick and of the dead. When He shall "send His Angels, and they shall gather His elect from all corners of the earth," (Matt. xxiv. 31), shall "gather the wheat into the barn, and the tares to the fire." (Matt. xiii. 30.) And then, and never till then, shall be the fulness indeed, when God shall be not, as now He is, somewhat in every one, but "all in all." (1 Cor. xv. 28.) "And there shall be neither time" nor season "any more." (Rev. x. 6.) No fulness then but the fulness of eternity, and in it the fulness of all joy. To which, in the several seasons of our being "gathered to our fathers," He vouchsafes to bring us; that as the year, so the fulness of our lives may end in a Christmas, a merry joyful feast, as that is! And so God make this to us, in Him!

2. JOSEPH HALL:

FROM *MEDITATIONS AND VOWS*

¶FAMED in his own time as the "English Seneca," Joseph Hall was perhaps the first satirist in the literature of his country and continues to be read for that reason. Born in 1574, he entered the priesthood of the Anglican Church and became Bishop of Norwich. Having experienced sorrow and poverty after the establishment of the Commonwealth, he died in 1656. He knew most of the prominent people of his time, and seems to have been a man of great learning and artistic ability. Hall's later work consists chiefly of sermons, in writing which he took rank beside the other great divines of his time.

The selections which follow are taken from *Meditations and Vows*, first published in 1606. This form of writing was very popular in the early seventeenth century, other examples being preserved in the works of men as disparate as Lancelot Andrewes and John Dekker. Hall's book has been much appreciated, as the number of editions suggests. It had good sense as well as true spiritual fervor. The text given here is somewhat modernized from the edition published in 1901 by Charles Sayle, whose labors in behalf of a revival of interest in the writings of Hall cannot be too warmly praised.*

* From *Meditations and Vows*. By Joseph Hall. Edited by Charles Sayle. London: Kegan, Paul, 1901.

CHAPTER I

FAITHFUL man hath three eyes. The first of sense, common to him with brute creatures: the second of reason, common to all men: the third, of faith, proper to his profession: whereof each looketh beyond other; and none of them medleth with the other's objects. For neither doth the eye of sense reach to intelligible things and matters of discourse: nor the eye of reason to those things which are supernatural and spiritual: neither doth faith looke downe, to things that may be sensibly seen. If thou discourse to a brute beast of the depths of Philosophy, never so plainly, he understands not, because they are beyond the view of his eye; which is only of sense: If to a mere carnall man, of divine things; he perceiveth not the things of God: neither in deed can do; because they are spiritually discerned. And therefore no wonder if those things seem unlikely, incredible, impossible, to him which the faithfull man (having a proportionable means of apprehension) doth as plainly see, as his eye doth any sensible thing. Tell a plain countrey-man, that the Sunne, or some higher or lesser starre is much bigger than his Cart-wheel; or, at least, so many scores bigger than the whole earth; hee laughes thee to scorne, as affecting admiration, with a learned untruth. Yet the Scholler, by the eye of reason, doth as plainely see, and acknowledge this truth, as that his hand is bigger than his Pen. What a thick mist, yea what a palpable, and more than Egyptian darkness, doth the natural man live in! what a world is there, that he doth not see at all! and how little doth he see in this, which is his proper element! There is no bodily thing but the brute creatures see as well as he, and some of them better. As for his eye of reason, how dim is it in those things which are best fitted to it! what one thing is there in nature, which he dooth perfectly know? what herb, or flower, or worm that he treads on, is there whose true essence he knoweth? No, not so much, as what is in his own bosom; what it is, where it is, or whence it is that gives Being to himself: but, for those things which concern the best World, he doth not so much as confusedly see them; neither knoweth whether they be. He sees no whit into

the great and awful Majesty of God. He discernes Him not in
all his creatures, filling the World with his infinite and glorious
presence. He sees not His wise providence over-ruling all things,
disposing all casuall events, ordering all sinful actions of men to
His own glory: He comprehends nothing of the beautie, majestie,
power and mercy of the Saviour of the World, sitting in his
humanity at his Father's right hand. He sees not the unspeakable
happiness of the glorified souls of the Saints. He sees not the
whole heavenly common-wealth of Angels (ascending and descending to the behoofe of God's children) waiting upon him at all
times invisibly (not excluded with closenesse of prisons, nor
desolatenesse of wildernesses) and the multitude of evil spirits
passing and standing by him, to tempt him unto evil: but, like
unto the foolish bird, when he hath hid his head that he sees nobody, he thinks himself altogether unseen; and then counts himself solitarie, when his eye can meet with no companion. It was
not without cause, that we call a meer folle a naturall. For, however worldlings have still thought Christians God's fooles, we
know them the fools of the World. The deepest Philosopher that
ever was (saving the reverence of the Schooles) is but an ignorant
sot, to the simplest Christian. For, the weakest Christian may, by
plain information, see somewhat into the greatest mysteries of
Nature; because he hath the eye of reason common with the best:
but the best Philosopher by all the demonstration in the World,
can conceive nothing of the mysteries of godliness, because he
utterly wants the eye of faith. Though my insight into matters
of the world be so shallow, that my simplicitie mooveth pitie, or
maketh sport unto others, it shall be my contentment and happinesse, that I see further into better matters. That which I see not,
is worthlesse; and deserves little better than contempt: that which
I see, is unspeakable, inestimable, for comfort, for glory.

II

It is strange to see the varieties and proportion of spiritual and
bodily Diets: There be some Creatures, that are fatted and delighted with Poysons; others live by nothing but Ayre; and some
(they say) by Fire; others will taste no Water, but muddy;
others feed on their fellowes, or perhaps on part of themselves:

others, on the excretions of nobler Creatures: some search into
the Earth for sustenance, or dive into the Waters; others content
themselves with what the upper earth yeelds them without violence: All these and more, are answered in the palate of the soul:
there be some (yea, the most) to whome sin, which is of a most
venomous nature, is both food and dainties; others think it the
only life, to feed on the Popular ayre of Applause; others, that
are never well out of the fire of Contentions, and that wilfully
trouble all Waters with their private Humours and Opinions;
others, whose Crueltie delights in Oppression, and Bloud: yea,
whose Envy gnawes upon their owne Hearts; others, that take
pleasure to revive the wicked and foul Heresies of the greater
wits of the former Times; others, whose worldly Mindes root
altogether in Earthly Cares; or who, not content with the ordi-
narie provision of Doctrine, affect obscure Subtilties, unknowne to
wiser Men: others, whose too indifferent Mindes feede on what
ever Opinion comes next to hand, without any careful disquisition
of Truth; so some feede foul: others (but few) clean and wholesome. As there is no Beast upon Earth, which hath not his like in
the Sea, and which perhaps is not in some sort parallelled in the
Plants of the Earth: so there is no Bestial disposition, which is
not answerably found in some men. Mankind therefore hath
within itself his Goates, Cameleons, Salamanders, Camels,
Wolves, Dogges, Swine, Moles, and what ever sorts of Beasts:
there are but a few men amongst men: to a wise man the shape
is not so much as the qualities. If I be not a Man within, in my
Choyses, Affections, Inclinations; it had been better for me to
have been a Beast without. A Beast is but like itself; but an evil
Man is half a Beast, and half a Devil.

III

ALL temporal things are troublesome: For if we have good things,
it is a trouble to forgo them; and when we see they must be
parted from, eyther we wish they had not been so good, or that
we never had enjoyed them. Yea, it is more trouble to lose them,
than it was before joy to possess them. If, contrarily, we have
evil things, their very presence is troublesome, and still we wish
that they were good, or that we were disburdened of them. So,

good things are troublesome in event, evil things in their use.
They in the future, these in present: they, because they shall come
to an end; these, because they do continue. Tell me; thy Wife
or thy Child lyes dying, and now makes up a loving and dutifull
life, with a kind and heavenly departure, whether hadst thou
rather, for their own part, she had been so good, or worse? Would
it have cost thee so many heartie sighes and teares, if she had
been perverse and disobedient? Yet if in her life time I put thee
to this choise, thou thinkest it no choise at all, in such inequalitie.
It is more torment (sayest thou) to live one unquiet month, than
it is pleasure to live an Age in love. Or if they live be yet dearer:
Thou hast lived to gray hayres, not hastened with care, but bred
with late succession of yeeres. Thy Table was ever covered with
varietie of Dishes: Thy Back softly and richly clad: Thou never
gavest denyall to eyther Skin or Stomacke: Thou ever favouredst
thy selfe; and Health, thee. Now Death is at thy Threshold, and
unpartially knockes at thy doore; doest thou not wish thou hadst
lived with Crusts, and been cloathed with Ragges? Wouldest not
thou have given a better welcome to Death, if he had found thee
lying upon a Pallet of Straw, and supping of Water-gruell; after
many painfull Nights, and many Sides changed in vain? Yet this
beggerly estate thou detestest in health, and pittiest in others, as
truly miserable. The summ is: A Beggar wisheth he might be a
Monarch, while he lives; and the greatest Potentate wisheth he
had lived a Beggar, when he comes to die: and, if Beggerie be to
have nothing; he shall be so in death, though he wished it not.
Nothing, therefore, but Eternitie can make perfect Miserie, but
Eternitie: for, as temporal good things afflict us in their ending;
so temporal sorrowes affoord us joy in the hope of their end.
What folly is this in us, to seek for our trouble, to neglect our
happinesse? I can be but well; and this, that I was well, shal one
day be grievous: Nothing shall please me, but that once I shall
be happy for ever.

IV

MEN make difference betwixt Servants, Friends, and Sonnes:
Servants, though near us in place, yet for their inferioritie are
not familiar: Friends, though by reason of their equalitie, and
our love, they are familiar; yet still we conceive of them, as others

from our selves: But Children we think of affectionately, as the devided pieces of our owne Bodyes. But all these are one to GOD: His Servants, are his Friends; his Friends, are his Sonnes; his Sonnes, his Servants. Many clayme Kindred of God, and profess Friendship to him: because these are priviledges without difficultie, and not without honour; all the tryall is in service. The other are most in affection, and therefore secret, and so may be dissembled; this consisting in action, must needs shew it selfe to the eyes of others: Yee are my Friends, if ye do whatsoever I command you. Friendship with God, is in service; and this service is in action. Many wear God's Cloth, that know not their Master, that never did good chare in his service: So that God has many Retayners, that weare his Liverie, for a countenance, never wait on his; whom he will never owne for Servants, eyther by Favour, or Wages: few Servants, and therefore few Sonnes. It is great favour in God, and great honor to me, that He will vouchsafe to make me the lowest Drudge in his Family; which place if I had not, and were a Monarch of Men, I were accursed. I desire no more, but to serve; yet, Lord, thou givest me more, to be Thy Sonne. I heare David say, "Seemeth it a small matter to you, to be the sonne in law to a King?" What is it then, Oh what is it, to be the true adopted Sonne of the King of Glory? Let me not now say as David of Saul, but as Saul's grand-child to David; Oh, what is Thy Servant, that Thou shouldest look upon such a dead Dogge as I am?

V

THE estate of Heavenely and Earthly things is plainly represented to us by the two Lights of Heaven, which are appointed to rule the Night and the Day. Earthly things are rightly resembled, by the Moon: which being neerest to the Region of Mortalitie, is ever in changes, and never lookes upon us twice with the same face; and when it is at the full is blemished with some dark blots, not capable of any illumination. Heavenly things are figured by the Sunne; whose great and glorious Light is both natural to itselfe, and ever constant. That other fickle and dim Starre is fit enough for the Night of Miserie, wherein we live here below. And this firm and beautifull Light is but good enough for that day of glory, which the Saints live in. If it be good living here, where our sorrowes are changed with joys; what is it to live above, where our joys change not? I cannot look upon the Body of the Sunne; and yet I cannot see at all without the Light of it. I cannot behold the glory of Thy Saints, O Lord; yet without the knowledge of it, I am blinde. If Thy Creature be so glorious to us here belowe; how glorious shall Thy self be to us, when we are above this Sunne? This Sunne shall not shine upward, where thy Glory shineth; the greater light extinguisheth the lesser. O Thou Sunne of Righteousnesse (which shalt only shine to me, when I am glorified), do Thou heat, enlighten, comfort me with the beames of they presence, till I be glorified. Amen.

3. JEREMY TAYLOR:

THE MYSTERIOUSNESS OF MARRIAGE

¶THE fame of Jeremy Taylor as a literary artist is firmly established. New editions of *Holy Living* and *Holy Dying,* his two prose masterpieces, continue to appear, and generous portions of his work are included in all the anthologies. But interest in the mellifluent writer tends to obscure the importance of the thinker and the theologian. Taylor was a scholarly man whose knowledge of traditional Christian teaching and whose insight into matters of the soul merit respect even today. Nowhere do these qualities appear to greater advantage than in the sermon reprinted here. It is representative of that religious eloquence of the seventeenth century which, abandoning the dialectic of Andrewes and the logical eloquence of Hall, created a lofty spiritual prose poetry of which Hooker, Fuller and Barrow were also masters.

Jeremy Taylor was born in 1613, and won fame as a Cambridge scholar. Later on he became Bishop of Down and participated in many of the stirring events of his time. His death in 1667 found him working at what would perhaps have been his greatest book. Among those of his writings not yet mentioned, the *Liberty of Prophesying* and *The Great Exemplar* are doubtless the most important. It remains to add that the Greek passages of the text have been omitted here.*

---

* From *The Mysteriousness of Marriage.* By Jeremy Taylor. Cambridge: Francis Walterson, 1928.

THE MYSTERIOUSNESS OF MARRIAGE

This is a great mystery, but I speak concerning Christ and the Church. Nevertheless, let every one of you in particular so love his wife even as himself, and the wife sees that she reverence her husband.—EPHESIANS V. 32, 33.

HE first blessing God gave to man was society; and that society was a marriage, and that marriage was confederate by God himself, and hallowed by a blessing: and at the same time, and for very many descending ages, not only by the instinct of nature, but by a superadded forwardness (God himself inspiring the desire), the world was most desirous of children, impatient of barrenness, accounting single life a curse, and a childless person hated by God. The world was rich and empty, and able to provide for a more numerous posterity than it had. When a family could drive their herds, and set their children upon camels, and lead them till they saw a fat soil watered with rivers, and there sit down without paying rent, they thought of nothing but to have great families, that their own relations might swell up to a patriarchate, and their children be enough to possess all the regions that they saw, and their grandchildren become princes, and themselves build cities and call them by the name of a child, and become the fountain of a nation.

This was the consequent of the first blessing, "Increase and multiply." The next blessing was the promise of the Messiah; and that also increased in men and women a wonderful desire of marriage: for as soon as God had chosen the family of Abraham to be the blessed line from whence the world's Redeemer should descend according to the flesh, every of his daughters hoped to have the honor to be his mother, or his grandmother, or something of his kindred; and to be childless in Israel was a sorrow to the Hebrew women, great as the slavery of Egypt, or their dishonors in the land of their captivity.

But when the Messiah was come, and the doctrine was published, and his ministers but few, and his disciples were to suffer persecution, and to be of an unsettled dwelling, and the nation of the Jews, in the bosom and society of which the Church especially did dwell, were to be scattered and broken all in pieces with fierce calamities, and the world was apt to calumniate and to suspect and dishonor Christians upon pretences and unreasonable jealousies, and that to all these purposes the state of marriage brought many inconvenieces; it pleased God in this new creation to inspire into the hearts of his servants a disposition and strong desire to lead a single life, lest the state of marriage should in that conjunction of things become an accidental impediment to the dissemination of the gospel, which called men from a confinement in their domestic charges to travel, and flight, and poverty, and difficulty, and martyrdom. Upon this necessity the Apostles and apostolical men published doctrines, declaring the advantages of single life, not by any commandment of the Lord, but by the spirit of prudence, for the present and then incumbent necessities, and in order to the advantages which did accrue to the public ministries and private piety.

Upon this occasion it grew necessary for the Apostle to state the question right, and to do honor to the holy rite of marriage, and to snatch the mystery from the hands of zeal and folly, and to place it in Christ's right hand, that all its beauties might appear, and a present convenience might not bring in a false doctrine, and a perpetual sin, and an intolerable mischief.

Marriage is a school and exercise of virtue; and though marriage hath cares, yet the single life hath desires, which are more troublesome and more dangerous, and often end in sin, while the cares are but instances of duty and exercises of piety; and therefore, if single life hath more privacy of devotion, yet marriage hath more necessities and more variety of it, and is an exercise of more graces. Here is the proper scene of piety and patience, of the duty of parents and the charity of relatives; here kindness is spread abroad, and love is united and made firm as a centre. Marriage is the nursery of heaven; the virgin sends prayers to God, but she carries but one soul to Him; but the state of marriage fills up the numbers of the elect, and hath in it the labor of love and the delicacies of friendship, the blessing of society and the union of hands and hearts; it hath in it less of beauty, but more of safety, than the single life; it hath more care, but less danger; it is more merry, and more sad; is fuller of sorrows, and fuller of joys; it lies under more burdens, but is supported by all the strengths of love and charity, and those burdens are delightful.

Marriage is the mother of the world, and preserves kingdoms, and fills cities and churches, and heaven itself. Celibate, like the fly in the heart of an apple, dwells in a perpetual sweetness, but sits alone, and is confined and dies in singularity; but marriage, like the useful bee, builds a house, and gathers sweetness from every flower, and labors and unites into societies and republics, and sends out colonies, and feeds the world with delicacies, and obeys their king, and keeps order, and exercises many virtues, and promotes the interest of mankind, and is that state of good things to which God hath designed the present constitution of the world.

They that enter into the state of marriage, cast a die of the greatest contingency, and yet of the greatest interest in the world, next to the last throw for eternity. Life or death, felicity or a lasting sorrow, are in the power of marriage. A woman indeed ventures most, for she hath no sanctuary to retire to from an evil husband; she must dwell upon her sorrow, and hatch the eggs which her own folly or infelicity hath produced; and she is more under it, because her tormentor hath a warrant of prerogative; and the woman may complain to God as subjects do of tyrant princes, but otherwise she hath no appeal in the causes of unkindness. And though the man can run from many hours of his sadness, yet he must return to it again; and when he sits among his neighbors, he remembers the objection that lies in his bosom, and he sighs deeply. The boys, and the pedlers, and the fruiterers, shall tell of this man, when he is carried to his grave, that he lived and died a poor wretched person.

The stags in the Greek epigram, whose knees were clogged with frozen snow upon the mountains, came down to the brooks of the valleys, hoping to thaw their joints with the waters of the stream; but there the frost overtook them, and bound them fast in ice till the young herdsman took them in their stranger snare. It is the unhappy chance of many men, finding many inconveniences upon the mountains of single life, they descend into the valleys of marriage to refresh their troubles, and there they

enter into fetters, and are bound to sorrow by the cords of a
man's or woman's peevishness. And the worst of the evil is, they
are to thank their own follies; for they fell into the snare by
entering an improper way. Christ and the Church were no in-
gredients in their choice. But as the Indian women enter into
folly for the price of an elephant, and think their crime war-
rantable, so do men and women change their liberty for a rich
fortune (like Eriphyle the Argive, she preferred gold before a
good man), and show themselves to be less than money, by over-
valuing that to all the content and wise felicity of their lives:
and when they have counted the money and their sorrows together, how willingly would they buy, with the loss of all that
money, modesty, or sweet nature, to their relative! The odd
thousand pounds would gladly be allowed in good-nature and
fair manners.

As very a fool is he that chooses for beauty principally; *"cui
sunt eruditi oculi, et stulta mens"* (as one said), whose eyes are
witty, and their souls sensual. It is an ill band of affections to
tie two hearts together by a little thread of red and white. And
they can love no longer but until the next ague comes; and they
are fond of each other, but, at the chance of fancy, or the small-
pox, or childbearing, or care, or time, or anything that can destroy
a pretty flower.

Man and wife are equally concerned to avoid all offences of
each other in the beginning of their conversation. Every little
thing can blast an infant blossom; and the breath of the south
can shake the little rings of the vine, when first they begin to
curl like the locks of a new-weaned boy; but when by age and
consolidation they stiffen into the hardness of a stem, and have
by the warm embraces of the sun, and the kisses of heaven,
brought forth their clusters, they can endure the storms of the
north, and the loud noises of a tempest, and yet never be broken.
So are the early unions of an unfixed marriage; watchful and
observant, jealous and busy, inquisitive and careful, and apt to
take alarm at every unkind word. For infirmities do not manifest
themselves in the first scenes, but in the succession of a long
society; and it is not chance or weakness when it appears at
first, but it is want of love or prudence, or it will be so ex-
pounded; and that which appears ill at first, usually affrights

the inexperienced man or woman, who makes unequal conjectures, and fancies mighty sorrows by the proportions of the new and early unkindness. It is a very great passion, or a huge folly, or a certain want of love, that cannot preserve the colors and beauties of kindness so long as public honesty requires a man to wear their sorrows for the death of a friend.

Plutarch compares a new marriage to a vessel before the hoops are on; everything dissolves their tender compaginations: but when the joints are stiffened and are tied by a firm compliance and proportioned bending, scarcely can it be dissolved without fire or the violence of iron. After the hearts of the man and the wife are endeared and hardened by a mutual confidence, and experience longer than artifice and pretence can last, there are a great many remembrances, and some things present, that dash all little unkindnesses in pieces. The little boy in the Greek epigram, that was creeping down a precipice, was invited to his safety by the sight of his mother's pap, when nothing else could entice him to return: and the bond of common children, and the sight of her that nurses which is most dear to him, and the endearments of each other in the course of a long society, and the same relation, is an excellent security to redintegrate and to call that love back, which folly and trifling accidents would disturb. When it is come thus far, it is hard untwisting the knot; but be careful in its first coalition that there be no rudeness done; for if there be, it will forever after be apt to start and to be diseased.

Let man and wife be careful to stifle little things, that as fast as they spring they be cut down and trod upon; for if they be suffered to grow by numbers, they make the spirit peevish, and the society troublesome, and the affections loose and easy by an habitual aversation. Some men are more vexed with a fly than with a wound; and when the gnats disturb our sleep, and the reason is disquieted, but not perfectly awakened, it is often seen that he is fuller of trouble than if, in the daylight of his reason, he were to contest with a potent enemy. In the frequent little accidents of a family, a man's reason cannot always be awake; and when his discourses are imperfect, and a trifling trouble makes him yet more restless, he is soon betrayed to the violence of passion. It is certain that the man or woman are ·in a state of weakness and folly then, when they can be troubled with a trifling accident; and therefore it is not good to tempt their affections when they are in that state of danger. In this case the caution is, to subtract fuel from the sudden flame; for stubble, though it be quickly kindled, yet it is soon extinguished, if it be not blown by a pertinacious breath, or fed with new materials. Add no new provocations to the accident, and do not inflame this, and peace will soon return, and the discontent will pass away soon, as the sparks from the collision of a flint; ever remembering, that discontents proceeding from daily little things do breed a secret undiscernible disease, which is more dangerous than a fever proceeding from a discerned notorious surfeit.

Let them be sure to abstain from all those things which by experience and observation they find to be contrary to each other. They that govern elephants, never appear before them in white; and the masters of bulls keep from them all garments of blood and scarlet, as knowing that they will be impatient of civil usages and discipline when their natures are provoked by their proper antipathies. The ancients in their marital hieroglyphics used to depict Mercury standing by Venus, to signify that by fair language and sweet entreaties the minds of each other should be united; and hard by them, *"suadam et gratias discripserunt,"* they would have all deliciousness of manners, compliance and mutual observance to abide.

Let the husband and wife infinitely avoid a curious distinction of mine and thine; for this hath caused all the laws, and all the suits, and all the wars in the world. Let them who have but one person have also but one interest. Corvinus dwells in a farm and receives all its profits, and reaps and sows as he pleases, and eats of the corn and drinks of the wine; it is his own: but all that also is his lord's, and for it Corvinus pays acknowledgment; and his patron hath such powers and uses of it as are proper to the lords; and yet for all this, it may be the king's too, to all the purposes that he can need, and is all to be accounted in the census, and for certain services and times of danger. So are the riches of a family; they are a woman's as well as a man's; they are hers for need, and hers for ornament, and hers for modest delight, and for the uses of religion and prudent charity: but the disposing them into portions of inheritance, the assignation of charges and governments, stipends and rewards, annuities and greater donatives, are the reserves of the superior right, and not to be invaded by the under-possessors.

As the earth, the mother of all creatures here below, sends up all its vapors and proper emissions at the command of the sun, and yet requires them again to refresh her own needs, and they are deposited between them both, in the bosom of a cloud, as a common receptacle, that they may cool his flames, and yet descend to make her fruitful: so are the proprieties of a wife to be disposed of by her lord; and yet all are for her provision, it being a part of his need to refresh and supply hers, and it serves the interest of both while it serves the necessities of either.

These are the duties of them both, which have common regards and equal necessities and obligations; and indeed there is scarce any matter of duty, but it concerns them both alike, and is only distinguished by names, and hath its variety by circumstances and little accidents: and what in one is called love, in the other is called reverence; and what in the wife is obedience, the same in the man is duty. He provides, and she dispenses; he gives commandments, and she rules by them; he rules her by authority, and she rules him by love; she ought by all means to please him, and he must by no means displease her. For as the heart is set in the midst of the body, and though it strikes to one side by the prerogative of nature, yet those throbs and constant motions are felt on the other side also, and the influence is equal to both: so it is in conjugal duties; some motions are to the one side more than to the other, but the interest is on both, and the duty is equal in the several instances.

The next inquiry is more particular, and considers the power and duty of the man. "Let every one of you so love his wife, even as himself"; she is as himself, the man hath power over her as over himself, and must love her equally. A husband's power over his wife is paternal and friendly, not magisterial and despotic. The wife is *"in perpetuâ tutelâ,"* under conduct and counsel; for the power a man hath is founded in the understanding, not in the will or force; it is not a power of coercion, but a power of advice, and that government that wise men have over those who are fit to be conducted by them. Thou art to be a father and a mother to her, and a brother: and great reason, unless the state of marriage should be no better than the condition of an orphan. For she that is bound to leave father and mother and brother for thee, either is miserable, like a poor fatherless child, or else ought to find all these, and more, in thee.

The dominion of a man over his wife is no other than as the soul rules the body; for which it takes a mighty care, and uses it with a delicate tenderness, and cares for it in all contingencies, and watches to keep it from all evils, and studies to make for it fair provisions, and very often is led by its inclinations and desires, and does never contradict its appetites but when they are evil, and then also not without some trouble and sorrow; and its government comes only to this: it furnishes the body with light and understanding, and the body furnishes the soul with hands and feet; the soul governs because the body cannot else be happy, but the government is no other than provision; as a nurse governs a child when she causes him to eat, and to be warm, and dry, and quiet. And yet even the very government itself is divided; for man and wife in the family are as the sun and moon in the firmament of heaven; he rules by day, and she by night, that is, in the lesser and more proper circles of her affairs, in the conduct of domestic provisions and necessary offices, and shines only by his light, and rules by his authority. And as the moon in opposition to the sun shines brightest, that is, then when she is in her own circles and separate regions, so is the authority of the wife then most conspicuous when she is separate and in her proper sphere; *"in gynæceo,"* in the nursery and offices of domestic employment. But when she is in conjunction with the sun her brother, that is, in that place and employment in which his care and proper offices are employed, her light is not seen, her authority hath no proper business. But else there is no difference; for they were barbarous people among whom wives were instead of servants; and it is a sign of impotency and weakness to force the camels to kneel for their load, because thou hast not spirit and strength enough to climb: to make the affections and evenness of a wife bend by the flexures of a servant, is a sign the man is not wise enough to govern when another stands by. And as amongst men and women humility is the way to be preferred, so it is in husbands; they shall prevail by cession, by sweetness and counsel, and charity and compliance. So that we

cannot discourse of the man's right without describing the measures of his duty; that, therefore, follows next.

"Let him love his wife even as himself":—that is his duty,
and the measure of it too; which is so plain, that, if he understands how he treats himself, there needs nothing be added concerning his demeanor towards her, save only that we add the
particulars in which holy Scripture instances this general commandment.

The first is, "Be not bitter against her"; and this is the least
index and signification of love; a civil man is never bitter against
a friend or a stranger, much less to him that enters under his
roof, and is secured by the laws of hospitality. But a wife does
all that and more: she quits all her interest for his love; she
gives him all that she can give; she is much the same person as
another can be the same, who is conjoined by love and mystery
and religion, and all that is sacred and profane. They have the
same fortune, the same family, the same children, the same
religion, the same interest, the same flesh; and therefore the
Apostle urges, "No man hateth his own flesh, but nourisheth and
cherisheth it"; and he certainly is strangely sacrilegious and a
violator of the rights of hospitality and sanctuary, who uses her
rudely, who is fled for protection not only to his house, but also
to his heart and bosom.

There is nothing can please a man without love; and if a
man be weary of the wise discourses of the Apostles, and of
the innocency of an even and a private fortune, or hates peace
or a fruitful year, he hath reaped thorns and thistles from the
choicest flowers of paradise; for nothing can sweeten felicity
itself, but love. But when a man dwells in love, then the breasts
of his wife are pleasant as the droppings upon the hill of Hermon, her eyes are fair as the light of heaven, she is a fountain
sealed, and he can quench his thirst, and ease his cares, and lay
his sorrow down upon her lap, and can retire home as to his
sanctuary and refectory, and his gardens of sweetness and chaste
refreshments.

No man can tell but he that loves his children, how many
delicious accents make a man's heart dance in the pretty conversation of those dear pledges; their childishness, their stammering,
their little angers, their innocence, their imperfections, their neces-

sities, are so many little emanations of joy and comfort to him that delights in their persons and society. But he that loves not his wife and children feeds a lioness at home, and broods a nest of sorrows; and blessing itself cannot make him happy: so that all the commandments of God enjoining a man to love his wife are nothing but so many necessities and capacities of joy. She that is loved is safe, and he that loves is joyful.

The husband should nourish and cherish her; he should refresh her sorrows and entice her fears into confidence and pretty arts of rest. But it will concern the prudence of the husband's love to make the cares and evils as simple and easy as he can, by doubling the joys and acts of a careful friendship, by tolerating her infirmities (because by so doing he either cures her, or makes himself better,) by fairly expounding all the little traverses of society and communication, by taking everything by the right handle, as Plutarch's expression is; for there is nothing but may be misinterpreted; and yet if it be capable of a fair construction, it is the office of love to make it. Love will account that to be well said which, it may be, was not so intended; and then it may cause it to be so, another time.

Hither also is to be referred that he secure the interest of her virtue and felicity by a fair example; for a wife to a husband is a line or superficies—it hath dimensions of its own, but no motion or proper affections; but commonly puts on such images of virtues or vices as are presented to her by her husband's idea: and if thou beest vicious, complain not that she is infected that lies in thy bosom; the interest of whose love ties her to transcribe thy copy, and write after the character of thy manners. Paris was a man of pleasure, and Helena was an adulteress, and she added covetousness upon her own account. But Ulysses was a prudent man, and a wary counsellor, sober and severe; and he efformed his wife into such imagery as he desired; and she was chaste as the snows upon the mountains, diligent as the fatal sisters, always busy, and always faithful; she had a lazy tongue and a busy hand.

Above all the instances of love let him preserve towards her an inviolable faith, and an unspotted chastity; for this is the marriage-ring; it ties two hearts by an eternal band; it is like the cherubim's flaming sword, set for the guard of paradise;

he that passes into that garden, now that it is immured by Christ and the Church, enters into the shades of death. No man must touch the forbidden tree, that in the midst of the garden, which is the tree of knowledge and life. Chastity is the security of love, and preserves all the mysteriousness like the secrets of a temple. Under this lock is deposited security of families, the union of affections, the repairer of accidental breaches. This is a grace that is shut up and secured by all arts of heaven and the defence of laws, the locks and bars of modesty, by honor and reputation, by fear and shame, by interest and high regards; and that contract that is intended to be forever is yet dissolved and broken by the violation of this. Nothing but death can do so much evil to the holy rites of marriage as unchastity and breach of faith can; and by the laws of the Romans a man might kill his daughter or his wife, if he surprised her in the breach of her holy vows, which are as sacred as the threads of life, secret as the privacies of the sanctuary, and holy as the society of angels. God that commanded us to forgive our enemies left it in our choice, and hath not commanded us to forgive an adulterous husband or a wife; but the offended party's displeasure may pass into an eternal separation of society and friendship. Now in this grace it is fit that the wisdom and severity of the man should hold forth a pure taper, that his wife may, by seeing the beauties and transparency of that crystal, dress her mind and her body by the light of so pure reflections. It is certain he will expect it from the modesty and retirement, from the passive nature and colder temper, from the humility and fear, from the honor and love, of his wife, that she be pure as the eye of heaven: and therefore it is but reason that the wisdom and nobleness, the love and confidence, the strength and severity of the man should be as holy and certain in this grace as he is a severe exactor of it at her hands, who can more easily be tempted by another, and less by herself.

These are the little lines of a man's duty, which, like threads of light from the body of the sun, do clearly describe all the regions of his proper obligations. Now, concerning the woman's duty, although it consists in doing whatsoever her husband commands, and so receives measures from the rules of his government, yet there are also some lines of life depicted upon her hands, by which she may read and know how to proportion out her duty to her husband.

The first is obedience. The man's authority is love, and the woman's love is obedience; for this obedience is no way founded in fear, but in love and reverence. We will add, that it is an effect of that modesty which, like rubies, adorns the necks and cheeks of women. It is modesty to advance and highly to honor them who have honored us by making us to be the companions of their dearest excellencies; for the woman that went before the man in the way of death, is commanded to follow him in the way of love; and that makes the society to be perfect, and the union profitable, and the harmony complete. A wife never can become equal but by obeying. A ruling woman is intolerable. But that is not all; for she is miserable, too: for it is a sad calamity for a woman to be joined to a fool or a weak person; it is like a guard of geese to keep the capitol; or as if a flock of sheep should read grave lectures to their shepherd, and give him orders when she shall conduct them to pasture. To be ruled by weaker people, to have a fool to one's master, is the fate of miserable and unblessed people: and the wife can be no ways happy unless she be governed by a prudent lord, whose commands are sober counsels, whose authority is paternal, whose orders are provisions, and whose sentences are charity.

The next line of the woman's duty is compliance, which St. Peter calls "the hidden man of the heart, the ornament of a meek and a quiet spirit"; and to it he opposes "the outward and pompous ornament of the body"; concerning which, as there can be no particular measure set down to all persons, but the proportions were to be measured by the customs of wise people, the quality of the woman, and the desires of the man; yet it is to be limited by Christian modesty and the usages of the more excellent and severe matrons. Menander in the comedy brings in a man turning his wife from his house because she stained her hair yellow, which was then the beauty. A wise woman should not paint. A studious gallantry in clothes cannot make a wise man love his wife the better. Such gayeties are fit for tragedies, but not for the uses of life. *"Decor occultus, et tecta venustas"*; that is the Christian woman's fineness, the hidden man of the heart, sweetness of manners, humble comportment, fair interpretation of all addresses, ready compliances, high opinion of him, and mean of herself.

To partake secretly, and in her heart, of all his joys and sorrows; to believe him comely and fair, though the sun hath drawn a cypress over him; (for as marriages are not to be contracted by the hands and eye, but with reason and the hearts, so are these judgments to be made by the mind, not by the sight); and diamonds cannot make the woman virtuous, nor him to value her who sees her put them off, then, when charity and modesty are her brightest ornaments.

And indeed those husbands that are pleased with indecent gayeties of their wives, are like fishes taken with ointments and intoxicating baits, apt and easy for sport and mockery, but useless for food; and when Circe had turned Ulysses's companions into hogs and monkeys, by pleasures and the enchantments of her bravery and luxury, they were no longer useful to her, she knew not what to do with them; but of wise Ulysses she was continually enamoured. Indeed the outward ornament is fit to take fools, but they are not worth the taking; but she that hath a wise husband must entice him to an eternal dearness by the veil of modesty, and the grave robes of chastity, the ornament of meekness, and the jewels of faith and charity: she must have no *"fucus"* but blushings; her brightness must be purity, and she must shine round about with sweetnesses and friendship, and she shall be pleasant while she lives, and desired when she dies. If not, her grave shall be full of rottenness and dishonor, and her memory shall be worse after she is dead: "after she is dead"; for that will be the end of all merry meetings; and I choose this to be the last advice to both.

Remember the days of darkness, for they are many; the joys of the bridal chambers are quickly past, and the remaining portion of the state is a dull progress, without variety of joys, but not without the change of sorrows; but that portion that shall enter into the grave must be eternal. It is fit that I should infuse a bunch of myrrh into the festival goblet, and after the Egyptian manner serve up a dead man's bones at a feast; I will only show it, and take it away again; it will make the wine bitter, but wholesome. But those married pairs that live, as remembering that they must part again, and give an account how they treat themselves and each other, shall at that day of their death be admitted to glorious espousals; and then they shall live again, be married to their Lord, and partake of his glories, with Abraham and Joseph, St. Peter and St. Paul, and all the married saints.

All those things that now please us shall pass from us, or we from them; but those things that concern the other life are permanent as the numbers of eternity: and although at the resurrection there shall be no relation of husband and wife, and no marriage shall be celebrated but the marriage of the Lamb; yet then shall be remembered how men and women passed through this state, which is a type of that; and from this sacramental union all holy pairs shall pass to the spiritual and eternal, where love shall be their portion, and joys shall crown their heads, and they shall lie in the bosom of Jesus, and in the heart of God to eternal ages.

4. WILLIAM LAW:

FROM *A SERIOUS CALL TO A DEVOUT AND HOLY LIFE*

¶WHEN William Law published his *Serious Call* in 1728, the religious life of England was at a low ebb. Rationalism and skepticism were in the ascendancy. The book immediately made a profound impression, Dr. Samuel Johnson telling his friends that reading it was the occasion of his first "thinking in earnest of religion after he became capable of rational inquiry." Almost every spiritual leader for generations thereafter learned to know and love the book. Thus we find Newman as a young man aided and influenced by it. And though John Wesley parted with Law, it is likely enough that both gave impetus to that movement of religious awakening which was to be termed Methodism.

The value of the *Serious Call* lies in the remarkable skill with which rational and mystical conceptions of the Christian life are blended. Later on Law himself was more definitely drawn to the mystics, becoming the leading English protagonist of the German "cobbler seer" Jakob Boehme. Of Law's other books, *The Way to Divine Knowledge* probably has the greatest appeal for the present time. The section reprinted here constitutes Chapter XI of the *Serious Call.**

---

* From *A Serious Call to a Devout and Holy Life*. By William Law. London: J. M. Dent, 1906.

A SERIOUS CALL TO A DEVOUT AND HOLY LIFE

OME people will perhaps object, that all these rules of holy living unto God in all that we do, are too great a restraint upon human life; that it will be made too anxious a state, by thus introducing a regard to God in all our actions; and that by depriving ourselves of so many seemingly innocent pleasures, we shall render our lives dull, uneasy, and melancholy.

To which it may be answered,

First, That these rules are prescribed for, and will certainly procure a quite contrary end. That instead of making our lives dull and melancholy, they will render them full of content and strong satisfactions. That by these rules, we only change the childish satisfactions of our vain and sickly passions, for the solid enjoyments and real happiness of a sound mind.

Secondly, That as there is no foundation for comfort in the enjoyments of this life, but in the assurance that a wise and good God governeth the world, so the more we find out God in every thing, the more we apply to Him in every place, the more we look up to Him in all our actions, the more we conform to His will, the more we act according to His wisdom, and imitate His goodness, by so much the more do we enjoy God, partake of the Divine nature, and heighten and increase all that is happy and comfortable in human life.

Thirdly, He that is endeavouring to subdue, and root out of his mind all those passions of pride, envy, and ambition, which religion opposes, is doing more to make himself happy, even in this life, than he that is contriving means to indulge them. For these passions are the causes of all the disquiets and vexations of human life: they are the dropsies and fevers of our minds, vexing them with false appetites, and restless cravings after such things as we do not want, and spoiling our taste for those things which are our proper good.

Do but imagine that you somewhere or other saw a man that proposed reason as the rule of all his actions; that had no desires but after such things as nature wants, and religion approves;

that was as pure from all the motions of pride, envy, and covetousness, as from thoughts of murder; that, in this freedom from worldly passions, he had a soul full of Divine love, wishing and praying that all men may have what they want of worldly things, and be partakers of eternal glory in the life to come. Do but fancy a man living in this manner, and your own conscience will immediately tell you, that he is the happiest man in the world, and that it is not in the power of the richest fancy to invent any higher happiness in the present state of life.

And, on the other hand, if you suppose him to be in any degree less perfect; if you suppose him but subject to one foolish fondness or vain passion, your own conscience will again tell you that he so far lessens his own happiness, and robs himself of the true enjoyment of his other virtues. So true is it, that the more we live by the rules of religion, the more peaceful and happy do we render our lives.

Again; as it thus appears that real happiness is only to be had from the greatest degrees of piety, the greatest denials of our passions, and the strictest rules of religion; so the same truth will appear from a consideration of human misery. If we look into the world, and view the disquiets and troubles of human life, we shall find that they are all owing to our violent and irreligious passions.

Now all trouble and uneasiness is founded in the want of something or other: would we, therefore, know the true cause of our troubles and disquiets, we must find out the cause of our wants; because that which creates and increaseth our wants, does, in the same degree, create and increase our troubles and disquiets.

God Almighty has sent us into the world with very few wants; meat, and drink, and clothing, are the only things necessary in life; and as these are only our present needs, so the present world is well furnished to supply these needs.

If a man had half the world in his power, he can make no more of it than this; as he wants it only to support an animal life, so is it unable to do any thing else for him, or to afford him any other happiness.

This is the state of man,—born with few wants, and into a large world very capable of supplying them. So that one would reasonably suppose that men should pass their lives in content and thankfulness to God; at least, that they should be free from violent disquiets and vexations, as being placed in a world that has more than enough to relieve all their wants.

But if to all this we add, that this short life, thus furnished with all that we want in it, is only a short passage to eternal glory, where we shall be clothed with the brightness of Angels, and enter into the joys of God, we might still more reasonably expect that human life should be a state of peace, and joy, and delight in God. Thus it would certainly be, if reason had its full power over us.

But, alas! though God, and nature, and reason, make human life thus free from wants and so full of happiness; yet our passions, in rebellion against God, against nature and reason, create a new world of evils, and fill human life with imaginary wants, and vain disquiets.

The man of pride has a thousand wants, which only his own pride has created; and these render him as full of trouble as if God had created him with a thousand appetites, without creating any thing that was proper to satisfy them. Envy and ambition have also their endless wants, which disquiet the souls of men, and by their contradictory motions, render them as foolishly miserable, as those that want to fly and creep at the same time.

Let but any complaining, disquieted man, tell you the ground of his uneasiness, and you will plainly see that he is the author of his own torment; that he is vexing himself at some imaginary evil, which will cease to torment him as soon as he is content to be that which God, and nature, and reason, require him to be.

If you should see a man passing his days in disquiet, because he could not walk upon the water, or catch birds as they fly by him, you would readily confess that such a one might thank himself for such uneasiness. But now if you look into all the most tormenting disquiets of life, you will find them all thus absurd: where people are only tormented by their own folly, and vexing themselves at such things as no more concern them, nor are any more their proper good, than walking upon the water or catching birds.

What can you conceive more silly and extravagant, than to suppose a man racking his brains, and studying night and day how to fly?—wandering from his own house and home, wearying himself with climbing upon every ascent, cringing and courting everybody he meets to lift him up from the ground, bruising himself with continual falls, and at last breaking his neck?—— and all this from an imagination that it would be glorious to have the eyes of people gazing up at him, and mighty happy to eat, and drink, and sleep, at the top of the highest trees in the kingdom: would you not readily own that such a one was only disquieted by his own folly?

If you ask, what it signifies to suppose such silly creatures as these, as are nowhere to be found in human life?

It may be answered, that wherever you see an ambitious man, there you see this vain and senseless flyer.

Again: if you should see a man that had a large pond of water, yet living in continual thirst, not suffering himself to drink half a draught, for fear of lessening his pond; if you should see him wasting his time and strength, in fetching more water to his pond; always thirsty, yet always carrying a bucket of water in his hand, watching early and late to catch the drops of rain, gaping after every cloud, and running greedily into every mire and mud, in hopes of water, and always studying how to make every ditch empty itself into his pond: if you should see him grow grey and old in these anxious labours, and at last end a careful, thirsty life, by falling into his own pond; would you not say that such a one was not only the author of all his own disquiets, but was foolish enough to be reckoned amongst idiots and madmen? But yet foolish and absurd as this character is, it does not represent half the follies, and absurd disquiets, of the covetous man.

I could now easily proceed to show the same effects of all our other passions, and make it plainly appear that all our miseries, vexations, and complaints, are entirely of our own making, and that, in the same absurd manner, as in these instances of the covetous and ambitious man. Look where you will, you will see all worldly vexations, but like the vexation of him that was always in mire and mud in search of water to drink, when he had more at home than was sufficient for a hundred horses.

Cælia is always telling you how provoked she is, what intolerable, shocking things happen to her, what monstrous usage she suffers, and what vexations she meets with everywhere. She tells you that her patience is quite worn out, and there is no bearing the behaviour of people. Every assembly that she is at, sends her home provoked; something or other has been said, or done, that no reasonable, well-bred person ought to bear. Poor people that want her charity are sent away with hasty answers, not because she has not a heart to part with any money, but because she is too full of some trouble of her own to attend to the complaints of others. Cælia has no business upon her hands but to receive the income of a plentiful fortune; but yet, by the doleful turn of her mind, you would be apt to think that she had neither food nor lodging. If you see her look more pale than ordinary, if her lips tremble when she speaks to you, it is because she is just come from a visit, where Lupus took no notice at all of her, but talked all the time to Lucinda, who has not half her fortune. When cross accidents have so disordered her spirits, that she is forced to send for the doctor, to make her able to eat, she tells him in great anger at Providence, that she never was well since she was born, and that she envies every beggar that she sees in health.

This is the disquiet life of Cælia, who has nothing to torment her but her own spirit.

If you could inspire her with Christian humility, you need do no more to make her as happy as any person in the world. This virtue would make her thankful to God for half so much health as she has had, and help her to enjoy more for the time to come. This virtue would keep off tremblings of the spirits, and loss of appetite, and her blood would need nothing else to sweeten it.

I have just touched upon these absurd characters, for no other end but to convince you, in the plainest manner, that the strictest rules of religion are so far from rendering a life dull, anxious, and uncomfortable (as is above objected), that, on the contrary, all the miseries, vexations, and complaints, that are in the world, are owing to the want of religion; being directly caused by those absurd passions which religion teaches us to deny.

For all the wants which disturb human life, which make us uneasy to ourselves, quarrelsome with others, and unthankful to God; which weary us in vain labours and foolish anxieties; which carry us from project to project, from place to place, in a poor pursuit of we know not what, are the wants which neither God, nor nature, nor reason, hath subjected us to, but are solely infused into us by pride, envy, ambition, and covetousness.

So far, therefore, as you reduce your desires to such things as nature and reason require; so far as you regulate all the motions of your heart by the strict rules of religion, so far you remove yourself from that infinity of wants and vexations, which torment every heart that is left to itself.

Most people, indeed, confess that religion preserves us from a great many evils, and helps us in many respects to a more happy enjoyment of ourselves; but then they imagine that this is only true of such a moderate share of religion, as only gently restrains us from the excesses of our passions. They suppose that the strict rules and restraints of an exalted piety are such contradictions to our nature, as much needs make our lives dull and uncomfortable.

Although the weakness of this objection sufficiently appears from what hath been already said, yet I shall add one word more to it.

This objection supposes that religion, moderately practised, adds much to the happiness of life; but that such heights of piety as the perfection of religion requireth, have a contrary effect.

It supposes, therefore, that it is happy to be kept from the excesses of envy, but unhappy to be kept from other degrees of envy. That it is happy to be delivered from a boundless ambition, but unhappy to be without a more moderate ambition. It supposes, also, that the happiness of life consists in a mixture of virtue and vice, a mixture of ambition and humility, charity and envy, heavenly affection and covetousness. All which is as absurd as to suppose that it is happy to be free from excessive pains, but unhappy to be without more moderate pains; or that the happiness of health consisted in being partly sick and partly well.

For if humility be the peace and rest of the soul, then no one has so much happiness from humility, as he that is the most humble. If excessive envy is a torment of the soul, he most perfectly delivers himself from torment, that most perfectly extinguishes every spark of envy. If there is any peace and joy in doing any action according to the will of God, he that brings the most of his actions to this rule, does most of all increase the peace and joy of his life.

And thus it is in every virtue; if you act up to every degree of it, the more happiness you have from it. And so of every vice; if you only abate its excesses, you do but little for yourself; but if you reject it in all degrees, then you feel the true ease and joy of a reformed mind.

As for example: If religion only restrains the excesses of revenge, but lets the spirit still live within you in lesser instances, your religion may have made your life a little more outwardly decent, but not made you at all happier, or easier in yourself. But if you have once sacrified all thoughts of revenge, in obedience to God, and are resolved to return good for evil at all times, that you may render yourself more like to God, and fitter for His mercy in the kingdom of love and glory; this is a height of virtue that will make you feel its happiness.

Secondly, As to those satisfactions and enjoyments, which an exalted piety requireth us to deny ourselves, this deprives us of no real comfort of life.

For, 1st, Piety requires us to renounce no ways of life, where we can act reasonably, and offer what we do to the glory of God. All ways of life, all satisfactions and enjoyments, that are within these bounds, are no way denied us by the strictest rules of piety. Whatever you can do, or enjoy, as in the presence of God, as His servant, as His rational creature that has received reason and knowledge from Him; all that you can perform conformably to a rational nature, and the will of God, all this is allowed by the laws of piety. And will you think that your life will be uncomfortable unless you may displease God, be a fool, and mad, and act contrary to that reason and wisdom which He has implanted in you?

And as for those satisfactions which we dare not offer to a holy God, which are only invented by the folly and corruption of the world, which inflame our passions, and sink our souls into grossness and sensuality, and render us incapable of the Divine favour, either here or hereafter; surely it can be no uncomfortable state of life to be rescued by religion from such self-murder, and to be rendered capable of eternal happiness.

Let us suppose a person destitute of that knowledge which we have from our senses, placed somewhere alone by himself, in the midst of a variety of things which he did not know how to use; that he has by him bread, wine, water, golden dust, iron chains, gravel, garments, fire, etc. Let it be supposed that he has no knowledge of the right use of these things, nor any direction from his senses how to quench his thirst, or satisfy his hunger, or make any use of the things about him. Let it be supposed, that in his drought he puts golden dust into his eyes; when his eyes smart, he puts wine into his ears; that in his hunger, he puts gravel into his mouth; that in pain, he loads himself with the iron chains; that feeling cold, he puts his feet in the water; that being frighted at the fire, he runs away from it; that being weary, he makes a seat of his bread. Let it be supposed, that through his ignorance of the right use of the things that are about him, he will vainly torment himself whilst he lives, and at last die, blinded with dust, choked with gravel, and loaded with irons. Let it be supposed that some good being came to him, and showed him the nature and use of all the things that were about him, and gave him such strict rules of using them, as would certainly, if observed, make him the happier for all that he had, and deliver him from the pains of hunger, and thirst, and cold.

Now could you with any reason affirm, that those strict rules of using those things that were about him, had rendered that poor man's life dull and uncomfortable?

Now this is in some measure a representation of the strict rules of religion; they only relieve our ignorance, save us from tormenting ourselves, and teach us to use everything about us to our proper advantage.

Man is placed in a world full of variety of things; his ignorance makes him use many of them as absurdly as the man that put dust in his eyes to relieve his thirst, or put on chains to remove pain.

Religion, therefore, here comes in to his relief, and gives him strict rules of using everything that is about him; that by so using them suitably to his own nature, and the nature of the things, he may have always the pleasure of receiving a right benefit from them. It shows him what is strictly right in meat, and drink, and clothes; and that he has nothing else to expect from the things of this world, but to satisfy such wants of his own; and then to extend his assistance to all his brethren, that, as far as he is able, he may help all his fellow-creatures to the same benefit from the world that he hath.

It tells him that this world is incapable of giving him any other happiness; and that all endeavours to be happy in heaps of money, or acres of land, in fine clothes, rich beds, stately equipage, and show and splendour, are only vain endeavours, ignorant attempts after impossibilities, these things being no more able to give the least degree of happiness, than dust in the eyes can cure thirst, or gravel in the mouth satisfy hunger; but, like dust and gravel misapplied, will only serve to render him more unhappy by such an ignorant misuse of them.

It tells him that although this world can do no more for him than satisfy these wants of the body, yet that there is a much greater good prepared for man than eating, drinking, and dressing; that it is yet invisible to his eyes, being too glorious for the apprehension of flesh and blood; but reserved for him to enter upon, as soon as this short life is over; where, in a new body formed to an angelic likeness, he shall dwell in the light and glory of God to all eternity.

It tells him that this state of glory will be given to all those that make a right use of the things of this present world, who do not blind themselves with golden dust, or eat gravel, or groan under loads of iron of their own putting on; but use bread, water, wine, and garments, for such ends as are according to nature and reason; and who, with faith and thankfulness, worship the kind Giver of all that they enjoy here, and hope for hereafter.

Now can any one say that the strictest rules of such a religion as this debar us of any of the comforts of life? Might it not as justly be said of those rules that only hinder a man from choking himself with gravel? For the strictness of these rules only consists in the exactness of their rectitude.

Who would complain of the severe strictness of a law that, without any exception, forbad the putting of dust into our eyes? Who could think it too rigid, that there were no abatements? Now this is the strictness of religion; it requires nothing of us strictly, or without abatements, but where every degree of the thing is wrong, where every indulgence does us some hurt.

If religion forbids all instances of revenge, without any exception, it is because all revenge is of the nature of poison; and though we do not take so much as to put an end to life, yet if we take any at all, it corrupts the whole mass of blood, and makes it difficult to be restored to our former health.

If religion commands an universal charity, to love our neighbour as ourselves, to forgive and pray for all our enemies without any reserve; it is because all degrees of love are degrees of happiness, that strengthen and support the Divine life of the soul, and are as necessary to its health and happiness, as proper food is necessary to the health and happiness of the body.

If religion has laws against laying up treasures upon earth, and commands us to be content with food and raiment, it is because every other use of the world is abusing it to our own vexation, and turning all its conveniences into snares and traps to destroy us. It is because this plainness and simplicity of life secures us from the cares and pains of restless pride and envy, and makes it easier to keep that straight road that will carry us to eternal life.

If religion saith, "Sell that thou hast, and give to the poor," it is because there is no other natural or reasonable use of our riches, no other way of making ourselves happier for them; it is because it is as strictly right to give others that which we do not want ourselves, as it is right to use so much as our own wants require. For if a man has more food than his own nature requires, how base and unreasonable is it to invent foolish ways of wasting it, and make sport for his own full belly, rather than let his fellow-creatures have the same comfort from food which he hath had. It is so far, therefore, from being a hard law of religion, to make this use of our riches, that a reasonable man would rejoice in that religion which teaches him to be happier in that which he gives away, than in that which he keeps for himself; which teaches him to make spare food and raiment be greater blessings to him, than that which feeds and clothes his own body.

If religion requires us sometimes to fast, and deny our natural appetites, it is to lessen that struggle and war that is in our nature, it is to render our bodies fitter instruments of purity, and more obedient to the good motions of Divine grace; it is to dry up the springs of our passions that war against the soul, to cool the flame of our blood, and render the mind more capable of Divine meditations. So that although these abstinences give some pain to the body, yet they so lessen the power of bodily appetites and passions, and so increase our taste of spiritual joys, that even these severities of religion, when practised with discretion, add much to the comfortable enjoyment of our lives.

If religion calleth us to a life of watching and prayer it is because we live amongst a crowd of enemies, and are always in need of the assistance of God. If we are to confess and bewail our sins, it is because such confessions relieve the mind, and restore it to ease; as burdens and weights taken off the shoulders, relieve the body, and make it easier to itself. If we are to be frequent and fervent in holy petitions, it is to keep us steady in the sight of our true God, and that we may never want the happiness of a lively faith, a joyful hope, and well-grounded trust in God. If we are to pray often, it is that we may be often happy in such secret joys as only prayer can give; in such communications of the Divine Presence, as will fill our minds with all the happiness that beings not in Heaven are capable of.

Was there anything in the world more worth our care, was there any exercise of the mind, or any conversation with men, that turned more to our advantage than this intercourse with God, we should not be called to such a continuance in prayer. But if a man considers what it is that he leaves when he retires to devotion, he will find it no small happiness to be so often relieved from doing nothing, or nothing to the purpose; from dull idleness, unprofitable labour, or vain conversation. If he considers that all that is in the world, and all that is doing in it, is only for the body, and bodily enjoyments, he will have reason to rejoice at those hours of prayer, which carry him to higher consolations, which raise him above these poor concerns, which open to his mind a scene of greater things, and accustom his soul to the hope and expectation of them.

If religion commands us to live wholly unto God, and to do all to His glory, it is because every other way is living wholly against ourselves, and will end in our own shame and confusion of face.

As everything is dark, that God does not enlighten; as everything is senseless, that has not its share of knowledge from Him;

as nothing lives, but by partaking of life from Him; as nothing exists, but because He commands it to be; so there is no glory or greatness, but what is of the glory and greatness of God.

We indeed may talk of human glory as we may talk of human life, or human knowledge: but as we are sure that human life implies nothing of our own but a dependent living in God, or enjoying so much life in God; so human glory, whenever we find it, must be only so much glory as we enjoy in the glory of God.

This is the state of all creatures, whether men or Angels; as they make not themselves, so they enjoy nothing from themselves: if they are great, it must be only as great receivers of the gifts of God; their power can only be so much of the Divine power acting in them; their wisdom can be only so much of the Divine wisdom shining within them; and their light and glory, only so much of the light and glory of God shining upon them.

As they are not men or Angels, because they had a mind to be so themselves, but because the will of God formed them to be what they are; so they cannot enjoy this or that happiness of men or Angels, because they have a mind to it, but because it is the will of God that such things be the happiness of men, and such things the happiness of Angels. But now if God be thus all in all; if His will is thus the measure of all things, and all natures; if nothing can be done, but by His power; if nothing can be seen, but by a light from Him; if we have nothing to fear, but from His justice; if we have nothing to hope for, but from His goodness; if this is the nature of man, thus helpless in himself; if this is the state of all creatures, as well those in Heaven as those on earth; if they are nothing, can do nothing, can suffer no pain, nor feel any happiness, but so far, and in such degrees, as the power of God does all this; if this be the state of things, then how can we have the least glimpse of joy or comfort, how can we have any peaceful enjoyment of ourselves, but by living wholly unto that God, using and doing everything conformably to His will? A life thus devoted unto God, looking wholly unto Him in all our actions, and doing all things suitable to His glory, is so far from being dull and uncomfortable, that it creates new comforts in everything that we do.

On the contrary, would you see how happy they are who live according to their own wills, who cannot submit to the dull and melancholy business of a life devoted unto God; look at the man in the parable, to whom his Lord had given one talent.

He could not bear the thoughts of using his talent according to the will of Him from whom he had it, and therefore he chose to make himself happier in a way of his own. "Lord," says he, "I knew thee, that thou art an hard man, reaping where thou hadst not sown, and gathering where thou hadst not strawed: and I was afraid, and went and hid thy talent in the earth! lo, there thou hast that is thine."

His Lord, having convicted him out of his own mouth, despatches him with this sentence, "Cast the unprofitable servant into outer darkness: there shall be weeping and gnashing of teeth." [1]

Here you see how happy this man made himself, by not acting wholly according to his Lord's will. It was, according to his own account, a happiness of murmuring and discontent; I knew thee, says he, that thou wast an hard man: it was a happiness of fears and apprehensions; I was, says he, afraid: it was a happiness of vain labours and fruitless travels; I went, says he, and hid thy talent; and after having been awhile the sport of foolish passions, tormenting fears, and fruitless labour, he is rewarded with darkness, eternal weeping, and gnashing of teeth.

Now this is the happiness of all those who look upon a strict and exalted piety, that is, a right use of their talent, to be a dull and melancholy state of life.

They may live a while free from the restraints and directions of religion; but, instead thereof, they must be under the absurd government of their passions: they must, like the man in the parable, live in murmurings and discontents, in fears and apprehensions. They may avoid the labour of doing good, of spending their time devoutly, of laying up treasures in Heaven, of clothing the naked, of visiting the sick; but then they must, like this man, have labours and pains in vain, that tend to no use or advantage, that do no good either to themselves or others; they must travel, and labour, and work, and dig, to hide their talent in the earth. They must, like him, at their Lord's coming, be convicted out

[1] Matt. xxv. 24, 25, 30.

of their own mouths, be accused by their own hearts, and have everything that they have said and thought of religion, be made to show the justice of their condemnation to eternal darkness, weeping, and gnashing of teeth.

This is the purchase that they make, who avoid the strictness and perfection of religion, in order to live happily.

On the other hand, would you see a short description of the happiness of a life rightly employed, wholly devoted to God, you must look at the man in the parable to whom his Lord had given five talents. "Lord," says he, "thou deliveredst unto me five talents; behold, I have gained beside them five talents more. His Lord said unto him, Well done, thou good and faithful servant; thou hast been faithful over a few things, I will make thee ruler over many things: enter thou into the joy of thy Lord."

Here you see a life that is wholly intent upon the improvement of the talents, that is devoted wholly unto God, is a state of happiness, prosperous labours, and glorious success. Here are not, as in the former case, any uneasy passions, murmurings, vain fears, and fruitless labours. The man is not toiling and digging in the earth for no end or advantage; but his pious labours prosper in his hands, his happiness increases upon him; the blessing of five becomes the blessing of ten talents; and he is received with a "Well done, good and faithful servant: enter thou into the joy of thy Lord."

Now as the case of these men in the parable left nothing else to their choice, but either to be happy in using their gifts to the glory of the Lord, or miserable by using them according to their own humours and fancies; so the state of Christianity leaves us no other choice.

All that we have, all that we are, all that we enjoy, are only so many talents from God: if we use them to the ends of a pious and holy life, our five talents will become ten, and our labours will carry us into the joy of our Lord; but if we abuse them to the gratifications of our own passions, sacrificing the gifts of God to our own pride and vanity, we shall live here in vain labours and foolish anxieties, shunning religion as a melancholy thing, accusing our Lord as a hard master, and then fall into everlasting misery.

We may for a while amuse ourselves with names and sounds,

and shadows of happiness; we may talk of this or that greatness and dignity; but if we desire real happiness, we have no other possible way to it but by improving our talents, by so holily and piously using the powers and faculties of men in this present state, that we may be happy and glorious in the powers and faculties of Angels in the world to come.

How ignorant, therefore, are they of the nature of religion, of the nature of man, and the nature of God, who think a life of strict piety and devotion to God to be a dull uncomfortable state; when it is so plain and certain that there is neither comfort nor joy to be found in anything else!

5. JOHN HENRY NEWMAN:
FROM THE *APOLOGIA PRO VITA SUA*

¶By common consent the *Apologia pro Vita Sua,* in which Newman narrated his spiritual and religious history, is one of the greatest of all autobiographies. Logically, therefore, it should have been included in the first part of the present book; but upon second thought the editor deemed it advisable to place selections from Newman in their proper setting, which is English literature. The *Apologia* was first published in 1864, as a way of replying to certain criticisms of the Catholic position made by the Rev. Charles Kingsley. Newman had entered the Catholic Church in 1846, after a period of fame as the brilliant leader of the "Oxford Movement," or movement to reform the Anglican Church in accordance with ideas held by a group of earnest theologians at the university. Born in 1801, Newman soon gave evidence of a great and deeply religious mind. He died in 1890, after having written many books, struggled in behalf of many causes and suffered no little for his convictions. He was made a Cardinal by Pope Leo XIII.

Of necessity the *Apologia pro Vita Sua* is largely controversial. Newman explains why he took certain steps—notably that which brought him into the Catholic Church—and defends himself for having taken them. But the writing, lucid and dense, reasonable and passionate alike, succeeds primarily in helping us to know an utterly sincere and extraordinarily gifted human being. For the special purpose of this volume, two passages have been selected. The first gives a simple and appealing outline of Newman's youth. The second states his conclusions on one of the most important of all problems. Taken together, these passages seem to be fairly representative of the book as a whole, though this really demands reading from beginning to end.*

---

* From *Apologia pro Vita Sua.* By John Henry Newman. New York: Longmans, Green and Company. N.D.

APOLOGIA PRO VITA SUA

I

WAS brought up from a child to take great delight in reading the Bible; but I had no formed religious convictions till I was fifteen. Of course I had perfect knowledge of my catechism.

After I was grown up, I put on paper such recollections as I had of my thoughts and feelings on religious subjects, at the time that I was a child and a boy. Out of these I select two, which are at once the most definite among them, and also have a bearing on my later convictions.

In the paper to which I have referred, written either in the long vacation of 1820, or in October 1823, the following notices of my school days were sufficiently prominent in my memory for me to consider them worth recording:—"I used to wish the Arabian Tales were true: my imagination ran on unknown influences, on magical powers, and talismans. . . . I thought life might be a dream, or I an Angel, and all this world a deception, my fellow-angels by a playful device concealing themselves from me, and deceiving me with the semblance of a material world."

Again, "Reading in the Spring of 1816 a sentence from [Dr. Watts's] 'Remnants of Time,' entitled 'the Saints unknown to the world,' to the effect, that 'there is nothing in their figure or countenance to distinguish them,' etc., etc., I supposed he spoke of Angels who lived in the world, as it were disguised."

The other remark is this: "I was very superstitious, and for some time previous to my conversion" [when I was fifteen] "used constantly to cross myself on going into the dark."

Of course I must have got this practice from some external source or other; but I can make no sort of conjecture whence; and certainly no one had ever spoken to me on the subject of the Catholic religion, which I only knew by name. The French master was an *émigré* priest, but he was simply made a butt, as French masters too commonly were in that day, and spoke English very imperfectly. There was a Catholic family in the village, old maiden ladies we used to think; but I knew nothing but their name. I have of late years heard that there were one or two Catholic boys in the school; but either we were carefully kept from knowing this, or the knowledge of it made simply no impression on our minds. My brother will bear witness how free the school was from Catholic ideas.

I had once been into Warwick Street Chapel, with my father, who, I believe, wanted to hear some piece of music; all that I bore away from it was the recollection of a pulpit and a preacher and a boy swinging a censer.

When I was at Littlemore, I was looking over old copy-books of my school days, and I found among them my first Latin Verse-Book; and in the first page of it there was a device which almost took my breath away with surprise. I have the book before me now, and have just been showing it to others. I have written in the first page, in my schoolboy hand, "John H. Newman, February 11th, 1811, Verse Book;" then follow my first verses. Between "Verse" and "Book" I have drawn the figure of a solid cross upright, and next to it, what may indeed be meant for a necklace, but what I cannot make out to be anything else than a set of beads suspended, with a little cross attached. At this time I was not quite ten years old. I suppose I got the idea from some romance, Mrs. Radcliffe's or Miss Porter's; or from some religious picture; but the strange thing is, how, among the thousand objects which meet a boy's eyes, these in particular should so have fixed themselves in my mind, that I made them thus practically my own. I am certain there was nothing in the churches I attended, or the prayer books I read, to suggest them. It must be recollected that churches and prayer books were not decorated in those days as I believe they are now.

When I was fourteen, I read Paine's tracts against the Old Testament, and found pleasure in thinking of the objections which were contained in them. Also, I read some of Hume's essays; and perhaps that on Miracles. So at least, I gave my father to understand; but perhaps it was a brag. Also, I recollect copying out some French verses, perhaps Voltaire's, against the immortality of the soul, and saying to myself something like "How dreadful, but how plausible!"

When I was fifteen (in the autumn of 1816) a great change of thought took place in me. I fell under the influences of a

definite creed, and received into my intellect impressions of
dogma, which, through God's mercy, have never been effaced or
obscured. Above and beyond the conversations and sermons of
the excellent man, long dead, who was the human means of this
beginning of divine faith in me, was the effect of the books which
he put into my hands, all of the school of Calvin. One of the
first books I read was a work of Romaine's; I neither recollect
the title nor the contents, except one doctrine, which of course I
do not include among those which I believe to have come from
a divine source, viz. the doctrine of final perseverance. I received
it at once, and believed that the inward conversion of which I
was conscious (and of which I still am more certain than that I
have hands and feet) would last into the next life, and that I was
elected to eternal glory. I have no consciousness that this belief
had any tendency whatever to lead me to be careless about pleasing God. I retained it till the age of twenty-one, when it gradually
faded away; but I believe that it had some influence on my
opinions, in the direction of those childish imaginations which I
have already mentioned, viz. in isolating me from the objects
which surrounded me, in confirming me in my mistrust of the
reality of material phenomena, and making me rest in the thought
of two and two only supreme and luminously self-evident beings,
myself and my Creator;—for while I considered myself predestined to salvation, I thought others simply passed over, not
predestined to eternal death. I only thought of the mercy to
myself.

The detestable doctrine last mentioned is simply denied and
abjured, unless my memory strangely deceives me, by the writer
who made a deeper impression on my mind than any other, and
to whom (humanly speaking) I almost owe my soul—Thomas
Scott of Aston Sandford. I so admired and delighted in his writings, that, when I was an undergraduate, I thought of making a
visit to his parsonage, in order to see a man whom I so deeply
revered. I hardly think I could have given up the idea of this
expedition, even after I had taken my degree; for the news of his
death in 1821 came upon me as a disappointment as well as a
sorrow. I hung upon the lips of Daniel Wilson, afterwards
Bishop of Calcutta, as in two sermons at St. John's Chapel he gave
the history of Scott's life and death. I had been possessed of his

essays from a boy; his commentary I bought when I was an undergraduate.

What, I suppose, will strike any reader of Scott's history and writings, is his bold unworldliness and vigorous independence of mind. He followed truth wherever it led him, beginning with Unitarianism, and ending in a zealous faith in the Holy Trinity. It was he who first planted deep in my mind that fundamental truth of religion. With the assistance of Scott's essays, and the admirable work of Jones of Nayland, I made a collection of Scripture texts in proof of the doctrine, with remarks (I think) of my own upon them, before I was sixteen; and a few months later I drew up a series of texts in support of each verse of the Athanasian Creed. These papers I have still.

Besides his unworldliness, what I also admired in Scott was his resolute opposition to Antinomianism, and the minutely practical character of his writings. They show him to be a true Englishman, and I deeply felt his influence; and for years I used almost as proverbs what I considered to be the scope and issue of his doctrine, "Holiness before peace," and "Growth is the only evidence of life."

Calvinists make a sharp separation between the elect and the world; there is much in this that is parallel or cognate to the Catholic doctrine; but they go on to say, as I understand them, very differently from Catholicism,—that the converted and the unconverted can be discriminated by man, that the justified are conscious of their state of justification, and that the regenerate cannot fall away. Catholics on the other hand shade and soften the awful antagonism between good and evil, which is one of their dogmas, by holding that there are different degrees of justification, that there is a great difference in point of gravity between sin and sin, that there is the possibility and the danger of falling away, and that there is no certain knowledge given to any one that he is simply in a state of grace, and much less that he is to persevere to the end:—of the Calvinistic tenets the only one which took root in my mind was the fact of heaven and hell, divine favour and divine wrath, of the justified and the unjustified. The notion that the regenerate and the justified were one and the same, and that the regenerate, as such, had the gift of perseverance, remained with me not many years, as I have said already.

This main Catholic doctrine of the warfare between the city
of God and the powers of darkness was also deeply impressed
upon my mind by a work of a very opposite character, Law's
"Serious Call."

From this time I have given a full inward assent and belief to
the doctrine of eternal punishment, as delivered by our Lord
Himself, in as true a sense as I hold that of eternal happiness;
though I have tried in various ways to make that truth less terrible
to the reason.

Now I come to two other works, which produced a deep impression on me in the same autumn of 1816, when I was fifteen years
old, each contrary to each, and planting in me the seeds of
an intellectual inconsistency which disabled me for a long course
of years. I read Joseph Milner's Church History, and was nothing
short of enamoured of the long extracts from St. Augustine and
the other Fathers which I found there. I read them as being the
religion of the primitive Christians: but simultaneously with
Milner I read Newton on the Prophecies, and in consequence
became most firmly convinced that the Pope was the Antichrist
predicted by Daniel, St. Paul, and St. John. My imagination was
stained by the effects of this doctrine up to the year 1843; it had
been obliterated from my reason and judgment at an earlier date;
but the thought remained upon me as a sort of false conscience.
Hence came that conflict of mind, which so many have felt besides
myself;—leading some men to make a compromise between two
ideas, so inconsistent with each other—driving others to beat out
the one idea or the other from their minds—and ending in my
own case, after many years of intellectual unrest, in the gradual
decay and extinction of one of them—I do not say its violent
death, for why should I not have murdered it sooner, if I murdered it at all?

I am obliged to mention, though I do it with great reluctance,
another deep imagination, which at this time, the autumn of 1816,
took possession of me—there can be no mistake about the fact;—
viz. that it was the will of God that I should lead a single life.
This anticipation, which has held its ground almost continuously
ever since—with the break of a month now and a month then,
up to 1829, and, after that date, without any break at all—was
more or less connected in my mind, with the notion that my

calling in life would require such a sacrifice as celibacy involved; as, for instance, missionary work among the heathen, to which I had a great drawing for some years. It also strengthened my feeling of separation from the visible world, of which I have spoken above.

II

STARTING then with the being of a God (which, as I have said, is as certain to me as the certainty of my own existence, though when I try to put the grounds of that certainty into logical shape, I find a difficulty in doing so in mood and figure to my satisfaction), I look out of myself into the world of men, and there I see a sight which fills me with unspeakable distress. The world seems simply to give the lie to that great truth, of which my whole being is so full; and the effect upon me, is, in consequence, as a matter of necessity, as confusing as if it denied that I am in existence myself. If I looked into a mirror, and did not see my face, I should have the sort of feeling which actually comes upon me, when I look into this living busy world, and see no reflexion of its Creator. This is, to me, one of the great difficulties of this absolute primary truth, to which I referred just now. Were it not for this voice, speaking so clearly in my conscience and my heart, I should be an atheist, or a pantheist, or a polytheist when I looked into the world. I am speaking for myself only; and I am far from denying the real force of the arguments in proof of a God, drawn from the general facts of human society, but these do not warm me or enlighten me; they do not take away the winter of my desolation, or make the buds unfold and the leaves grow within me, and my moral being rejoice. The sight of the world is nothing else than the prophet's scroll, full of "lamentations, and mourning, and woe."

To consider the world in its length and breadth, its various history, the many races of man, their starts, their fortunes, their mutual alienation, their conflicts; and then their ways, habits, governments, forms of worship; their enterprises, their aimless courses, their random achievements and acquirements, the impotent conclusion of long-standing facts, the tokens so faint and broken, of a superintending design, the blind evolution of what turn out to be great powers or truth, the progress of things, as if from unreasoning elements, not towards final causes, the greatness and littleness of man, his far-reaching aims, his short duration, the curtain hung over his futurity, the disappointments of life, the defeat of good, the success of evil, physical pain, mental anguish, the prevalence and intensity of sin, the pervading idolatries, the corruptions, the dreary hopeless irreligion, that condition of the whole race, so fearfully yet exactly described in the Apostle's words, "having no hope and without God in the world" —all this is a vision to dizzy and appal; and inflicts upon the mind the sense of a profound mystery, which is absolutely beyond human solution.

What shall be said to this heart-piercing, reason-bewildering fact? I can only answer, that either there is no Creator, or this living society of men is in a true sense discarded from His presence. Did I see a boy of good make and mind, with the tokens on him of a refined nature, cast upon the world without provision, unable to say whence he came, his birthplace or his family connections, I should conclude that there was some mystery connected with his history, and that he was one, of whom, from one cause or other, his parents were ashamed. Thus only should I be able to account for the contrast between the promise and condition of his being. And so I argue about the world;—*if* there be a God, *since* there is a God, the human race is implicated in some terrible aboriginal calamity. It is out of joint with the purposes of its Creator. This is a fact, a fact as true as the fact of its existence; and thus the doctrine of what is theologically called original sin becomes to me almost as certain as that the world exists, and as the existence of God.

And now, supposing it were the blessed and loving will of the Creator to interfere in this anarchical condition of things, what are we to suppose would be the methods which might be necessarily or naturally involved in His object of mercy? Since the world is in so abnormal a state, surely it would be no surprise to me, if the interposition were of necessity equally extraordinary— or what is called miraculous. But that subject does not directly come into the scope of my present remarks. Miracles as evidence, involve an argument; and of course I am thinking of some means which does not immediately run into argument. I am rather asking what must be the face-to-face antagonist, by which to withstand and baffle the fierce energy of passion and the all-corroding, all-dissolving scepticism of the intellect in religious inquiries? I have no intention at all to deny, that truth is the real object of our reason, and that, if it does not attain to truth, either the premiss or the process is in fault; but I am not speaking of right reason, but of reason as it acts in fact and concretely in fallen man. I know that even the unaided reason, when correctly exercised, leads to a belief in God, in the immortality of the soul, and in a future retribution; but I am considering it actually and historically; and in this point of view, I do not think I am wrong in saying that its tendency is towards a simple unbelief in matters of religion. No truth, however sacred, can stand against it, in the long run; and hence it is that in the pagan world, when our Lord came, the last traces of the religious knowledge of former times were all but disappearing from those portions of the world in which the intellect had been active and had had a career.

And in these latter days, in like manner, outside the Catholic Church things are tending, with far greater rapidity than in that old time from the circumstance of the age, to atheism in one shape or other. What a scene, what a prospect, does the whole of Europe present at this day! and not only Europe, but every government and every civilisation through the world, which is under the influence of the European mind! Especially, for it most concerns us, how sorrowful, in the view of religion, even taken in its most elementary, most attenuated form, is the spectacle presented to us by the educated intellect of England, France, and Germany! Lovers of their country and of their race, religious men, external to the Catholic Church, have attempted various expedients to arrest fierce wilful human nature in its onward course, and to bring it into subjection. The necessity of some form of religion for the interests of humanity, has been generally acknowledged: but where was the concrete representative of things invisible, which would have the force and toughness necessary to be a breakwater against the deluge? Three centuries ago the establishment of religion, material, legal, and social, was generally adopted as the best expedient for the purpose, in those countries which separated from the Catholic Church; and for a long time it was successful; but now the crevices of those establishments are admitting the enemy. Thirty years ago, education was relied upon: ten years ago there was a hope that wars would cease for ever, under the influence of commercial enterprise and the reign of the useful and fine arts; but will any one venture to say that there is anything anywhere on this earth, which will afford a fulcrum for us, whereby to keep the earth from moving onwards?

The judgment, which experience passes on establishments or education, as a means of maintaining religious truth in this anarchical world, must be extended even to Scripture, though Scripture be divine. Experience proves surely that the Bible does not answer a purpose, for which it was never intended. It may be accidentally the means of the conversion of individuals; but a book, after all, cannot make a stand against the wild living intellect of man, and in this day it begins to testify, as regards its own structure and contents, to the power of that universal solvent, which is so successfully acting upon religious establishments.

Supposing then it to be the Will of the Creator to interfere in human affairs, and to make provisions for retaining in the world a knowledge of Himself, so definite and distinct as to be proof against the energy of human scepticism, in such a case—I am far from saying that there was no other way—but there is nothing to surprise the mind, if He should think fit to introduce a power into the world, invested with the prerogative of infallibility in religious matters. Such a provision would be a direct, immediate, active, and prompt means of withstanding the difficulty; it would be an instrument suited to the need; and, when I find that this is the very claim of the Catholic Church, not only do I feel no difficulty in admitting the idea, but there is a fitness in it, which recommends it to my mind. And thus I am brought to speak of the church's infallibility, as a provision, adapted by the mercy of the Creator, to preserve religion in the world, and to restrain that freedom of thought, which of course in itself is one of the greatest of our natural gifts, and to rescue it from its own suicidal excesses. And let it be observed that, neither here nor in what follows, shall I have occasion to speak directly of the revealed body of truths, but only as they bear upon the defence of natural religion. I say, that a power, possessed of infallibility in religious teaching, is happily adapted to be a working instrument, for smiting hard and throwing back the immense energy of the aggressive intellect:—and in saying this, as in the other things that I have to say, it must still be recollected that I am all along bearing in mind my main purpose, which is a defence of myself.

I am defending myself here from a plausible charge brought against Catholics, as will be seen better as I proceed. The charge is this:—that I, as a Catholic, not only make profession to hold doctrines which I cannot possibly believe in my heart, but that I also believe in the existence of a power on earth, which at its own will imposes upon men any new set of *credenda*, when it pleases, by a claim to infallibility; in consequence, that my own thoughts are not my own property; that I cannot tell that to-morrow I may not have to give up what I hold to-day, and that the necessary effect of such a condition of mind must be a degrading bondage, or a bitter inward rebellion relieving itself in secret infidelity, or the necessity of ignoring the whole subject of religion in a sort of disgust, and of mechanically saying everything that the Church says, and leaving to others the defence of it. As then I have above spoken of the relation of my mind towards the Catholic Creed, so now I shall speak of the attitude which it takes up in the view of the Church's infallibility.

And first, the initial doctrine of the infallible teacher must be an emphatic protest against the existing state of mankind. Man had rebelled against his Maker. It was this that caused the divine interposition: and the first act of the divinely accredited messenger must be to proclaim it. The Church must denounce rebellion as of all possible evils the greatest. She must have no terms with it; if she would be true to her Master, she must ban and anathematise it. This is the meaning of a statement which has furnished matter for one of those special accusations to which I am at present replying: I have, however, no fault at all to confess in regard to it; I have nothing to withdraw, and in consequence I here deliberately repeat it. I said, "The Catholic Church holds it better for the sun and moon to drop from heaven, for the earth to fail, and for all the many millions on it to die of starvation in extremest agony, as far as temporal affliction goes, than that one soul, I will not say, should be lost, but should commit one single venial sin, should tell one wilful untruth, or should steal one poor farthing without excuse." I think the principle here enunciated to be the mere preamble in the formal credentials of the Catholic Church,

as an Act of Parliament might begin with a *"Whereas."* It is because of the intensity of the evil which has possession of mankind, that a suitable antagonist has been provided against it; and
the initial act of that divinely-commissioned power is of course
to deliver her challenge and to defy the enemy. Such a preamble
then gives a meaning to her position in the world, and an interpretation to her whole course of teaching and action.

In like manner she has ever put forth, with most energetic dis-
tinctness, those other great elementary truths, which either are an
explanation of her mission or give a character to her work. She
does not teach that human nature is irreclaimable, else wherefore
should she be sent? not that it is to be shattered and reversed, but
to be extricated, purified, and restored; not that it is a mere mass
of evil, but that it has the promise of great things, and even now
has a virtue and a praise proper to itself. But in the next place she
knows and she preaches that such a restoration, as she aims at
effecting in it, must be brought about, not simply through any
outward provision of preaching and teaching, even though it be
her own, but from a certain inward spiritual power or grace im-
parted directly from above, and which is in her keeping. She has
it in charge to rescue human nature from its misery, but not simply
by raising it upon its own level, but by lifting it up to a higher
level than its own. She recognises in it real moral excellence
though degraded, but she cannot set it free from earth except by
exalting it towards heaven. It was for this end that a renovating
grace was put into her hands, and therefore from the nature of
the gift, as well as from the reasonableness of the case, she goes
on, as a further point, to insist, that all true conversion must begin
with the first springs of thought, and to teach that each individual
man must be in his own person one whole and perfect temple of
God, while he is also one of the living stones which build up a
visible religious community. And thus the distinctions between
nature and grace, and between outward and inward religion, become two further articles in what I have called the preamble of
her divine commission.

Such truths as these she vigorously reiterates, and perti-
naceously inflicts upon mankind; as to such she observes no half-
measures, no economical reserve, no delicacy or prudence. "Ye
must be born again," is the simple, direct form of words which

she uses after her Divine Master; "your whole nature must be re-born, your passions, and your affections, and your aims, and your conscience, and your will, must all be bathed in a new element, and reconsecrated to your Maker, and, the last not the least, your intellect." It was for repeating these points of her teaching in my own way, that certain passages of one of my volumes have been brought into the general accusation which has been made against my religious opinions. The writer has said that I was demented if I believed, and unprincipled if I did not believe, in my statement that a lazy, ragged, filthy, story-telling beggar-woman, if chaste, sober, cheerful, and religious, had a prospect of heaven, which was absolutely closed to an accomplished statesman, or lawyer, or noble, be he ever so just, upright, generous, honourable, and conscientious, unless he had also some portion of the divine Christian grace; yet I should have thought myself defended from criticism by the words which our Lord used to the chief priests, "The publicans and harlots go into the kingdom of God before you." And I was subjected again to the same alternative of imputations, for having ventured to say that consent to an unchaste wish was indefinitely more heinous than any lie viewed apart from its causes, its motives, and its consequences; though a lie, viewed under the limitation of these conditions, is a random utterance, an almost outward act, not directly from the heart, however disgraceful it may be, whereas we have the express words of our Lord to the doctrine that "whoso looketh on a woman to lust after her, hath committed adultery with her already in his heart." On the strength of these texts I have surely as much right to believe in these doctrines as to believe in the doctrine of original sin, or that there is a supernatural revelation, or that a Divine Person suffered, or that punishment is eternal.

Passing now from what I have called the preamble of that grant of power, with which the Church is invested, to that power itself, Infallibility, I make two brief remarks: on the one hand, I am not here determining anything about the essential seat of that power, because that is a question doctrinal, not historical and practical; nor, on the other hand, am I extending the direct subject-matter, over which that power has jurisdiction, beyond religious opinion:—and now as to the power itself.

This power, viewed in its fullness, is as tremendous as the giant evil which has called for it. It claims, when brought into exercise in the legitimate manner, for otherwise of course it is but dormant, to have for itself a sure guidance into the very meaning of every portion of the divine message in detail, which was committed by our Lord to His apostles. It claims to know its own limits, and to decide what it can determine absolutely and what it cannot. It claims, moreover, to have a hold upon statements not directly religious, so far as this, to determine whether they indirectly relate to religion, and, according to its own definitive judgment, to pronounce whether or not, in a particular case, they are consistent with revealed truth. It claims to decide magisterially, whether infallibly or not, that such and such statements are or are not prejudicial to the apostolic *depositum* of faith, in their spirit or in their consequences, and to allow them, or condemn and forbid them, accordingly. It claims to impose silence at will on any matters, or controversies, of doctrine, which on its own *ipse dixit* it pronounces to be dangerous, or inexpedient, or inopportune. It claims that whatever may be the judgment of Catholics upon such acts, these acts should be received by them with those outward marks of reverence, submission, and loyalty, which Englishmen, for instance, pay to the presence of their sovereign, without public criticism on them, as being in their matter inexpedient, or in their manner violent or harsh. And lastly, it claims to have the right of inflicting spiritual punishment, of cutting off from the ordinary channels of the divine life, and of simply excommunicating, those who refuse to submit themselves to its formal declarations. Such is the infallibility lodged in the Catholic Church, viewed in the concrete, as clothed and surrounded by the appendages of its high sovereignty: it is, to repeat what I said above, a supereminent prodigious power sent upon earth to encounter and master a giant evil.

6. COVENTRY PATMORE:

"KNOWLEDGE AND SCIENCE," FROM *THE ROD, THE ROOT AND THE FLOWER*

¶ONE result of the Oxford Movement, in which Cardinal New-man took the most prominent part, was to encourage the writing of mystical verse by poets who studied the literature of the Christian mystical tradition. A good example is the life and work of Coventry Patmore (1823-1896), whose best writing ranks with that of Tennyson and Browning. Interested in both science and religion, Patmore early decided to become the "poet of married love" in which he beheld an allegory of the relations between the world and the soul as well as of the soul and God. His most important poems are, no doubt, *The Angel in the House* (a metrical romance in four parts) and *The Unknown Eros* (a sequence of mystical odes). Patmore married three times, his union with his second wife coinciding with his entry into the Catholic Church.

The passage quoted here is from one of Patmore's several prose books, *The Rod, the Root and the Flower*. This is a compilation of short, aphoristic essays on mystical and aesthetic topics. He was, as will be seen, concerned with lofty doctrine which he strove to express in what he called "hard sayings." But the reader will observe that both thought and diction are searchingly human, deriving excellence from a careful study of the heart of man no less than from theology, "the mistress of sciences." *

---

* From *The Rod, the Root and the Flower*. By Coventry Patmore. London: George Bell and Sons, 1923.

KNOWLEDGE AND SCIENCE

I

F WE would find in God that full satisfaction of all our desires which He promises, we must believe *extravagantly*, *i.e.*, as the Church and the Saints do; and must not be afraid to follow the doctrine of the Incarnation into all its *natural* consequences. Those who fear to call Mary the "Mother of God" simply do not believe in the Incarnation at all; but we must go further, and believe His word when He rebuked the people for regarding her as exclusively His Mother, declaring that every soul who received Him with faith and love was also, in union with Her, His Mother, the Bride of the Holy Spirit. We must not be afraid to believe that this Bride and Mother, with whom we are identified, is "Regina Cœli," as well as "Regina Mundi"; and that this Queen of Heaven and Earth is simply a pure, natural woman; and that one of our own race, and each of us, in union with her, has been made "a little lower than the angels," in order to be "crowned with honour and glory" far beyond the honour and glory of the highest and His purely spiritual creatures. "It is not written that He has taken hold (or united Himself) with any of the angels"; but of the lowest of His spiritual creatures, who alone is also flesh, "He has taken hold"; and the Highest has found His ultimate and crowning felicity in a marriage of the flesh as well as the Spirit; and in this infinite contrast and intimacy of height with depth and spirit with flesh He, who is very Love, finds, just as ordinary human love does, its final rest and the full fruition of its own life; and the joy of angels is in contemplating, and sharing by perfect sympathy with humanity, that glory which humanity alone actually possesses. This, the literal doctrine of the Church and the Scriptures, sounds preposterous in the ears of nearly all "Christians" even; and yet its actual truth has been realised, even in this life, as something far more than a credible promise, by those who have received the message of their Angel with somewhat of the faith of Mary, and to each of whom it has been said: "Blessed art thou because thou hast believed; for there shall be a performance of the

things which have been promised to thee." Let Christians leave off thinking of the Incarnation as a thing past, or a figure of speech, and learn to know that it consists for them in their becoming the intimately and humanly beloved of a divine and yet human Lover; and His local paradise and heaven of heavens.

II

"My heart is enlarged, I see, I wonder, I abound; my sons come from afar, and my daughters rise up at my side." This is the knowledge, the *personal* knowledge of God, which immediately follows the first great and uncompromising sacrifice of the Soul to Him. The heart becomes an ocean of knowledge actually perceived. All that previously was confessed by faith is seen far more clearly than external objects are seen by the natural eye. Sons, that is, corroborative truths, come from afar; the most remote facts of past experience and of science are confirmations strong as proofs of Holy Writ; and daughters, all natural affections and desires, find suddenly their interpretation, justification, and satisfaction, and are henceforward as "the polished corners of the Temple."

III

When once God "has made known to us the Incarnation of His Son Jesus Christ by the message of an Angel," that is to say, when once it has become, not an article of abstract faith, but a fact discerned in our own bodies and souls, we are made sharers of the Church's infallibility; for our reasoning is thenceforward from discerned reality to discerned reality, and not from and to those poor and always partially fallacious and misleading signs of realities, thoughts which can be formulated in words. Though he may express himself erroneously, no man, so taught, can be otherwise than substantially orthodox, and he is always willing and glad to submit his expressions to the sole assessor of verbal truth, whose judgments have never been convicted of inconsistency, even by the most hostile and malevolent criticism.

IV

"Eternity," says Aquinas, "is the entire, simultaneous, and perfect possession of a life without end." God goes forth from simplicity into all particulars of reality; man returns from all his peculiar and partial apprehensions of reality to God, and *his* eternity is "the entire, simultaneous, and perfect possession of a life" which is the synthesis of all the real apprehensions, or perceptions of good, which he has acquired here. Hence the acquisition of knowledge is the first business of mortal life,—not knowledge of "facts," but of realities, which none can ever begin to know until he knows that all knowledge but the knowledge of God is vanity.

V

"GOD," writes a Persian Poet, "is at once the mirror and the mirrored, the Lover and the Beloved." Every Soul was created to be, if it chose, a participator of this felicity, *i.e.*, of "the glory which the Son had with the Father before the beginning of the world." *This* is the sum total of "mysticism," or true "science"; and he who has not attained, through denial of himself, to some *sensible* knowledge of this felicity, in reality knows nothing; for all knowledge, worthy of the name, is nuptial knowledge.

VI

"THAT which He shows you in secret proclaim on the housetops," —not to others, but to yourself. The most remote, undefined, and (if you do not fix them in your consciousness, by reflection, affirmation, and corroboration) evanescent thoughts, are commonly "secrets" which are, of all others, the most important and life-affecting.

VII

"No prophecy is of private interpretation." We must believe nothing in religion but what has been declared by the Church, but many things declared by the Church must be spoken by the Spirit in the Soul before she can hear them in the word of the Church. Her orthodoxy, then, consists in this, that she must try what she hears in herself by that word, in which all is contained, either explicitly or implicitly. This is not hard, for the one deep calls to the other, and the Spirit knows what the Spirit speaks. Flavour and palate, perfume and nostrils, are not closer correlatives than are revelation and human consciousness.

VIII

PLATO's cave of shadows is the most profound and simple statement of the relation of the natural to the spiritual life ever made.
Men stand with their backs to the Sun, and they take the shadows
cast by it upon the walls of their cavern for realities. The shadows,
even, of heavenly realities are so alluring as to provoke ardent
desires, but they cannot satisfy us. They mock us with unattain-
able good, and our natural and legitimate passions and instincts,
in the absence of their true and substantial satisfactions, break
forth into frantic disorders. If we want fruition we must turn our
backs on the shadows, and gaze on their realities in God.

It may be added that, when we have done this, and are weary
of the splendours and felicities of immediate reality, we may turn
again, from time to time, to the shadows, which, having thus
become intelligible, and being attributed by us to their true origin,
are immeasurably more satisfying than they were before, and
may be delighted in without blame. This is the "evening joy,"
the joy of contemplating God in His creatures, of which the
theologians write; and this purified and intelligible joy in the
shadow—which has now obtained a core of substance—is not only
the hundredfold "promise of this life also," but it is, as the
Church teaches, a large part of the joy of the blest.

IX

Knowledge purifies. There are two kinds of impurity: impurity
of will, which is sin; and impurity of ignorance, which makes
that the Angels themselves are said to be impure in the sight of
God. For essential purity is order, and there can be no perfection
of order without knowledge of what is the right order of things
within us; and the purest of created beings has still to pray
"Order all things in me strongly and sweetly from end to end."
There are in man many floating islands of good, like that of
Delos, but he cannot have a perfect conscience concerning them,
and they are not safe ground on which to build the temple of
God, until they are chained to the bottom of the sea of the senses
and perceptions by ordered knowledge. The impurity of ignorance
is in none so manifest as in the devout; for they *act* on their
ignorance, and fill themselves and others with miserable scruples

and hard thoughts of God, and are as apt to call good evil as other men are to call evil good.

X

"Unless above himself he can erect himself, how mean a thing is man." He that sets himself with his whole heart on this task, will find at some stage or other of the work, that, like Abraham, he has to offer up his first-born, his dearest possession, his "ruling love," whatever that may be. He must actually lift the knife,—not so much to prove his sincerity to God as to himself; for no man who has not thus won assurance of himself can advance surely. But he will find that he has killed a ram, and that his first-born is safe, and exalted by this offering to be the father of a great nation; and he will understand why God called the place in which this sacrifice was offered "The land of vision."

XI

What discredits the idea of "Revelation" most with those who doubt or reject it, is the denial that it is communicated to the whole world. Whereas it is expressly affirmed, in the very first words of St. John's Gospel, that this "Light lighteth every one that cometh into the world," only they have loved darkness better than light. A *Witness* to a revelation is a different thing; and that religion has the best claims upon us which professes, as Christianity does, to be mainly a Witness of that original and universal light.

XII

After the main dogmas, which are of faith, the teaching of theologians is very largely derived from facts of psychology within the reach of every one who chooses to pay the cost. For example, one of the most important of these facts is that there are four states or aspects of the Soul towards God; states or aspects which rapidly and inevitably succeed each other, and recur almost daily in the life of every Soul which is doing its full duty. The theologians call these states by those times of the day to which they strikingly correspond: Morning, Noon, Evening, and Night. The Morning is the mood of glad, free, and hopeful worship, supplication, and thanksgiving; the Noon is the perfect state of contemplation, or spiritual fruition; this cannot be sustained, say the theologians, even by the Angels for very long, and it passes into the "Evening joy," in which the Soul turns, not from God, but to God in His creatures—to all natural delights, rendered natural indeed by supernatural insight. Lastly, Night is that condition of the Soul which, in this stage of being, occupies by far the greatest part of the lives even of the most holy, but which will have no existence when the remains of corruption which cause the darkness shall have passed away. "The wicked," however, "have no bonds in their death," and this terrible and daily recurring trial is as little known to them as that other after which the "Bride" sighed: "Show me where Thou pasturest Thy sheep in the noonday."

XIII

THE "touch" of God is not a figure of speech. "Touch," says Aquinas, "applies to spiritual as well as to material things." The same authority says, "Touch is the sense of alimentation, taste that of savour." A perfect life ends, as it begins, in the simplicity of infancy: it knows nothing of God on whom it feeds otherwise than by touch and taste. The fullness of intelligence is the obliteration of intelligence. God is then our honey, and we, as St. Augustine says, are His; and who wants to understand honey or requires the *rationale* of a kiss? "The Beatific Vision," says St. Bernard, "is not seen by the eyes, but is a substance which is sucked as through a nipple."

XIV

To the living and affirmative mind, difficulties and unintelligibilities are as dross, which successively rises to the surface, and dims the splendour of ascertained and perceived truth, but which is cast away, time after time, until the molten silver remains unsullied; but the negative mind is lead, and, when all its formations of dross are skimmed away, nothing remains.

XV

I ONCE asked a famous theologian why he did not preach the love and knowledge of God from his pulpit as he had been discoursing of them for a couple of hours with me, instead of setting forth

Doctrine hard
In which Truth shows herself as near a lie
As can comport with her divinity.

He answered that, if he were to do so, his whole congregation would be living in mortal sin before the end of the week. It is true. The work of the Church in the world is, not to teach the mysteries of life, so much as to persuade the soul to that arduous degree of purity at which God Himself becomes her teacher. The work of the Church ends when the knowledge of God begins.

XVI

WHEN the state which the theologians call "Perfection" is attained, and life is from good to truth instead of from truth to good, the connection between truth ceases to be an intellectual necessity. Not only the "earth," or mass of related knowledge, but "the multitude of the isles is thine." Every discerned good is assured truth and safe land, whether its subaqueous connection with the main continent is demonstrable or not. "Love and do what you like." "Habitual grace" knows how to suck the baits off the hooks of the Devil, and can take up adders without being bitten.

XVII

THERE is a perfectly simple test by which you may know whether you have attained the region of divine perception. The particular sayings and narratives of Scripture, which have seemed, if we would confess it, the most utter nonsense and absurdity, or mere figures of speech, will gradually become centres of ineffable light, and self-evident truths of being; there will be no more doubt as to your seeing the right meaning than there is about the key that fits the lock, or the answer, when given, to an ingenious enigma; and these sayings and narratives, from being habitually passed over as hopelessly unmeaning or as "Eastern" hyperboles and *façons de parler*, will carry henceforward the only instructions worth listening to.

IV

ENGLISH RELIGIOUS POETRY

=

1. EDMUND SPENSER:

AN HYMNE of *HEAVENLY BEAUTIE*

¶It is hardly necessary to say much here concerning the life (1553-1599) of Edmund Spenser, Elizabethan poet and courtier. The melodious organ music of the *Faërie Queene*, a poem in which the descriptive power of English speech is revealed as nowhere else, is a matter of common knowledge; and there is no lover of old verse whom the stanzas of the *Shepherd's Calendar* and the sonnets of the *Amoretti* have not haunted. The *Hymne* here reprinted is one of four in which Spenser attempted to set forth a complete Platonic doctrine of human conduct. Man is aware of the beauties of earth and takes delight in them, but his enjoyment will soon pall if he does not lift his eyes from the "shadow" to the "Divine reality." This last is the explanation of all things and at the same time the sublime goal towards which the soul tends.

Spenser is peculiarly the poet in whom the traditional Catholic point of view blends with the special beliefs and aspirations of Puritanism. This has been pointed out repeatedly, and is especially worthy of note in connection with the present *Hymne*. Catholics have praised it warmly; Protestants have claimed it for their own. The conclusion to which one must arrive is that in all probability the poem is a statement of Christian belief pure and simple. Fervor is blended with dictional beauty:—it is a prayer set to music without notes. It has seemed best to adhere to the form of Spenserian English, all attempts to modernize which result in failure.*

---

* From *The Faërie Queene, The Shepheards Calendar, together with the Other Works of England's Arch-Poet, Edm. Spenser*. London, 1611. *The Complete Works of Spenser:* Globe Edition. Macmillan, N. Y. Also The Cambridge Edition: Houghton Mifflin Co., Boston.

AN HYMNE OF HEAVENLY BEAUTIE

OVE, lift me up upon thy golden wings
From this base world unto thy heavens hight,
Where I may see those admirable things
Which there thou workest by thy soveraine might,
Farre above feeble reach of earthly sight,
That I thereof an heavenly Hymne may sing
Unto the God of Love, high heavens King.

Many lewd layes (ah! woe is me the more!)
In praise of that mad fit which fooles call Love,
I have in th' heat of youth made heretofore,
That in lights wits did loose affection move;
But all those follies now I do reprove,
And turned have the tenor of my string,
The heavenly prayses of true Love to sing.

And ye that wont with greedy vaine desire
To reade my fault, and, wondring at my flame,
To warme your selves at my wide sparckling fire,
Sith now that heat is quenched, quench my blame,
And in her ashes shrowd my dying shame;
For who my passed follies now pursewes,
Beginnes his owne, and my old fault renewes.

Before this worlds great frame, in which all things
Are now containd, found any being-place,
Ere flitting Time could wag his eyas wings
About that mightie bound which doth embrace
The rolling spheres, and parts their houres by space,
That High Eternall Powre, which now doth move
In all these things, mov'd in it selfe by love.

It lovd it selfe, because it selfe was faire;
(For fair is lov'd;) and of it self begot
Like to it selfe his eldest Sonne and Heire,
Eternall, pure, and voide of sinfull blot,
The firstling of His joy, to whom no iot.

Of loves dislike or pride was to be found,
Whom He therefore with equall honour crownd.

With Him he raignd, before all time prescribed,
In endlesse glorie and immortall might,
Together with that Third from them derived,
Most wise, most holy, most almightie Spright!
Whose kingdomes throne no thoughts of earthly wight
Can comprehend, much lesse my trembling verse
With equall words can hope it to reherse.

Yet, O most blessed Spirit! pure lampe of light,
Eternall spring of grace and wisedom trew,
Vouchsafe to shed into my barren spright
Some little drop of thy celestiall dew,
That may my rymes with sweet infuse embrew,
And give me words equall unto my thought,
To tell the marveiles by thy mercie wrought.

Yet being pregnant still with powrefull grace,
And full of fruitfull Love, that loves to get
Things like himselfe, and to enlarge his race,
His second brood, though not of powre so great,
Yet full of beautie, next He did beget,
And infinite increase of angels bright,
All glistring glorious in their Makers light.

To them the heavens illimitable hight
(Not this round heaven, which we from hence behold,
Adornd with thousand lamps of burning light,
And with ten thousand gemmes of shyning gold,)
He gave as their inheritance to hold,
That they might serve Him in eternall blis,
And be partakers of those ioyes of His.

There they in their trinall triplicities
About Him wait, and on His will depend,
Either with nimble wings to cut the skies,
When He them on His messages doth send,
Or on His owne dread presence to attend,
Where they behold the glorie of His light,
And caroll hymnes of love both day and night.

Both day, and night, is unto them all one;
For He His beames doth unto them extend,
That darkness there appeareth never none;
Ne hath their day, ne hath their blisse, an end,
But there their termelesse time in pleasure spend;
Ne ever should their happinesse decay,
Had not they dar'd their Lord to disobay.

But pride, impatient of long resting peace,
Did puffe them up with greedy bold ambition,
That they gan cast their state how to increase
Above the fortune of their first condition,
And sit in Gods own seat without commission:
The brightest angel, even the child of Light,
Drew millions more against their God to fight.

Th' Almighty, seeing their so bold assay,
Kindled the flame of His consuming yre.
And with His onely breath them blew away
From heavens hight, to which they did aspyre,
To deepest hell, and lake of damned fyre,
Where they in darknesse and dread horror dwell,
Hating the happie light from which they fell.

So that next off-spring of the Makers love,
Next to Himselfe in glorious degree,
Degendering to hate, fell from above
Through pride; (for pride and love may ill agree;)
And now of sinne to all ensample bee:
How then can sinfull flesh itselfe assure,
Sith purest angels fell to be impure?

But that Eternall Fount of love and grace,
Still flowing forth His goodnesse unto all,
Now seeing left a waste and emptie place
In His wyde pallace, through those angels fall,
Cast to supply the same, and to enstall
A new unknown colony therein,
Whose root from earths base groundworke should begin.

Therefore of clay, base, vile, and next to nought,
Yet form'd by wondrous skill, and by His might,
According to an heavenly patterne wrought,
Which he had fashiond in his wise foresight,
He man did make, and breathd a living spright
Into his face, most beautiful and fayre,
Endewed with wisedomes riches, heavenly, rare.

Such He him made, that he resemble might
Himselfe, as mortall thing immortall could;
Him to be lord of every living wight
He made by love out of his owne like moulde,
In whom he might his mightie selfe-behould;
For love doth love the thing belov'd to see,
That like it selfe in lovely shape may bee.

But man, forgetfull of his Makers grace
No lesse than angels, whom he did ensew,
Fell from the hope of promist heavenly place,
Into the mouth of Death, to sinners dew,
And all his off-spring into thraldome threw,
Where they for ever should in bonds remaine
Of never-dead yet ever-dying paine.

Till that great Lord of Love, which him at first
Made of meere love, and after liked well,
Seeing him lie like creature long accurst
In that deep horor of despeyred hell,
Him, wretch, in doole would let no lenger dwell,
But cast out of that bondage to redeeme,
And pay the price, all were his debt extreeme.

Out of the bosome of eternall blisse,
In which He reigned with His glorious Syre,
He downe descended, like a most demisse
And abiect thrall, in fleshes fraile attyre,
That He for him might pay sinnes deadly hyre,
And him restore unto that happie state
In which he stood before his haplesse fate.

In flesh at first the guilt committed was,
Therefore in flesh it must be satisfyde;
Nor spirit, nor angel, though they man surpas,
Could make amends to God for mans misguyde,
But onely man himselfe, who selfe did slyde:
So, taking flesh of sacred virgins wombe,
For mans deare sake He did a man become.

And that most blessed bodie, which was borne
Without all blemish or reproachfull blame,
He freely gave to be both rent and torne
Of cruell hands, who with despightfull shame
Revyling Him, that them most vile became,
At length Him nayled on a gallow-tree,
And slew the lust by most uniust decree.

O huge and most unspeakeable impression
Of Loves deep wound, that pierst the piteous hart
Of that deare Lord with so entyre affection,
And, sharply launching every inner part,
Dolours of death into His soule did dart,
Doing him die that never it deserved,
To free His foes, that from His heast had swerved!

What hart can feel least touch of so sore launch,
Or thought can think the depth of so deare wound?
Whose bleeding sourse their streames yet never staunch,
But still do flow, and freshly still redownd,
To heale the sores of sinfull soules unsound,
And clense the guilt of that infected cryme
Which was enrooted in all fleshly slyme.

O blessed Well of Love! O Floure of Grace!
O glorious Morning-Starre! O Lampe of Light!
Most lively image of thy Fathers face,
Eternal King of Glorie, Lord of Might,
Meeke Lambe of God, before all worlds behight,
How can we Thee requite for all this good?
Or what can prize that Thy most precious blood?

Yet nought Thou ask'st in lieu of all this love,
But love of us, for guerdon of thy paine:
Ay me! what can us lesse than that behove?
Had He required life for us againe,
Had it beene wrong to ask His owne with gaine?
He gave us life, He it restored lost;
Then life were least, that us so little cost.

But He our life hath left unto us free,
Free that was thrall, and blessed that was band;
Ne ought demaunds by that we loving bee,
As He Himselfe hath lov'd us afore-hand,
And bound thereto with an eternall band,
Him first to love that was so dearely bought,
And next our brethren, to his image wrought.

Him first to love great right and reason is,
Who first to us our life and being gave,
And after, when we fared had amisse,
Us wretches from the second death did save;
And last, the food of life, which new we have,
Even He Himselfe, in his dear sacrament,
To feede our hungry soules, unto us lent.

Then next, to love our brethren, that were made
Of that selfe mould, and that self Maker's hand,
That we, and to the same again shall fade,
Where they shall have like heritage of land,
However here on higher steps we stand,
Which also were with selfe-same price redeemed
That we, however of us light esteemed.

And were they not, yet since that loving Lord
Commaunded us to love them for His sake,
Even for His sake, and for His sacred word,
Which in His last bequest He to us spake,
We should them love, and with their needs partake;
Knowing that, whatsoere to them we give,
We give to Him by whom we all doe live.

Such mercy He by His most holy reede
Unto us taught, and to approve it trew,
Ensampled it by His most righteous deede,
Shewing us mercie (miserable crew!)
That we the like should to the wretches shew,
And love our brethren; thereby to approve
How much, Himselfe that loved us, we love.

Then rouze thy selfe, O Earth! out of thy soyle,
In which thou wallowest like to filthy swyne,
And doest thy mynd in durty pleasures moyle;
Unmindfull of that dearest Lord of thyne;
Lift up to Him thy heavie clouded eyne,
That thou this soveraine bountie mayst behold,
And read, through love, His mercies manifold.

Beginne from first, where He encradled was
In simple cratch, wrapt in a wad of hay,
Betweene the toylfull oxe and humble asse,
And in what rags, and in how base aray,
The glory of our heavenly riches lay,
When Him the silly shepheards came to see,
Whom greatest princes sought on lowest knee.

From thence reade on the storie of His life,
His humble carriage, His unfaulty wayes,
His cancred foes, His fights, His toyle, His strife,
His paines, His povertie, His sharpe assayes,
Through which He past His miserable dayes,
Offending none, and doing good to all,
Yet being malist both by great and small.

And look at last, how of most wretched wights
He taken was, betrayd, and false accused,
How with most scornfull taunts, and fell despights
He was revyld, disgrast, and foule abused;
How scourgd, how crownd, how buffeted, how brused;
And, lastly, how twixt robbers crucifyde,
With bitter wounds through hands, through feet, and syde!

Then let thy flinty hart, that feeles no paine,
Empierced be with pittifull remorse,
And let thy bowels bleede in every vaine,
At sight of His most sacred heavenly corse,
So torne and mangled with malicious forse;
And let thy sould, whose sins His sorrows wrought,
Melt into teares, and grone in grieved thought.

With sence wherof, whilest so thy softened spirit
Is inly toucht, and humbled with meeke zeale
Through meditation of His endlesse merit,
Lift up thy mind to th' Author of thy weale,
And to His soveraine mercie doe appeale;
Learne Him to love that loved thee so deare,
And in thy brest His blessed image beare.

With all thy hart, with all thy soule and mind,
Thou must Him love, and His beheasts embrace;
All other loves, with which the world doth blind
Weake fancies, and stirre up affections base,
Thou must renounce and utterly displace,
And give thy selfe unto Him full and free,
That full and freely gave Himselfe to thee.

Then shalt thou feele thy spirit so possest,
And ravisht with devouring great desire
Of His dear selfe, that shall thy feeble brest
Inflame with love, and set thee all on fire
With burning zeale, through every part entire,
That in no earthly thing thou shalt delight,
But in His sweet and amiable sight.

Thenceforth all worlds desire will in thee dye,
And all earthes glorie, on which men do gaze,
Seeme durt and drosse in thy pure-sighted eye,
Compar'd to that celestiall beauties blaze,
Whose glorious beames all fleshly sense doth daze
With admiration of their passing light,
Blinding the eyes, and lumining the spright.

Then shall thy ravisht soul inspired bee
With heavenly thoughts, farre above humane skil,
And thy bright radiant eyes shall plainely see
Th' idee of His pure glorie present still
Before thy face, that all thy spirits shall fill
With sweete enragement of celestiall love,
Kindled through sight of those faire things above.

2. JOHN DONNE:

HOLY SONNETS

¶THE religious poetry of John Donne (1573-1631) is notable for the drama it outlines in a manner calculated to wring from all of us the confession: "There speaks a part of me!" It is verse of a man torn between Heaven and Hell, between the delights of the world and peace in submission to the Divine will. This poet's earlier verse had been, often enough, carnal and sophisticated, though always lit up with flashes of an intense love of purity. His later work, however, is almost purely spiritual in quality. *Holy Sonnets*, written about 1617, express a soul torn between the ecstasies and the discomforts of conversion. They constitute perhaps the greatest, certainly the most realistic, of all spiritual sonnet sequences. Of course they do not breathe the peace of the mystics; but such phrases as "Batter my heart, three-person'd God" can never be forgotten.

It remains to add that Donne, who sought preferment and curiously enough found it only in the English Church from association with which he long struggled to be free, was for a time the Dean of St. Paul's, London. There he became known as a great, if tortuous and tortured, preacher. His verse was not published until 1633, though it was passed round and read prior to that time. During the nineteenth century, his work was well-nigh neglected, but with the opening of the twentieth a veritable Donne furore began, culminating in a measure with the publication of H. J. G. Grierson's definitive edition of the poems.*

* From *The Poems of John Donne*. Edited by H. J. G. Grierson. Oxford: Clarendon Press, 1912.

HOLY SONNETS

I

HOU hast made me, and shall Thy work decay?
Repair me now, for now mine end doth haste,
I run to death, and death meets me as fast,
And all my pleasures are like yesterday;
I dare not move my dim eyes any way,
Despair behind, and death before doth cast
Such terror, and my feeble flesh doth waste
By sin in it, which it towards hell doth weigh;
Only Thou art above, and when towards Thee
By Thy leave I can look, I rise again;
But our old subtle foe so tempteth me,
That not one hour myself I can sustain;
Thy Grace may wing me to prevent his art,
And thou like Adamant draw mine iron heart.

II

As due by many titles I resign
Myself to Thee, O God, first I was made
By Thee, and for Thee, and when I was decay'd
Thy blood bought that, the which before was Thine;
I am Thy son, made with Thyself to shine,
Thy servant, whose pains thou hast still repaid,
Thy sheep, Thine Image, and, till I betray'd
Myself, a temple of Thy Spirit divine;
Why doth the devil then usurp on me?
Why doth he steal, nay ravish that 's Thy right?
Except Thou rise and for Thine own work fight,
Oh I shall soon despair, when I do see
That Thou lov'st mankind well, yet wilt not choose me,
And Satan hates me, yet is loth to lose me.

III

O MIGHT those sighs and tears return again
Into my breast and eyes, which I have spent,
That I might in this holy discontent

Mourn with some fruit, as I have mourn'd in vain;
In mine Idolatry what showers of rain
Mine eyes did waste? what griefs my heart did rent?
That sufferance was my sin; now I repent;
'Cause I did suffer I must suffer pain.
Th' hypdroptic drunkard, and night-scouting thief,
The itchy Lecher, and self-tickling proud
Have the remembrance of past joys, for relief
Of coming ills. To poor me is allow'd
No ease; for, long, yet vehement grief hath been
Th' effect and cause, the punishment and sin.

IV

Oh my black Soul! now thou art summoned
By sickness, death's herald, and champion;
Thou art like a pilgrim, which abroad hath done
Treason, and durst not turn to whence he is fled,
Or like a thief, which till death's doom be read,
Wisheth himself delivered from prison;
But damn'd and hal'd to execution,
Wisheth that still he might be imprisoned.
Yet grace, if thou repent, thou canst not lack;
But who shall give thee that grace to begin?
Oh make thyself with holy mourning black,
And red with blushing, as thou art with sin;
Or wash thee in Christ's blood, which hath this might
That being red, it dyes red souls to white.

V

I am a little world made cunningly
Of Elements, and an Angelic sprite,
But black sin hath betray'd to endless night
My world's both parts, and, oh, both parts must die.
You which beyond that heaven which was most high
Have found new spheres, and of new lands can write,
Pour new seas in mine eyes, that so I might
Drown my world with my weeping earnestly,
Or wash it if must be drown'd no more:
But oh it must be burnt! alas the fire

Of lust and envy have burnt it heretofore,
And made it fouler; let their flames retire,
And burn me, O Lord, with a fiery zeal
Of Thee and Thy house, which doth in eating heal.

VI

THIS is my play's last scene, here heavens appoint
My pilgrimage's last mile; and my race
Idly, yet quickly run, hath this last pace,
My span's last inch, my minute's latest point,
And gluttonous death, will instantly unjoint
My body, and soul, and I shall sleep a space,
But my ever-waking part shall see that face,
Whose fear already shakes my every joint:
Then, as my soul, to heaven her first seat, takes flight,
And earth-born body, in the earth shall dwell,
So, fall my sins, that all may have their right,
To where they 're bred, and would press me, to hell.
Impute my righteous, thus purg'd of evil,
For thus I leave the world, the flesh, the devil.

VII

AT the round earth's imagin'd corners, blow
Your trumpets, Angels, and arise, arise
From death, you numberless infinities
Of souls, and to your scatter'd bodies go,
All whom the flood did, and fire shall o'erthrow,
All whom war, dearth, age, agues, tyrannies,
Despair, law, chance, hath slain, and you whose eyes,
Shall behold God, and never taste death's woe.
But let them sleep, Lord, and me mourn a space,
For, if above all these, my sins abound,
'Tis late to ask abundance of Thy grace,
When we are there; here on this lowly ground,
Teach me how to repent; for that 's as good
As if Thou hadst seal'd my pardon, with Thy blood.

VIII

IF faithful souls be alike glorified
As Angels, then my father's soul doth see
And adds this even to full felicity,
That valiantly I hell's wide mouth o'erstride:
But if our minds to these souls be descried
By circumstances, and by signs that be
Apparent in us, not immediately,
How shall my mind's white truth by them be try'd?
They see idolatrous lovers weep and mourn,
And vile blasphemous Conjurers to call
On Jesus' name, and Pharisaical
Dissemblers feign devotion. Then turn
O pensive soul, to God, for He knows best
Thy true grief, for He put it in my breast.

IX

IF poisonous minerals, and if that tree,
Whose fruit threw death on else immortal us,
If lecherous goats, if serpents envious
Cannot be damn'd; alas! why should I be?
Why should intent or reason, born in me,
Make sins, else equal, in me more heinous?
And mercy being easy, and glorious
To God; in His stern wrath, why threatens He?
But who am I, that dare dispute with Thee
O God? Oh! of thine only worthy blood,
And my tears, make a heavenly Lethean flood,
And drown in it my sin's black memory;
That Thou remember them, some claim as debt,
I think it mercy, if Thou wilt forget.

X

DEATH be not proud, though some have called thee
Mighty and dreadful, for, thou art not so,
For, those, whom thou think'st, thou dost overthrow,
Die not, poor death, nor yet canst thou kill me.
From rest and sleep, which but thy pictures be,

Much pleasure, then from thee, much more must flow,
And soonest our best men with thee do go,
Rest of their bones, and soul's delivery.
Thou art slave to Fate, Chance, kings, and desperate men,
And dost with poison, war, and sickness dwell,
And poppy, or charms can make us sleep as well,
And better than thy stroke; why swell'st thou then?
One short sleep past, we wake eternally,
And death shall be no more; death, thou shalt die.

XI

Spit in my face you Jews, and pierce my side,
Buffet, and scoff, scourge, and crucify me,
For I have sinn'd, and sinn'd, and only He,
Who could do no iniquity, hath died:
But by my death can not be satisfied
My sins, which pass the Jews' impiety:
They kill'd once an inglorious man, but I
Crucify him daily, being now glorified.
Oh let me then, His strange love still admire:
Kings pardon, but He bore our punishment.
And Jacob came cloth'd in vile harsh attire
But to supplant, and with gainful intent:
God cloth'd himself in vile man's flesh, that so
He might be weak enough to suffer woe.

XII

Why are we by all creatures waited on?
Why do the prodigal elements supply
Life and food to me, being more pure than I,
Simple, and further from corruption?
Why brook'st thou, ignorant horse, subjection?
Why dost thou bull, and boar so sillily
Dissemble weakness, and by one man's stroke die,
Whose whole kind, you might swallow and feed upon?
Weaker I am, woe is me, and worse than you,
You have not sinn'd, nor need be timorous.
But wonder at a greater wonder, for to us
Created nature doth these things subdue,

But their Creator, whom sin, nor nature tied,
For us, His Creatures, and His foes, hath died.

XIII

WHAT if this present were the world's last night?
Mark in my heart, O Soul, where thou dost dwell,
The picture of Christ crucified, and tell
Whether that countenance can thee affright,
Tears in His eyes quench the amazing light,
Blood fills His frowns, which from His pierc'd head fell.
And can that tongue adjudge thee unto hell,
Which pray'd forgiveness for His foes' fierce spite?
No, no; but as in my idolatry
I said to all my profane mistresses,
Beauty, of pity, foulness only is
A sign of rigour: so I say to thee,
To wicked spirits are horrid shapes assign'd,
This beauteous form assures a piteous mind.

XIV

BATTER my heart, three-person'd God; for, you
As yet but knock, breathe, shine, and seek to mend;
That I may rise, and stand, o'erthrow me, and bend
Your force, to break, blow, burn and make me new.
I, like an usurp'd town, to another due,
Labour to admit you, but Oh, to no end,
Reason your viceroy in me, me should defend,
But is captiv'd, and proves weak or untrue.
Yet dearly I love you, and would be loved fain,
But am betroth'd unto your enemy:
Divorce me, untie, or break that knot again,
Take me to you, imprison me, for I
Except you enthral me, never shall be free,
Nor ever chaste, except you ravish me.

XV

WILT thou love God, as He thee? then digest,
My Soul, this wholesome meditation,
How God the Spirit, by Angels waited on

In heaven, doth make His Temple in thy breast.
The Father having begot a Son most blest,
And still begetting (for he ne'er begun)
Hath deign'd to choose thee by adoption,
Coheir to His glory, and Sabbath's endless rest;
And as a robb'd man, which by search doth find
His stol'n stuff sold, must lose or buy it again:
The Son of glory came down, and was slain,
Us whom He had made, and Satan stol'n, to unbind.
'Twas much, that man was made like God before,
But, that God should be made like man, much more.

XVI

FATHER, part of His double interest
Unto Thy kingdom, Thy son gives to me,
His jointure in the knotty Trinity
He keeps, and gives to me His death's conquest.
This Lamb, whose death, with life the world hath blest,
Was from the world's beginning slain, and He
Hath made two Wills, which with the Legacy
Of His and Thy kingdom, do Thy Sons invest.
Yet such are Thy laws, that men argue yet
Whether a man those statutes can fulfil;
None doth; but all-healing grace and spirit
Revive again what law and letter kill.
Thy law's abridgement, and Thy last command
Is all but love; Oh let this last Will stand!

XVII

SINCE she whom I lov'd hath paid her last debt
To Nature, and to hers, and my good is dead,
And her Soul early into heaven ravished,
Wholly on heavenly things my mind is set,
Here the admiring her my mind did whet
To seek Thee, God; so streams do show their head;
But though I have found Thee, and Thou my thirst has fed,
A holy thirsty dropsy melts me yet.
But why should I beg more Love, when as Thou
Dost woo my soul for hers; off'ring all Thine:

And dost not only fear lest I allow
My Love to Saints and Angels, things divine,
But in Thy tender jealousy dost doubt
Lest the World, Flesh, yea Devil, put Thee out.

XVIII

SHOW me, dear Christ, Thy Spouse, so bright and clear.
What! is it She, which on the other shore
Goes richly painted? or which rob'd and tore
Laments and mourns in Germany and here?
Sleeps she a thousand, then peeps up one year?
Is she self truth and errs? now new, now outwore?
Doth she, and did she, and shall she evermore
On one, on seven, or on no hill appear?
Dwells she with us, or like adventuring knights
First travail we to seek and then make Love?
Betray kind husband thy spouse to our sights,
And let mine amorous soul court thy mild Dove,
Who is most true, and pleasing to thee, then
When she is embrac'd and open to most men.

XIX

OH, to vex me, contraries meet in one;
Inconstancy unnaturally hath begot
A constant habit; that when I would not
I change in vows, and in devotion.
As humorous is my contrition
As my profane Love, and as soon forgot:
As riddlingly distemper'd, cold and hot,
As praying, as mute; as infinite, as none.
I durst not view heaven yesterday; and to-day
In prayers, and flattering speeches I court God:
To-morrow I quake with true fear of His rod.
So my devout fits come and go away
Like a fantastic Ague: save that here
Those are my best days, when I shake with fear.

3. EDWARD BENLOWES:

THEOPHILA'S LOVE SONG

¶THE poem offered herewith is, perhaps, one of the *curiosa* of English literature. It forms part of a volume of mystical verse first published in 1652, then almost forgotten, and finally definitively resurrected by George Saintsbury, whose *Minor Caroline Poets* (1905) included it. To Professor Saintsbury's book the present editor is indebted both for his knowledge of the poem and for the text offered. Benlowes is a typical seventeenth-century "metaphysical poet" in his fondness for unusual constructions and elisions. But there is no other writer of the time, not even Crashaw, who writes verse in such complete awareness of the great Christian mystical tradition. *Theophila* as a whole describes the experiences of a soul which has elected to turn from the world to God. The present "Song" describes the moment of highest ecstasy following consciousness of the Divine Love.

Edward Benlowes was born about 1603 and died in 1676. Little is known concerning his life, excepting that the last eight years of it were spent in Oxford where he was known as an assiduous reader who was often in need of even the necessities of life. Since he was born wealthy, it is assumed that his fortune was lavished on hospitality (for which he appears to have been famous), or employed to collect a library, or lost during the Civil War. During many years he professed the Catholic faith, but it is generally agreed that he died a Protestant. Benlowes is the author of other works, most of them in Latin.*

---

* From *Minor Poets of the Caroline Period*. Edited by George Saintsbury. Oxford: Clarendon Press, 1905.

THEOPHILA'S LOVE SONG

ELF! Oh, how mean an harmony it breeds!
Jesus! All names this Name of names exceeds!
This Name's God's mercy at full sea, 'tis Love's
High tow'r, Joy's loadstone; this, my spirit
    moves.
Hark: 'Rise, my love, my fair one, come away;
Ling'ring breeds loss; I am thy Leader, Light, and Way.'

What speed Speed's self can make, soul, fly withal;
Greatness and goodness most magnetical!
Shoot, like a flash of fire, to th' ruby wine,
His precious blood, transcendently Divine!
(How poor those costly pearls were, drunk by some)
My LORD, drink Blood to me! Let it to th' world's health come!

All hope's unanchor'd but in That. Thou art,
'Bove Indies' womb, rich to my love-sick heart!
Flesh-fair endowments are but skin-deep brags,
Varnish'd corruption; wealth is but Care's bags;
The bag imposthumed chokes. Gold, Beauty, Fame
Are sublunary mists to Saints' seraphic flame.

Jesus! This fans my fire, which has at best
But grains of incense, pounds of interest.
Go, int'rest; take the principal, Thine own:
Divine Love loves Thy loveliness alone!
What flames to Thine proportionable be!
Lord, hadst not first lov'd man, man could not have lov'd Thee!

Why lov'st us, but because THOU wouldst? Oh, why
For lepers would Thee Undefilèd die?
That pen was dipt i' th' standish of thy Blood,
Which wrote th' indenture of our termless good!
Oh Love, 'bove wish! Never such Love enroll'd!
Who think their utmost flames enough for Thee, are cold.

Whose Highness did not to be low disdain,
Yet, when at lowest highest did remain!
Who bow'dst Heav'n's altitude, refresh with flow'rs,
With Jesse's sov'reign flow'r, my fainting pow'rs,
Which sink (as shaft-struck hart emboss'd) twixt grief,
And joy: grief for my sin, joy for Thy free relief.

Wrack'd is with bitter-sweet extremes my mind,
Shell'd, sheath'd, cag'd, coffin'd in her treacherous friend;
Her always tempting mass of flesh she bears,
Her hopes, did they not sprout from Thee, were fears:
Hope, Thou perfume of lovers, for Thy sake
Love's generous, throws at all: life's but a petty stake;

Scarce worth the prize. Love makes two spirits but one;
Me, counterpart to Thy indenture, own;
I, active then as light, tread air and flame,
Without or wing, or chariot; and disclaim
All the faint sweets of earth. Thy Spirit views
How in Love's torrid zone Thy swelt'ring martyr stews.

Row me, ye dove-wing'd oars, whom Hope does buoy,
To wish'd-for hav'n, flowing with tides of joy!
Yet wish I not, my Joy, Thy joys above,
Merely for joy; nor pleasures of Thy Love,
Only for love of pleasure. No, let free
Spiritual languors teem! fruitful, yet virgins be!

Give, give me children, or I die! Love, rest
Thy head upon the pillows of my breast!
When me Thou shalt impregn'd with virtues make
A fruitful Eden, all the fruitage take!
Thy passion, Jonathan, below did move;
Rapt spirits, in high excess, flame with intensest love!

My life is hid with Thee in God! Descry
Thyself, O Thou, my plighted Spouse, that I
May ever glorious be! That my joy'd soul
With Thee may make up marriage! and my whole

Self Thee for Bridegroom have! My hope still sends
Up 'Come,' that I may enter with Thy feasted friends!

Oh, that long-long'd for Come! oh, Come! mine eyes,
Love's sentinels, watch, like officious spies!
Strike sparks of joy t' inflame Love's tinder! make
The exile view her home, the dreamer wake!
Tears raise the fire of Love! Ease sighs of air,
Fire's passion, wat'ry tears, and earthy self-despair!

My sighs, condens'd to drops, compute hours spent!
Cancel the lease of my clay tenement,
Which pays dear rent of groans! oh, grant a writ
Of ease! I languish out, not live! Permit
A pass to Sion's Mount! But, I resign
My green-sick will, though sick of Love, to that of Thine!

Waitings, which ripen hopes, are not delays;
Presence how great, how true's Love, absence says:
While lungs my breath shall organ, I'll press still
Th' exinanition of my o'ergrown will.
'Behold, I quickly come.' O'erjoy'd I'm here!
Oh, Come! Till then, each day's an age, each hour a year.

Jesu! (That Name's Joy's essence!) hasten on!
Throng amorous sights for dissolution!
Fastidious earth, avaunt; with love-plumes soar,
My soul, to meet thy Spouse. Canst wish for more?
Only come! give a ring! re-echo then,
'Oh, Come. Even so, Lord Jesu, Come! Amen. Amen.'

4. RICHARD CRASHAW:

HYMN TO THE ADORABLE ST. TERESA

¶WHEN the Puritans beheaded King Charles and proceeded to re-organize Cambridge University according to their spirit, Richard Crashaw (1616-1650) was one of fifty-five Fellows ejected. He thereupon left for France, was received into the Catholic Church, became a priest and died in Italy. While at the University he had gained renown as a poet, preacher and divine. Cowley and others were his devoted friends. Several volumes of his had met with warm praise, and it was characteristic of the time that he should have written as well in Latin as in English. *The Delights of the Muses* and *Sacred Poems* are perhaps his most illustrious works in the mother tongue, while *Epigrammata Sacra* contains some of the finest Latin poems ever written in England.

The present *Hymn* is usually thought to be characteristic of Crashaw at his best. It is less replete with "conceits" and over-sensuous imagery than are some of his other poems, and it contains epigrammatic lines of extraordinary vigor and depth. The poem was occasioned by reflections caused by reading the works of St. Teresa of Avila. Of course the original version was written while Crashaw was still an Anglican. After becoming a Catholic, he thought it well to append some lines which alter nothing in the first poem but add some thoughts and lines of striking beauty. The continued references to Spain were occasioned by the feeling against that country which still ran high in Protestant England.*

---

* From the *Poems of Richard Crashaw*. Edited by A. R. Waller. Cambridge: Cambridge University Press, 1904.

HYMN TO THE ADORABLE ST. TERESA

A HYMN TO THE NAME AND HONOR OF THE ADMIRABLE
SAINT TERESA

OVE, thou art absolute sole lord
Of life and death. To prove the word,
We'll now appeal to none of all
Those thy old soldiers, great and tall,
Ripe men of martyrdom, that could reach down
with strong arms their triumphant crown,
Such as could with lusty breath
Speak loud into the face of death
Their great Lord's glorious name; to none
Of those whose spacious bosoms spread a throne
For love at large to fill; spare blood and sweat,
And see him take a private seat,
Making his mansion in the mild
And milky soul of a soft child.
  Scarce has she learned to lisp the name
Of martyr, yet she thinks it shame
Life should so long play with that breath
Which spent can buy so brave a death.
She never undertook to know
What death with love should have to do;
Nor has she e'er yet understood
Why to show love she should shed blood;
Yet though she cannot tell you why,
She can love and she can die.
  Scarce has she blood enough to make
A guilty sword blush for her sake;
Yet has she 'a heart dares hope to prove
How much less strong is death than love.
  Be love but there, let poor six years
Be posed with the maturest fears
Man trembles at, you straight shall find
Love knows no nonage, nor the mind.
'Tis love, not years or limbs that can

Make the martyr or the man.
　　　Love touched her heart, and lo it beats
High, and burns with such brave heats,
Such thirsts to die, as dares drink up
A thousand cold deaths in one cup.
Good reason, for she breathes all fire;
Her weak breast heaves with strong desire
Of what she may with fruitless wishes
Seek for amongst her mother's kisses.
　　　Since 'tis not to be had at home,
She'll travel to a martyrdom.
No home for hers confesses she
But where she may a martyr be.
　　　She'll to the Moors, and trade with them
For this unvalued diadem.
She'll offer them her dearest breath,
With Christ's name in't, in change for death.
She'll bargain with them, and will give
Them God, teach them how to live
In him; or if they this deny,
For him she'll teach them how to die.
So shall she leave amongst them sown
Her Lord's blood, or at least her own.
　　　Farewell then, all the world, adieu!
Teresa is no more for you.
Farewell, all pleasures, sports, and joys,
Never till now esteemèd toys,
Farewell, whatever dear may be,
Mother's arms or father's knee;
Farewell house and farewell home,
She's for the Moors and martyrdom!
　　　Sweet, not so fast! lo, thy fair spouse
Whom thou seek'st with so swift vows
Calls thee back, and bids thee come
T' embrace a milder martyrdom.
　　　Blest powers forbid thy tender life
Should bleed upon a barbarous knife;
Or some base hand have power to race
Thy breast's chaste cabinet and uncase

A soul kept there so sweet; oh no,
Wise heav'n will never have it so:
Thou art love's victim, and must die
A death more mystical and high;
Into love's arms thou shalt let fall
A still surviving funeral.
His is the dart must make the death
Whose stroke shall taste thy hallowed breath;
A dart thrice dipped in that rich flame
Which writes thy spouse's radiant name
Upon the roof of heav'n, where aye
It shines, and with a sovereign ray
Beats bright upon the burning faces
Of souls, which in that name's sweet graces
Find everlasting smiles. So rare,
So spiritual, pure, and fair
Must be th' immortal instrument
Upon whose choice point shall be sent
A life so loved; and that there be
Fit executioners for thee,
The fair'st and first-born sons of fire,
Blest seraphim, shall leave their choir
And turn love's soldiers, upon thee
To exercise their archery.
    Oh, how oft shalt thou complain.
Of a sweet and subtle pain,
Of intolerable joys,
Of a death in which who dies
Loves his death, and dies again,
And would forever so be slain,
And lives and dies, and knows not why
To live, but that he thus may never leave to die.
    How kindly will thy gentle heart
Kiss the sweetly killing dart!
And close in his embraces keep
Those delicious wounds, that weep
Balsam to heal themselves with. Thus
When these thy deaths, so numerous,
Shall all at last die into one,

And melt thy soul's sweet mansion
Like a soft lump of incense, hasted
By too hot a fire, and wasted
Into perfuming clouds, so fast
Shalt thou exhale to heav'n at last
In a resolving sigh; and then,
Oh, what? Ask not the tongues of men;
Angels cannot tell; suffice,
Thyself shall feel thine own full joys
And hold them fast forever. There
So soon as thou shalt first appear,
The moon of maiden stars, thy white
Mistress, attended by such bright
Souls as thy shining self, shall come
And in her first ranks make thee room;
Where 'mongst her snowy family
Immortal welcomes wait for thee.

  Oh, what delight when revealed life shall stand
And teach thy lips heav'n with his hand,
On which thou now mayst to thy wishes
Heap up thy consecrated kisses.
What joys shall seize thy soul when she,
Bending her blessed eyes on thee,
Those second smiles of heaven, shall dart
Her mild rays through thy melting heart!

  Angels, thy old friends, there shall greet thee,
Glad at their own home now to meet thee.

  All thy good works which went before
And waited for thee at the door
Shall own thee there, and all in one
Weave a constellation
Of crowns, with which the King, thy spouse,
Shall build up thy triumphant brows.

  All thy old woes shall now smile on thee,
And thy pains sit bright upon thee;
All thy sorrows here shall shine,
All thy sufferings be divine;
Tears shall take comfort and turn gems,
And wrongs repent to diadems.

Even thy deaths shall live, and new
Dress the soul that erst they slew;
Thy wounds shall blush to such bright scars
As keep account of the Lamb's wars.
    Those rare works where thou shalt leave writ
Love's noble history, with wit
Taught thee by none but him, while here
They feed our souls, shall clothe thine there.
Each heav'nly word by whose hid flame
Our hard hearts shall strike fire, the same
Shall flourish on thy brows, and be
Both fire to us and flame to thee,
Whose light shall live bright in thy face
By glory, in our hearts by grace.
    Thou shalt look round about and see
Thousands of crowned souls throng to be
Themselves thy crown; sons of thy vows,
The virgin-births with which thy sovereign spouse
Made fruitful thy fair soul, go now
And with them all about thee, bow
To him. Put on, he'll say, put on,
My rosy love, that thy rich zone
Sparkling with the sacred flames
Of thousand souls whose happy names
Heav'n keeps upon thy score. Thy bright
Life brought them first to kiss the light
That kindled them to stars. And so
Thou with the Lamb, thy Lord, shalt go,
And wheresoe'er he sets his white
Steps, walk with him those ways of light
Which who in death would live to see
Must learn in life to die like thee.

An apology for the foregoing hymn, as having been writ when
    the author was yet among the Protestants

Thus have I back again to thy bright name
(Fair flood of holy fires!) transfused the flame

I took from reading thee; 'tis to thy wrong,
I know, that in my weak and worthless song
Thou here art set to shine where thy full day
Scarce dawns. O pardon if I dare to say
Thine own dear books are guilty, for from thence
I learned to know that love is eloquence.
That hopeful maxim gave me heart to try
If, what to other tongues is tuned so high,
Thy praise might not speak English too; forbid,
By all thy mysteries that here lie hid,
Forbid it, mighty love! let no fond hate
Of names and words so far prejudicate.
Souls are not Spaniards too; one friendly flood
Of baptism blends them all into a blood.
Christ's faith makes but one body of all souls,
And love's that body's soul; no law controls
Our free traffic for heav'n; we may maintain
Peace, sure, with piety, though it come from Spain.
What soul soe'er, in any language, can
Speak heav'n like hers is my soul's countryman.
Oh, 'tis not Spanish, but 'tis heav'n she speaks!
'Tis heaven that lies in ambush there, and breaks
From thence into the wond'ring reader's breast,
Who feels his warm heart hatched into a nest
Of little eagles and young loves, whose high
Flights scorn the lazy dust and things that die.
　　　There are enow whose draughts, as deep as hell,
Drink up all Spain in sack. Let my soul swell
With thee, strong wine of love! Let others swim
In puddles; we will pledge this seraphim
Bowls full of richer blood than blush of grape
Was ever guilty of; change we too our shape,
My soul: some drink from men to beasts—oh, then
Drink we till we prove more, not less, than men,
And turn not beasts but angels. Let the king
Me ever into these his cellars bring,
Where flows such wine as we can have of none
But him who trod the wine-press all alone,

Wine of youth, life, and the sweet deaths of love;
Wine of immortal mixture, which can prove
Its tincture from the rosy nectar; wine
That can exalt weak earth, and so refine
Our dust that at one draught mortality
May drink itself up, and forget to die.

5. GEORGE HERBERT:
THE CHURCH PORCH

¶THE seventeenth century witnessed a revival of religious poetry, due in large measure to the impetus given by George Herbert. He was not merely a genuine poet, but also a genuine mystic whose life in the Anglican Church reminds one frequently of the spirit in which St. Francis de Sales served the Catholic Church. Herbert was born in 1593, and educated at Cambridge. After his ordination to the ministry he suffered considerably from ill health and was forced to seek leisure. It was largely during the time diverted from the "cure of souls" that his poetry seems to have been written. His personality was of extraordinary sweetness and charm. It is interesting to note that the success of his verse was in no small measure due to the esteem in which he was held as a man by other literary people. Herbert died in 1632.

The Church Porch, reprinted here, forms the introduction (the "Perirrhanterium" Herbert himself styled it) of a volume of poetry that set forth the virtues, difficulties, feasts and joys of the Christian life. It is a remarkably complete exposition of these rules by means of which the soul can prepare itself for progress towards God. Nowhere else in English is there so reasonable and wise a treatise on this subject. Naturally, the reader will also note the unusual quality of Herbert's imagery, which can use very plain, homely things to illustrate a theme of almost unearthly loftiness. The author is never merely a poet, but he is nevertheless unfailingly a poet.*

* From *The Works of George Herbert*. Edited by the Rev. Robert Aris Willmott. London: George Routledge. N.D.

THE CHURCH PORCH

HOU, whose sweet youth and early hopes en-
    hance
    Thy rate and price, and mark thee for a
    treasure,
Hearken unto a Verser, who may chance
Rhyme thee to good, and make a bait of pleasure:
  A verse may find him, who a sermon flies,
  And turn delight into a sacrifice.

Beware of lust; it doth pollute and foul
Whom God in Baptism washed with His own blood;
It blots thy lesson written in thy soul;
The holy lines cannot be understood.
  How dare those eyes upon a Bible look,
  Much less towards God, whose lust is all their book?

Abstain wholly, or wed. Thy bounteous Lord
Allows thee choice of paths; take no by-ways;
But gladly welcome what He doth afford;
Not grudging that thy lust hath bounds and stays.
  Continence hath his joy; weigh both, and so
  If rottenness have more, let Heaven go.

If God had laid all common, certainly
Man would have been the encloser; but since now
God hath impaled us, on the contrary
Man breaks the fence, and every ground will plough.
  O, what were man, might he himself misplace!
  Sure to be cross, he would shift feet and face.

Drink not the third glass,—which thou canst not tame
When once it is within thee, but before
Mayst rule it as thou list,—and pour the shame,
Which it would pour on thee, upon the floor.
  It is most just to throw that on the ground
  Which would throw me there if I keep the round.

He that is drunken, may his mother kill
Big with his sister; he hath lost the reins,
Is outlawed by himself; all kind of ill
Did with his liquor slide into his veins.
    The drunkard forfeits Man, and doth divest
    All worldly right, save what he hath by Beast.

Shall I, to please another's wine-sprung mind,
Lose all mine own? God hath given me a measure
Short of his can and body; must I find
A pain in that wherein he finds a pleasure?
    Stay at the third glass; if thou lose thy hold,
    Then thou art modest, and the wine grows bold.

If reason move not gallants, quit the room—
All in a shipwreck shift their several way;
Let not a common ruin thee intomb:
Be not a beast in courtesy, but stay,—
    Stay at the third cup, or forego the place:
    Wine above all things doth God's stamp deface.

Yet, if thou sin in wine or wantonness,
Boast not thereof, nor make thy shame thy glory.
Frailty gets pardon by submissiveness;
But he that boasts shuts that out of his story;
    He makes flat war with God, and doth defy
    With his poor clod of earth the spacious sky.

Take not His Name, Who made thy mouth, in vain;
It gets thee nothing, and hath no excuse.
Lust and wine plead a pleasure, avarice gain;
But the cheap swearer through his open sluice
    Lets his soul run for nought, as little fearing:
    Were I an Epicure, I could bate swearing.

When thou dost tell another's jest, therein
Omit the oaths, which true wit cannot need;
Pick out of tales the mirth, but not the sin,
He pares his apple that will cleanly feed.

Play not away the virtue of that Name,
Which is thy best stake, when griefs make thee tame.

The cheapest sins most dearly punished are,
Because to shun them also is so cheap;
For we have wit to mark them, and to spare.
O crumble not away thy soul's fair heap!
    If thou wilt die, the gates of hell are broad;
    Pride and full sins have made the way a road.

Lie not; but let thy heart be true to God,
Thy mouth to it, thy actions to them both:
Cowards tell lies, and those that fear the rod;
The stormy-working soul spits lies and froth.
    Dare to be true. Nothing can need a lie;
    A fault, which needs it most, grows two thereby.

Fly idleness; which yet thou canst not fly
By dressing, mistressing, and compliment.
If those take up thy day, the sun will cry
Against thee; for his light was only lent.
    God gave thy soul brave wings; put not those feathers
    Into a bed, to sleep out all ill weathers.

Art thou a magistrate? then be severe;
If studious, copy fair what Time hath blurred,
Redeem truth from his jaws: if soldier,
Chase brave employments with a naked sword
    Throughout the world. Fool not; for all may have,
    If they dare try, a glorious life, or grave.

O England, full of sin, but most of sloth!
Spit out thy phlegm, and fill thy breast with glory;
Thy gentry bleats, as if thy native cloth [1]
Transfused a sheepishness into thy story;
    Not that they all are so, but that the most
    Are gone to grass, and in the pasture lost.

[1] A reference to the wool trade, for which in Herbert's time England had already long been noted.

This loss springs chiefly from our education:
Some till their ground, but let weeds choke their sons;
Some mark a partridge, never their child's fashion;
Some ship them over, and the thing is done.
    Study this art, make it thy great design;
    And if God's image move thee not, let thine.

Some great estates provide, but do not breed
A mastering mind; so both are lost thereby:
Or else they breed them tender, make them need
All that they leave; this is flat poverty:
    For he that needs five thousand pound to live
    Is full as poor as he that needs but five.[1]

The way to make thy son rich is to fill
His mind with rest, before his trunk with riches:
For wealth without contentment climbs a hill,
To feel those tempests which fly over ditches;
    But if thy son can make ten pound his measure,
    Then all thou addest may be called his treasure.

When thou dost purpose aught within they power,
Be sure to do it, though it be but small;
Constancy knits the bones, and makes us stour
When wanton pleasures beckon us to thrall.
    Who breaks his own bond forfeiteth himself;
    What nature made a ship, he makes a shelf.

Do all things like a man, not sneakingly;
Think the king sees thee still; for his King does.
Simpering is but a lay hypocrisy;
Give it a corner, and the clue undoes.
    Who fears to do ill sets himself to task;
    Who fears to do well sure should wear a mask.

---

[1] The same thought occurs in St. 30:
      "Who cannot live on twenty pound a-year,
        Cannot on forty."

Look to thy mouth; diseases enter there.
Thou hast two sconces: if thy stomach call,
Carve, or discourse; do not a famine fear:
Who carves is kind to two; who talks, to all.
    Look on meat, think it dirt, then eat a bit,
    And say withal, "Earth to earth I commit."

Slight those who say, amidst their sickly healths,
"Thou livest by rule." What doth not so but man?
Houses are built by rule, and Commonwealths.
Entice the trusty sun, if that you can,
    From his ecliptic line; beckon the sky!
    Who lives by rule, then, keeps good company.

Who keeps no guard upon himself is slack,
And rots to nothing at the next great thaw.
Man is a shop of rules, a well-trussed pack,
Whose every parcel under-writes a law.[1]
    Lose not thyself, nor give thy humours way;
    God gave them to thee under lock and key.

By all means use sometimes to be alone;
Salute thyself; see what thy soul doth wear;
Dare to look in thy chest, for 'tis thine own,
And tumble up and down what thou find'st there:
    Who cannot rest till he good fellows find,
    He breaks up house, turns out of doors his mind.

Be thrifty, but not covetous: therefore give
Thy need, thine honour, and thy friend his due.
Never was scraper brave man. Get to live;
Then live, and use it; else it is not true
    That thou hast gotten. Surely use alone
    Makes money not a contemptible stone.

---

[1] Parcel is here used in its original sense of little piece or portion. The sense of the passage seems to be that no rule of the moral nature can be transgressed without disorganizing the whole system.

Never exceed thy income. Youth may make
Even with the year; but Age, if it will hit,
Shoots a bow short, and lessens still his stake,
As the day lessens, and his life with it.
    Thy children, kindred, friends upon thee call:
    Before thy journey fairly part with all.

Yet in thy thriving still misdoubt some evil,
Lest gaining gain on thee, and make thee dim
To all things else. Wealth is the conjuror's devil,
Whom, when he thinks he hath, the devil hath him.
    Gold thou mayest safely touch; but if it stick
    Unto thy hands, it woundeth to the quick.

What skills it, if a bag of stones or gold
About thy neck do drown thee? Raise thy head;
Take stars for money,—stars not to be told
By any art, yet to be purchasèd.
    None is so wasteful as the scraping dame;
    She loseth three for one,—her soul, rest, fame.

By no means run in debt: take thine own measure.
Who cannot live on twenty pound a-year,
Cannot on forty; he's a man of pleasure,
A kind of thing that's for itself too dear.
    The curious unthrift makes his cloth too wide,
    And spares himself, but would his tailor chide.

Spend not on hopes. They that by pleading clothes
Do fortunes seek when worth and service fail,
Would have their tale believèd for their oaths,
And are like empty vessels under sail.
    Old courtiers know this: therefore set out so,
    As all the day thou mayst hold out to go.

In clothes, cheap handsomeness doth bear the bell;
Wisdom's a trimmer thing than shop e'er gave.
Say not, then, "This with that lace will do well;"
But, "This with my discretion will be brave."
    Much curiousness is a perpetual wooing,
    Nothing with labour, folly long a-doing.

Play not for gain, but sport. Who plays for more
Than he can lose with pleasure, stakes his heart;
Perhaps his wife's too, and whom she hath bore:
Servants and churches also play their part.
    Only a herald, who that way doth pass,
    Finds his cracked name at length in the church glass.

If yet thou love game at so dear a rate,
Learn this, that hath old gamesters dearly cost:
Dost lose? rise up; dost win; rise in that state:
Who strive to sit out losing hands are lost.
    Game is a civil gunpowder, in peace
    Blowing up houses with their whole increase.

In conversation boldness now bears sway:
But know, that nothing can so foolish be
As empty boldness: therefore, first essay
To stuff thy mind with solid bravery;
    Then march on gallant: get substantial worth;
    Boldness gilds finely, and will set it forth,

Be sweet to all. Is thy complexion sour?
Then keep such company; make them thy allay;
Get a sharp wife, a servant that will lour:
A stumbler stumbles least in rugged way.
    Command thyself in chief. He life's war knows,
    Whom all his passions follow, as he goes.

Catch not at quarrels. He that dares not speak
Plainly and home is coward of the two.
Think not thy fame at every twitch will break;
By great deeds show that thou canst little do—
    And do them not: that shall thy wisdom be;
    And charge thy temperance into bravery.

If that thy fame with every toy be posed,[1]
'Tis a thin web, which poisonous fancies make:
But the great soldier's honour was composed

[1] Posed = puzzled or perplexed.

Of thicker stuff, which would endure a shake.
  Wisdom picks friends; civility plays the rest:
  A toy shunned cleanly passeth with the best.

Laugh not too much; the witty man laughs least;
For wit is news only to ignorance.
Less at thine own things laugh, lest in the jest
Thy person share, and the conceit advance:
  Make not thy sport abuses; for the fly
  That feeds on dung is colourèd thereby.

Pick out of mirth, like stones out of thy ground,
Profaneness, filthiness, abusiveness;
These are the scum, with which coarse wits abound:
The fine may spare these well, yet not go less.
  All things are big with jest; nothing that's plain
  But may be witty, if thou hast the vein.

Wit's an unruly engine, wildly striking
Sometimes a friend, sometimes the engineer;
Hast thou the knack? pamper it not with liking;
But if thou want it, buy it not too dear.
  Many affecting wit beyond their power,
  Have got to be a dear fool for an hour.

A sad wise valour is the brave complexion
That leads the van and swallows up the cities.
The giggler is a milkmaid, whom infection
Or a fired beacon frighteneth from his ditties.
  Then he's the sport: the mirth then in him rests,
  And the sad man is cock of all his jests.

Towards great persons use respective boldness; [1]
That temper gives them theirs, and yet doth take
Nothing from thine; in service, care or coldness
Doth ratably thy fortunes mar or make.
  Feed no man in his sins; for adulation
  Doth make thee parcel-devil in damnation.

---

[1] Respective boldness = pay the respect due to their several persons, positions and stations.

Envy not greatness; for thou makest thereby
Thyself the worse, and so the distance greater.
Be not thine own worm; yet such jealousy
As hurts not others, but may make thee better,
   Is a good spur. Correct thy passion's spite;
   Then may the beasts draw thee to happy light.

When baseness is exalted, do not bate
The place its honour for the person's sake;
The shrine is that which thou dost venerate,
And not the beast that bears it on his back.
   I care not though the Cloth of State should be
   Not of rich arras but mean tapestry.

Thy friend put in thy bosom; wear his eyes
Still in thy heart, that he may see what's there.
If cause require thou art his sacrifice,
Thy drops of blood must pay down all his fear:
   But love is lost, the way of friendship's gone,
   Though David had his Jonathan, Christ His John.

Yet be not surety, if thou be a father:
Love is a personal debt; I cannot give
My children's right, nor ought he take it: rather
Both friends should die than hinder them to live.
   Fathers first enter bonds to Nature's ends,
   And are her sureties ere they are a friend's.

If thou be single, all thy goods and ground
Submit to love; but yet not more than all:
Give one estate, as one life. None is bound
To work for two, who brought himself to thrall.
   God made me one man: love makes me no more,
   Till labour come and make my weakness score.

In thy discourse, if thou desire to please,
All such is courteous, useful, new, or witty:
Usefulness comes by labour, wit by ease;
Courtesy grows in Court, news in the city:
   Get a good stock of these, then draw the card
   That suits him best of whom thy speech is heard.

Entice all neatly to what they know best;
For so thou dost thyself and him a pleasure;—
But a proud ignorance will lose his rest
Rather than show his cards;—steal from his treasure
   What to ask further: doubts well-raised do lock
   The speaker to thee, and preserve thy stock.

If thou be master-gunner, spend not all
That thou canst speak at once, but husband it,
And give men turns of speech; do not forestall
By lavishness thine own and others' wit,
   As if thou mad'st thy will: a civil guest
   Will no more talk all than eat all the feast.

Be calm in arguing: for fierceness makes
Error a fault, and truth discourtesy.
Why should I feel another man's mistakes
More than his sicknesses, or poverty?
   In love I should; but anger is not love,
   Nor wisdom neither; therefore gently move.

Calmness is great advantage; he that lets
Another chafe, may warm him at his fire,
Mark all his wanderings, and enjoy his frets,
As cunning fencers suffer heat to tire.
   Truth dwells not in the clouds; the bow that's there
   Doth often aim at, never hit the sphere.

Mark what another says; for many are
Full of themselves, and answer their own notion.
Take all into thee; then with equal care
Balance each dram of reason, like a potion.
   If truth be with thy friend, be with them both,
   Share in the conquest, and confess a troth.

Be useful where thou livest, that they may
Both want and wish thy pleasing presence still.
Kindness, good parts, great places, are the way
To compass this. Find out men's wants and will,
   And meet them there. All worldly joys go less
   To the one joy of doing kindnesses.

Pitch thy behaviour low, thy projects high;
So shalt thou humble and magnanimous be:
Sink not in spirit; who aimeth at the sky
Shoots higher much than he that means a tree.
    A grain of glory mixed with humbleness
    Cures both a fever and lethargicness.

Let thy mind still be bent, still plotting where
And when and how the business may be done.
Slackness breeds worms; but the sure traveller,
Though he alights sometimes, still goeth on.
    Active and stirring spirits live alone;
    Write on the others "Here lies such a one."

Slight not the smallest loss, whether it be
In love or honour; take account of all:
Shine like the sun in every corner: see
Whether thy stock of credit swell or fall.
    Who say "I care not," those I give for lost:
    And to instruct them 'twill not quit the cost.

Scorn no man's love, though of a mean degree;
Love is a present for a mighty king;
Much less make any one thine enemy.
As guns destroy, so may a little sling.
    The cunning workman never doth refuse
    The meanest tool that he may chance to use.

All foreign wisdom doth amount to this,
To take all that is given, whether wealth,
Or love, or language; nothing comes amiss;
A good digestion turneth all to health:
    And then, as far as fair behaviour may,
    Strike off all scores; none are so clear as they.

Keep all thy native good, and naturalise
All foreign of that name; but scorn their ill;
Embrace their activeness, not vanities:

Who follows all things, forfeiteth his will.
  If thou observest strangers in each fit,
  In time they'll run thee out of all thy wit.

Affect in things about thee cleanliness,
That all may gladly board thee, as a flower.
Slovens take up their stock of noisomeness
Beforehand, and anticipate their last hour.
  Let thy mind's sweetness have his operation
  Upon thy body, clothes, and habitation.

In alms regard thy means, and others' merit;
Think heaven a better bargain than to give
Only thy single market-money for it;
Join hands with God to make a man to live,
  Give to all something; to a good poor man,
  Till thou change names, and be where he began.

Man is God's image; but a poor man is
Christ's stamp to boot; both images regard.
God reckons for him, counts the favour His;
Write, "So much given to God"; thou shalt be heard.
  Let thy alms go before, and keep heaven's gate
  Open for thee; or both may come too late.

Restore to God His due in tithe and time;
A tithe purloined cankers the whole estate.
Sundays observe; think when the bells do chime,
'Tis angels' music; therefore come not late.
  God then deals blessings: if a king did so,
  Who would not haste, nay give, to see the show?

Twice on the day His due is understood;
For all the week thy food so oft He gave thee
Thy cheer is mended; bate not of the food,
Because 'tis better, and perhaps may save thee.
  Thwart not the Almighty God; O, be not cross!
  Fast when thou wilt; but then 'tis gain, not loss.

Though private prayer be a brave design,
Yet public hath more promises, more love;
And love's a weight to hearts, to eyes a sign.
We all are but cold suitors; let us move
    Where it is warmest. Leave thy six and seven;
    Pray with the most; for where most pray is heaven.

When once thy foot enters the Church, be bare;
God is more there than thou; for thou art there
Only by His permission: then beware,
And make thyself all reverence and fear.
    Kneeling ne'er spoiled silk stocking; quit thy state;
    All equal are within the Church's gate.

Resort to sermons, but to prayers most:
Praying's the end of preaching. O, be drest;
Stay not for the other pin! Why, thou hast lost
A joy for it worth worlds. Thus Hell doth jest
    Away thy blessings, and extremely flout thee,
    Thy clothes being fast, but thy soul loose about thee.

In time of service seal up both thine eyes,
And send them to thy heart; that, spying sin,
They may weep out the stains by them did rise:
Those doors being shut, all by the ear comes in.
    Who marks in church-time others' symmetry,
    Makes all their beauty his deformity.

Let vain or busy thoughts have there no part;
Bring not thy plough, thy plots, thy pleasures thither.
Christ purged His Temple; so must thou thy heart:
All worldly thoughts are but thieves met together
    To cozen thee. Look to thy actions well;
    For churches either are our Heaven or Hell.

Judge not the preacher, for he is thy judge;
If thou mislike him, thou conceiv'st him not.
God calleth preaching folly: do not grudge
To pick out treasures from an earthen pot.
    The worst speak something good; if all want sense,
    God takes a text, and preacheth patience.

He that gets patience, and the blessing which
Preachers conclude with, hath not lost his pains.
He that by being at Church escapes the ditch,
Which he might fall in by companions, gains.
    He that loves God's abode, and to combine
    With saints on earth, shall one day with them shine.

Jest not at preacher's language or expression;
How know'st thou but thy sins made him miscarry?
Then turn thy faults and his into confession:
God sent him, whatsoe'er he be; O, tarry,
    And love him for his Master; his condition,
    Though it be ill, makes him no ill physician.

None shall in Hell such bitter pangs endure
As those who mock at God's way of salvation:
Whom oil and balsams kill, what salve can cure?
They drink with greediness a full damnation.
    The Jews refusèd thunder, and we, folly;
    Though God do hedge us in, yet who is holy?

Sum up at night what thou hast done by day,
And in the morning what thou hast to do;
Dress and undress thy soul; mark the decay
And growth of it; if with thy watch that too
    Be down, then wind up both: since we shall be
    Most surely judged, make thy accounts agree.

In brief, acquit thee bravely, play the man;
Look not on pleasures as they come, but go;
Defer not the least virtue: life's poor span
Make not an ell by trifling in thy woe.
    If thou do ill, the joy fades, not the pains;
    If well, the pain doth fade, the joy remains.

6. JOHN HENRY NEWMAN:

THE DREAM OF GERONTIUS

¶NEWMAN, dedicating his collected verse to Edward Badeley in 1867, professed inability to distinguish between his poems from the point of view of their artistic merit. But many of these lyrics were faithful reflections of moods which had played a part in the "religious movement" which had formed so integral a part of his life; and some have kept their charm for many succeeding generations. *Lead Kindly Light* is surely one of the best-known hymns in the English language. Of almost equal popularity is the *Dream of Gerontius*, here reprinted. Newman was at first tempted to cast it aside, but was persuaded to let the editor of the London *Month* have it for publication in his magazine.

Since then it has often been reprinted. General "Chinese" Gordon carried it with him on his campaigns, and many another famous man virtually learned it by heart. The poem has no great æsthetic value, but there is little other meditation literature in English to compare with it. "Gerontius" means, of course, "aging man." It was written at a time (1865) when Newman himself, though destined to live many more years, felt that his powers were flagging and that death was near at hand.*

---

* From *Verses on Various Occasions*. By John Henry Newman. London: Longmans, Green and Co., 1890.

THE DREAM OF GERONTIUS

§ I.

GERONTIUS

ESU, MARIA—I am near to death,
    And Thou art calling me; I know it now.
Not by the token of this faltering breath,
    This chill at heart, this dampness on my brow,
    (Jesu, have mercy! Mary, pray for me!)
    'Tis this new feeling, never felt before,
(Be with me, Lord, in my extremity!)
    That I am going, that I am no more.
'Tis this strange innermost abandonment,
    (Lover of souls! great God! I look to Thee,)
This emptying out of each constituent
    And natural force, by which I come to be.
Pray for me, O my friends; a visitant
    Is knocking his dire summons at my door,
The like of whom, to scare me and to daunt,
    Has never, never come to me before;
'Tis death,—O loving friends, your prayers!—'tis he! . . .
As though my very being had given way,
    As though I was no more a substance now,
And could fall back on nought to be my stay,
    (Help, loving Lord! Thou my sole Refuge, Thou,)
And turn no whither, but must needs decay
    And drop from out the universal frame
Into that shapeless, scopeless, blank abyss,
    That utter nothingness, of which I came:
This is it that has come to pass in me;
    Oh, horror! this it is, my dearest, this;
So pray for me, my friends, who have not strength to pray.

ASSISTANTS

Kyrie eleïson, Christe eleïson, Kyrie eleïson.
Holy Mary, pray for him.
All holy Angels, pray for him.

Choirs of the righteous, pray for him.
Holy Abraham, pray for him.
St. John Baptist, St. Joseph, pray for him.
St. Peter, St. Paul, St. Andrew, St. John,
All Apostles, all Evangelists, pray for him.
All holy Disciples of the Lord, pray for him.
All holy Innocents, pray for him.
All holy Martyrs, all holy Confessors,
All holy Hermits, all holy Virgins,
All ye Saints of God, pray for him.

GERONTIUS

Rouse thee, my fainting soul, and play the man;
    And through such waning span
Of life and thought as still has to be trod,
    Prepare to meet thy God.
And while the storm of that bewilderment
    Is for a season spent,
And, ere afresh the ruin on me fall,
    Use well the interval.

ASSISTANTS

Be merciful, be gracious; spare him, Lord.
Be merciful, be gracious; Lord, deliver him.
From the sins that are past;
  From Thy frown and Thine ire;
      From the perils of dying;
      From any complying
      With sin, or denying
      His God, or relying
    On self, at the last;
    From the nethermost fire;
  From all that is evil;
  From power of the devil;
  Thy servant deliver,
  For once and for ever.

By Thy birth, and by Thy Cross,
Rescue him from endless loss;

By Thy death and burial,
Save him from a final fall;
By Thy rising from the tomb,
  By Thy mounting up above,
  By the Spirit's gracious love,
Save him in the day of doom.

GERONTIUS

Sanctus fortis, Sanctus Deus,
  De profundis oro te,
Miserere, Judex meus,
  Parce mihi, Domine.
Firmly I believe and truly
  God is three, and God is One;
And I next acknowledge duly
  Manhood taken by the Son.
And I trust and hope most fully
  In that Manhood crucified;
And each thought and deed unruly
  Do to death, as He has died.
Simply to His grace and wholly
  Light and life and strength belong,
And I love, supremely, solely,
  Him the holy, Him the strong.
Sanctus fortis, Sanctus Deus,
  De profundis oro te,
Miserere, Judex meus,
  Parce mihi, Domine.
And I hold in veneration,
  For the love of Him alone,
Holy Church, as His creation,
  And her teachings, as His own.
And I take with joy whatever
  Now besets me, pain or fear,
And with a strong will I sever
  All the ties which bind me here.
Adoration aye be given,
  With and through the angelic host,

To the God of earth and heaven,
    Father, Son, and Holy Ghost.
Sanctus fortis, Sanctus Deus,
    De profundis oro te,
Miserere, Judex meus,
    Mortis in discrimine.

I can no more; for now it comes again,
That sense of ruin, which is worse than pain,
That masterful negation and collapse
Of all that makes me man; as though I bent
Over the dizzy brink
Of some sheer infinite descent;
Or worse, as though
Down, down for ever I was falling through
The solid framework of created things,
And needs must sink and sink
Into the vast abyss. And, crueller still,
A fierce and restless fright begins to fill
The mansion of my soul. And, worse and worse,
Some bodily form of ill
Floats on the wind, with many a loathsome curse
Tainting the hallow'd air, and laughs, and flaps
Its hideous wings,
And makes me wild with horror and dismay.
O Jesu, help! pray for me, Mary, pray!
Some Angel, Jesu! such as came to Thee
In Thine own agony. . . .
Mary, pray for me. Joseph, pray for me. Mary, pray for me.

ASSISTANTS

Rescue him, O Lord, in this his evil hour,
As of old so many in Thy gracious power:—(Amen.)
Enoch and Elias from the common doom; (Amen.)
Noe from the waters in a saving home; (Amen.)
Abraham from th' abounding guilt of Heathenesse; (Amen.)
Job from all his multiform and fell distress; (Amen.)
Isaac, when his father's knife was raised to slay; (Amen.)

Lot from burning Sodom on its judgment-day; (Amen.)
Moses from the land of bondage and despair; (Amen.)
Daniel from the hungry lions in their lair; (Amen.)
And the Children Three amid the furnace-flame; (Amen.)
Chaste Susanna from the slander and the shame; (Amen.)
David from Golia and the wrath of Saul; (Amen.)
And the two Apostles from their prison-thrall; (Amen.)
Thecla from her torments; (Amen:)
                              —so to show Thy power,
Rescue this Thy servant in his evil hour.

GERONTIUS

Novissima hora est; and I fain would sleep.
The pain has wearied me . . . Into Thy hands,
O Lord, into Thy hands . . . .

THE PRIEST

Proficiscere, anima Christiana, de hoc mundo!
Go forth upon thy journey, Christian soul!
Go from this world! Go, in the Name of God
The Omnipotent Father, who created thee!
Go in the Name of Jesus Christ, our Lord,
Son of the living God, who bled for thee!
Go, in the Name of the Holy Spirit, who
Hath been pour'd out on thee! Go, in the name
Of Angels and Archangels; in the name
Of Thrones and Dominations; in the name
Of Princedoms and of Powers; and in the name
Of Cherubim and Seraphim, go forth!
Go, in the name of Patriarchs and Prophets;
And of Apostles and Evangelists,
Of Martyrs and Confessors; in the name
Of Holy Monks and Hermits; in the name
Of Holy Virgins; and all Saints of God,
Both men and women, go! Go on thy course;
And may thy place to-day be found in peace,
And may thy dwelling be the Holy Mount
Of Sion:—through the Same, through Christ, our Lord.

§ 2

SOUL OF GERONTIUS

I went to sleep; and now I am refresh'd,
A strange refreshment: for I feel in me
An inexpressive lightness, and a sense
Of freedom, as I were at length myself,
And ne'er had been before. How still it is!
I hear no more the busy beat of time,
No, nor my fluttering breath, nor struggling pulse;
Nor does one moment differ from the next.
I had a dream; yes:—some one softly said
"He's gone;" and then a sigh went round the room.
And then I surely heard a priestly voice
Cry "Subvenite;" and they knelt in prayer.
I seem to hear him still; but thin and low,
And fainter and more faint the accents come,
As at an ever-widening interval.
Ah! whence is this? What is this severance?
This silence pours a solitariness
Into the very essence of my soul;
And the deep rest, so soothing and so sweet,
Hath something too of sternness and of pain.
For it drives back my thoughts upon their spring
By a strange introversion, and perforce
I now begin to feed upon myself,
Because I have nought else to feed upon.—

Am I alive or dead? I am not dead,
But in the body still; for I possess
A sort of confidence which clings to me,
That each particular organ holds its place
As heretofore, combining with the rest
Into one symmetry, that wraps me round,
And makes me man; and surely I could move,
Did I but will it, every part of me.
And yet I cannot to my sense bring home
By very trial, that I have the power.

'Tis strange; I cannot stir a hand or foot,
I cannot make my fingers or my lips
By mutual pressure witness each to each,
Nor by the eyelid's instantaneous stroke
Assure myself I have a body still.
Nor do I know my very attitude,
Nor if I stand, or lie, or sit, or kneel.

So much I know, not knowing how I know,
That the vast universe, where I have dwelt,
Is quitting me, or I am quitting it.
Or I or it is rushing on the wings
Of light or lightning on an onward course,
And we e'en now are million miles apart.
Yet . . . is this peremptory severance
Wrought out in lengthening measurements of space,
Which grow and multiply by speed and time?
Or am I traversing infinity
By endless subdivision, hurrying back
From finite towards infinitesimal,
Thus dying out of the expansive world?

Another marvel: some one has me fast
Within his ample palm; 'tis not a grasp
Such as they use on earth, but all around
Over the surface of my subtle being,
As though I were a sphere, and capable
To be accosted thus, a uniform
And gentle pressure tells me I am not
Self-moving, but borne forward on my way.
And hark! I hear a singing; yet in sooth
I cannot of that music rightly say
Whether I hear, or touch, or taste the tones.
Oh, what a heart-subduing melody!

ANGEL

My work is done,
My task is o'er,
And so I come,
Taking it home,

For the crown is won,
    Alleluia,
For evermore.
My work is done,

My Father gave
    In charge to me
        This child of earth
        E'en from its birth,
To serve and save,
    Alleluia,
    And saved is he.

This child of clay
    To me was given,
        To rear and train
        By sorrow and pain
In the narrow way,
    Alleluia,
    From earth to heaven.

SOUL

It is a member of that family
Of wondrous beings, who, ere the worlds were made,
Millions of ages back, have stood around
The throne of God:—he never has known sin
But through those cycles all but infinite,
Has had a strong and pure celestial life,
And bore to gaze on the unveil'd face of God,
And drank from the everlasting Fount of truth,
And served Him with a keen ecstatic love.
Hark! he begins again.

ANGEL

O Lord, how wonderful is depth and height,
    But most in man, how wonderful Thou art!
With what a love, what soft persuasive might
    Victorious o'er the stubborn fleshly heart,
    Thy tale complete of saints Thou dost provide,
    To fill the thrones which angels lost through pride!

He lay a grovelling babe upon the ground,
     Polluted in the blood of his first sire,
With his whole essence shatter'd and unsound,
     And coil'd around his heart a demon dire,
Which was not of his nature, but had skill
To bind and form his op'ning mind to ill.

Then I was sent from heaven to set right
     The balance in his soul of truth and sin,
And I have waged a long relentless fight,
     Resolved that death-environ'd spirit to win,
Which from its fallen state, when all was lost,
Had been repurchased at so dread a cost.

Oh, what a shifting parti-colour'd scene
     Of hope and fear, of triumph and dismay,
Of recklessness and penitence, has been
     The history of that dreary, life-long fray!
And oh, the grace to nerve him and to lead,
How patient, prompt, and lavish at his need!

O man, strange composite of heaven and earth!
     Majesty dwarf'd to baseness! fragrant flower
Running to poisonous seed! and seeming worth
     Cloking corruption! weakness mastering power!
Who never art so near to crime and shame,
As when thou hast achieved some deed of name;—

How should ethereal natures comprehend
     A thing made up of spirit and of clay,
Were we not task'd to nurse it and to tend,
     Link'd one to one throughout its mortal day?
More than the Seraph in his height of place,
The Angel-guardian knows and loves the ransom'd race.

SOUL

Now know I surely that I am at length
Out of the body; had I part with earth,
I never could have drunk those accents in,
And not have worshipp'd as a god the voice
That was so musical; but now I am

So whole of heart, so calm, so self-possess'd,
With such a full content, and with a sense
So apprehensive and discriminant,
As no temptation can intoxicate.
Nor have I even terror at the thought
That I am clasp'd by such a saintliness.

ANGEL

All praise to Him, at whose sublime decree
    The last are first, the first become the last;
By whom the suppliant prisoner is set free,
    By whom proud first-borns from their thrones are cast;
Who raises Mary to be Queen of heaven,
While Lucifer is left, condemn'd and unforgiven.

§ 3

SOUL

I will address him. Mighty one, my Lord,
My Guardian Spirit, all hail!

ANGEL

                All hail, my child!
My child and brother, hail! what wouldest thou?

SOUL

I would have nothing but to speak to thee
For speaking's sake. I wish to hold with thee
Conscious communion; though I fain would know
A maze of things, were it but meet to ask,
And not a curiousness.

ANGEL

          You cannot now
Cherish a wish which ought not to be wish'd.

SOUL

Then I will speak. I ever had believed
That on the moment when the struggling soul

Quitted its mortal case, forthwith it fell
Under the awful Presence of its God,
There to be judged and sent to its own place.
What lets me now from going to my Lord?

ANGEL

Thou art not let; but with extremest speed
Art hurrying to the Just and Holy Judge:
For scarcely art thou disembodied yet.
Divide a moment, as men measure time,
Into its million-million-millionth part,
Yet even less than that the interval
Since thou didst leave the body; and the priest
Cried "Subvenite," and they fell to prayer;
Nay, scarcely yet have they begun to pray.

For spirits and men by different standards mete
The less and greater in the flow of time.
By sun and moon, primeval ordinances—
By stars which rise and set harmoniously—
By the recurring seasons, and the swing,
This way and that, of the suspended rod
Precise and punctual, men divide the hours,
Equal, continuous, for their common use.
Not so with us in the immaterial world;
But intervals in their succession
Are measured by the living thought alone,
And grow or wane with its intensity.
And time is not a common property;
But what is long is short, and swift is slow,
And near is distant, as received and grasp'd
By this mind and by that, and every one
Is standard of his own chronology.
And memory lacks its natural resting-points
Of years, and centuries, and periods.
It is thy very energy of thought
Which keeps thee from thy God.

SOUL

Dear Angel, say,
Why have I now no fear at meeting Him?
Along my earthly life, the thought of death
And judgment was to me most terrible.
I had it aye before me, and I saw
The Judge severe e'en in the Crucifix.
Now that the hour is come, my fear is fled;
And at this balance of my destiny,
Now close upon me, I can forward look
With a serenest joy.

ANGEL

It is because
Then thou didst fear, that now thou dost not fear,
Thou hast forestall'd the agony, and so
For thee the bitterness of death is past.
Also, because already in thy soul
The judgment is begun. That day of doom,
One and the same for the collected world,—
That solemn consummation for all flesh,
Is, in the case of each, anticipate
Upon his death; and, as the last great day
In the particular judgment is rehearsed,
So now, too, ere thou comest to the Throne,
A presage falls upon thee, as a ray
Straight from the Judge, expressive of thy lot.
That calm and joy uprising in thy soul
Is first-fruit to thee of thy recompense,
And heaven begun.

§ 4

SOUL

But hark! upon my sense
Comes a fierce hubbub, which would make me fear
Could I be frighted.

ANGEL

We are now arrived
Close on the judgment-court; that sullen howl
Is from the demons who assemble there.
It is the middle region, where of old
Satan appeared among the sons of God,
To cast his jibes and scoffs at holy Job.
So now his legions throng the vestibule,
Hungry and wild, to claim their property,
And gather souls for hell. Hist to their cry.

SOUL

How sour and how uncouth a dissonance!

DEMONS

Low-born clods
   Of brute earth,
      They aspire
To become gods,
   By a new birth,
And an extra grace,
   And a score of merits,
      As if aught
Could stand in place
      Of the high thought,
   And the glance of fire
Of the great spirits,
The powers blest,
   The lords by right,
      The primal owners,
      Of the proud dwelling
   And realm of light,—
Dispossess'd,
Aside thrust,
      Chuck'd down
   By the sheer might
Of a despot's will,
      Of a tyrant's frown,

Who after expelling
Their hosts, gave,
Triumphant still,
And still unjust,
Each forfeit crown
To psalm-droners,
And canting groaners,
To every slave,
And pious cheat,
And crawling knave,
Who lick'd the dust
Under his feet.

ANGEL

It is the restless panting of their being;
Like beasts of prey, who, caged within their bars,
In a deep hideous purring have their life,
And an incessant pacing to and fro.

DEMONS

The mind bold
And independent,
The purpose free,
So we are told,
Must not think
To have the ascendant.
What's a saint?
One whose breath
Doth the air taint
Before his death;
A bundle of bones,
Which fools adore,
Ha! ha!
When life is o'er;
Which rattle and stink,
E'en in the flesh.
We cry his pardon!
No flesh hath he;
Ha! ha!

For it hath died,
'Tis crucified
Day by day,
Afresh, afresh,
Ha! ha!
That holy clay,
Ha! ha!
This gains guerdon,
So priestlings prate,
Ha! ha!
Before the Judge,
And pleads and atones
For spite and grudge,
And bigot mood,
And envy and hate,
And greed of blood.

SOUL

How impotent they are! and yet on earth
They have repute for wondrous power and skill;
And books describe, how that the very face
Of the Evil One, if seen, would have a force
Even to freeze the blood, and choke the life
Of him who saw it.

ANGEL

In thy trial-state
Thou hadst a traitor nestling close at home,
Connatural, who with the powers of hell
Was leagued, and of thy senses kept the keys,
And to that deadliest foe unlock'd thy heart.
And therefore is it, in respect to man,
Those fallen ones show so majestical.
But, when some child of grace, Angel or Saint,
Pure and upright in his integrity
Of nature, meets the demons on their raid,
They scud away as cowards from the fight.
Nay, oft hath holy hermit in his cell,
Not yet disburden'd of mortality,

Mock'd at their threats and warlike overtures;
Or, dying, when they swarm'd, like flies, around,
Defied them, and departed to his Judge.

DEMONS

Virtue and vice,
    A knave's pretence,
        'Tis all the same;
        Ha! ha!
            Dread of hell-fire,
    Of the venomous flame,
               A coward's plea.
Give him his price,
            Saint though he be,
Ha! ha!
    From shrewd good sense
            He'll slave for hire
    Ha! ha!
        And does but aspire
To the heaven above
        With sordid aim,
And not from love.
           Ha! ha!

SOUL

I see not those false spirits; shall I see
My dearest Master, when I reach His Throne?
Or hear, at least, His awful judgment-word
With personal intonation, as I now
Hear thee, not see thee, Angel? Hitherto
All has been darkness since I left the earth;
Shall I remain thus sight-bereft all through
My penance-time? If so, how comes it then
That I have hearing still, and taste, and touch,
Yet not a glimmer of that princely sense
Which binds ideas in one, and makes them live?

ANGEL

Nor touch, nor taste, nor hearing hast thou now;
Thou livest in a world of signs and types,
The presentations of most holy truths,
Living and strong, which now encompass thee.
A disembodied soul, thou hast by right
No converse with aught else beside thyself;
But, lest so stern a solitude should load
And break thy being, in mercy are vouchsafed
Some lower measures of perception,
Which seem to thee, as though through channels brought,
Through ear, or nerves, or palate, which are gone.
And thou art wrapp'd and swathed around in dreams,
Dreams that are true, yet enigmatical;
For the belongings of thy present state,
Save through such symbols, come not home to thee.
And thus thou tell'st of space, and time, and size,
Of fragrant, solid, bitter, musical,
Of fire, and of refreshment after fire;
As (let me use similitude of earth,
To aid thee in the knowledge thou dost ask)—
As ice which blisters may be said to burn.
Nor hast thou now extension, with its parts
Correlative,—long habit cozens thee,—
Nor power to move thyself, nor limbs to move.
Hast thou not heard of those, who after loss
Of hand or foot, still cried that they had pains
In hand or foot, as though they had it still?
So it is now with thee, who hast not lost
Thy hand or foot, but all which made up man.
So will it be, until the joyous day
Of resurrection, when thou wilt regain
All thou hast lost, new-made and glorified.
How, even now, the consummated Saints
See God in heaven, I may not explicate;
Meanwhile, let it suffice thee to possess
Such means of converse as are granted thee,
Though, till that Beatific Vision, thou art blind;

For e'en thy purgatory, which comes like fire,
Is fire without its light.

SOUL

His will be done!
I am not worthy e'er to see again
The face of day; far less His countenance,
Who is the very sun. Natheless in life,
When I looked forward to my purgatory,
It ever was my solace to believe,
That, ere I plunged amid the avenging flame,
I had one sight of Him to strengthen me.

ANGEL

Nor rash nor vain is that presentiment;
Yes,—for one moment thou shalt see thy Lord.
Thus will it be: what time thou art arraign'd
Before the dread tribunal, and thy lot
Is cast for ever, should it be to sit
On His right hand among His pure elect,
Then sight, or that which to the soul is sight,
As by a lightning-flash, will come to thee,
And thou shalt see, amid the dark profound,
Whom thy soul loveth, and would fain approach,—
One moment; but thou knowest not, my child,
What thou dost ask: that sight of the Most Fair
Will gladden thee, but it will pierce thee too.

SOUL

Thou speakest darkly, Angel; and an awe
Falls on me, and a fear lest I be rash.

ANGEL

There was a mortal, who is now above
In the mid-glory: he, when near to die,
Was given communion with the Crucified,—
Such, that the Master's very wounds were stamp'd
Upon his flesh; and, from that agony
Which thrill'd through body and soul in that embrace,

Learn that the flame of the Everlasting Love
Doth burn ere it transform. . . .

§ 5

. . . Hark to those sounds!
They come of tender beings angelical,
Least and most childlike of the sons of God.

FIRST CHOIR OF ANGELICALS

Praise to the Holiest in the height,
    And in the depth be praise:
In all His words most wonderful;
    Most sure in all His ways.

To us His elder race He gave
    To battle and to win,
Without the chastisement of pain,
    Without the soil of sin.

The younger son He will'd to be
    A marvel in His birth:
Spirit and flesh his parents were;
    His home was heaven and earth.

The Eternal bless'd His child, and arm'd
    And sent him hence afar,
To serve as champion in the field
    Of elemental war.

To be His Viceroy in the world
    Of matter, and of sense;
Upon the frontier, towards the foe
    A resolute defence.

ANGEL

We now have pass'd the gate, and are within
The House of Judgment; and whereas on earth
Temples and palaces are form'd of parts
Costly and rare, but all material,
So in the world of spirits nought is found,

To mould withal, and form into a whole,
But what is immaterial; and thus
The smallest portions of this edifice,
Cornice, or frieze, or balustrade, or stair,
The very pavement is made up of life—
Of holy, blessed, and immortal beings,
Who hymn their Maker's praise continually.

SECOND CHOIR OF ANGELICALS

Praise to the Holiest in the height,
   And in the depth be praise:
In all His words most wonderful;
   Most sure in all His ways!

Woe to thee, man! for he was found
   A recreant in the fight;
And lost his heritage of heaven,
   And fellowship with light.

Above him now the angry sky,
   Around the tempest's din;
Who once had Angels for his friends,
   Had but the brutes for kin.

O man! a savage kindred they;
   To flee that monster brood
He scaled the seaside cave, and clomb
   The giants of the wood.

With now a fear, and now a hope,
   With aids which chance supplied,
From youth to eld, from sire to son,
   He lived, and toil'd, and died.

He dreed his penance age by age;
   And step by step began
Slowly to doff his savage garb,
   And be again a man.

And quicken'd by the Almighty's breath,
   And chasten'd by His rod,

And taught by angel-visitings,
    At length he sought his God;

And learn'd to call upon His Name,
    And in His faith create
A household and a father-land,
    A city and a state.

Glory to Him who from the mire,
    In patient length of days,
Elaborated into life
    A people to His praise!

SOUL

The sound is like the rushing of the wind—
The summer wind—among the lofty pines;
Swelling and dying, echoing round about,
Now here, now distant, wild and beautiful;
While, scatter'd from the branches it has stirr'd
Descend ecstatic odours.

THIRD CHOIR OF ANGELICALS

Praise to the Holiest in the height,
    And in the depth be praise:
In all His words most wonderful;
    Most sure in all His ways!

The Angels, as beseemingly
    To spirit-kind was given,
At once were tried and perfected,
    And took their seats in heaven.

For them no twilight or eclipse;
    No growth and no decay:
'Twas hopeless, all-ingulfing night,
    Or beatific day.

But to the younger race there rose
    A hope upon its fall;
And slowly, surely, gracefully,
    The morning dawn'd on all.

And ages, opening out, divide
    The precious, and the base,
And from the hard and sullen mass
    Mature the heirs of grace.

O man! albeit the quickening ray,
    Lit from his second birth,
Makes him at length what once he was,
    And heaven grows out of earth;

Yet still between that earth and heaven—
    His journey and his goal—
A double agony awaits
    His body and his soul.

A double debt he has to pay—
    The forfeit of his sins:
The chill of death is past, and now
    The penance-fire begins.

Glory to Him, who evermore
    By truth and justice reigns;
Who tears the soul from out its case,
    And burns away its stains!

ANGEL

They sing of thy approaching agony,
Which thou so eagerly didst question of:
It is the face of the Incarnate God
Shall smite thee with that keen and subtle pain;
And yet the memory which it leaves will be
A sovereign febrifuge to heal the wound;
And yet withal it will the wound provoke,
And aggravate and widen it the more.

SOUL

Thou speakest mysteries; still methinks I know
To disengage the tangle of thy words:
Yet rather would I hear thy angel voice,
Than for myself be thy interpreter.

ANGEL

When then—if such thy lot—thou seest thy Judge,
The sight of Him will kindle in thy heart
All tender, gracious, reverential thoughts.
Thou wilt be sick with love, and yearn for Him,
And feel as though thou couldst but pity Him,
That one so sweet should e'er have placed Himself
At disadvantage such, as to be used
So vilely by a being so vile as thee.
There is a pleading in His pensive eyes
Will pierce thee to the quick, and trouble thee.
And thou wilt hate and loathe thyself; for, though
Now sinless, thou wilt feel that thou hast sinn'd,
As never thou didst feel; and wilt desire
To slink away, and hide thee from His sight:
And yet wilt have a longing eye to dwell
Within the beauty of His countenance
And these two pains, so counter and so keen,—
The longing for Him, when thou seest Him not;
The shame of self at thought of seeing Him,—
Will be thy veriest, sharpest purgatory.

SOUL

My soul is in my hand: I have no fear,—
In His dear might prepared for weal or woe.
But hark! a grand, mysterious harmony:
It floods me like the deep and solemn sound
Of many waters.

ANGEL

　　　　　We have gain'd the stairs
Which rise towards the Presence-chamber; there
A band of mighty Angels keep the way
On either side, and hymn the Incarnate God.

ANGELS OF THE SACRED STAIRS

Father, whose goodness none can know, but they
　　Who see Thee face to face,

By man hath come the infinite display
Of thy victorious grace;
But fallen man—the creature of a day—
Skills not that love to trace.
It needs, to tell the triumph Thou hast wrought,
An Angel's deathless fire, an Angel's reach of thought.

It needs that very Angel, who with awe,
Amid the garden shade,
The great Creator in His sickness saw,
Soothed by a creature's aid,
And agonized, as victim of the Law
Which He Himself had made;
For who can praise Him in His depth and height,
But he who saw Him reel amid that solitary fight?

SOUL

Hark! for the lintels of the presence-gate
Are vibrating and echoing back the strain.

FOURTH CHOIR OF ANGELICALS

Praise to the Holiest in the height,
And in the depth be praise:
In all His words most wonderful;
Most sure in all His ways!

The foe blasphemed the Holy Lord,
As if He reckon'd ill,
In that He placed His puppet man
The frontier place to fill.

For, even in his best estate,
With amplest gifts endued,
A sorry sentinel was he,
A being of flesh and blood.

As though a thing, who for his help
Must needs possess a wife,
Could cope with those proud rebel hosts
Who had angelic life.

And when, by blandishment of Eve,
  That earth-born Adam fell,
He shriek'd in triumph, and he cried,
  "A sorry sentinel;

"The Maker by His word is bound,
  Escape or cure is none;
He must abandon to his doom,
  And slay His darling son."

ANGEL

And now the threshold, as we traverse it,
Utters aloud its glad responsive chant.

FIFTH CHOIR OF ANGELICALS

Praise to the Holiest in the height
  And in the depth be praise:
In all His words most wonderful;
  Most sure in all His ways!

O loving wisdom of our God!
  When all was sin and shame,
A second Adam to the fight
  And to the rescue came.

O wisest love! that flesh and blood
  Which did in Adam fail,
Should strive afresh against the foe,
  Should strive and should prevail;

And that a higher gift than grace
  Should flesh and blood refine,
God's Presence and His very Self,
  And Essence all-divine.

O generous love! that He who smote
  In man for man the foe,
The double agony in man
  For man should undergo;

And in the garden secretly,
  And on the cross on high,

Should teach His brethren and inspire
To suffer and to die.

§ 6

ANGEL

Thy judgment now is near, for we are come
Into the veilèd presence of our God.

SOUL

I hear the voices that I left on earth.

ANGEL

It is the voice of friends around thy bed,
Who say the "Subvenite" with the priest.
Hither the echoes come; before the Throne
Stands the great Angel of the Agony,
The same who strengthen'd Him, what time He knelt
Lone in that garden shade, bedew'd with blood.
That Angel best can plead with Him for all
Tormented souls, the dying and the dead.

ANGEL OF THE AGONY

Jesu! by that shuddering dread which fell on Thee;
Jesu! by that cold dismay which sicken'd Thee;
Jesu! by that pang of heart which thrill'd in Thee;
Jesu! by that mount of sins which crippled Thee;
Jesu! by that sense of guilt which stifled Thee;
Jesu! by that innocence which girdled Thee;
Jesu! by that sanctity which reign'd in Thee;
Jesu! by that Godhead which was one with Thee;
Jesu! spare these souls which are so dear to Thee;
Souls, who in prison, calm and patient, wait for Thee;
Hasten, Lord, their hour, and bid them come to Thee,
To that glorious Home, where they shall ever gaze on Thee.

SOUL

I go before my Judge. Ah! ...

ANGEL

                     ... Praise to His Name!
The eager spirit has darted from my hold,
And with the intemperate energy of love,
Flies to the dear feet of Emmanuel;
But, ere it reach them, the keen sanctity,
Which with its effluence, like a glory, clothes
And circles round the Crucified, has seized,
And scorch'd, and shrivell'd it; and now it lies
Passive and still before the awful Throne.
O happy, suffering soul! for it is safe,
Consumed, yet quicken'd, by the glance of God.

SOUL

Take me away, and in the lowest deep
         There let me be,
And there in hope the lone night-watches keep,
         Told out for me.
There, motionless and happy in my pain,
         Lone, not forlorn,—
There will I sing my sad perpetual strain,
         Until the morn.
There will I sing, and soothe my stricken breast,
         Which ne'er can cease
To throb, and pine, and languish, till possest
         Of its Sole Peace.
There will I sing my absent Lord and Love:—
         Take me away,
That sooner I may rise, and go above,
And see Him in the truth of everlasting day.

§ 7

ANGEL

Now let the golden prison ope its gates,
Making sweet music, as each fold revolves
Upon its ready hinge. And ye, great powers,
Angels of Purgatory, receive from me

My charge, a precious soul, until the day,
When, from all bond and foreiture released,
I shall reclaim it for the courts of light.

SOULS IN PURGATORY

1. Lord, Thou hast been our refuge: in every generation;
2. Before the hills were born, and the world was: from age to age Thou art God.
3. Bring us not, Lord, very low: for Thou hast said, Come back again, ye sons of Adam.
4. A thousand years before Thine eyes are but as yesterday: and as a watch of the night which is come and gone.
5. The grass springs up in the morning: at evening tide it shrivels up and dies.
6. So we fail in Thine anger: and in Thy wrath are we troubled.
7. Thou hast set our sins in Thy sight: and our round of days in the light of Thy countenance.
8. Come back, O Lord! how long: and be entreated for Thy servants.
9. In Thy morning we shall be filled with Thy mercy: we shall rejoice and be in pleasure all our days.
10. We shall be glad according to the days of our humiliation: and the years in which we have seen evil.
11. Look, O Lord, upon Thy servants and on Thy work: and direct their children.
12. And let the beauty of the Lord our God be upon us: and the work of our hands, establish Thou it.

Glory be to the Father, and to the Son: and to the Holy Ghost.
As it was in the beginning, is now, and ever shall be: world without end. Amen.

ANGEL

Softly and gently, dearly-ransom'd soul,
    In my most loving arms I now enfold thee,
And, o'er the penal waters, as they roll,
    I poise thee, and I lower thee, and hold thee.

And carefully I dip thee in the lake,
    And thou, without a sob or a resistance,

Dost through the flood thy rapid passage take,
　　Sinking deep, deeper, into the dim distance.

Angels, to whom the willing task is given,
　　Shall tend, and nurse, and lull thee, as thou liest;
And masses on the earth, and prayers in heaven,
　　Shall aid thee at the Throne of the Most Highest.

Farewell, but not for ever! brother dear,
　　Be brave and patient on thy bed of sorrow;
Swiftly shall pass thy night of trial here,
　　And I will come and wake thee on the morrow.

7. FRANCIS THOMPSON:
TWO ODES

¶Of Francis Thompson's *Hound of Heaven* Sir Edward Burne-Jones said: "Since Gabriel Rossetti's *Blessed Damosel* no mystical words have so touched me." Similar experiences are recorded during all of the more than forty years which have followed the publication of this masterpiece. It is at once a profession of faith, an admission of human weakness and guilt, and a sermon to all artists and writers. The "Hound" is God, whose love pursues the soul. Less well known, the *Orient Ode* is also a truly great mystical poem. The theme is the incarnation of Jesus, which Thompson views as the central fact in human history and life—the meeting of God and man in communal being.

Thompson is the only modern English Catholic poet of first-rate importance to have been born (1859) in the Church. For a time he studied theology, but was advised to abandon his idea of becoming a priest. He also failed as a student of medicine. Thereupon he went to London and led the life of an outcast and struggling litterateur. An article sent to Mr. Wilfrid Meynell aroused that editor's attention, and the reclamation of Thompson began. Though by this time a victim of disease and laudanum, he lived long enough to complete a considerable body of verse, a number of treatises and many literary essays. He died in 1907.*

---

* From *Complete Poetical Works of Francis Thompson.* New York: Charles Scribner's Sons; also Dodd, Mead & Company.

THE HOUND OF HEAVEN

FLED Him, down the nights and down the days;
    I fled Him, down the arches of the years;
    I fled Him, down the labyrinthine ways
       Of my own mind; and in the mist of tears
    I hid from Him, and under running laughter.
            Up vistaed hopes I sped;
            And shot, precipitated,
Adown Titanic glooms of chasmèd fears,
  From those strong Feet that followed, followed after.
      But with unhurrying chase,
      And unperturbèd pace,
    Deliberate speed, majestic instancy,
      They beat—and a Voice beat
      More instant than the Feet—
  'All things betray thee, who betrayest Me.'

      I pleaded, outlaw-wise,
By many a hearted casement, curtained red,
  Trellised with intertwining charities;
(For, though I knew His love Who followèd,
      Yet was I sore adread
Lest, having Him, I must have naught beside.)
But, if one little casement parted wide,
  The gust of His approach would clash it to:
  Fear wist not to evade, as Love wist to pursue.
Across the margent of the world I fled,
  And troubled the gold gateways of the stars,
  Smiting for shelter on their clangèd bars;
      Fretted to dulcet jars
And silvern chatter the pale ports o' the moon.
I said to Dawn: Be sudden—to Eve: Be soon;
  With thy young skiey blossoms heap me over
      From this tremendous Lover—
Float thy vague veil about me, lest He see!
I tempted all His servitors, but to find

My own betrayal in their constancy,
In faith to Him their fickleness to me,
  Their traitorous trueness, and their loyal deceit.
To all swift things for swiftness did I sue;
  Clung to the whistling mane of every wind.
      But whether they swept, smoothly fleet,
      The long savannahs of the blue;
          Or whether, Thunder-driven,
          They clanged his chariot 'thwart a heaven,
Plashy with flying lightnings round the spurn o' their feet:—
  Fear wist not to evade as Love wist to pursue.
          Still with unhurrying chase,
          And unperturbèd pace,
      Deliberate speed, majestic instancy,
          Came on the following Feet,
          And a Voice above their beat—
'Naught shelters thee, who wilt not shelter **Me**.'

I sought no more that after which I strayed
          In face or man or maid;
But still within the little children's eyes
          Seems something, something that replies,
They at least are for me, surely for me!
I turned me to them very wistfully:
But just as their young eyes grew sudden fair
          With dawning answers there,
Their angel plucked them from me by the hair.
'Come then, ye other children, Nature's—share
With me' (said I) 'your delicate fellowship;
          Let me greet you lip to lip,
          Let me twine with you caresses,
              Wantoning
          With our Lady-Mother's vagrant tresses,
              Banqueting
          With her in her wind-walled palace,
          Underneath her azured daïs,
          Quaffing, as your taintless way is,
              From a chalice

Lucent-weeping out of the dayspring.'
    So it was done:
I in their delicate fellowship was one—
Drew the bolt of Nature's secrecies.
      I knew all the swift importings
      On the wilful face of skies;
      I knew how the clouds arise
      Spumèd of the wild sea-snortings;
        All that's born or dies
      Rose and drooped with; made them shapers
Of mine own moods, or wailful or divine;
      With them joyed and was bereaven.
      I was heavy with the even,
      When she lit her glimmering tapers
      Round the day's dead sanctities.
      I laughed in the morning's eyes.
I triumphed and I saddened with all weather,
      Heaven and I wept together,
And its sweet tears were salt with mortal mine;
Against the red throb of its sunset-heart
      I laid my own to beat,
      And share commingling heat;
But not by that, by that, was eased my human smart.
In vain my tears were wet on Heaven's grey cheek.
For ah! we know not what each other says,
      These things and I; in sound *I* speak—
Their sound is but their stir, they speak by silences.
Nature, poor stepdame, cannot slake my drouth;
      Let her, if she would owe me,
Drop yon blue bosom-veil of sky, and show me
      The breasts o' her tenderness:
Never did any milk of hers once bless
        My thirsting mouth.
        Nigh and nigh draws the chase.
        With unperturbèd pace,
      Deliberate speed, majestic instancy;
        And past those noisèd Feet
        A voice comes yet more fleet—
      'Lo! naught contents thee, who content'st not Me.'

Naked I wait Thy love's uplifted stroke!
My harness piece by piece Thou hast hewn from me,
  And smitten me to my knee;
 I am defenceless utterly.
 I slept, methinks, and woke,
And, slowly gazing, find me stripped in sleep.
In the rash lustihead of my young powers,
 I shook the pillaring hours
And pulled my life upon me; grimed with smears,
I stand amid the dust o' the mounded years—
My mangled youth lies dead beneath the heap.
My days have crackled and gone up in smoke,
Have puffed and burst as sun-starts on a stream.
  Yea, faileth now even dream
The dreamer, and the lute the lutanist;
Even the linked fantasies, in whose blossomy twist
I swung the earth a trinket at my wrist,
Are yielding; cords of all too weak account
For earth with heavy griefs so overplussed.
  Ah! is Thy love indeed
A weed, albeit an amaranthine weed,
Suffering no flowers except its own to mount?
  Ah! must—
  Designer infinite!—
Ah! must Thou char the wood ere Thou canst limn with it?
My freshness spent its wavering shower i' the dust;
And now my heart is as a broken fount,
Wherein tear-drippings stagnate, spilt down ever
  From the dank thoughts that shiver
Upon the sighful branches of my mind.
  Such is; what is to be?
The pulp so bitter, how shall taste the rind?
I dimly guess what Time in mists confounds;
Yet ever and anon a trumpet sounds
From the dim battlements of Eternity;
Those shaken mists a space unsettle, then
Round the half-glimpsèd turrets slowly wash again.
  But not ere him who summoneth
  I first have seen, enwound

With glooming robes purpureal, cypress-crowned;
His name I know, and what his trumpet saith.
Whether man's heart or life it be which yields
          Thee harvest, must Thy harvest-fields
          Be dunged with rotten death?
               Now of that long pursuit
               Comes on at hand the bruit;
          That Voice is round me like a bursting sea:
               'And is thy earth so marred,
               Shattered in shard on shard?
          Lo, all things fly thee, for thou fliest Me!
          Strange, piteous, futile thing!
Wherefore should any set thee love apart?
Seeing none but I makes much of naught' (He said),
'And human love needs human meriting:
          How hast thou merited—
Of all man's clotted clay the dingiest clot?
          Alack, thou knowest not
How little worthy of any love thou art!
Whom wilt thou find to love ignoble thee,
          Save Me, save only Me?
All which I took from thee I did but take,
          Not for thy harms,
But just that thou might'st seek it in My arms.
          All which thy child's mistake
Fancies as lost, I have stored for thee at home:
          Rise, clasp My hand, and come!'
     Halts by me that footfall:
     Is my gloom, after all,
Shade of His hand, outstretched caressingly?
     'Ah, fondest, blindest, weakest,
     I am He Whom thou seekest!
Thou dravest love from thee, who dravest Me.'

ORIENT ODE

          Lo, in the sanctuaried East,
          Day, a dedicated priest

In all his robes pontifical exprest,
Lifteth slowly, lifteth sweetly,
From out its Orient tabernacle drawn,
Yon orbèd sacrament confest
Which sprinkles benediction through the dawn;
And when the grave procession's ceased,
The earth with due illustrious rite
Blessed,—ere the frail fingers featly
Of twilight, violet-cassocked acolyte,
His sacerdotal stoles unvest—
Sets, for high close of the mysterious feast,
The sun in august exposition meetly
Within the flaming monstrance of the West.

O salutaris hostia,
Quæ cœli pandis ostium!
Through breachèd darkness' rampart, a
Divine assaulter, art thou come!
God whom none may live and mark!
Borne within thy radiant ark,
While the Earth, a joyous David,
Dances before thee from the dawn to dark.
The moon, O leave, pale ruined Eve;
Behold her fair and greater daughter [1]
Offers to thee her fruitful water,
Which at thy first white *Ave* shall conceive!

Thy gazes do on simple her
Desirable allures confer;
What happy comelinesses rise
Beneath thy beautifying eyes!
Who was, indeed, at first a maid
Such as, with sighs, misgives she is not fair,
And secret views herself afraid,
Till flatteries sweet provoke the charms they swear:
Yea, the gazes, blissful Lover,
Make the beauties they discover!

[1] The earth.

What dainty guiles and treacheries caught
From artful promptings of love's artless thought
Her lowly loveliness teach her to adorn,
When thy plumes shiver against the conscious gates of morn!

And so the love which is thy dower,
(Earth, though her first-frightened breast
Against the exigent boon protest
For she, poor maid, of her own power
Was nothing in herself, not even love,
But an unwitting void thereof),
Gives back to thee in sanctities of flower;
And holy odours do her bosom invest,
That sweeter grows for being prest:
Though dear recoil, the tremorous nurse of joy,
From thine embrace still startles coy,
Till Phosphor lead, at thy returning hour,
The laughing captive from the wishing West.

Nor the majestic heavens less
Thy formidable sweets approve,
Thy dreads and thy delights confess,
That do draw, and that remove.
Thou as a lion roar'st, O Sun,
Upon the satellite's vexèd heels;
Before thy terrible hunt thy planets run;
Each in his frighted orbit wheels,
Each flies through inassuageable chase,
Since the hunt o' the world begun,
The puissant approaches of thy face,
And yet thy radiant leash he feels.
Since the hunt o' the world begun,
Lashed with terror, leashed with longing,
The mighty course is ever run;
Pricked with terror, leashed with longing,
Thy rein they love, and thy rebuke they shun.
Since the hunt o' the world began,
With love that trembleth, fear that loveth,

Thou join'st the woman to the man;
And Life with Death
In obscure nuptials moveth,
Commingling alien yet affinèd breath.

Thou art the incarnated Light
Whose Sire is aboriginal, and beyond
Death and resurgence of our day and night;
From him is thy viceregent wand
With double potency of the black and white.
Giver of Love, and Beauty, and Desire,
The terror, and the loveliness, and purging,
The deathfulness and lifefulness of fire!
Samson's riddling meanings merging
In thy twofold sceptre meet:
Out of the minatory might,
Burning Lion, burning Lion,
Comes the honey of all sweet,
And out of thee, the Eater, comes forth meat.
And though, by thine alternate breath,
Every kiss thou dost inspire
Echoeth
Back from the windy vaultages of death;
Yet thy clear warranty above
Augurs the wings of death too must
Occult reverberations stir of love
Crescent, and life incredible;
That even the kisses of the just
Go down not unresurgent to the dust.
Yea, not a kiss which I have given,
But shall triumph upon my lips in heaven,
Or cling a shameful fungus there in hell.

Know'st thou me not, O Sun? Yea, well
Thou know'st the ancient miracle,
The children know'st of Zeus and May;
And still thou teachest them, O splendid Brother,
To incarnate, the antique way,
The truth which is their heritage from their Sire

In sweet disguise of flesh from their sweet Mother.
My fingers thou hast taught to con
Thy flame-chorded psalterion,
Till I can translate into mortal wire—
Till I can translate passing well—
The heavenly harping harmony,
Melodious, sealed, inaudible,
Which makes the dulcet psalter of the world's desire.
Thou whisperest in the Moon's white ear,
And she does whisper into mine,—
By night together, I and she—
With her virgin voice divine,
The things I cannot half so sweetly tell
As she can sweetly speak, I sweetly hear.

By her, the Woman, does Earth live, O Lord,
Yet she for Earth, and both in Thee.
Light out of Light!
Resplendent and prevailing Word
Of the Unheard!
Not unto thee, great Image, not to thee
Did the wise heathen bend an idle knee;
And in an age of faith grown frore
If I too shall adore,
Be it accounted unto me
A bright sciential idolatry!
God has given thee visible thunders
To utter thine apocalypse of wonders;
And what want I of prophecy,
That at the sounding from thy station
Of thy flagrant trumpet, see
The seals that melt, the open revelation?
Or who a God-persuading angel needs,
That only heeds
The rhetoric of thy burning deeds?
Which but to sing, if it may be,
In worship-warranting moiety,
So I would win
In such a song as hath within

A smouldering core of mystery,
Brimmèd with nimbler meanings up
Than hasty Gideons in their hands may sup;—
Lo, my suit pleads
That thou, Isaian coal of fire,
Touch from yon altar my poor mouths' desire,
And the relucent song take for thy sacred meeds.

To thine own shape
Thou round'st the chrysolite of the grape,
Bind'st thy gold lightnings in his veins;
Thou storest the white garners of the rains.
Destroyer and preserver, thou
Who medicinest sickness, and to health
Art the unthankèd marrow of its wealth;
To those apparent sovereignties we bow
And bright appurtenances of thy brow!
Thy proper blood dost thou not give,
That Earth, the gusty Mænad, drink and dance?
Art thou not life of them that live?
Yea, in a glad twinkling advent, thou dost dwell
Within our body as a tabernacle!
Thou bittest with thine ordinance
The jaws of Time, and thou dost mete
The unstable treading of his feet.
Thou to thy spousal universe
Art Husband, she thy Wife and Church;
Who in most dusk and vidual curch,
Her Lord being hence,
Keeps her cold sorrows by thy hearse.
The heavens renew their innocence
And morning state
But by thy sacrament communicate;
Their weeping night the symbol of our prayers,
Our darkened search,
And sinful vigil desolate.
Yea, biune in imploring dumb,
Essential Heavens and corporal Earth await;
The Spirit and the Bride say: Come!

Lo, of thy Magians I the least
Haste with my gold, my incenses and myrrhs,
To thy desired epiphany, from the spiced
Regions and odorous of Song's traded East.
Thou, for the life of all that live
The victim daily born and sacrificed;
To whom the pinion of this longing verse
Beats but with fire which first thyself didst give,
To thee, O Sun—or is't perchance to Christ?

Ay, if men say that on all high heaven's face
The saintly signs I trace
Which round my stolèd altars hold their solemn place,
Amen, amen! For oh, how could it be,—
When I with wingèd feet had run
Through all the windy earth about,
Quested its secret of the sun,
And heard what things the stars together shout,—
I should not heed thereout
Consenting counsel won:—
'By this, O Singer, know we if thou see.
When men shall say to thee: Lo! Christ is here,
When men shall say to thee: Lo! Christ is there,
Believe them: yea, and this—then art thou seer,
When all thy crying clear
Is but: Lo here! lo there!—ah me, lo everywhere!'